SECOND EDITION

Methods of Teaching Bookkeeping– Accounting

WITHDRAWN

by

LEWIS D. BOYNTON

Professor of Business Education
Central Connecticut State College
New Britain, Connecticut

SOUTH-WESTERN
PUBLISHING CO.

CINCINNATI   DALLAS   CHICAGO   NEW ROCHELLE, N. Y.   BURLINGAME, CALIF.

X80

233521

METHODS OF TEACHING
BOOKKEEPING-ACCOUNTING

PREFACE

Purpose

The purpose of this textbook is threefold:

1. To help the beginning bookkeeping teacher who has had little or no background in the principles and methods of teaching.

2. To supplement the limited special coverage and help that is given to future bookkeeping teachers in a general or composite undergraduate methods course.

3. To challenge the experienced bookkeeping teacher in the up-to-dateness of his knowledge and the classroom procedures he uses in the teaching of this specialized subject area.

Need

This is a day of large masses of people to be taught, of constantly increasing subject matter to be mastered, of an urgent need for higher and higher levels of competency. It is also an era of a continuing knowledge explosion. It is necessary that time not be wasted in the bookkeeping-accounting classroom by uninformed teachers using outmoded procedures. It is necessary that teaching be characterized by efficiency, up-to-dateness, and the development of the kind of people who will easily and effectively assume the responsibilities of the working world. It should be obvious, therefore, that the *methods* by which the future workers in any vocational area are taught are of exceedingly great importance.

The methods used in teaching a subject can either forever limit a student to mediocre performance *or* open up the wide world of professional activity. The methods used can develop students into resentful and routine followers of orders *or* produce eager and inquiring minds. Educational waste and personal damage is obvious in the case of an aspiring speed typist permitted to hunt and peck; a future chef who spends class time copying recipes but never has the chance to cook anything; a student in driver education who knows all the laws and the rules of driving but has never driven in downtown traffic. Educational waste is equally obvious in the bookkeeping-accounting classroom where the teacher concentrates solely on rigid rules, unalterable procedures, and rote memorization of principles; where the teacher would rather resign than permit a free discussion of the application of bookkeeping-accounting principles to everyday living or go through the ordeal of a field trip to a computer center.

There have been years of research and development of materials in all of the specialized areas of business education, including bookkeeping-accounting. The teacher, new or experienced, is condemned to making all the mistakes of the past if he is ignorant of what has gone before, what is currently being practiced, and what the future may hold. The uninformed teacher concentrating on the subject matter in the book and disdaining a look at methods of presenting that subject matter will be oblivious to, among other things, new teaching materials, the infinite resources of a community, government funds available for use in improving vocational training, the relationship of bookkeeping-accounting to the field of automated data processing, and the ultimate satisfaction of seeing students develop into desirable members of a business community.

This book is designed to help all bookkeeping teachers, whatever their background of experience, become better teachers through the use of better methods.

Development

Part I (Chapters 1-13) of this textbook, "Foundations for the Teaching of Bookkeeping-Accounting," is aimed at helping both beginning and experienced teachers to deal adequately with all of the basic factors that should be taken into consideration for:

1. Justifying the teaching of manual bookkeeping-accounting in an emerging age of automated data processing.

2. Planning the content of the course for any school.
3. Planning the day-to-day teaching and learning activities.
4. Determining when and to whom the subject should be taught.
5. Determining the effectiveness of the teaching and the learning.
6. Keeping abreast of meaningful research as well as educational and business trends affecting bookkeeping-accounting instruction.

Part II (Chapters 14-24), "Guidelines for Teaching Special Areas of Bookkeeping-Accounting," deals with specific suggestions for teaching selected subject matter areas of bookkeeping-accounting. In the main, these include topics which seem to create the greatest challenge to teachers.

Because there is no single best way for a topic to be taught, the author presents the teaching suggestions in this section with the hope that they may (1) help experienced teachers not satisfied with their success in these areas, and (2) help beginning teachers to overcome their initial difficulties—so that in the beginning they have a way of teaching such topics. But with experience should come discrimination and the selection of a method which suits the individual teacher.

Changes

This book is an outgrowth of the thoughts presented in the first edition of *Methods of Teaching Bookkeeping*. Since the first edition, changes have occurred, and trends have emerged in both education and in business. These newer developments and challenges have required this revision to be a major one.

Fourteen of the sixteen original chapters have been retained. All fourteen have been up-dated and have undergone extensive revision. Ten new chapters have been added. Six of these help to make up the series of how-to-teach chapters in Part II dealing with special areas or topics in a first-year bookkeeping course. Chapter 24, for example, suggests the extent of the responsibility of the teacher for teaching about automated data processing and presents day-to-day subject matter outlines for help in such teaching.

Acknowledgments

An important factor in the production of this revised edition was the encouragement of colleagues who used the previous edition and, in recent years, kept prodding by asking, "When are you going to revise your methods book?" I also acknowledge with appreciation the contributions to this revised edition stemming from the many problems, challenges, and ideas shared with me in my methods courses and at professional meetings by both beginning and experienced teachers. Special recognition is given to Manlio Jannace, Head of the Data Center, and to Howard Ward, instructor of automated data processing at Central Connecticut State College for their views about the teaching of automated data processing at the high school level.

Surpassing all other acknowledgments is that to my wife. While she claims not to know the difference between a *debit* and a *credit*, and does not, she does know when a thought or idea has not been clearly written. As a result, her reading and criticizing the manuscript, her own writing or rewriting of some troublesome spots, and her constant encouragement were invaluable.

LEWIS D. BOYNTON

METHODS OF TEACHING
BOOKKEEPING-ACCOUNTING

Contents

Chapter   Page

Part I

Foundations for the Teaching of Bookkeeping-Accounting

Part II

Guidelines for Teaching Special Areas

Appendixes

INTRODUCTION

Part I of this textbook is devoted to the broad and basic principles which form the foundation of the teaching of bookkeeping-accounting.

Every bookkeeping-accounting teacher needs to have an appreciation of the place and the importance of bookkeeping-accounting as a vocation, as a background of related information for helping students learn how business operates, and as a specialized course in the high school curriculum. (Hereafter the term "bookkeeping-accounting" generally will be abbreviated "B-A" when used with words such as "teacher" and "course.") The B-A teacher must have knowledge about and enthusiasm for his subject. He needs to have a clear, up-to-date, and unbiased understanding of the place of manual bookkeeping-accounting today and of the teaching of the course in an emerging age of computers and automated data processing. Chapters 1 through 3 are devoted to this necessary background which is not covered in subject matter courses. They are designed to take the B-A course beyond the confines of the classroom. They are aimed at giving the breadth of view and knowledge necessary for developing both the prospective teacher and the experienced teacher into something more than textbook followers.

Planning is one of the essentials for learning to teach well—for improving one's teaching. Teachers in training need to know specifically how bookkeeping-accounting can be taught. Teachers in service need to know how they can improve their teaching. What do you do? What do you say? How do you plan?

1

What equipment, what teaching and learning "tools," what supplies are available, and which are best? How can you effectively teach both the bright and the dull, the fast and the slow, and not just teach the average students in your class? What is a good testing program? Who should get an "A"? Who should fail? The answers to these and to other questions are revealed in Chapters 4 through 10.

New developments in both education and in business affect the teaching of business subjects. Every B-A teacher has the responsibility of keeping up to date with such changes. By meeting this responsibility, the teacher brings his opinion and his influence to bear upon emerging trends, upon controversial issues, and upon research findings. The last three chapters in Part I of this textbook, Chapters 11 through 13, are concerned with these important phases affecting B-A instruction.

THE STATUS OF BOOKKEEPING-ACCOUNTING

Chapter 1

A Challenge to the Teacher

There never has been a more exciting and challenging age in which to be a B-A teacher. Today's business world is an international one with incredible machines to help its employees meet the needs and desires of an exploding world population. The boundaries of the world have been extended into space, and the phenomenal knowledge explosion is stepping up the pace, quality, and demands of education. New ways to teach people are being explored—computer assisted instruction, auto-teaching devices, programmed media, television, and innumerable audio-visual materials. In such a complicated civilization, young people need vigorous, sensitive teaching and guidance to help them find their places in the fast-moving streams of the working world.

The role of the B-A teacher has never been more vital. The complexity of our age demands for its very existence the keeping of many records with infallible accuracy. It demands the interpretation of these records with comprehensive, analytic judgment. The people who keep these records must be well educated and masters of B-A principles and procedures.

The challenge, therefore, of the B-A teacher is to see and feel the excitement of the growing business world and to implant in his students both desire and knowledge—the desire to contribute their best to this world and the knowledge which tells them how. It is hoped that from the classes of such teachers will come the alert, keen-thinking, personable office workers needed in today's business world.

3

The Changing Image of the Bookkeeper

What is the image of the present-day bookkeeper or accounting clerk which the teacher might have in mind as he seeks to mold the potential office workers of his community?

The bookkeeper of a hundred years ago is easily and clearly pictured. He was to be seen in the corner of an office, wearing an eyeshade, perched on a high stool, bent over a tall, slanting desk with two inkwells (red and black), recording figures in large books with a quill pen. He was solely responsible for the total business records of his employer. If he worked for one of the larger firms of that era, he might have had an apprentice or two assisting him.

One gets the feeling that the owners or managers of the businesses in those days tolerated the bookkeeping clerk but did not depend very heavily upon the results of his work for their decisions. The image of yesterday's bookkeeper is like that of Bob Cratchit, Ebenezer Scrooge's bookkeeper in Dickens' *Christmas Carol.*

The bookkeeper of today cannot be pictured as clearly as the bookkeeper of a hundred years ago. He is to be found in thousands of different kinds of offices all over the world. (The majority of today's offices are small with one or two employees; a small percentage are quite large with thousands of employees.) He may

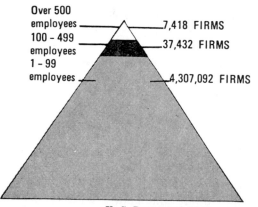

U. S. Department of Commerce
Illustrated in *Nation's Business* (April, 1965) p. 84

**Figure 1—1. Comparison of number of employees
and firms**

also be an individual keeping the books of his own business in a local service station, on a farm, in a beauty salon, in a doctor's office, or at home.

In the smaller offices and local service businesses, the bookkeeper may enjoy the privilege of controlling the entire B-A cycle from original entry to the preparation of financial statements. He probably has some mechanical assistant at his side—an adding or calculating machine suitable to his particular needs. When certain periodic or repetitive data become burdensome, he may turn to a professional accounting service which will process the material rapidly on more sophisticated machines than his office may be able to afford. In the large offices of many corporations, where employers are concerned with the recording of thousands of transactions and the keeping of the additional records required by federal and state governments, the B-A process has been broken down into a number of small duties comparable to the assembly line work of the factories. Numerous workers perform these duties and often each holds the title of "bookkeeper" or "accounting clerk." Some do nothing but post to the accounts A through G of the accounts receivable ledger, others to the accounts H through L, and so on. Some have the sole responsibility of preparing the payroll and keeping employee records. Similarly, different persons in the same office have the duties of keeping special journals, handling cash, checking invoices, operating office machines, preparing statements, and so on. Each of them performs B-A duties— duties ranging in difficulty from simply copying numbers to analyzing transactions and preparing statements that show the results of business operations.

In certain segments of the B-A process and in the large companies which must deal with massive recording loads, electronic machines may take over the laborious, repetitive work. In this instance, we may find the work of the bookkeeper or accountant a matter of thinking how best to use the machines to accomplish what needs to be done. With his knowledge of B-A principles, such a person may help in the programming of what a machine is to do and may analyze the meaning of the results.

The management of businesses and governments today lean heavily upon the work of the bookkeeper and accountant to help in planning and in making decisions. Without meaningful records and someone to interpret them, the present colossus of enterprise would certainly fall.

So in the space of a century, the single image of the bookkeeper with his eyeshade and quill pen, laboriously copying figures, has given way to a multi-image of posting clerks, payroll clerks, manual bookkeepers, and machine bookkeepers, working in air-conditioned rooms with machine and electronic power to do their will.

International Business Machines Corporation

Figure 1—2. Early bookkeeper and contemporary bookkeeper

The similarity, the sameness in the duties performed by some of the clerical workers with different titles is illustrated by the following job descriptions supplied by the Dictionary of Occupational Titles.[1]

Bookkeeper (clerical) I. 210:388. *full-charge bookkeeper; general book-keeper.* Keeps records of financial transactions of establishment: Verifies and enters details of transactions as they occur or in chronological order in account and cash journals from items, such as sales slips, invoices, check stubs, inventory records, and requisitions. Summarizes details on separate ledgers, using

---

[1] U.S. Department of Labor, *Dictionary of Occupational Titles*, Volume I, *Definitions of Titles* (3d ed., Washington: U.S. Government Printing Office, 1965).

adding machine, and transfers data to general ledger. Balances books and compiles reports to show statistics, such as cash receipts and expenditures, accounts payable and receivable, profit and loss and other items pertinent to operation of business. Calculates employee wages from plant records or time-cards and makes up checks or withdraws cash from bank for payment of wages. May prepare withholding, Social Security, and other tax reports. May compute, type, and mail monthly statements to customers. May complete books to or through trial balance. May operate calculating and bookkeeping machines.

Bookkeeper (clerical) II. 210-388. Keeps one section of set of financial records, performing duties as described under BOOKKEEPER I. May be designated according to section of bookkeeping records kept, such as *Accounts-Payable Bookkeeper; Accounts-Receivable Bookkeeper;* . . . See volume II for additional titles.

Accounting Clerk (clerical) 219.488. Performs variety of routine calculating, posting, and typing duties to accomplish accounting: Posts details of business transactions, such as allotments, disbursements, deductions from payrolls, pay and expense vouchers, remittances paid and due, checks, and claims. Totals accounts, using adding machine, computes and records interest charges, refunds, cost of lost or damaged goods, freight or express charges, rentals, and similar items. May type vouchers, invoices, account statements, payrolls, periodic reports, and other records. May be designated according to type of accounting performed as *Abstract-Examination Clerk* (insurance); *Accounts-Payable Clerk; Accounts-Receivable Clerk; Rent and Miscellaneous Remittance Clerk* (insurance); *Tax-Record Clerk* (light, heat, & power); *Ticket; Rebate Clerk* (motor trans.; r.r. trains). See volume II for additional titles.

The following cross referencing included in Volume I of the *Dictionary of Occupational Titles* further illustrates the sameness of bookkeeping work that is performed by clerical workers under different job titles.

> **Accounting Clerk, Pay Roll** (banking) *see* Accounting Clerk (clerical).
>
> **Accounting Clerk, Trust** (banking) *see* Accounting Clerk (clerical).
>
> **Accounts-Payable Bookkeeper** (clerical) *see* Bookkeeper II.
>
> **Accounts-Payable Clerk** (clerical) *see* Accounting Clerk.
>
> **Accounts-Receivable Bookkeeper** (clerical) *see* Bookkeeper II.
>
> **Accounts-Receivable Clerk** (clerical) *see* Accounting Clerk.

While the different titles given to clerical workers doing book-keeping and accounting work can be confusing, the *Dictionary of Occupational Titles* is able to maintain a clear distinction between persons engaged in the *profession* of accounting and those engaged in *occupations* of a clerical nature, regardless of whether the job title that is used is "bookkeeper," or "accounting clerk," or something else.

The Challenge in the Bookkeeping-Accounting Class

Each year over a half-million students begin the study of bookkeeping-accounting. Some will become bookkeepers. However, there are many students in B-A classes who do not intend to become vocational bookkeepers but who need bookkeeping-accounting in order to function more effectively in the jobs for which they are preparing—the secretarial or distributive education students; the girls who will get married and be family budget makers; the students who will eventually run the small businesses throughout the country.

Are the students in B-A classes being satisfactorily helped with the kind of business procedures and knowledge that all future office workers should get from today's B-A course? Are they being given a true picture of the requirements and opportunities in this field of work? Is their instruction such that they will be able to apply the basic principles they learn to their own small business, to a small segment of a big corporation's operations, to the planning of programs for bookkeeping by machine, to the secretarial and general office work they may be called upon to do, or to their own personal affairs?

The nature of bookkeeping-accounting in today's scheme of things and the numerous reasons for which students enter B-A classes create many problems in the determination of content and method in the modern classroom and form a constant challenge to the B-A teacher. It is to these problems and stimulating challenges that this text is directed.

Levels of Work in Bookkeeping-Accounting

The scope of bookkeeping is wide and its activities varied, as may be inferred from the preceding paragraphs. It is defined as the "art or practice" of keeping a systematic record of business transactions.

This "art or practice" is being taught to students in the high schools in courses labeled *record keeping, bookkeeping, bookkeeping and accounting,* and *accounting.* The drawing of a sharp dividing line between record keeping, bookkeeping, and accounting is impossible. It does seem, however, that the handling and the recording of business transactions and the use made of such records in the business office are on three rather distinct levels. These duties may all be performed by one person in a small office, or the different aspects may each be performed by different individuals. The three classifications of *record keeping, bookkeeping,* and *accounting* are presented for two purposes: (1) so that the reader knows what the author is referring to when these terms are used in this text, and (2) to show what is believed to be a logical and descriptive breakdown of these areas. Additional remarks as to the distinction between the terms *bookkeeping* and *accounting* are found starting on page 316 under the topic, *"Bookkeeping" Versus "Accounting" as a High School Course Title.* In the remainder of this text, the terms describing the work of these three levels will be used according to the following descriptions.

Record keeping. Under this term is classed the work of posting clerks or entry bookkeepers, payroll clerks, clerks who fill out forms, clerks who take a number from one form or column and place it in another column or on another form, and clerks who routinely operate or monitor bookkeeping machines. In the main, such persons usually are dealing with *parts* or segments of the bookkeeping cycle. Many, if not most, of such office workers need not understand the other functions of the bookkeeping cycle in order to do their job and earn their salary, although as much understanding of the total bookkeeping process as possible is desirable from the point of view of enabling such workers to advance and appreciate the part they play in their job. If a serious attempt is ever made to standardize the classification of such workers, the term *junior bookkeeper* might be considered for a worker who performs such routine, segmentary bookkeeping duties.

Bookkeeping. Under this term is classed the work of office employees who are concerned with the whole or the major picture of a firm's business transactions—not just the parts. For example, in addition to understanding and being able to handle any of the segments described above under record keeping, these employees should have the ability to maintain journals and ledgers, take a trial balance, make adjusting entries, balance, rule, and close accounts, and prepare necessary statements or reports that reflect the condition of the business. While some firms employ public or private accountants and do not require their bookkeepers to perform all of these duties, all-round bookkeepers must have an understanding of the bookkeeping cycle and the principles underlying the records needed for completing this cycle—records necessary to show (1) what a firm is worth (the balance sheet) and (2) how it got that way (the income statement). These all-round bookkeepers could be labeled *senior bookkeepers.*

Accounting. Here we move into a professional field made up of persons who have been trained to *interpret* (to a higher degree than the senior bookkeeper) the meaning of business transactions and bookkeeping records, to *audit* accounts and records, to *advise* and supply help in systematizing the kinds of accounts, forms, books, and records best suited for individual businesses. They may also work with specialists in planning programs for electronic computers. We also have specialists trained in various fields such as estate accounting, tax accounting, cost accounting, and municipal or government accounting.

In general, the teaching of record keeping and bookkeeping-accounting is done on the high school level and the teaching of accounting principles on the college or professional school level. Some teachers claim that accounting instruction begins when the student first starts to analyze and interpret accounts—which could be the first or second month of the first year's introduction to bookkeeping. Nevertheless it must be recognized that accountants, as described above, are not produced from merely one or even two years of high school study of this subject regardless of what it is called.

High schools are now offering courses in machine bookkeeping and computer operation. An operational knowledge of a machine will not make either a bookkeeper or an accountant. The machine is a tool of operation. The bookkeeper or accountant must have the knowledge which allows him to command a total view of the entire process in all its ramifications, including the use of machines.

The Importance of Bookkeeping-Accounting in Today's World

Is bookkeeping, the first commercial subject to enter the high school in 1824,[2] as important and necessary today as it has been in the past?

---

[2] Harry D. Kitson, *Commercial Education in Secondary Schools* (New York: Ginn and Company, 1929), p. 40.

Before this century, and for the first several decades of this century, bookkeeping was primarily an optional tool of management. Then a sole proprietorship or a partnership kept records merely for its own knowledge and benefit in administering the business. Corporations, at that time, also kept books for this reason and because they were accountable to their stockholders. Businessmen today are more management-wise, and therefore are more aware of the value of information available in good B-A records and the use to which this information can be put. Furthermore, federal, state, and local governments have stepped into the B-A picture by requiring the businessman as well as the private individual to keep records of business transactions.

Numerous laws are being passed that relate to such things as sales taxes, excise taxes, income taxes, social security, workmen's compensation, and wages and hours of employment. All of these laws have added to the volume of B-A work that is required and to the complexity of the B-A procedures. Furthermore, in addition to withholding from employees' wages the amounts required by the government for social security and income taxes, businesses often agree with their employees to withhold amounts for other purposes, such as insurance, hospital care, union dues, and bond purchases. Therefore, many businesses, which in the past did or did not keep books as they chose, now have no option and must not only keep accurate records but also must keep them in a manner required by law.

It is quite obvious not only that bookkeeping-accounting is more important in our economy today, but that also there is more of it in both the business world and in the home.

There is an ever-increasing need of personal records—records of birth, schooling, earnings from the first job to retirement, expenses, savings, and so on until death and after.

Governments of nations must keep large numbers of records about people, world food needs, international loans, world relief funds, population growth, and ventures into space.

Accounting becomes an international problem when firms establish branches in other countries and when international cooperative ventures such as the Common Market are instituted. Accounting laws and practices vary from country to country, and international agreement on accounting procedures are vital in order to interpret financial statements intelligently for purposes not only of business but also of political decision. Secret reserves and unlimited depreciation of assets are two examples of areas in which international accounting procedures vary widely and cause many problems of interpretation.

While these facts do not immediately affect the teaching of bookkeeping-accounting in an American high school, the knowledge of them widens the horizons of the teacher and should give a dimension of vision to his teaching. It should also indicate that bookkeeping-accounting cannot be taught in a vacuum, that it must continually be related to the daily activities of people, business, and government.

All of this means that today's high school student of vocational bookkeeping-accounting has a wider market for his services and a greater potential future than previously, and he can also find ample use for such knowledge and skill in his personal and future family life.

A knowledge of bookkeeping-accounting has importance not only for the vocational bookkeeper or the person training to become a bookkeeper but for others also. Such understanding can be important and helpful to the typist who types statements and materials dealing with financial transactions; to the secretary who takes dictation and transcribes information dealing with business transactions and records; to the file clerk who stores and must find business records quickly; to the salesperson who records cash and charge transactions and who is concerned with inventories and sales taxes; to the person planning to operate his own farm, garage, television repair shop, beauty parlor, or store; and to the management of any business. Lack of proper records and the lack of understanding of records is one of the most frequent causes of business failure. Finally, the importance of bookkeeping-accounting is related to the individual and family budgetkeeper who has difficulty living within a fixed income, keeping a checking account, preparing personal income tax statements, recording and reporting social security deductions from the pay of domestic employees, and the like.

Bookkeeping-Accounting Employment Outlook

The Need for Employment Information

If an instructor is teaching a vocational subject, it is obvious that he should have up-to-date information about the employment situation in the vocational area in which he is teaching. Without this information his guidance of students is questionable, and his teaching of the subject matter lacks authority.

This is an era of rapid change in employment patterns. The application of office automation to the mountains of clerical work which must be done is shifting employment needs, and it is not yet clear just what the result will be. Some say office automation eliminates jobs, which it does; but others point out that it also helps create new jobs, as do swollen population numbers and the increasing needs and desires of the world. What some of these jobs are and exactly what training they will require is not yet completely clear.

So it becomes a challenge for a B-A teacher to keep informed about office employment and to show wisdom in the assessment of information available to him. He should not be carried off too easily in the current of excitement for the "latest thing."

A teacher, like the driver of a car, needs to look back at what he has passed, around him at the present situation, and ahead in order to predict what might happen in the future occupations of those he teaches. With this view in all directions, his decisions in the area of guidance and educational planning should have the quality of soundness.

The figures which the United States Government makes available concerning employment classifies bookkeepers under the term "Clerical and kindred workers"; and in turn, "Clerical and kindred workers" are classified under "White-Collar Workers." The term "white-collar" has been applied generally to office workers because their jobs do not require special work clothes. Craftsmen are labeled "blue-collar" workers. Figure 1–3 shows the percentage of civilian white-collar workers compared with the percentage of civilian blue-collar workers.

Growth of white-collar workers. A look to the past shows that the large grouping of white-collar workers, which included bookkeepers, has increased in number markedly and constantly since

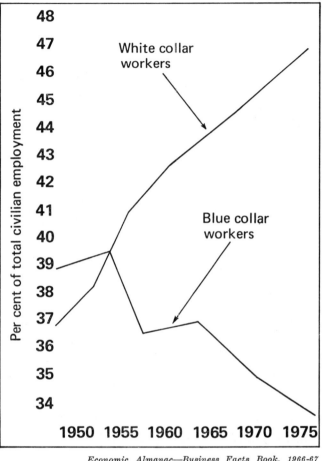

Economic Almanac—Business Facts Book, 1966-67
National Industrial Conference Board.

Figure 1—3. Comparison of white-collar workers and blue-collar workers

1900. The Bureau of Labor Statistics, United States Department of Labor, provides these figures:

Between 1900 and 1950, the number of white-collar workers increased by more than 300 percent, while blue-collar and service workers both increased by less than 150 percent. Thus, by 1950, white-collar workers accounted for 42 percent of the nonagricultural labor force, whereas blue-collar and service workers had dropped to 47 percent and 12 percent, respectively.[3]

Growth of clerical field. Within the white-collar group, the clerical field in which bookkeepers are grouped has shown the largest growth.

The greatest gains in white-collar employment between 1900 and 1950 occurred among clerical workers, who rose from the smallest to the largest white-collar group during this half century. By 1950, they accounted for one out of every three white-collar workers. Employment in stenographic, typing, and secretarial occupations alone increased elevenfold during the first half of the century. Such great increases were due in part to the greater volume of record-keeping required in all phases of industrial activity and to the expansion of industries such as banking, insurance, and government, where accurate and detailed records are particularly important.[4]

After 1950, the growth still continued in the large overall classification of white-collar workers.

The 1950's brought a continuation of the long-term upward trend in employment of white-collar workers. Between 1950 and 1960, total nonagricultural employment rose 17 percent, from 52.2 million to 61.1 million. During the same period, white-collar employment rose 27 percent, from 22.4 million to 28.5 million, reaching 47 percent of total nonagricultural employment by 1960 (table 2).[5]

From 1950 to 1960, the clerical field, too, showed well-defined increases, but not as great as between 1900-1950.

Clerical employment increased by 32 percent over the decade, reaching 9.7 million in 1960. Although this rate was substantial, it was much lower than in earlier decades. Greatly expanded use of tabulating machines, computers, and other office equipment such as duplicating machines probably helped to curtail the growth of clerical workers in the 1950's.[6]

---

[3] Carol Barry, U.S. Department of Labor, Bureau of Labor Statistics, "The White-Collar Worker in the 20th Century," a reprint from *Occupational Outlook Quarterly*, Vol. 5, No. 2 (Washington: U.S. Government Printing Office, May, 1961), p. 1.
[4] *Ibid.*, p. 2.
[5] *Ibid.*
[6] *Ibid.*

The 1968-69 edition of the *Occupational Outlook Handbook* reported that, "Almost 12 million people were employed in clerical or some closely related kind of work in early 1966."[7] It also summarized the 1966 employment picture in major clerical occupations with the following chart.

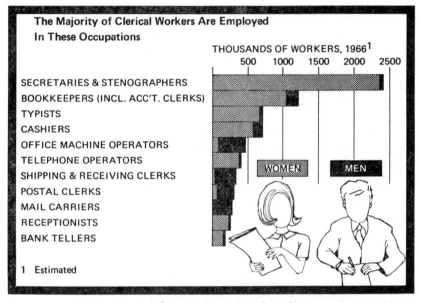

Figure 1—4. Employment in major clerical occupations

Bookkeeping employment. The Institute for Research, devoted to vocational research, makes this statement about bookkeeping employment.

> Statistics show there are at least a million persons in the general field of bookkeeping, and approximately a hundred different kinds of bookkeeping positions. . . .
>
> Women outnumber men in this career, in a ratio of about two to one. Specialized machines, however, are drawing men into bookkeeping, particularly in higher level positions, whch have to do with programming or setting up the machines.[8]

---

[7] U.S. Department of Labor, Bureau of Labor Statistics, *Occupational Outlook Handbook*, Bulletin No. 1550 (1968-69 ed.; Washington: U.S. Government Printing Office, 1968), p. 245.

[8] The Institute for Research, *Bookkeeper and Bookkeeping Machine Operator—Careers (Including Operation of Data Processing Machines)*, Research No. 115 (Chicago: 1968), p. 5.

B-A teachers who might object to the amount of space in high school texts devoted to bookkeeping for retail establishments, or who are tempted to shift the emphasis of their vocational course to training for bookkeeping work in large offices, should be aware that, "Well over one-third of all bookkeeping workers are employed by retail stores or wholesale houses." [9]

The United States Department of Labor reports further that one-fifth of the workers are employed by manufacturing companies, and about one-sixth by finance, insurance, and real estate firms.[10] The Department also states that, "Substantial numbers are employed also by public utility companies and construction firms and in other business and professional offices." [11]

Employment outlook for clerical workers. While the *rate* of growth in the future for white-collar workers cannot be expected to be as great as between 1900 and 1960, *growth* in employment in this general area is predicted for the years ahead. The 1968-69 edition of the *Occupational Outlook Handbook* states:

> Employment in clerical occupations is expected to rise moderately during the rest of the 1960's and through the 1970's. As employment rises to meet the needs of an expanding economy, more than 325,000 new positions in clerical and related occupations will be added each year. An even greater number of clerical workers will be needed each year to replace those who retire or leave their job for other reasons.[12]

In an article pointing out some of the more promising job opportunities that will be available through the 1970's to the high school graduate, the following statement is made:

> Employment in clerical occupations is expected to rise moderately through the 1970's. However, employee turnover is especially high among clerical workers because many of them are young women who work for only a few years and then leave their jobs because of family responsibilities. Employment opportunities will be numerous for secretaries and stenographers, typists, and bookkeeping and

---

[9] U.S. Department of Labor, Bureau of Labor Statistics, "Employment Outlook for Bookkeeping Workers, Office Machine Operators," *Occupational Outlook Handbook,* a reprint of Bulletin No. 1300-17 (Washington: 1961), p. 1.

[10] *Ibid.*

[11] *Ibid.*

[12] *Occupational Outlook Handbook,* Bulletin No. 1550, *op. cit.,* p. 246.

accounting clerks. Though less numerous than the traditional clerical occupations, office jobs associated with electronic computers show the fastest growth.[13]

Employment outlook for bookkeepers. The United States Department of Labor has this to say in its 1968-69 *Occupational Outlook Handbook* about the employment outlook for bookkeepers specifically.

> The number of bookkeeping workers is expected to increase moderately during the rest of the 1960's and through the 1970's. The number of openings to be filled is expected to exceed 75,000 each year as new jobs are created and replacements are needed for employees who retire or stop working for other reasons. Additional thousands of workers will be needed annually to replace bookkeeping workers who transfer to other types of employment.
>
> Employment in this field is expected to rise mainly as a result of the long-term growth of business and recordkeeping needs resulting from population expansion and economic prosperity. The increasing use of electronic data processing equipment and other mechanized bookkeeping machines, however, is expected to limit somewhat the growth of employment requirements for bookkeeping workers. Many types of machines such as posting machines, punchcard machines, and electronic computers can process accounting and bookkeeping data more accurately, rapidly, and economically than can be done by hand. Nevertheless, the need for bookkeeping workers will probably outpace the laborsaving impact of office machines over the next 10 to 15 years.[14]

Employment outlook for accountants. While high school teachers cannot turn out accountants, it is logical to assume that some of their B-A students may continue their study into the field of accounting. Therefore, in order to guide students effectively, a knowledge of the employment outlook for the accountant is of value to the teacher. According to the Bureau of Labor Statistics, "Accountants numbered about 500,000 in early 1967, of whom about 100,000 were certified public accountants. Accounting is one of the largest fields of professional employment for men. Only about 2 percent of the CPA's, and less than 10 percent of all accountants

---

[13] Russell B. Flanders, "Jobs with a Future for High School Graduates," *Occupational Outlook Quarterly* (February, 1968), pp. 27-28.

[14] *Occupational Outlook Handbook,* Bulletin No. 1550, *op. cit.,* p. 254.

are women." [15] This latter statement offers a sharp contrast to book-keeping employment where women predominate.

The Bureau of Labor Statistics further reports:

> Employment opportunities for accountants are expected to be excellent through the 1970's. As many as 12,000 accountants may be needed annually during this period to replace those who retire, die, or transfer to other occupations. Provided no major setback occurs in the general level of business activity, at least an equal number of accountants probably will be needed each year due to growth in the occupation. Demand for college-trained accountants will rise faster than demand for people without this broad background of training, because of the growing complexity of business accounting requirements. However, graduates of business and other schools which offer thorough training in accounting should have good job prospects during this period, also.

> Accounting employment is expected to expand rapidly in the 1970's because of such factors as the greater use of accounting information in business management; complex and changing tax systems; the growth in size and number of business corporations required to provide financial reports to stockholders; and the increasing use of accounting services by small business organizations.

> The computer is having a major effect on the accounting profession. Electronic data processing systems are replacing manual preparation of accounting records and financial statements. As a result the need for junior accountants at the lower level may be reduced or eliminated. On the other hand, computers can process vast quantities of routine data which will require the employment of additional accountants so that these data can be analyzed. Also, the computer is expected to bring about radical changes in management information systems and decision-making processes in large companies. Additional highly-trained accountants will be required to prepare, administer and analyze the information made available by these systems.[16]

It would seem that after all the statistics have been read and assessed there is going to be a continuing need for workers in bookkeeping at all levels—from the routine clerical type of book-keeper to the college trained accountant. The compilers of the statistics imply that in a complicated world bookkeeping and

---

15 *Ibid.*, p. 32.
16 *Ibid.*, pp. 33-34.

accounting are becoming more complicated, too. So it seems that there is a real need for B-A teachers who understand the complex situation and who can convey their knowledge to others.

The working conditions of the bookkeeper. In a career research on the work of the bookkeeper, this statement is made indicating the wide area of employment in bookkeeping:

> Bookkeeping is so essential to modern business that persons in this vocation find employment in every community, large and small. There are also part-time, free-lance bookkeepers, who have their own businesses and service small or special accounts, and others who specialize in complicated types of bookkeeping.[17]

What are the general conditions of work in this wide area? The hours of work per week vary with the type of business, size of the firm, and the community in which the firm is located. Some bookkeepers, like accountants, are often obliged to work under pressure at certain periods of the year. For the bookkeeper, this is usually toward the end of the month and at income tax reporting time. At these times it is not uncommon for them to work extra hours, sometimes without extra pay, balancing and closing the books, preparing statements, sending out bills, and the like. Vacations for bookkeepers follow the usual pattern for other office workers in the community. This is commonly a one- or two-week paid vacation after six months or a year of successive employment. Most companies offer retirement plans and have hospital insurance, unemployment insurance, Social Security, and Workmen's Compensation.

The bookkeeper's job is a confining one, and the routine of the work will not vary much. However, in the larger offices a capable bookkeeper may find his position a stepping-stone to becoming a department head, an office manager, an accountant, an auditor, a comptroller, a treasurer, or a credit and collections manager.

The salaries that bookkeepers or accounting clerks receive will vary according to the level of work done, the size of the organization, and the kind of locality in which the organization is situated.

---

[17] The Institute for Research, *loc. cit.*

Large cities have jobs paying higher salaries than do small communities, and manufacturing concerns usually pay higher salaries than other kinds of business. The Institute for Research reports, "A comparison of salaries in a recent survey showed beginning bookkeepers and bookkeeping machine operators received from $70 to $85 a week. A full-time hand bookkeeper receives around $100 a week; a bookkeeping machine operator, from $395 to $400 a month." [18]

The report continues:

> A survey of fifty metropolitan areas showed the average monthly pay for hand bookkeepers to be from $250 to $500 a month. A beginner starts at a minimum rate, and receives an increase in salary at the end of a three-month period if satisfactory, according to the survey.

Bookkeepers have not been organized into a national labor union. In some of the larger metropolitan offices and in a few small offices, however, bookkeepers, along with other office workers, have been faced with the decision of joining or not joining a union that encompasses their area of employment.

Personal traits of a bookkeeper. Bookkeepers or accounting clerks must have a liking for figures and an aptitude for working with them. Even though there are machines to perform tedious tasks, some calculation by hand will be necessary.

The Institute for Research indicates some personal qualities desirable in a bookkeeper which the teacher might note for purposes of guidance.

> Patience is an important quality for the bookkeeper. Many times, a small and elusive error will throw long columns of figures out of balance, and it will take much checking before the error is discovered.
>
> An alert mind is essential, as are the abilities to reason and concentrate. Where his office is not off by itself, the bookkeeper must be able to ignore all distractions, and become absorbed in his own particular work.
>
> Accuracy is highly important. The accuracy of every transaction must be determined constantly. This requires a methodical nature with orderly and systematic habits. Legibility of handwriting and neatness are important.

---

[18] *Ibid.*, p. 16.

The bookkeeper must have a good memory, and the ability to get to the bottom of troublesome problems. In a small organization, the bookkeeper has to know all the departments and divisions of the business, and where to go for all necessary information.

Tact and discretion are important personal qualifications, for the bookkeeper often deals with fellow employees, customers, or clientele. Salaries of employees, known to the bookkeeper, should not be discussed, nor should private company matters of which he is aware be divulged.[19]

These descriptions emphasize the fact that a bookkeeper's work is of a confidential nature and of great importance, requiring a trustworthy person with a deep sense of responsibility. It is the teacher's responsibility to convey this concept of a bookkeeper's work to those who study with him.

Need for study of individual community. The status of B-A employment is not complete for the individual teacher until he has specific information about the particular community in which his school functions. The facts and figures presented in this chapter are characteristic of the United States as a whole, but a study of the individual community may present a somewhat different situation which must be taken into account in planning a school program. It becomes a responsibility of the teacher, therefore, to inform himself as well as his school of the employment scene in his own particular community. The resources available to the B-A teacher in his local community and the use of these resources in his teaching are discussed in Chapter 8, *School and Community Resources.*

STUDY QUESTIONS

1. What are the conditions of today which make the role of the B-A teacher a vital one?

2. If a person tells you he is a bookkeeper, why can you not today be sure of exactly what he does in an office?

---

[19] *Ibid.,* p. 16.

3. What are the situations in the modern office that create problems in content and method in the B-A classroom?

4. Where, besides in a business office, is B-A work performed?

5. What are the major differences between *record keeping, bookkeeping,* and *accounting?*

6. State at least three major reasons why the need for B-A work has increased in recent years.

7. Give several illustrations of how a knowledge and skill of bookkeeping can be of real value to people who are not, or do not plan to become, vocational bookkeepers?

8. Why should a B-A teacher keep abreast of office employment opportunities?

9. What type of workers are labeled "white-collar" workers by the United States Government when making employment classifications? "blue-collar" workers?

10. What were the reasons for the tremendous growth of the clerical field between the years 1900-1960?

11. Why has the growth rate of clerical workers since 1960 to the present not been as rapid as in earlier years?

12. In what type of business are most of the bookkeepers in this country employed? About how many?

13. What predictions concerning employment for future bookkeepers does the United States Department of Labor make? Will electronic machines have an effect?

14. What is the employment outlook for accountants?

15. What are the characteristics of a bookkeeper's work that might cause people to like it? What characteristics might cause others to dislike it?

16. What are some of the personal qualities that are desirable for a potential bookkeeper or accounting clerk to have before entering the B-A field?

17. Why is it important for the high school B-A instructor to know what is going on in the business field in his own community?

DISCUSSION QUESTIONS

1. It has been said that because of the coming of automated data processing the position of a bookkeeper will disappear. Do you agree?

2. What are the advantages to the B-A teacher of his having a clear picture of bookkeeping in the United States? in his own community?

3. By what different ways and means can a B-A teacher find out about the work and the pay of bookkeepers in his community?

4. Suppose one of your high school students had an opportunity to do bookkeeping work before studying the subject and challenged you with the statement, "But we didn't do it that way in the office where I worked." How would you answer him?

5. Discuss the differences in the characteristics that might be required in the work of a bookkeeper and an accountant as indicated by the nature of the work described in this chapter.

6. What advantages and disadvantages do you see for office workers being members of a labor union?

7. What part can or should B-A teachers play in helping to raise the pay standards of bookkeepers?

8. Discuss the possibility of manual bookkeeping in the year 2000.

PROJECTS

1. Interview two or more B-A workers employed in different size offices and write a report on the similarities and the differences in the work they do.

2. Interview a secretary, a salesperson, and either the manager or owner of a service station, a small garage, a beauty shop, or a farm for the purpose of finding out and reporting how a knowledge of bookkeeping is of help to each in his work.

3. Analyze the "Help Wanted" advertisements in several newspapers (preferably metropolitan) calling for people with bookkeeping ability. Classify these results as to characteristics, abilities, pay, etc. Summarize your findings, and state your conclusions.

4. From the latest United States Census report secure the employment figures for bookkeepers in your state and the nearest large city. Compare with other office occupations and with industrial employment.

5. Prepare a paper on "The Present Status of Bookkeeping-Accounting Work in My Community."

6. Prepare a paper on "The Present Status of Bookkeeping-Accounting Employment in My Community."

7. Interview an accountant and a bookkeeper and report on (a) their reactions to the offering of B-A courses in high school, and (b) what they believe the basic content of such courses should be.

8. Interview several local businessmen who are employers of B-A workers and report on their beliefs about the need for B-A courses in the high school.

SELECTED REFERENCES

Barry, Carol. U.S. Department of Labor, Bureau of Labor Statistics. "The White-Collar Worker in the 20th Century." A reprint from *Occupational Outlook Quarterly.* V (May, 1967), 1.

Blackstone, Bruce I., and Emanuel Weinstein. "Factors Affecting Bookkeeping and Accounting as a Career," *Developing Vocational Competency in Bookkeeping and Accounting.* Eastern Business Teachers Assn. Yearbook, Vol. 40, Chap. 1 (New York: New York University Bookstore, 1967).

Careers—Bookkeeper and Bookkeeping Machine Operator. Chicago: The Institute for Research, 1968.

Carlson, Arthur E. "A Career in Bookkeeping and Accounting," *Business Education Forum.* XVIII (January, 1964), 10-11.

Durham, Winfred. "Relation of Bookkeeping Instructions to the Duties Performed by Bookkeepers," *Balance Sheet.* XLIII (November, 1961), 105-106, 144.

Flanders, Russell B. "Jobs With a Future for High School Graduates," *Occupational Outlook Quarterly.* XII (February, 1968), 27-28.

Hertzfeld, Arthur. "Aptitudes, Personality Traits, and Educational Preparation Essential to Successful Employment," *Developing Vocational Competency in Bookkeeping and Accounting,* Eastern Business Teachers Assn. Yearbook, Vol. 40, Chap. 2 (New York: New York University Bookstore, 1967).

Kitson, Harry D. *Commercial Education in Secondary Schools.* New York: Ginn and Co., 1929.

Kuklinski, Walda M. "What Executives Say About Bookkeeping," *Business Education Forum.* XXII (February, 1968), 19.

U.S. Department of Labor. *Dictionary of Occupational Titles,* Vol. I. *Definitions of Titles,* 3d ed. Washington: U.S. Government Printing Office, 1965.

U.S. Department of Labor, Bureau of Labor Statistics. *Occupational Outlook Handbook,* 1968-1969 ed. Washington: U.S. Government Printing Office, 1968.

Weaver, David H. "Are My Bookkeeping Students Ready for Jobs?" *Business Teacher.* XLIV (March-April, 1967), 4-5.

Bookkeeping Enrollments

Public High Schools

Next to typewriting, the B-A course continues to be the most popular business course in student enrollments in the public high schools of the United States. The latest national survey of offerings and enrollments in high school subjects conducted by the United States Office of Education was for the year 1960-61.

Comparative enrollments in public high school bookkeeping courses for the years 1948-49 and 1960-61 were as follows:

	Pupils Enrolled *			
Bookkeeping Course	1948-49 [1] Total	1948-49 Percentage	1960-61 [2] Total	1960-61 Percentage
First year	398,081	84.3	562,370 **	89.2
Second year	69,637	14.7	64,936	10.3
Third and Fourth years ..	4,445 ***	1.0	3,408	.5
TOTALS	472,163	100.0	630,714	100.0

 * Includes pupils enrolled in half-year courses. Enrollments in half-year courses amounted to about 2½ percent of the total enrollments. Alaska and Hawaii are not included in the 1948-49 figures.
 ** Includes 709 students reported as enrolled in "General Bookkeeping." This term was described in correspondence with the U.S. Office of Education as, ". . . a basic course in bookkeeping."
 *** This figure reported in the 1948-49 survey as "Third Year" enrollees, not as "Third and Fourth years."

[1] U.S. Office of Education, "Offerings and Enrollments in High School Subjects 1948-49," *Biennial Survey of Education in the United States, 1948-50* (Washington: U.S. Government Printing Office, 1951), chap. v.
[2] U.S. Office of Education, *Summary of Offerings and Enrollments in Public Secondary Schools* (Washington: U.S. Government Printing Office, June, 1964).

During 1960-61, 630,714 students were enrolled in public high school bookkeeping courses. This is an increase of 158,551 over the 472,163 bookkeeping course enrollees reported in the previous survey of 1948-49.

While these comparative figures show a substantial increase of 33% in the bookkeeping enrollments during this twelve-year span, the total pupil population during this time was increasing about twice as fast. Reasons why the increase in bookkeeping enrollments lags behind the increase in school population are supplied later in this chapter.

It is worth noting from the preceding two surveys that of the total students enrolled in bookkeeping courses, about 5 percent fewer were proceeding to an advanced bookkeeping course in 1960-61 than in 1948-49. There is some likelihood, however, that this trend may have been reversed since the 1960-61 survey as a result of the enactment of the Vocational Education Act of 1963. This act, which is discussed in Chapter 13, made federal funds available for the first time to reimburse high schools offering vocational office training. As a result, the next national survey may show that the stimulus of the federal monies available under the Vocational Education Act of 1963 has caused increased enrollments in vocational business courses, including bookkeeping courses.

Nonpublic High Schools

In addition to the 630,714 students enrolled in public high school bookkeeping courses reported in the 1960-61 survey, a survey [3] of nonpublic secondary schools in 1961-62 disclosed the following:

Bookkeeping Course	Pupils Enrolled *	
	1961-62	Percentage
First year	53,026	89.5
Second year	6,108	10.3
Third and Fourth years	123	.2
TOTAL	59,257	100.0

* Includes pupils enrolled in half-year courses. Those in half-year courses were less than 2 percent of the total.

[3] U.S. Office of Education, *Subject Offerings and Enrollments, Grades 9-12, Nonpublic Secondary Schools, 1961-62* (Washington: U.S. Government Printing Office, 1965).

About 90 percent of these enrollments were in Roman Catholic secondary schools. The remainder was distributed somewhat equally between other-church related schools and non-church related schools.

If the total bookkeeping enrollments of all secondary schools in the United States are combined, both public and nonpublic, at the start of the 1960's there was a total of close to 700,000 students studying bookkeeping.

Years of Bookkeeping-Accounting Offered

Extent of Bookkeeping-Accounting Offerings Vary

The enrollment statistics for B-A courses indicate very clearly that all students do not study the subject for the same length of time. It is also true that all high schools do not offer the same length of training in bookkeeping-accounting. Some offer it for one year, some provide two years, and a relatively few provide more than two years of instruction. What are the reasons for this variation in course offerings by secondary schools?

The First-Year Course Is Most Popular

There are three principal reasons why the very great majority of students who enroll in B-A courses do so for only one year. These are as follows:

1. Many students cannot take an advanced course because some high schools do not find it feasible to offer more than one year of B-A instruction. This opinion is derived from the national enrollment figures listed on a previous page.

2. Most schools that offer various sequences in their business education curriculum, such as stenographic, selling, or clerical, require students majoring in such sequences to take one year of B-A instruction. One year is generally considered sufficient for such students planning to enter sales or office work.

3. Some students who complete a first-year course find that they lack the interest or the ability for studying an advanced course.

The Advanced Bookkeeping-Accounting Courses Are More Selective

B-A courses beyond the first year have vocational bookkeeping and accounting as their major aim. Such primarily vocational preparation is open, as a general rule, only to those students who possess the potentialities for success in this vocation or who are planning to go on to study accounting in college. It is generally agreed, therefore, that students who have shown limited aptitude and interest in first-year bookkeeping-accounting, or who have not proven themselves capable in this field, should be discouraged from continuing the subject.

Advanced B-A courses are not equally popular in all sections of the United States. For example, a study of enrollment figures supplied for the various states in the national survey [4] of 1960-61 will show that while high schools in New England and the Middle Atlantic states account for about a quarter of the total enrollments in first-year bookkeeping-accounting, their enrollments in advanced courses amount to nearly two-thirds of the national enrollments in these courses. One reason for this difference may be traced to the comparative density of population and size of high schools in different states or sections of the country. Another reason would seem to be a difference in educational philosophy on the comparative emphasis or importance given to vocational education.

Improvised Ways of Offering High School Bookkeeping-Accounting Instruction

Many schools because of their size, limited enrollment, and the type of community they serve cannot educationally or financially justify more than one year of B-A instruction. To offer a strictly or predominately vocational second-year course to three or four qualified students whom the community might absorb into such vocational employment often is not the best use of time and funds. Extremely small schools might offer a similar argument against a one-year course.

One successful solution that some schools have found to this problem is to offer a diversified occupations training program. In such a program the too few students for a separate course in bookkeeping-accounting, auto mechanics, carpentry, and other subjects are grouped into one class for what help and guidance an especially qualified teacher is able to give the group. This training may be supplemented by an apprenticeship situation in a part-time job under a capable employer.

---

[4] United States Office of Education, *Summary of Offerings and Enrollments in Public Secondary Schools, loc. cit.*

Another successful solution of the problem of very small classes is the method that is known as supervised correspondence. Under this plan a number of students, each possibly studying a different subject, are brought together in one class where they work under the supervision of a teacher. The teacher need not be qualified to teach all the subjects that are being studied because each student uses instructions and lesson plans provided by the correspondence center, often a state university or college. The supervising teacher makes certain that the work is being completed according to instructions, does some routine checking, and mails to the correspondence center all work that is to be graded. This work is then returned with the comments and the suggestions of the grader. The supervising teacher also administers the tests that are sent out by the correspondence center, but the tests, like the daily work, are graded at the correspondence center.

Supervised correspondence is of sufficient importance that the National Association of Secondary School Principals published a bulletin dealing exclusively with this subject.[5] This method has been found very helpful to schools not otherwise able to offer all subjects required to meet the needs of their pupils.

Another type of compromise that some small high schools use as a solution for meeting community and student needs is to offer B-A courses every other year. The 1960-61 national survey [6] indicated that a total of 840 public high schools reported first-year and general bookkeeping courses offered in alternate years, but not in 1960-61. This survey also showed that a total of 35 schools reported the offering of second-year B-A courses every other year, but not in 1960-61. When second-year bookkeeping-accounting is offered on alternate years, the first-year course must be available in the tenth year so that these students who must postpone for one year taking the second course can do so in their last or twelfth year.

Still another educational compromise is to teach the first- and second-year courses together—in one classroom at the same time. Such compromises raise a question of educational values. Do the advantages of these practices outweigh the disadvantages? Perhaps these decisions are best reached on an individual community and school basis.

---

[5] *The Bulletin of the National Association of Secondary School Principals*, Vol. 36, No. 190 (December, 1952).

[6] United States Office of Education, *Summary of Offerings and Enrollments in Public Secondary Schools, loc. cit.*

One Versus Two Years of High School Bookkeeping-Accounting

Some schools improvise and compromise in order to supply a second year of advanced vocational bookkeeping-accounting. Others offer only one year of bookkeeping-accounting through considered choice rather than necessity. Who is right? Should there be more than a one-year course? The answer is not the same for all schools. Many high schools can justify a second-year course. The right answer for an individual school depends upon the facts present in the community served by the school.

The degree to which affirmative answers are forthcoming to the following questions would be some indication of the need for and the justification of a second-year B-A course.

1. Is there a sufficient need in the community for persons trained in this special area to justify such training? (A survey of employment needs would supply the factual answer to this basic question.)

2. Do enough former graduates now working in the business community favor such a course—feel that they were "short changed" by the lack of such a course when they were in high school? (A follow-up study of former graduates would supply factual answers to this question.)

3. Are the local employers of office workers in favor of such a course being offered in the high school?

4. Does the local school system offer more than one year of vocational training in one or more other courses such as carpentry, typewriting, auto mechanics, agriculture, stenography, and home economics? If so, doesn't the school then have as much responsibility for providing a second-year course in bookkeeping-accounting?

There is little doubt that many schools offering only one year of bookkeeping-accounting could justify a second year on the evidence of affirmative answers that they could compile to the above questions. But there are arguments pro and con to this problem. Some administrators claim that the high school can best benefit the student by giving him more of a well-rounded education rather than by having him spend a second year in a specialized vocational area. Vocationalists, second-year B-A teachers, and others reply that vocational training is one of the major purposes of education and therefore an integral part of general education. They believe that without preparation for earning a living in this age of specialization, one is not generally educated.

There are some educators who say that, just as there was a trend away from three- and four-year bookkeeping courses in the high school several decades ago, today there is a trend away from two years of high school bookkeeping-accounting. The comparative enrollment figures for the years 1948-49 and 1960-61 on the first page of this chapter tend to support such a claim. But as stated earlier, it is likely that federal funds from the Vocational Education Act of 1963 have stimulated enrollments in bookkeeping courses in recent years.

More Than Two Years of High School Bookkeeping-Accounting

When high schools offer more than two years of B-A instruction, they perhaps would find it challenging to provide proof that such courses are more worthwhile than other courses which the student could be taking. How many students who took a third year of bookkeeping-accounting secured office jobs solely because they had this additional year? How many such students advanced on the job more rapidly or were paid more money because of this extra third year? Did it cause those who went on to college accounting courses to make a better college record than those who had only two years of bookkeeping-accounting in high school?

One study, some years ago, answered this last question by stating in its conclusions that the learning of accountancy is not improved in any way by any additional training in bookkeeping beyond two years in high school. At the same time it should be mentioned that several studies have been made which show that students who have studied bookkeeping-accounting in high school generally earn better than average grades in their introductory college accounting courses. Furthermore, ". . . some schools have worked out an arrangement with higher educational institutions whereby second-year bookkeeping students are permitted to take placement examinations in accounting at the college or university. If they do well in these examinations, they are given advanced standing for college accounting and are permitted to enter second- or third-semester college accounting (courses) depending upon the scores they make on the college placement tests."[7] High schools offering more than two years of bookkeeping-accounting owe their students and themselves proof of the relative value of such courses above other courses which the students might take instead.

This is not to deny or oppose the value of giving all vocational students a reserve in knowledge and skill beyond the initial job requirements. It is merely to claim that two years of good B-A instruction for the average high school student is a maximum which can and should supply such a reserve. Some very able teachers dealing with very able students accomplish this in less than two years.

Post-High School Bookkeeping-Accounting Instruction

Where the ever-increasing junior or community colleges and technical institutes have established themselves, there has been a definite trend to move specialized education, including vocational bookkeeping-accounting, into the 13th and 14th grades of these post-high school institutions. This upgrading of bookkeeping-accounting to the junior college level is bound to have a bearing on the enrollments in high school courses. It is perhaps a major reason why enrollments in high school B-A courses have not increased in the same proportion as overall high school enrollments for the past several decades.

The upgrading trend is a logical one because employers generally prefer to hire more mature workers than those represented by the usual high school graduate. This trend will also release time for offering a more complete general education program in an already crowded high school curriculum. However, just as long as there are students who leave school at high school age or at the completion of their high school studies, there will be a need for vocational preparation in the high school. Therefore, while this upgrading trend is probably causing a decrease in the high school enrollment of some vocational B-A courses, the possibility of such courses being removed entirely from the high school curriculum cannot be foreseen.

---

[7] Hamden L. Forkner, Robert M. Swanson, and Robert J. Thompson, *The Teaching of Bookkeeping*, Monograph 101 (Cincinnati: South-Western Publishing Co., 1960), p. 3.

Record Keeping

The teaching of record keeping and the place of record keeping courses in the high school curriculum is discussed in Chapter 13, "Developing Trends Affecting Bookkeeping-Accounting Instruction," starting on page 331 under the topic *Downgrading the Subject Matter of Bookkeeping-Accounting.*

Grade Placement

The logical and ideal place to teach any skill or vocational subject is immediately before it is to be put to use. A vocational B-A student should not complete his specialized preparation in the tenth or eleventh grade and then have a one- or two-year forgetting period before he graduates from high school, gets a job, and puts his knowledge and skill to work. Furthermore, specialized preparation, which is rightly placed in the last years of high school, should be available to certain *deserving* and *capable* students in their tenth or eleventh year *if it is known* that they will leave high school before they reach the eleventh or twelfth year. In other words, programming of students into vocational courses should be sufficiently flexible so as not to deny certain capable students who will leave high school before graduation an opportunity for vocational preparation.

One study concerning when students started to enroll in specialized vocational business courses reported the following.

Only basic business subjects are being taught in the ninth and tenth years, and specialization begins in the eleventh year. Of the seventy-five school districts investigated, thirty-eight offer either general business or business arithmetic in the ninth grade, while forty-eight schools offered these courses in the tenth grade. The table below shows the number of schools in which sequences begin in the ninth, tenth, and eleventh years, respectively.

Years in Which Specialization Begins	No. of Schools
Ninth Year	3
Tenth Year	12
Eleventh Year	54

It is an interesting fact that the three schools in which specialization began in the ninth year offered only two sequences—bookkeeping and stenography. Of the twelve schools in which specialization began in the tenth year, eleven offered only bookkeeping and stenographic sequences. Specialization before the eleventh grade is not recommended. . . .[8]

Related Business Education Subjects

Importance of Related Business Subjects

The United States Department of Labor in its 1968-69 *Occupational Outlook Handbook* indicates the importance of other office education courses for B-A workers in addition to a course in bookkeeping-accounting.

> In selecting workers for bookkeeping jobs, most employers prefer high school graduates who have taken business arithmetic and bookkeeping. Some prefer applicants who have completed a post-high school business training program or junior college. Training which includes typewriting and the use of office machines is often very helpful, since many bookkeeping workers perform a variety of office duties.
>
> In many small establishments, one *general bookkeeper* (D.O.T. 210.388) does all of the analysis, recording, and other work necessary to keep a complete set of books. Although employees in positions of this kind may use simple office equipment such as adding machines, they do most of their work by hand. Often they also file, answer the telephone, prepare and mail out customers' bills, and perform other general office work.[9]

Enrollments in Business Subjects

Business education courses that B-A majors are either required to take or may elect to take vary with the offerings and requirements of individual high schools. The following national enrollment figures for the common courses under the supervision of business education departments when the surveys were made reflect their popularity and the trend in popularity between the twelve-year span of these two surveys.

---

[8] John C. Roman, *The Business Curriculum*, Monograph 100 (Cincinnati: South-Western Publishing Co., 1960), p. 45.

[9] U.S. Department of Labor, Bureau of Labor Statistics, *Occupational Outlook Handbook*, Bulletin No. 1550 (1968-69 ed.; Washington: U.S. Government Printing Office, 1968), p. 253.

A COMPARATIVE SUMMARY
of
OFFERINGS AND ENROLLMENTS IN
BUSINESS EDUCATION SUBJECTS
of
PUBLIC SECONDARY SCHOOLS
1948-49 and 1960-61

	Pupils Enrolled *	
Subject **	Total [10] 1948-49	Total [11] 1960-61
Typewriting	1,216,142	1,902,592
Bookkeeping	472,163	630,714
Shorthand	421,635	550,321
General Business	279,577	461,793
Business Arithmetic	249,690	298,941
Office Practice	108,201	189,935
Business Law	130,585	167,101
Clerical Practice	—	95,992
Business English	56,620	91,717
Office Machines	—	89,986
Salesmanship	50,475	49,338
Economic Geography	90,045	41,567
Consumer Education	38,872	40,520
Retailing	28,170	40,312
Cooperative Office Training	21,452	13,904
Advertising	6,208	2,838

* Includes pupils enrolled in half-year courses. Alaska and Hawaii not included in 1948-49 figures.
** Listed in order of popularity during the 1960-61 survey.

Typewriting. Studies have been made to show the frequency of various activities performed by office workers. Using the typewriter is one of the most common office activities. As a result of these studies and because of the level of typewriting required, most bookkeepers or accounting clerks can acquire sufficient skill within one year. Therefore, it seems essential that all high school B-A majors be required to learn to typewrite. An examination of

[10] United States Office of Education, *Biennial Survey of Education in the United States 1948-50, loc. cit.*

[11] United States Office of Education, *Summary of Offerings and Enrollments in Public Secondary Schools, loc. cit.*

courses of study shows such a requirement is a common element in most high school B-A sequences throughout the country.

Shorthand. Stenography as a vocation is separate from bookkeeping-accounting. In occasional small businesses, however, employers sometimes seek workers who possess a combination of office skills, including stenography, typewriting, and bookkeeping-accounting. Since this stenographic employment "requirement" is not a general one, the answer to the problem will undoubtedly vary from community to community. Therefore, schools could and should find the right answer by surveying their communities or graduates to determine if such training should be offered to the vocational B-A students in their schools.

In the main, however, (1) because of the already "tight" high school curriculum with its many required courses, and (2) because students who have a strong aptitude and interest in bookkeeping-accounting may not possess similar strengths in shorthand, and vice versa, and (3) because shorthand skill adds little to one's understanding of business and how it operates—has little value unless used vocationally—it is questionable that any school should make shorthand a requirement for those students with a vocational interest in bookkeeping-accounting.

General business. (Sometimes called basic business or junior business.) General business is, next to typewriting, the most popular of all social or related business subjects open to or required of B-A students. It is most often found in the ninth grade. Some schools, however, offer it in the tenth year, and a few permit or require juniors and seniors to fit it into their programs. General business, like general science, general mathematics, and other generalized high school subjects, should, when it is properly organized along the lines of common personal business experiences and properly taught, be required of all high school students, not just business education students. Frequently, however, the aims of this course are so specialized that it deserves no such status as a general education course.

In either case, whether general business has such a general aim as "to provide training in consumer business activities in which all persons engage," or a more specialized aim, such as "to provide a knowledge of business practices and principles for vocational use," future B-A students should, in general, be required to take general business.

Business arithmetic. Business arithmetic is also a very popular related business education course in the high schools of the country. A knowledge of arithmetic is necessary to the understanding and performing of bookkeeping-accounting. Business arithmetic is most commonly found in the ninth and tenth years, with a few schools offering it in the eleventh and twelfth years. Most students who are required to take business arithmetic or have the opportunity to elect it, enroll in it either the year immediately before they start their B-A instruction or take it concurrently with their first year of bookkeeping-accounting. Some teachers believe that business arithmetic should be learned immediately before the first year of B-A instruction, while others think it should be taught in a course concurrently with the first-year course.

Both sides of this controversy are discussed on page 308. Remarks on the teaching of business arithmetic and its relationship to B-A instruction will be found on pages 308-311.

Clerical office practice. In some schools there are clerical office practice courses called office machines, general clerical practice, office practice, and secretarial practice. These courses are commonly found in the twelfth year and have as their major aim the purpose of rounding out the vocational office preparation of students majoring in the B-A or the secretarial sequences. For example, some high schools that terminate their B-A courses at the end of the eleventh year require their B-A students to take training in courses called office practice, or clerical practice, or office machines during the twelfth year. Such courses, in addition to teaching common vocational office practices, require these students to keep their B-A knowledge and skills in practice through the use of assigned problems and materials for use on the machines and the like. In this way a year of forgetting can be eliminated, and B-A knowledge and skill can be reinforced. Schools that follow such practice cannot be criticized for forcing a year of forgetting upon their vocational B-A students.

In other schools office practice is a twelfth-year course for students who could not and did not succeed at the start of the secretarial or B-A sequences. The major purpose of this course is continuing office training in the simpler office skills and knowledges. The merit of caring for "failures" of the bookkeeping-accounting and the secretarial sequences in this manner has much to justify it. There is more general clerical work being done by general clerical workers in the offices of the country than there is bookkeeping-accounting and stenographic work combined. But when the office practice course is comprised wholly or in a large part of such students, its status in the curriculum is not improved if it earns the label, "For Low Ability Only."

A third group, made up primarily of large city high schools, has started giving this area of clerical training a higher status in the curriculum than that of a single course. For the past decade or two, such schools have been installing a clerical sequence in their business offerings. This clerical sequence parallels the older and more familiar bookkeeping, stenographic, and sales sequences. The illustration on page 42, showing the business education programs in the Syracuse (New York) high schools pictures this. It is worth noting that just as the clerical practice program has started to achieve its rightful place in the curriculums of large city high schools, the coming of automation to the office is likely to have its most telling effect in this area of routine and repetitive work.

Business law and other social business subjects. Business law, economics, economic geography, and consumer education or consumer economics are other courses frequently elected or required of students majoring in bookkeeping-accounting. It would be a rare school that would offer all of these courses. Furthermore, aside from business law, these courses are frequently offered in the social studies department of the high school rather than the business education department.

Bookkeeping-Accounting Programs
in
High Schools of Different Size

Bookkeeping-Accounting Programs Vary

No one curriculum can be set up that will suit the needs of all communities. Similarly, the various common high school programs such as business education, college preparatory, general, and industrial or vocational, will not only vary from state to state, but from city to city, as well as from school to school within the same city or school district.

Common patterns do, however, exist. One study [12] reported the following three business education programs as representative of three different sized high schools.

THE SMALL HIGH SCHOOL

Basic Business Curriculum

    Typewriting (one year) .... Grade 11
    Business Law (one semester) .... Grade 12
    Consumer Economics (one semester) ...... Grade 12

Stenographic Curriculum

    Shorthand (one year) .... Grade 12
    Office Practice (one year) .... Grade 12

General Clerical Curriculum

    Bookkeeping (one year) .... Grade 12
    Office Practice (one year) .... Grade 12

THE MEDIUM-SIZED HIGH SCHOOL

Three-, Four-, or Five-Teacher Business Education Department
(Vocational business pupils majoring in the stenographic sequence)

Grade 10	Grade 11	Grade 12
Business Mathematics	Bookkeeping I	Business English
General Business	Shorthand I	Business Law
	Typewriting I	Office Practice
		Shorthand II
		Typewriting II

(Vocational business pupils majoring in the bookkeeping-clerical sequence)

Grade 10	Grade 11	Grade 12
Business Mathematics	Bookkeeping I	Bookkeeping II
General Business	Principles of Selling	Business Law
	Typewriting I	Office Practice

---

[12] Roman, *op. cit.*, pp. 15-18.

THE LARGE HIGH SCHOOL
BUSINESS EDUCATION PROGRAMS IN THE SYRACUSE PUBLIC SCHOOLS

YEAR	COLLEGE PREPARATORY FOR**		BUSINESS PROGRAMS IN				GENERAL BUSINESS
	Secretarial Science	Business Administration	STENOGRAPHY***	BOOK-KEEPING	GENERAL CLERICAL	SALES	THREE UNIT BUSINESS CHOICE
9th Grade	English Ec. World Gen. Science Gen. Business El. Algebra		English Ec. World Gen. Science Gen. Business				English Ec. World Gen. Science Gen. Bus. or Algebra
10th Grade	English Wld. History Math. 10 Biology Language		English Wld. History Bus. Arithmetic Typewriting				English Wld. Hist. Bus. Choice
11th Grade	English Amer. Hist. Shorthand I Typewriting Language	English Amer. Hist. Bookkeep. I Typewriting Language	English Amer. Hist. Shorthand I Ofc. Prac. I Health*	English Amer. Hist. Bookkeep. I Ofc. Prac. I Health*	English Amer. Hist. Ofc. Prac. I Bookkeep. I Health*	English Amer. Hist. Salesmanship Bookkeep. I Health*	English Amer. Hist. Bus. Choice Health*
12th Grade	English Amer. Hist.* Bus. Law* Shtd. II & Transcrip.	English Amer. Hist.* Bus. Law* Bookkeep. II or Ofc. Prac. I or Salesmansh.	English Amer. Hist.* Shorthand II & Transcr. Bus. Law*	English Amer. Hist.* Bookkeep. II Bus. Law*	English Amer. Hist.* Ofc. Prac. II Bus. Law*	English Amer. Hist.* Merchandising Bus. Law*	English Amer. Hist.* Bus. Choice
Recommended Electives	Bookkeep. I Speech* Bus. Mgmt.*	Speech* Bus. Mgmt.*	9th — Homemaking or Industrial Arts 10th — Art* & Music* or 1 year of either 11th or 12th — Speech*; Home & Family Living*; Bus. Mgmt.*; Bookkeeping I strongly recommended for Steno. major				Confer with counselor

* Indicates a one-semester course

** Enrollment only with approval of counselor

*** Ninth- and tenth-grade English average of 80 per cent required

Curriculum Requirements Are More Flexible Today

Not many years ago when programming an entering high school student, the common practice was to place him in a selected curriculum—on a prescribed "track." Through testing, guidance, and parental or student choice the student was then labeled as being either "College Preparatory," "Commercial," or "General." The commercial students were then similarly placed on such other "tracks" as *secretarial* or *bookkeeping*. Being placed on one of these "tracks" in some schools resulted in a rigid adherence to prescribed courses in each "track" or curriculum.

In 1960, however, it was reported: "The majority of American high schools offer an elective-sequence curriculum in business education. The elective-sequence curriculum pattern indicates that there is no specific curriculum, only a good selection of business subjects, selected by the students through the guidance of the business teachers and the homeroom advisers." [13] While this 1960 report is perhaps still true today, the requirements of the Vocational Education Act of 1963, as discussed in Chapter 13, are probably influencing some schools to return to more strongly prescribed vocational business curriculums.

The possibility of this return to more strongly prescribed vocational high school business curriculums is further supported by the prescribed recommendations contained in the report of the extensive national study, "Curricular Implications of Automated Data Processing for Educational Institutions." [14] Furthermore, at a time when some educators have been wondering about the status of high school bookkeeping-accounting in an age of expanding automated data processing, it is indeed significant when a study of this scope and stature, centering its attention on automated data processing in the curriculum, recommends not only that a bookkeeping course be included in an ADP curriculum,[15] but that a course in Data Processing Applications ". . . should be coordinated with Bookkeeping and Business and Office Procedures." [16]

---

[13] *Ibid.*
[14] F. Kendrick Bangs, Principal Investigator, *Curricular Implications of Automated Data Processing for Educational Institutions* (Boulder, Colorado: University of Colorado, 1968).
[15] *Ibid.*, p. 3.
[16] *Ibid.*, p. 5.

The elective-sequence curriculum possesses the flexibility for programming the more able business students and those who are late academic "bloomers" into courses that will supply them with the greatest challenge as well as the best preparation for meeting college entrance requirements. If, however, the guidance is weak or if it is biased for or against any particular area of education, the disadvantages of the elective-sequence curriculum become apparent.

B-A and other business teachers must give first consideration to that large majority of their students who will not go on to college. Today, however, with the increasing demands for going to college and the correspondingly rising admissions standards, high school business students with college potential should be identified early and encouraged to take courses that will help them with their possible entrance into college. The elective-sequence curriculum helps to make this possible.

Another way to help the student who is interested in business, but has his eye on a future college education, is to suggest a high school curriculum which takes both interests into consideration. The college-preparatory curriculum for business students that are outlined in the first two columns of the illustration on page 42 do this.

Unless business teachers supply such individual help and guidance in the programming of business students, they are not in a very strong position when they appeal for more able students to be guided into business programs.

Cooperative Work Experience Programs

Bookkeeping, like other vocations, was learned in earlier times by the apprenticeship method. Under this method bookkeeping was learned the hard, laborious way. There was no organized approach to learning. The apprentice "picked up" his knowledge and skill from month to month and year to year as scattered duties were assigned to him. He was not learning under a trained teacher. His learnings and skill were limited to the type and the level of bookkeeping work performed in the specific business where he was employed.

This apprenticeship method, however, had some advantages that have never been fully duplicated by a formal training in school. Some of these advantages were:

1. Working with "live" material—keeping real books and working with figures and bookkeeping problems that had real meaning and importance—not just practice or theoretical problems.

2. The incentive for making good on the job—not just in school.

3. The incentive of earning wages while learning.

Today, some high schools are providing these advantages of the old apprenticeship method without incurring any of the disadvantages. They do this by arranging to have their twelfth-year B-A students get on-the-job experiences and training in programs called "Cooperative Work Experience Programs." These programs can operate in various ways and for various lengths of time. In general, however, the better programs possess the following characteristics:

1. Qualified twelfth-year B-A students get or are assigned to part-time B-A jobs in offices in the community.

2. Some programs have the students spending one-half day in school and one-half day (usually the afternoon) on the job. In other programs the students work after school and on Saturdays, or attend school and work on alternate weeks.

3. Since the students are under the direction and coordination of the school, they are operating within the curriculum and school (diploma) credit is given for such experience.

4. The students are paid by the employer for their services.

5. A B-A teacher is assigned as a coordinator of this program and keeps in touch with employers to learn how the students are doing (their strengths and shortcomings) and to see that such students are receiving fair treatment and worth-while experiences.

6. These cooperative work-experience students meet daily in a class that is usually taught by the coordinating teacher. One major aim of this class should be to coordinate and use the experiences the students are having on the job with formal B-A instruction. Much of the time spent in such a class often involves remedial teaching—alleviating the weaknesses disclosed by their on-the-job experiences. These areas are discovered through the coordinator's visits and meetings with employers and through written reports or rating forms made to the school by the employers.

Most businessmen, when clearly informed of the purposes and practices of this type of program, have, in general, been cooperative and enthusiastic about such training of possible future employees. It should be readily understood, however, why some businessmen are reluctant to have inexperienced students working on their books. As a result, the work experience for B-A students centers on routine clerical work rather than a full fledged assignment to B-A work. Some experience with routine clerical work can prove valuable to many students who have never before worked in an office. Coordinators should be alert, however, to insure that the nonbookkeeping experiences of their co-op students are worthwhile office experiences and that the program is not weakened by their students failing to experience something close to the on-the-job work situation of a bookkeeper or accounting clerk.

The teacher-coordinator, in order to have time to visit employers and students on the job, should not be assigned the same teaching load as other teachers.

Tryout Courses for Prospective Bookkeeping-Accounting Students

It is a common practice in vocational high schools to require freshmen who are not sure of their choice of vocation to have tryout or exploratory experiences in various vocational areas. For example, a school that offers vocational training in carpentry, auto mechanics, machine shop practice, and the like, often programs entering students into each of these courses for a few weeks or months of initial experiences in the learning of these vocations. The logical purpose of this is to help the student arrive at a more considered judgment of his liking for such work and a more considered judgment in his choice of preparation for a future vocation.

Some high schools offering vocational business programs have tried the same plan for students considering office occupations. Such schools have given these students an opportunity of a few weeks or more of an introduction to "learn" whether they like or prefer to typewrite, to keep books, or to write shorthand. Such tryout experiences in general have not proven to be of value in helping to guide the right students into or out of these three vocational business education areas.

Arguments against such tryout experiences for prospective vocational business students seem to have more validity than those that favor such courses. Three, six, or eight weeks of tryout experiences in each of these business areas are not enough to give most students the feeling of confidence and a sense of achievement. Before the time that the student is about to "get the feel" of the typewriter, the shorthand outlines, the bookkeeping cycle, and before the satisfaction of understanding and achievement is reached, he is cut short of these experiences which are basically important to his decision for going on or not. As a result, some students who might eventually find success and happiness in one of these office vocations exclaim, after such experiences, "Not for me!" Others who do choose to specialize in one of these areas as a result of a tryout course frequently seem to make their decision on the basis of the personality and influence of the teacher rather than a true appreciation of and liking for the particular subject chosen.

Tryout courses for such vocational areas as carpentry and auto mechanics are more likely to be successful. In such courses there are short units of learning and skill that can be mastered and directly applied to similar or related tasks in these fields. A student can build a bookcase or make mechanical repairs to cars and within a few weeks experience a feeling of success—of achievement—in such work. As a result, he can more fairly appraise his liking for such work. If good tryout courses in bookkeeping-accounting are to be developed, such courses cannot expect to be successful unless they, too, offer such results rather than merely duplicate the introductory weeks of a first-year B-A class.

It seems possible and probable that good, short, tryout or prognostic courses in bookkeeping-accounting will some day be developed. Thus far, none have been reported that have proven to be sound. Until experiments on this problem disclose facts in support of such tryout courses, schools, in general, should probably not adopt them.

Bookkeeping-Accounting in the Core Curriculum

The personal-use phases of bookkeeping-accounting—home or personal budget records and procedures, personal checking accounts and bank reconciliation statements, and personal income tax records and reporting—involve common learnings and skills that everyone should possess. Such learnings are most effective when acquired close to their time of use. The time required to teach such information and skills on a personal-use level does not justify a separate course in this area for everybody. The business educator, however, should be alert to the three existing possibilities for contributing such learnings to all students. One possibility is in the general business course which should be required of everyone. Since this course is usually offered in the ninth or tenth year, it is not at a time closest to when the students would put such training to immediate use. Another possibility is the consumer economics (consumer education) course which, if offered in the high school, is frequently closer to the time of graduation than is the general business course.

The other opportunity could be in those schools offering a core program of common learnings for all students. If such a program extends throughout the three or four years of high school, such training should be included near the close of the students' high school experiences.

STUDY QUESTIONS

1. Which, if any, high school business courses have higher enrollments than bookkeeping-accounting?

2. What are the three principal reasons why the very great majority of first-year B-A students do not take a second- or a third-year B-A course?

3. What is a diversified occupations training program? a supervised correspondence program?

4. How do some small high schools with low B-A enrollments improvise in order to offer B-A courses for a few students?

5. How can a school determine whether or not it should provide a second-year B-A course?

6. Why has the increase in community colleges had an effect on the enrollments in high school B-A courses?

7. Why is it questionable that a school make shorthand a requirement for students majoring in bookkeeping-accounting?

8. What is the difference between a *track* curriculum pattern and an *elective-sequence* curriculum pattern?

9. What are the three possibilities for teaching personal use phases of bookkeeping to *all* students in the high school?

10. What is the best year or years to offer B-A courses in the high school? Why?

11. What related business subjects are most commonly taken by B-A students?

12. What are the major arguments in support of a course in general clerical practice?

13. What are the advantages of a high school work experience program?

14. What are the major characteristics of a cooperative work experience program?

15. What is meant by a tryout course for prospective B-A students?

16. Why have brief tryout courses for prospective B-A students not proven to be very satisfactory?

17. Why is it not safe to predict that future tryout courses for prospective B-A students will never prove satisfactory?

DISCUSSION QUESTIONS

1. How many years of bookkeeping-accounting should be offered to high school students?

2. Why are advanced B-A courses beyond the first year more popular in eastern than western high schools?

3. Who should be responsible for taking the initiative for determining the need for more than one year of high school B-A instruction—the local board of education? parents? employers of office workers? the school superintendent or principal? the faculty of the business education department? the B-A teacher(s)?

4. Should students who plan to go on to college be permitted or encouraged to take bookkeeping-accounting in high school?

5. What business education courses in the high school curriculum should vocational B-A students be *required* to take? *encouraged* to take? Why?

6. Would the establishment of a general clerical practices course or sequence be the best solution for preparing office workers who are not interested or cannot succeed in the B-A and shorthand courses?

7. Are there significant differences between courses called *office practice, clerical practice,* and *office machines?* Should one or more be required of B-A majors? Explain.

8. What dangers might exist for vocational high school students who follow a flexible, elective-sequence curriculum pattern?

9. How should a parent be answered who objects to her son being enrolled in a cooperative work experience program on the basis that, "I am sending him to high school to study and learn, not to spend part of his time away from school working on a job."?

PROJECTS

1. Prepare a paper on "The Place and Status of Bookkeeping-Accounting in the Curriculum at _____ High School." Include (a) a clear statement of the present situation; (b) a statement of strengths and weaknesses; (c) conclusions; (d) recommendations.

2. Prepare a paper in support of an ideal sequence of business courses which you would recommend for all B-A majors at either (a) a specific high school with which you are familiar, or (b) a large metropolitan high school.

3. Outline and explain the steps in a plan that you would recommend to a school which was sincere in wanting to determine whether their business curriculum should offer two years of B-A instruction instead of one year.

4. Outline the advantages and the disadvantages of both a "track" curriculum pattern and an elective-sequence curriculum pattern. State your conclusions and recommendations.

5. Prepare a paper which summarizes the status of "Bookkeeping-Accounting in the High School Curriculums of (*your state*)." Indicate your recommendations for changes.

6. Draw up a complete plan for establishing a cooperative work experience program for B-A students in your high school.

SELECTED REFERENCES

Balance in the Curriculum, Assn. for Supervision and Curriculum Development Yearbook. Washington: National Education Assn., 1961.

Bangs, F. Kendrick, Principal Investigator. *Curricular Implications of Automated Data Processing for Educational Institutions.* Boulder, Colorado: University of Colorado, 1968. (Available from Executive Secretary, Delta Pi Epsilon, Gustavus Adolphus College, St. Peter, MN 56082.)

Coleman, Brendan, and Helen H. Green. "Teach Your Undergraduate Methods Students About Adult Education Programs," *The Journal of Business Education.* XLIII (November, 1967), 63-64.

Forkner, Hamden L., Robert M. Swanson, and Robert J. Thompson. *The Teaching of Bookkeeping,* Monograph 101. Cincinnati: South-Western Publishing Company, 1960.

"Future Curriculums in Business Education," *National Business Education Quarterly.* XXXV (Summer, 1967), 11-22.

Griffitts, Horace F. "Vocational Office Education—Developing a Block Program," *The Journal of Business Education.* XLIII (April, 1968), 278-280.

Kuklinski, Walda M. "What Executives Say About Bookkeeping," *Business Education Forum.* XXII (February, 1968), 19-20.

Musselman, Vernon A., and J. Marshall Hanna. "Place of Bookkeeping and Accounting in the Curriculum," *Teaching Bookkeeping and Accounting,* Chapter 1. New York: Gregg Publishing Division, McGraw-Hill Book Company, Inc., 1960.

Roman, John C. *The Business Curriculum,* Monograph 100 (Revised). Cincinnati: South-Western Publishing Company, 1966.

Rossomando, Frederic W. "Modern Bookkeeping Curriculum Patterns," *Developing Vocational Competency in Bookkeeping and Accounting,* Eastern Business Teachers Association Yearbook, Vol. 40, 33-46. New York: New York University Bookstore, 1967.

The Bulletin of the National Association of Secondary School Principals.
XXXVI (December, 1952).

United States Department of Labor, Bureau of Labor Statistics. *Occu-pational Outlook Handbook,* 1968-69 Edition. Washington: U.S. Government Printing Office, 1968.

United States Office of Education. "Offerings and Enrollments in High School Business Subjects 1948-49," *Biennial Survey of Education in the United States,* Chapter 5. Washington: U.S. Government Printing Office, 1951.

——————. "Subject Offerings and Enrollments in Public Secondary Schools." Washington: U.S. Government Printing Office, 1965.

——————. "Subject Offerings and Enrollments, Grades 9-12, Non-public Secondary Schools, 1961-62." Washington: U.S. Government Printing Office, 1965.

Wilsing, Weston C. *Is Business Education in the Public High Schools Meeting the Needs and Desires of Businessmen?* Monograph 99. Cincinnati: South-Western Publishing Co., 1960.

OBJECTIVES OF BOOKKEEPING-ACCOUNTING INSTRUCTION— WHO SHOULD STUDY BOOKKEEPING-ACCOUNTING AND WHY

Chapter 3

Bookkeeping-Accounting Is a Specialized Course

Bookkeeping-accounting is a specialized area of education. The instruction given is primarily designed to train people to perform in a particular area of business skill. There are inherent in the course, however, learnings of personal use and of general educational value. Family and personal budgetkeeping, personal tax records and reporting, and personal bank records and reconciliation statements are examples of common topics with which all students should be familiar. Such common personal-use areas in bookkeeping-accounting can be taught to the average student in less than a semester. It therefore does not seem a wise use of educational time to guide high school students into a full-year or semester course in bookkeeping-accounting for the *sole* purpose of acquiring the personal-use knowledges and skills that can be taught within several months. Such learnings, having educational values for all students, are best presented in a general education course required of all students. These learnings may also be included in a core program in those schools having such a curriculum.

The teacher should be aware of the information that can be used by everyone, and first-year B-A students should be shown the relationship between vocational and personal-use bookkeeping. But such an awareness does not remove the course from a specialized, predominately vocational area of education nor place it in the field of general education. The student entering the course should be able (1) to anticipate an educational experience that will prepare him to derive his livelihood from B-A activity in business; (2) to acquire the B-A knowledge and skill which may be required in such positions as general clerk, secretary, and typist; (3) to acquire the B-A knowledge and skill necessary for the successful operation of a business of his own; (4) to apply this vocational knowledge to personal business problems; (5) to develop qualities of personality that will enhance the ranks of an important segment of the business world.

The Objectives of Bookkeeping-Accounting Instruction

There is no phase in B-A instruction that outranks the importance of the objectives of the course. No teacher teaches without some aim or purpose. No student learns without some aim or purpose. The kind and caliber of the teacher's aims will condition the kind and quality of teaching and learning. The caliber of the pupil's aims will condition what he learns as well as how well he learns it. The aims of the B-A teacher and the aims and needs of the B-A student have an effect upon the aims and behavior of each other.

Teachers' aims or purposes range all the way from earning a living and covering materials in a textbook, to giving each individual student under their tutorage the optimum help and encouragement for growth and development. Students' aims or purposes range all the way from being in school just to meet attendance laws or because of parental insistence, to being there to get the most and best education the school has to offer.

Just as the bookkeeper must understand the bookkeeping equation if he is to achieve his goal as a successful bookkeeper, so the teacher should understand the following equation dealing with behavior.

BEHAVIOR = knowledge + skills + attitudes

One way, therefore, to think of the B-A course objectives is to think in terms of the behavior to be affected—the knowledge to be gained, the skills to be acquired, and the attitudes to be formed.

The truly professionally minded teacher will consider the reasons why a B-A course is offered, why individual students are in the course, how the course can best help and prepare them for their future lives. He will arrange to see that course objectives are established and that the students are aware of the goals to be achieved and share in their establishment. He will work with the students towards achieving these objectives. This teacher will, in addition to arranging for setting up course or group goals, also be observing and studying the needs of individual students as the course progresses, and determine individual objectives for certain students. For example, he sees that John needs to improve his penmanship, that Mary is reticent and reluctant to recite orally, or that Jack never associates or works with other boys. Accordingly, individual objectives are decided, and plans are made to overcome the individual shortcomings of these pupils. Students under such a teacher will learn because of him, not in spite of him.

Objectives are seldom reached by chance. The teacher consciously or unconsciously decides the direction in which he wishes to go and the things he desires to accomplish. Through his actions in the classroom he reaches for what he believes to be desirable. The teacher is not only a communicator but a model. If he does not see anything important, or helpful, or interesting about bookkeeping-accounting, he is not likely to stimulate others with a feeling of interest in the subject. The National Education Association says that every statement of educational purposes, including this one, depends upon the judgment of some person or group as to what is good and what is bad, what is true and what is false, what is ugly and what is beautiful, what is valuable and what is worthless, in the conduct of human affairs. Objectives are, essentially, a statement of preferences, choices, values. These preferences are exercised, these choices made, these values arranged in a variety of ways.

The variety of ways in which bookkeeping's numerous objectives have been listed and published are legion. Sometimes the lists are so long and so all-inclusive of educational objectives in general that if the term "bookkeeping" were removed from the lists of some objectives, the title of almost any other course in the high school could be substituted and would fit equally well. This practice, while having the advantage of enumerating each classroom teacher's responsibilities, has the possible disadvantage of losing the major aims of a specialized course, such as bookkeeping-accounting, among the subsidiary or secondary aims.

One study,[1] when summarizing its findings about the objectives of bookkeeping instruction, reported, "When bookkeeping job opportunities have decreased, the consensus has shifted to emphasis of broader vocational and nonvocational objectives; when job opportunities have increased, the consensus has returned to emphasis of vocational objectives." Some teachers who taught bookkeeping during the depression years of the 1930's will recall how in those years and for a long time thereafter it was common practice to justify a bookkeeping course on nearly every basis but the vocational. At that time, in some communities, the course was justified on the basis of its relationship to health, worthy use of leisure time, civic responsibility, citizenship, and other such general objectives of education as may be found in the Seven Cardinal Principles and the publications of the Educational Policies Commission. These general aims appeared over and over again in the lists of objectives for the teaching of bookkeeping and by virtue of such repetition, they began to take on a value and importance equal to and sometimes greater than the vocational objectives of the course. As these general objectives were developed in bookkeeping instruction, the vocational aims became subordinated in many instances, and the vocational strength of the bookkeeping course was weakened.

For some time now, with good job opportunities being present for bookkeeping-accounting and office work, and with federal funds being made available to subsidize vocational office training, the pendulum has been swinging back in strong favor of a predominately vocational objective for the B-A course. Since it has taken nearly a full generation of teachers to get the pendulum back where it belongs, it seems in order to caution new B-A teachers about the dangers of neglecting the vocational student and the vocational objective.

With this thought in mind, the following four major objectives are suggested as concise, balanced aims for the average first-year B-A course.

[1] Ruth A. Wallace, *The Rationale for Bookkeeping and Accounting in Public School Curriculums, 1821-1961* (M.A. thesis, San Jose State College, California, 1961), p. 299.

First-Year Bookkeeping-Accounting Objectives

Four Major Objectives of the First-Year Course

1. The vocational objective. Some students enroll for the B-A course because they plan to become vocational, on-the-job book-keepers. They plan that their principal livelihood will be derived from B-A activity in business. There is no doubt that the vocational aspirations of these pupils make the vocational objective essential, if not paramount, in classes containing such students. The subject matter and materials of instruction should be directly related to bookkeeping-accounting as it is practiced in present-day business offices. To do otherwise would be ignoring the needs of these potential bookkeepers and defeating for them the most valid of all reasons for studying bookkeeping-accounting.

2. The related vocational objective. Some students enroll in bookkeeping-accounting because they plan to become office or store workers and know that an understanding of some bookkeeping principles and skills may be helpful or required in such positions as general clerk, salesclerk, cashier, typist, secretary, and junior programmer. Some students similarly enroll in bookkeeping-accounting because they plan or hope to operate a business of their own, and they know that some bookkeeping knowledge and skill will benefit them in such endeavors. Some students plan to go on to college to study accounting or business administration and therefore take bookkeeping-accounting as prevocational or preprofessional education.

In most such cases, even though the student is not planning to become an on-the-job bookkeeper, it would appear that these students' bookkeeping needs and understandings are primarily vocational in nature and scope. Most of them not only need to learn what B-A instruction has to offer about business understandings and practices generally, but they also need to understand and be able to perform at least the simpler on-the-job duties and skills of a vocational bookkeeper that can be covered in a first-year course.

One of the shortcomings in B-A teaching materials and instruction is failure to relate first-year subject matter to the work of the prospective salesclerk, typist, secretary, and automated process worker. Most schools that require or urge these and other prospective business workers to have a year of bookkeeping-accounting do so with the guiding remark, "A knowledge of bookkeeping and accounting will be helpful," and then fail to indicate in a meaningful manner just how it will be helpful. Since bookkeeping-accounting has as a primary objective the goal of giving related vocational assistance to business workers, the teacher is obliged to be specific in helping such students realize and reach this goal.

It should be pointed out that we do not know which office workers may be called upon in their future positions to perform on-the-job bookkeeping duties and which of these workers will merely use their knowledge advantageously as general and helpful background information. Because we do not know this and because we do know that one year of good B-A instruction can bring them to a fairly high level of vocational competency, it seems obligatory that they be helped to acquire the highest degree of vocational B-A skill that their capacities and one year of study will allow. For some, such knowledge and skill will immediately or shortly be put to work; for others it will constitute a vocational reserve upon which they can draw when necessary.

Some writers prefer to class some of the above reasons for studying bookkeeping-accounting, such as keeping one's own records of farm income and expenses or keeping one's own books in a store, a garage, or a service station, as personal-use bookkeeping. This is done on the basis that these persons are keeping books and records for themselves—therefore, personal-use bookkeeping. Such persons, however, need as much vocational knowledge and skill for keeping the books of their own businesses as would be needed by a professional bookkeeper whom they might call in to keep the books of their businesses. The writer opposes such a classification of personal-use bookkeeping as another educational development that seeks to justify the aim of a course in personal-use bookkeeping at the expense of weakening the vocational or related vocational objectives of bookkeeping-accounting.

3. **The personal-use objective.** Surveys show that many high school as well as college students make a living in different vocations or professions than they had originally planned. Many students in the B-A class will never use their knowledge and skill on

the job or in their own business efforts. Much of the time spent by such students in a bookkeeping class could be charged as lost if they have little or no application for the knowledge and skill that was acquired there. There is, however, excellent opportunity for application of such learnings in their everyday living. Every person, like every business, must not only earn a living, but must manage to live on what he earns. Individuals and families, like businesses, do this best when they plan and budget wisely, keep helpful and necessary records, and follow good business practices. Many of these business practices are covered under Objectives 1 and 2 on page 57. However, it is the rare student who sees and can apply these practices to personal or family use without some specific guidance and help in doing so. It seems imperative, therefore, that the objective of personal-use bookkeeping should be included for all students in a first-year B-A course, regardless of the reason for which they are enrolled.

Perhaps a few students might enroll in a B-A course for this reason alone, but, to repeat an earlier statement, "It . . . does not seem a wise use of educational time to guide high school students into a full-year or semester course in bookkeeping for the sole purpose of acquiring the personal-use bookkeeping knowledges and skills that can be taught within a few months."

The three objectives just stated help set the standards and show the scope of B-A subject matter coverage. The fourth and final objective suggested for all first-year B-A classes is aimed at helping to meet those goals of education in general that are related to vocational success and sometimes transcend the subject matter in a specific vocational course.

4. The general education objective. Most, if not all, students who enroll in bookkeeping-accounting have needs to be met that are not related to the subject matter. For example, some are uncooperative; some do not get along well with other students; some use incorrect English; some are unable orally to express themselves clearly; some have poor habits of cleanliness, health, dress, and courtesy; some are addicted to tardiness, laziness, and carelessness; some are lonely; some are dishonest. Although a particular course such as English or health education may have major objectives for meeting some of these needs, correcting or improving these traits is not the sole responsibility of one teacher or of one course. They are the responsibilities of all teachers, of all courses, of education in general. Often, however, what is every teacher's job becomes no one's responsibility. One way to see that this is not the case in the B-A class is to set up a specific course objective for helping to meet these needs.

If there are B-A teachers or prospective B-A teachers who oppose this general education objective on the grounds that their sole responsibility to pupils is to teach them bookkeeping-accounting and make them personally or vocationally competent, they should consider the following question: "Is a bookkeeper or any other office worker vocationally competent who is discharged from his job or is denied advancement because he is careless, tardy, dishonest, frequently absent for causes other than illness, sloppy and unclean in dress and appearance, lacks loyalty and initiative, is irresponsible, lazy, can't get along with fellow employees, is uncooperative, and so on?" The answer is obvious and it becomes apparent that desirable personal qualities are a vital element in vocational competency. A skill-trained person is not necessarily a vocationally competent bookkeeper or office worker. The most expert of skill training is not sufficient for job success. Therefore, business education should also plan the continuing improvement of the general education that is present or potential in its vocational courses. The process of specific vocational business training should be so planned that it will include experiences which will contribute to the development of successful group activity, assumption of responsibility, ability to make decisions and take initiative, and all the other general characteristics of successful workers in all areas of endeavor.

The meeting of some of these general pupil needs can be more important to individual youngsters than having them achieve the subject matter objectives. They can and must be met, however, in a manner that supports or reinforces the previous three objectives rather than supplants them. The vocational needs of the class members must still remain the paramount objective.

The Motivational Objective of the First-Year Course

The previous four major objectives meet the needs of pupils studying bookkeeping-accounting with the exception of those students who are present because of parental insistence, merely because the course is required, just to "fill in" a schedule, to be with a friend, or for other reasons that may not generally be conducive or stimulating to learning. Students who start a B-A course with such questionable reasons probably begin with a negative attitude. Where these and other students enter B-A classes without knowing very much about the advantages or objectives of such a course, it would seem wise to start the course with a *motivational objective*. The purpose of this objective would be *to help bring students to an awareness of the advantages and various reasons for studying bookkeeping-accounting.*

This additional objective was not included in the suggested list for all classes because, although it is expected that the instructor will teach in a manner which stimulates, sustains, and increases interest in the subject, this initial and motivational objective for studying bookkeeping-accounting should be reached outside the class before the students enroll in it. Every student, before he enrolls for a B-A course or for any other specialized vocational course, should have the opportunity to study about major vocations, including business vocations. He should have the opportunity of studying the advantages and the disadvantages of particular vocations that interest him and the opportunity of arriving at a deep personal desire for studying the special subject of his choice. This objective could be part of a general or basic business course, a vocational or occupational information course, or a unit in the ninth or tenth grade of schools with a core curriculum.

But if the personnel of any special B-A class warrants it, the motivational objective should guide the teacher in planning his initial lessons. The first two of the sample lesson plans in Chapter 14 suggest ways to begin the course with the motivational objective in mind.

Subsidiary Objectives of the First-Year Course

Under any of the previous four major objectives the individual teacher can place supplementary aims that are compatible and which he desires for clarification. For example, the vocational aim of preparing on-the-job bookkeepers or accounting clerks cannot be fully achieved unless the student is accurate in simple arithmetic, writes legibly, is able to understand and use common business forms, understands the bookkeeping cycle, and the like. Similarly, the prospective business stenographer or typist has not achieved the optimum from the related vocational objective unless she has, among other things, acquired a good vocabulary and learned the various forms, rulings, and alignments of statements showing the condition of the business—unless she has been given assignments that include the typing of balance sheets, income statements, payrolls and such other related bookkeeping information that she will be called upon to type in business. The personal-use objective will not be fully achieved unless personal-use bookkeeping material, knowledge, and skill are used and developed.

A determination of the individual needs of his students will decide for the teacher what these subsidiary aims will be. They will vary from school to school. For example, the teacher in a central or county high school comprised chiefly of farm children would center the related vocational aim primarily on the business records of farm income and expense. Likewise the personal-use objective would center on personal and family budgeting, and the like, for farm families.

Examples of Published Lists of the First-Year Course Objectives

In addition to serving as goals to be achieved, detailed lists of course objectives serve as self-evaluating check lists for periodical appraisal of one's teaching success. Consider, for example, the following statement and list of fine objectives produced by experienced teachers and published by Colorado's Department of Education.

If an objective of a course is realized, the student should act or behave in a specific way as a result of the realization of the objective. Specific objectives are stated in terms of what behavior or action is expected from the student at the termination of an activity. The student who has studied bookkeeping for one school year should be able to:

1. Identify business papers and explain their use in business.
2. Analyze business transactions in terms of their effect on the business.
3. Make correct entries (from business papers and/or from a narrative of business transactions) in a two-column general journal, in a multi-column journal (combined cash journal), or in special journals with a variety of special columns.

4. Post from the various journals used to accounts in general and/or subsidiary ledgers.
5. Take a trial balance and recognize what a trial balance proves.
6. Locate and correct journalizing and posting errors.
7. Prove the accuracy of postings to control accounts and subsidiary ledgers.
8. Prepare work sheets involving simple adjustments.
9. Journalize and post adjusting and closing entries.
10. Prepare simple financial statements.
11. Rule accounts.
12. Prove the accuracy of his work at various stages of the bookkeeping cycle, e.g., before posting columnar journals, after posting to general and subsidiary ledger accounts, reconcile his bank statement.
13. Classify accounts.
14. Reconstruct transactions from account entries.
15. Write legibly and neatly.
16. Spell and use bookkeeping terms correctly.
17. Compute with reasonable speed and accuracy.
18. Prepare an income tax report that an average individual might have to make.
19. Secure from the records information that would be needed for state and federal government reports, e.g., sales tax, and amounts withheld for income tax and social security.
20. Use an adding machine or calculator with reasonable efficiency in doing bookkeeping work.
21. Be knowledgeable in the use of machines in processing business data and be aware of the future of automation related to bookkeeping.
22. Recognize his limitations of bookkeeping knowledge and obtain help of experts on complex problems.[2]

A similar, but shorter, list of first-year course objectives, issued by the Pennsylvania Department of Public Instruction as a guide for its B-A teachers, is shown on page 64.

---

[2] Colorado Department of Education, Division of Elementary and Secondary Education, *A Guide for Teaching Bookkeeping in Colorado Schools* (Denver: 1968), p. vii.

PENNSYLVANIA DEPARTMENT OF PUBLIC INSTRUCTION

Bookkeeping for Business Education Departments in
Pennsylvania's Public Schools
Objectives of the First-Year Course

1. To gain insight into the operation, function, and internal workings of a business enterprise.
2. To build a foundation in bookkeeping principles and terminology which can be used if accounting is chosen as a vocation.
3. To give enough background so a set of books for a small business, with a single proprietor, can be maintained.
4. To establish an understanding of how the basic principles of bookkeeping can be adapted to personal and social use.
5. To show the relationship of all bookkeeping forms to the entire bookkeeping cycle from the opening entries to the post-closing trial balance.
6. To develop habits of accuracy, independent thinking, legibility, neatness, promptness, and thoroughness.
7. To teach attitudes of cooperativeness, intellectual honesty, wholesome respect for business as an institution, and the opportunities business offers for employment.
8. To indicate how a properly kept set of records can provide the necessary information for the preparation of a tax return for either a private individual or a business enterprise.
9. To serve as an exploratory course to determine the interest in and aptitude for the opportunities offered by accounting as a profession.
10. To provide information that can be used in any line of business.
11. To develop an understanding of how to prepare, read, and interpret simple business reports and financial statements.[3]

Figure 3—1. Course objectives for first-year bookkeeping

---

[3] Pennsylvania Department of Public Instruction, *Bookkeeping for Business Education Departments in Pennsylvania's Public Schools*, Bulletin 273 (Harrisburg: The Department, 1958), p. 2.

Objectives of the First-Year Course—A Summary Opinion of Business Education Leaders

The following was one of many issues in a study presented to "current business leaders in business education" for the purpose of determining their opinions.

> If one year of bookkeeping is offered in the public secondary school, should the primary objective be initial job competency; personal and social use; a combination of vocational competency and personal use; or preparation for college accounting? [4]

The summary of the check sheet responses to the above issue indicated that the primary objective of a one-year bookkeeping course in the public secondary school should be to provide:

(Number)		
8	(21.0 per cent)	(a) initial job competency as an office worker.
1	(2.6 per cent)	(b) initial job competency as a bookkeeper.
2	(5.3 per cent)	(c) personal- and social-use values.
22	(57.9 per cent)	(d) a combination of initial job competency and personal and social use with emphasis on the vocational objective.
3	(7.9 per cent)	(e) a combination of initial job competency and personal and social use with emphasis on the personal and social use.
1	(2.6 per cent)	(f) preparation for college accounting.
1	(2.6 per cent)	(g) understanding the business enterprise.

Teaching Economic Concepts in Bookkeeping

A review of the literature on the teaching of bookkeeping for the past thirty years shows that some bookkeeping teachers have strong feelings about teaching economic principles in bookkeeping classes. This is worth special mention as a possible subsidiary aim falling under the aegis of the general education objective. B-A teachers who believe in integrating economic concepts in their bookkeeping classes can benefit from Griffith's following suggestions:

1. Develop a philosophy to weave economic understanding into bookkeeping instruction so that bookkeeping knowledge will not be hindered.
2. Identify the concepts that should be included in the bookkeeping instruction.

---

[4] Jerre E. Gratz, *Major Issues in Business Education*, Monograph 106 (Cincinnati: South-Western Publishing Co., 1962), pp. 4-7.

3. Determine where the concepts should be integrated in the book-keeping text.
4. Decide what teaching procedures to use.
5. Test for results.[5]

The following statements from a recent study that examined the practicability of introducing economic concepts in the book-keeping class are worth noting:

> Introducing economic materials within the course work of book-keeping classes, without further reinforcement, did not appear to increase the students' knowledge of economics. This might support an assumption that students tend to concentrate more on material they know will form a part of their tests rather than on supplementary material.
>
> If it is desired to include these (principles of economics) in the bookkeeping class, it is recommended that they be made a part of the normal testing program and reflected in the grades of students.[6]

Second-Year Bookkeeping-Accounting Objectives

At the end of one year of B-A study based upon sound and achieved objectives, most students in the course who are not planning to become on-the-job bookkeepers should have attained, within their abilities and reasons for being in the course, the optimum benefits from their study of the subject. This, primarily, would leave only those students planning to become bookkeepers, those planning to study business administration or accounting in college, and others who might possess a strong desire to learn more about the more technical phases of bookkeeping-accounting and its relationship to business practices (such as those hoping to operate a business of their own), as the three possible kinds of students wanting or needing more bookkeeping-accounting.

In schools offering a second year of bookkeeping-accounting, these latter kinds of students could, if they have shown sufficient interest and ability the first year, be permitted or encouraged to continue for a second year. No one should be permitted to prepare for a vocation unless he possesses the potentialities for success in

---

[5] Bob B. Griffith, "Bookkeeping Builds Basic Economic Concepts," *Journal of Business Education* (March, 1964), p. 233.

[6] William C. Mickelson, *The Practicability of Introducing Economic Concepts in Bookkeeping* (Master's thesis, Mankato State College, Mankato, Minnesota, December, 1966), pp. 35-36.

that vocation, or, stated in another way, unless he can be fitted for useful employment. To do otherwise would be a waste of the student's time and efforts and a waste of educational time and money.

The second-year B-A course should, therefore, have as its primary objective that of continuing the preparation of competent, on-the-job bookkeepers. Two of the four major objectives listed for the first-year course are essential for meeting this primary aim: (1) the vocational objective and (2) the general education objective. The other two objectives of the first-year course, the related vocational and personal-use objectives, then become secondary or subsidiary objectives. Since an extension of both of these latter objectives into the second-year course could prove beneficial for some, if not most, of the second-year students, they should not be discarded entirely.

Preparation for College Accounting

Another objective that has been getting special attention in recent years and seems to have its greatest application for the second-year course is that of preparing students for college accounting. Such an objective is supported by the following picture:

> In large schools where there is a sufficient number of students who have the interest and aptitude for advanced study, students should be encouraged to take the second year. It is interesting to note in this connection that some schools have worked out an arrangement with higher educational institutions whereby second-year bookkeeping students are permitted to take placement examinations in accounting at the college or university. If they do well on these examinations, they are given advanced standing for college accounting and are permitted to enter second- or third-semester college accounting depending upon the scores they make on the college placement tests.[7]

Such an arrangement can encourage better students to enroll in high school B-A courses. When this happens, the status of B-A courses is improved in the eyes of the students, guidance counselors, and faculty.

---

[7] Hamden L. Forkner, Robert M. Swanson, and Robert J. Thompson, *The Teaching of Bookkeeping*, Monograph 101 (Cincinnati: South-Western Publishing Co., 1960), p. 3.

Most of the accounting associations in the various states will supply teachers and guidance counselors with appropriate local information about requirements for careers in accounting. An additional aid for use in counseling students who are contemplating careers in accounting and business is the *Accounting Orientation Test for High School Students.* This test is a part of the testing program that is sponsored by the American Institute of Certified Public Accountants.[8]

There is a possibility that the degree to which high school B-A courses encourage students to continue with a study of college accounting has been slighted. For example, in a special survey of 775 undergraduate and graduate college accounting students, it was found that 214 or 27.6%, ". . . had an introductory course to accounting at the secondary level,"[9] and that 10% of the total respondents gave specific credit to their high school bookkeeping classes for attracting them to the field of accounting.

Two cautions, however, are in order for those schools that use the preparation-for-college-accounting objective to encourage college-bound students to enroll in high school B-A courses. First, many colleges and universities require respectable scores on the "College Board" examinations. The student should never be given the opportunity to say that he "failed" his "College Boards" and thus was not admitted to the college of his choice because he enrolled in bookkeeping-accounting instead of some basic college preparatory course designed to help him score higher on the "College Boards." This would not be the case of the able college-bound student who took bookkeeping-accounting in addition to the recommended college preparatory courses. Neither would it be the case if he were planning to enter a college which did not require the taking of the "College Boards."

The other caution which seems in order is that high schools offering only one year of B-A instruction will need to supplement the material in a first-year text before they can expect, with any degree of certainty, their college-bound students to be able to pass accounting placement examinations that would exempt them from first-semester college accounting. While it has been reported

---

[8] AICPA Testing Project Office, The Psychological Corporation, 304 East 45th Street, New York, NY 10017.

[9] Ray M. Powell, 'Career Choices Among Beta Alpha Psi Members," *The Accounting Review* (July, 1966) p. 527.

numerous times that students with a year or more of successful bookkeeping-accounting in high school do, on the average, earn better grades in first-semester college accounting courses than college accounting students without a high school background in bookkeeping-accounting, studies are now available which point out that subject matter coverage in introductory high school B-A texts do not match the sophistication or the coverage in introductory college accounting texts.

One study which compared introductory high school B-A textbooks with elementary college accounting textbooks contained the following recommendation:

> Further research is needed to determine what factors can be included in the high school bookkeeping course to make high school bookkeeping acceptable, or more acceptable, by colleges and universities as preparation for college accounting. Specific practices and procedures included in elementary college accounting but not included in high school bookkeeping need to be identified and included in the high school bookkeeping course.[10]

A more recent and similar study to that of Lund's mentioned above, recommended:

> For bookkeeping teachers who want their bookkeeping course structured in the framework of accounting concepts or theory, the bookkeeping course must be enriched from sources other than bookkeeping textbooks to include certain topics exclusive to accounting textbooks.[11]

This latter study concluded its recommendations as follows:

> Further research should be made on the style and type of illustrations and topics most appropriate to bookkeeping textbooks and accounting texts. This is especially true for schools that utilize advanced placement.[12]

---

[10] Erling Lund, *High School Bookkeeping as Preparation for College Accounting Based on a Comparison of Selected High School Bookkeeping Textbooks with Selected Elementary College Accounting Textbooks* (Master's thesis, University of Washington, 1962), p. 63.

[11] David Allen Bydalek, *A Comparative Analysis of Two High School Elementary Bookkeeping Texts and Two College Elementary Accounting Texts to Determine Commonality and Emphasis of Selected Topics* (Master's thesis, Northern Illinois University, DeKalb, 1966), pp. 52-53.

[12] *Ibid.*

Special attention should be called to the fact that both studies mentioned above compared the subject matter coverage in first-year high school B-A texts with the subject matter coverage in first-year college accounting textbooks. Much, if not most, of the coverage found in first-year college accounting that is not found in first-year high school texts is found in second-year high school B-A textbooks.

The Interpretative Bookkeeping-Accounting Objective

The "Why" Versus the "How" of Bookkeeping-Accounting Instruction

A parallel exists today in the criticism that has been leveled both at college accounting teachers and at high school B-A teachers. The same criticism on these two distinct educational levels is that too much emphasis is being placed on teaching the *how* of keeping business records and not enough on the *why*.

In some ways, high school bookkeeping-accounting is frequently influenced by trends in college accounting. There is a trend now on the college level, stimulated in part by the so-called "Pierson Report," to cut down on the time devoted to much of the routine procedures of bookkeeping and accounting. Several quotes from this study of university-college programs in business administration follow.

> . . . the core courses in accounting and statistics all too often stress elementary techniques in handling records, preparing reports, and answering day-to-day operating questions. In the first-year accounting course, for example, considerable attention is often given to working out bookkeeping procedures and to discussing the techniques and records employed in recording, classifying, and summarizing simple business transactions.[13]

> Presumably, introductory courses in accounting and statistics developed along these lines are thought to provide the best preparation for students who want to do more intensive work in these two areas, though even from the viewpoint of future majors such courses are being increasingly questioned. From the point of view of nonmajors, however, there seems little doubt that the emphasis on mechanics and techniques is a serious mistake. Indeed, attention

---

[13] Frank C. Pierson and Others. *The Education of American Businessmen* (New York: Mc-Graw-Hill Book Company, Inc., 1959), p. 209.

ought to be centered on accounting and statistics as aids to management in reaching decisions, with special reference to their uses as tools for coordinating different aspects of management decision making. Viewed in this light, accounting becomes an extremely important instrument for analyzing sales policy questions, pricing problems, capital expenditures programs, debt-financing methods, etc.[14]

High school teachers who might believe that their B-A courses should, therefore, follow a similar trend, should pause to consider the following strong caution which Pierson then makes about attempting to achieve a managerial objective with the adult, undergraduate college student.

> There is no denying that to give (college) accounting and statistics a strong managerial emphasis at the undergraduate level raises serious difficulties, not only because beginning students lack minimal technical preparation in these two subjects, but also because they have little or no familiarity with general management problems.[15]

People concerned with high school B-A instruction have also voiced concern about the heavy emphasis frequently given to the routine, recordative phase of bookkeeping.

> One of the greatest faults found in the teaching of bookkeeping lies in the emphasis placed by a teacher on the "how" rather than the "why." Many teachers emphasize *how* bookkeeping records are kept rather than *why* certain transactions are recorded as they are. The teacher by emphasizing the *how* is in reality training a bookkeeper. It is doubtful that a bookkeeping course in high school can be justified by this emphasis alone.[16]

The question here is not one of teachers opposing the teaching of more bookkeeping understanding. The issue centers on balance. How much of the *how* must a student do before he can best understand the *why*? Who has made a study to prove what is the right amount of *how* and the right amount of *why*? While there are as yet no proven answers to these questions, each B-A teacher should face the challenge and give a critical appraisal of what his objective is along these lines.

---

[14] *Ibid.*, p. 210.
[15] *Ibid.*
[16] Lloyd V. Douglas, James T. Blanford, and Ruth I. Anderson, *Teaching Business Subjects* (Englewood Cliffs, New Jersey: Prentice-Hall, Inc., 1958), p. 355.

The Interpretive Objective

One way that teachers can be sure to give deserving emphasis to the *why* of financial records and of B-A procedures is to make this a subsidiary objective which cuts across all major objectives of B-A instruction. Understanding the *why* of the procedures is to understand the cause, the reason, the purpose. To interpret is to explain the *why*. What, therefore, is the place of the interpretive objective in B-A teaching? How far should teachers go, or try to go, in teaching students to analyze and interpret?

Such a question is similar to "How much bookkeeping should be learned within a year? two years?" The best answer to either question is, "As much as is reasonably possible." Teachers who are concerned about interpretive bookkeeping are most likely conscientious ones searching for ways of strengthening and improving their courses. As such, they deserve a more helpful answer than, "Teach as much as is reasonably possible."

What are common problems in bookkeeping-accounting involving decision, analysis, explanation, or interpretation—problems that are not the daily routine of bookkeeping work which teachers might consider for coverage in high school courses? Moving from the simple to the more complex, these, in part, might be listed as follows:

1. Can students interpret a choice of account title?

   For example, why would one of the following account titles be chosen as "best" for establishing such a new account as freight, freight expense, freight and cartage, freight and drayage, freight in, delivery expense, freight out, cartage?

2. Can students interpret when new accounts should be established?

   For example,

   (a) When is it best to have a single expense account for depreciation and when should a separate depreciation account be established for each asset that depreciates?

   (b) When is it best to have a separate account for purchases returns *and* purchases allowances? Sales returns *and* sales allowances?

   (c) When and why should a petty cash account be established?

3. Can students explain errors and corrections?

4. Can students explain when it is best to have two, four, or another number of multi-columns in journals?

5. Can students explain when it is best to establish special journals?

6. Can students explain when it is best to establish special ledgers?

7. Can students interpret the function of each step in the book-keeping cycle and its relationship to each other step?

8. Can students explain the *why*, the reason and purpose, of each chapter in the text as it is completed?

9. Can students interpret financial statements?

10. Can students interpret written reports of financial statements?

Tonne supplies good illustrations of this interpretive objective when he says:

In studying the balance sheet the student should be taught to analyze the various items to determine the soundness of the business. He should, for example, understand (1) the function of cash and the relative amount required; (2) the problems of maintaining profitable inventories; (3) the disadvantage of too large inventories and the difficulties that go with hand-to-mouth buying; (4) the fact that accounts receivable, while listed as fluid assets, occasionally become solidified and thus fail in meeting current liabilities; (5) the justification for good will in a balance sheet and the extent to which it may be used merely to balance an inflated capitalization.

The same process of interpretation should be followed in studying the profit and loss statement. For example, in considering the sales section, the problem of sales returns may be treated as an unwarranted expense under some conditions. Again, in dealing with the cost-of-goods-sold section, the possibilities of various types of buying should be treated. Obviously, in learning the expense section, the student can learn to evaluate various problems, such as excess taxation, unjustified overhead, the extent to which high rent is justified, and the like.

The student should be led to recognize the problem of contingent liabilities, not only in the liabilities section of the balance sheet or in terms of discounting notes receivable, but also all through the operation of business. He should fully appreciate the unforeseen as the danger element in business. There is a constant possibility that the account that seems good may turn out to be uncollectible. Such risks should be analyzed carefully, so that the student can understand why some business costs cannot be avoided, and why, in fact, they must be faced courageously if the business is to make a profit.[17]

There is one area of student understanding and intepretation that has been infringed upon and weakened as a result of modern B-A teaching materials. Today, with the use of working papers, study guides, and practice sets, the students are constantly being handed tailor-made forms and materials. To the extent that this makes the students' work and learning easier, teachers rightly favor their use. If student work is limited to such tailor-made materials, however, if the student always finds the right kind of bookkeeping paper with the right number of lines and columns, with the headings and account names already filled in, it is similar to giving him problems with the solutions partially worked out. Furthermore, such exclusive use of tailor-made materials would eliminate some of the creativeness that might be exercised or encouraged in the B-A course. To urge that practice and interpretation in choice of deciding which column in multi-column journals should have what account titles and which accounts might be entered under sundries and the like, is not just to urge that the work be made more difficult for the student, but it is to urge that the student not be denied such learning experiences before he graduates from a B-A course.

It should be understood that the deeper one moves into the area of interpretation of bookkeeping the more he is moving into the field of accounting. As a result, teachers wishing to stress interpretative bookkeeping more strongly than most good high school textbooks should be clear in this objective and its value in relation to other objectives. For example, by striving for a deeper understanding of bookkeeping on the part of students, will the students

---

[17] Herbert A. Tonne. *Principles of Business Education,* 3d ed. (New York: Mc-Graw-Hill Book Company, Inc., 1961), pp. 289-90.

be shortchanged on other objectives—such as skill building or cutting down on the coverage of certain topical areas in the subject matter?

If the achievement of other objectives must be weakened or sacrificed in order for the student to reach a deeper comprehension of the bookkeeping covered, will this be to the student's advantage or disadvantage in his future employment? As able teachers analyze these questions, various correct answers will be reached. Some will say, "No! My course for my kinds of students is now well balanced as to objectives." Others will take the opposite stand. Perhaps a larger group, searching for ways of handling individual differences and ways of challenging their brighter students, will find that they can move some of their students deeper into the area of interpretative bookkeeping.

In summary, interpretation is a constant element in bookkeeping and can hardly be excluded from the study of the subject. There is a degree of interpretation and analysis that may be more accurately described as an accounting skill. The good B-A teacher will consider all the objectives of his course and so teach that a balance is maintained among these objectives.

Why Students Study Bookkeeping-Accounting

Students enroll in bookkeeping-accounting for a variety of reasons. When the teacher knows these reasons, he is in a better position to understand the needs of the students, to help determine the best objectives for the course, and to make the best choice of subject matter content to be covered in the course. He is also in a better position to guide students into or out of a B-A course or sequence.

One study which asked high school students why they enrolled in bookkeeping summarized the results of a questionnaire answered by 153 first-year bookkeeping students as shown on page 76.

This study shows that 78 percent of the students ("a" and "b") enrolled in bookkeeping for vocational or related vocational reasons. The remaining 34 students, or 22 percent, enrolled in bookkeeping for a variety of reasons. A study of some of these reasons raises two important questions. First, were some of these reasons sufficient or valid justification for enrolling or permitting the students to enroll in bookkeeping? Second, what did the

WHY STUDENTS STUDY BOOKKEEPING [18]

Reasons	First Choice	Second Choice	Grand Total
a. I expect to use the skill and information gained by taking this course for business (vocational) purposes immediately after I leave high school.	54	17	71
b. Although I am not planning to be a bookkeeper after graduation, but am planning to enter another career (secretary, selling, nursing, etc.), I think bookkeeping might help me in understanding my job.	65	23	88
c. I expect to use the skills and knowledge gained for purely personal reasons (i.e., keeping club records, personal budgeting).	6	18	24
d. Because I expect to major in business when I go to college.	5	4	9
e. Because I think that it would help me to earn my way through college.	1	0	1
f. Because I think that I would like to become a teacher.	0	0	0
g. Because my parents want me to take the course.	2	5	7
h. Because this course is required; I have to.	4	8	12
i. Because my friends are enrolled in this course or have urged me to take it.	0	2	2
j. Simply to "fill in" my schedule of classes at registration time.	1	4	5
k. Because I want to learn more about business generally.	12	65	77
l. (Fill in your own statement here if none of the above apply.)	3	7	10

teacher do about his objectives for taking care of the needs of those pupils who were in the course because ("g" and "h") they were inveigled or forced into taking it, or ("i" and "j") were enrolled for noneducational or questionable reasons?

These two problems are common ones faced by many, if not most, teachers: (1) how to see to it that only the "right" students are enrolled in B-A courses; (2) how to meet the needs of students in the course whose primary reasons for being there are not conducive to good bookkeeping learning. No perfect formula can be devised to care for the human equation involved in both of these problems. However, the B-A teacher who wants to improve

---

[18] Frederic T. Hawes, "Teacher, Whither Are You Bound—?" *Beacons on Business Education* (New Britain, Connecticut: Teachers College of Connecticut, January, 1950), p. 11.

his teaching, i.e., the learning of the class, and at the same time wants to make his task easier, can do much to arrive at a closer solution to these two problems. The first step that can be taken is an examination of the objectives toward which students and teachers should be working in the class.

Criteria for Enrolling Bookkeeping-Accounting Students

There are five major criteria or tests that can be considered as helpful in determining what students should be required or permitted to enroll in a B-A course. Stated in the form of questions requiring affirmative answers these are as follows:

1. Do the aims or objectives of the course fulfill the reason for enrolling the student? Schools that permit students without sound educational reasons to enroll in B-A courses should reexamine their vocational guidance principles and techniques. The motivational objective could be put to good use where student objectives are weak; or where the school, the teacher, or the student have no choice in the matter, such as students enrolling because of parental insistence.

2. Will the objectives of the course best help meet the educational or vocational plans of the student? Schools which require or encourage students preparing to become salesclerks, typists, and secretaries to enroll in bookkeeping-accounting for related vocational reasons, should be sure the course directly contributes to these students' vocational plans and education. Schools that have average-ability students planning to become vocational bookkeepers and have permitted their courses to deteriorate into low-level record keeping or personal-use courses primarily, should reexamine their B-A objectives to see if they are in balance and offer the greatest good to the greatest number of students.

3. Does the student have the degree of interest and ability necessary for reasonable success in the course? Students who do not have a level of interest or ability sufficient for deriving reasonable benefit from a specialized course would profit more from courses closer to their interest and ability. There are no prognostic tests nor interest tests that alone supply the answer as to which students will or will not succeed in a B-A course. The best current means for determining probable success in bookkeeping-accounting is derived from a consideration of multiple factors: the student's scholastic ability; past scholastic success; results of tests measuring I. Q., reading comprehension, vocational interest, and aptitude; and the reasons and strengths of the student's desire for studying bookkeeping-accounting. The best form of prognosis that is available for determining success in a B-A course is the consideration of a combination of these factors.

One solution for benefiting and meeting the needs of below-average or low-ability students who want to become office workers is to teach them in a special course, with its own special set of objectives, such business and general clerical skills and knowledges that are within their ability. The best solution is not to lower or change the objectives of a B-A course at the expense of average students.

4. Can the community's field of labor absorb the number of students enrolling in the course for the purpose of becoming vocational bookkeepers? The high school B-A course probably gives students the best understanding of how business functions. Furthermore, there are thousands and thousands of people, such as small-store and business proprietors, secretaries, and other office workers, who use the knowledge of bookkeeping-accounting in their work but who are not classified as bookkeepers because bookkeeping is not their major function. Therefore, when we consider the number of people, aside from vocational bookkeepers, who enter the business world and who will benefit from the study of bookkeeping-accounting, it is quite obvious that there should be many times more students studying bookkeeping than there are bookkeeping jobs in the community to be filled. As a result, it should be clear that this criterion applies only to those schools where there are more or considerably more students declaring themselves for becoming all-round vocational bookkeepers than there are such jobs to be filled in their communities.

There is, of course, no formula for an easy solution to the problem of supplying a community with the exact number of trained vocational bookkeepers that it needs each year. Some students will move and get jobs in other communities. Some will decide to accept other kinds of employment. There should, however, be a close relationship between the number of vocational bookkeepers trained in school and the number of available book-keeping jobs in the school community. A school's responsibility for good vocational guidance should cause it, when necessary, to attempt to keep the number of vocational bookkeeping graduates within reasonable bounds.

The individual school can probably best meet this criterion by an on-going study of the business needs of its community and good judgment in interpreting the results of such a study to determine what the B-A course enrollment of *students preparing to be vocational bookkeepers* should be.

5. Will the relative advantages or profit that the student can acquire from this course equal or outweigh the advantages which the student could derive from some other specialized course? All high school courses have some merit. Students could derive some advantages from each. Because in most high schools they cannot take all courses, a choice must be made. Certain courses will hold greater advantages for some students and less for others. If B-A teachers are meeting the major objectives of B-A instruction, they should welcome having the advantages of their course measured against the merits of any other course. They should cooperate in good, unbiased guidance for helping to see that the right student gets into the course which is best for him.

STUDY QUESTIONS

1. Why is the B-A course referred to as a specialized course?
2. Name several personal-use bookkeeping problems that every high school student should be taught to handle.
3. How can curriculum arrangements be made so that *all* students learn those phases of bookkeeping that are common problems of everyday living?
4. What are objectives?
5. Explain the statement, "No teacher teaches without some aim or purpose."
6. What are the four major objectives of a first-year B-A course?
7. What are some subsidiary objectives of a first-year B-A course?
8. Why, in addition to major B-A objectives, is it necessary for teachers to have subsidiary course objectives in mind?

9. When should a fifth major objective be considered for a first-year course?

10. How do major second-year B-A objectives differ from the major objectives of a first-year course?

11. Under what circumstances might college-bound students be encouraged to take a high school B-A course?

12. What major caution is offered about the degree of emphasis given on teaching the *how* of keeping business records as compared with the emphasis given to the teaching of the *why* of such records?

13. What is meant by the phrase "teaching interpretive bookkeeping-accounting"?

14. Describe five or six common interpretive bookkeeping-accounting problems.

15. How can the exclusive use of working papers and practice sets weaken a student's interpretive bookkeeping-accounting ability?

16. In what ways is it helpful to the teacher to know why students have enrolled in his B-A course?

17. What are four common reasons for students enrolling in a B-A course? Name other reasons and classify these as either "strong" or "weak" reasons.

18. What are the five criteria for enrolling students in a B-A course?

DISCUSSION QUESTIONS

1. Discuss the statement, "Everybody should know some bookkeeping, but not everybody should take a high school bookkeeping course."

2. If a high school sophomore in your homeroom who was a capable, well-rounded student with outstanding ability in music told you that his parents insisted on his taking bookkeeping-accounting even though he had no interest or desire to study the subject, how would you deal with the problem?

3. "All teachers should be teachers of children first and of subject matter second." What meaning and importance should this statement have for B-A teachers? How does it relate to the general education objective of B-A instruction?

4. What procedures would you advise for a teacher who knows at the start of his course that some of his students are not particularly pleased or interested to be starting the study of bookkeeping-accounting?

5. How likely do you believe it is for a teacher who has no particular liking for the subject of bookkeeping-accounting to be a good B-A teacher?

6. Should all B-A teachers plan to integrate the teaching of economic concepts in their classes?

7. Some colleges and universities require their freshmen and sophomores to concentrate on liberal arts courses and do not permit them to specialize in a major, such as accounting, until they become juniors in college. How, therefore, can high school B-A teachers defend as one of their objectives, *preparation for college accounting?*

8. What is the proper balance in a B-A class between the emphasis that should be given to the *HOW* and to the *WHY* of keeping business records?

9. If it is true that the deeper one moves into interpretative bookkeeping-accounting the deeper he is entering the field of accounting, then how far should teachers attempt to lead their pupils into interpretative bookkeeping-accounting?

10. How would you classify the four major objectives of a first-year B-A course in their order of importance?
Explain the reasons for your order of classification.

11. Discuss the various methods you could use to find out why students take bookkeeping-accounting.

12. Outline the procedures you would follow in setting up objectives for a B-A course.

13. Where should the major emphasis be placed in our B-A instruction—on theory or practice?

14. How can we prepare B-A pupils for the variety of procedures and forms that they will encounter on the job?

15. To what extent should the vocational business students, including B-A students, be educated for change—for changes in office procedures that cannot be foreseen at the time they are high school students?

PROJECTS

1. Interview three experienced high school guidance counselors and write a report on why they believe students should elect or be programmed into a B-A course.

2. Interview three experienced B-A teachers and write a report on their beliefs as to the control which the school should exercise in programming students into both first- and second-year B-A courses.

3. Analyze commonly used high school B-A textbooks and list, with supporting arguments, all of the topics or problems that are personal use in nature and should be taught to *all* students in the high school.

4. Prepare a paper outlining suggestive ways by which a first-year B-A course can be made more meaningful and helpful to the secretarial and/or distributive education students who are taking the course.

5. Read and compare the objectives set up for bookkeeping-accounting in your school, your city, your state.

6. Compare the objectives as stated in three different B-A textbooks.

7. Set up the objectives, both major and subsidiary, that you would like to see achieved in your class of first-year bookkeeping-accounting. At the end of the statement list the sources you consulted.

8. List the economic concepts that you believe should be included in (a) a first-year B-A course and (b) a second-year B-A course. Also, indicate the B-A topic to which you would relate each of these economic concepts.

9. Compare the topical content of a *first-semester* college accounting course (or text) with the topical content of a *first-year* high school B-A course (or text). Indicate what additional topics would have to be included in the high school course if the high school students were to be prepared to take a college placement test in accounting.

SELECTED REFERENCES

Brendel, LeRoy A. "Questions, Questions, Questions! Who's Got the Answers?" *Business Education Forum.* XIX (May, 1965), 23, 27.

Bydalek, David Allen. *A Comparative Analysis of Two High School Elementary Bookkeeping Texts and Two College Elementary Accounting Texts to Determine Commonality and Emphasis of Selected Topics.* Master's thesis. Northern Illinois University, DeKalb, 1966.

Colorado Department of Education, Division of Elementary and Secondary Education. "A Guide for Teaching Bookkeeping in Colorado Schools." Denver: The Department, 1968.

Cullor, Rachel, Virginia Davidson, Lee Gentry, Agnes Kinney, and Ronald Waterman. "Who Should Elect Bookkeeping," *Business Education Forum,* Vol. 22, March, 1968, p. 21. From *A Guide for Teaching Bookkeeping in Colorado Schools* published by Colorado Department of Education, 1968.

Dixon, Helen W. "Developing Traits, Attitudes and Work Habits in the Bookkeeping Classroom," *Business Education Forum.* XXI (March, 1967), 19-20.

Douglas, Lloyd V., James T. Blanford, and Ruth I. Anderson. *Teaching Business Subjects,* Chapter 9. Englewood Cliffs, New Jersey: Prentice-Hall, Inc., 1958.

Forkner, Hamden L., Robert M. Swanson, and Robert J. Thompson. *The Teaching of Bookkeeping,* Monograph 101. Cincinnati: South-Western Publishing Company, 1960.

Freeman, M. Herbert. "Outcomes in Developing Vocational Competence in Bookkeeping Occupations," *New Perspectives in Education for Business,* National Business Education Yearbook, No. 1. Washington: National Business Education Association, 1963, pp. 35-52.

Garrison, Lloyd L. "Economic Education Enrichment in the Bookkeeping Course," *Business Education Forum.* XVIII (April, 1964), 25.

Gratz, Jerre E. *Major Issues in Business Education,* Monograph 106. Cincinnati: South-Western Publishing Co., 1962.

Griffith, Bob B. "Bookkeeping Builds Basic Economic Concepts," *Journal of Business Education.* XXXIX (March, 1964), 233.

Hawes, Frederic T. "Teacher Whither Are You Bound—?" *Beacons on Business Education.* New Britain, Connecticut: Teachers College of Connecticut (January, 1950), 11.

House, Forest Wayne. *Factors Affecting Student Achievement in Beginning Bookkeeping in High School.* 1951 Delta Pi Epsilon Research Award. Oklahoma Agricultural and Mechanical College, 1953.

Howard, Alva. "The Relation of High School Bookkeeping to College Accounting," *The Balance Sheet.* XLV (October, 1963), 68-70.

Jasinski, Harry. "Bookkeeping as Preparation for Employment," *Selected Readings in Business and Office Occupations,* National Business Education Yearbook, No. 5 (Washington: National Business Education Association, 1967), 51-56.

Lund, Erling. *High School Bookkeeping as Preparation for College Accounting Based on a Comparison of Selected High School Bookkeeping Textbooks with Selected College Accounting Textbooks.* Master's thesis. University of Washington, 1962.

McIff, Lyle H. "Successful vs. Unsuccessful Performance in Introductory Accounting," *The Journal of Business Education.* XLIII (April, 1968), 272-273.

Mickelson, William C. *The Practicability of Introducing Economic Concepts in Bookkeeping.* Master's thesis. Mankato State College, Mankato, Minnesota, 1966.

Miller, Morris. "Trends in Objectives and Content of the First-Year Course in Bookkeeping," *Developing Vocational Competency in Bookkeeping and Accounting,* Eastern Business Teachers Association Yearbook, Vol. 40 (New York: New York University Bookstore, 1967), 47-63.

Nelson, Julius. "Trends in Objectives and Content of the Second-Year Course in Bookkeeping," *Developing Vocational Competency in Bookkeeping and Accounting,* Eastern Business Teachers Association Yearbook, Vol. 40 (New York: New York University Bookstore, 1967), 64-72.

Pennsylvania Department of Public Instruction. "Bookkeeping for Business Education Departments in Pennsylvania's Public Schools," Bulletin 273. Harrisburg: The Department, 1958.

Pierson, Frank C., and others. *The Education of American Businessmen.* New York: McGraw-Hill Book Co., Inc., 1959.

Plymire, Boyd G. "College Accounting for High School," *The Balance Sheet.* XLV (February, 1964), 259-260.

Powell, Ray M. "Career Choices Among Beta Alpha Psi Members," *The Accounting Review.* XLI (July, 1966), 523-524.

Stelter, Gayle A. "Include Basic Business and Economic Principles in Bookkeeping Classes," *The Balance Sheet.* XLIX (December, 1967), 156-157, 192.

Teel, Jesse F. "Enriching Bookkeeping Classes by Integrating Economics," *Selected Readings in Business and Office Occupations,* National Business Education Yearbook, No. 5 (Washington: National Business Education Association, 1967), 62-66.

Tonne, Herbert A. *Principles of Business Education,* Third Edition, Chapter 18. New York: Gregg Publishing Divison, McGraw-Hill Book Company, Inc., 1961.

Wallace, Ruth A. *The Rationale for Bookkeeping and Accounting in Public School Curriculums, 1821-1961.* M.A. thesis, San Jose State College California, 1961. As reported in *National Business Education Quarterly.* XL (Fall, 1962), 69.

Wilson, W. Harmon. "Some Danger Signs in Vocational Business Education," *The EBTA Journal.* IV (Spring, 1966), 50-51, 53.

THE LEARNING PROCESS AND THE TEACHING OF BOOKKEEPING-ACCOUNTING

Chapter 4

What Is Learning?

Over the centuries man has discovered bit by bit how people learn and has developed ways of teaching that utilize these discoveries. He has found that people learn differently. Because they learn differently, teachers must use a variety of methods in order to reach the various learning patterns of their students. Just telling or lecturing does not produce learning.

Man has found that people learn better when they are interested, and that a teacher can create interest; that people learn better when they are encouraged and rewarded rather than discouraged and punished; that they learn better when the goals are clear, realistic, attainable, and related to their personal interests and experiences. He has discovered that learning is better when what is to be learned is understood rather than simply memorized. He has discovered that the practice required to develop an ability must be thoughtful, analytical practice and not just sheer repetition.

There are, of course, many other discoveries about learning. It would be impossible to summarize here all that is known about learning. A continuing flow of information about how people learn is to be found in the writings and teachings of psychologists, educators, research workers in communication, business, anthropology, and any other field concerned with trying to find out why people behave as they do. The B-A teacher must make himself aware of this information through study, reading, and conversation. He must be receptive to new ideas about learning and new methods created to utilize these ideas.

Cronbach has listed seven concepts which are "central to the learning process," and he has suggested teachers' actions which are associated with each concept. These aspects of learning are presented below as a form of organization which the individual can follow when he thinks about learning problems and when he thinks about teaching methods in bookkeeping-accounting. It might also serve as a check list for a teacher to use when planning his teaching to be sure he has included and provided for all the aspects of learning.

**ACTS OF THE TEACHER ASSOCIATED WITH
EACH ASPECT OF LEARNING** [1]

Aspect of Learning	Teacher Activity
Situation	Selects and arranges material to which the pupil is to respond.
Personal characteristics	Uses aptitude tests and other data to judge what method and material the pupil is ready for.
Goal	Helps the pupil to understand what constitutes a desirable performance. Provides an encouraging atmosphere, sets attainable standards. Shows connections between the pupil's classwork and his personal aims.
Interpretation	Makes clear the characteristics of a desirable response. Arranges material meaningfully, and elaborates meanings by suitable explanation. Suggests suitable trial responses or methods of attack.
Action	Provides for the pupil to make active responses through practice, recitation, projects, etc.
Consequence	Monitors the pupil's performance to detect misunderstanding or faulty technique. Uses tests to show the pupil what progress he is making and what faults need to be overcome.
Reaction to thwarting	Reduces emotional tension. Assists the pupil to reinterpret. Studies the pupil individually to identify causes of difficulty.

The Learning Cycle

This listing of concepts central to the learning process suggests the presentation of a learning cycle in the manner of a B-A cycle (as illustrated on page 101). For each step in the cycle, basic principles of learning are given.

---

[1] Lee J. Cronbach, *Educational Psychology* (2d ed.; New York and Burlingame: Harcourt, Brace, and World, 1963), p. 83.

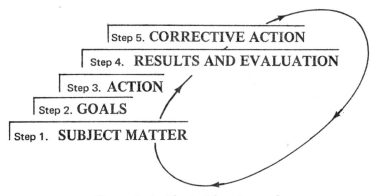

Figure 4—1. Chart of learning cycle

1. Subject matter. Subject matter in bookkeeping-accounting is determined by vocational practice and the larger goals of education. Psychologists point out that learning is more effective if some form or plan of total subject matter organization is apparent. The early presentation of the B-A cycle and referral to it throughout the course constantly gives an overall organization of B-A subject matter.

2. Goals. Activity or study directed toward worthwhile goals is the basis of education. It is desirable that such goals be constructed cooperatively by pupil and teacher. The teacher should know the character of good job performance and work with students in setting vocational goals. Students should be guided toward occupational and educational goals related to real interests and abilities.

3. Action. The actions which teachers take to teach and which pupils take to learn should be varied, directly related to vocational or personal use, and with emphasis on understanding the principles underlying the details of procedure.

4. Results and evaluation. Results of teaching and learning action should be known immediately after the action has taken place. How did we do? What was learned? What was not learned? What shall we do about it?—These are questions that should be asked and answered after each teaching and learning experience. Teachers and students should be continuously considering together the contribution of different experiences to the goals set.

5. Corrective action. Corrective action may be necessary for an entire class or limited to the individuals who did not achieve the goals set. If goals were not achieved, the teaching and learning experiences should be redesigned either for the whole group or for the individuals who did not learn. When goals are achieved, new goals should be established.

The aspects of learning are many. The psychologist says, "Learning, we are coming to understand, is not simply a matter of motivation, repetition, presentation, stimulation, conditioning, and the like, although, of course, all of these things are part of the problem. Learning, we are coming to understand, is a problem of total personality. It is a problem of an individual's personal discovery of meaning. . . . Learning may be defined as the discovery of personal meaning."[2] The learning cycle, therefore, just as the B-A cycle, needs this life-giving element of personal meaning to begin to function.

In bookkeeping and accounting, the principle of debit and credit or any of the other basic principles are probably never really learned until some relationship to the individual's personal experience is established. One adult reports that he passed with good grades through two years of high school bookkeeping and two years of college accounting, and one methods course in the teaching of bookkeeping-accounting. But today he claims that he doesn't know the relationship of right and left and debit and credit and really doesn't have any comprehension of basic bookkeeping-accounting principles. (Fortunately, he never became a B-A teacher.) His years of study taught him not bookkeeping-accounting, but how to pass courses in bookkeeping and accounting without learning the principles involved. If learning is the discovery of personal meaning, this may serve to explain why much of what people study in school has little effect on them.

The B-A subject matter is basically many interrelated principles of recording business transactions to show the effects on the condition of a business. The principles, of course, are illustrated and reinforced in any B-A text by problems and exercises and applications to various situations. When students can relate the principles

---

[2] *Ibid.*, p. 9.

to something which has real personal meaning to them, and then apply the principles where appropriate, we can assume learning has taken place. We cannot assume real B-A learning has occurred when all the students can do is recite rules, follow directions, memorize procedures, and be neat in preparing papers. We can only assume that they have learned to recite rules, follow directions, memorize procedures, and be neat.

Cronbach says, "The pupil who learns a prescription without understanding it will have difficulty in adapting it to a new situation. He may learn rapidly a procedure presented in a rote fashion. But . . . he is then less able to work out the proper procedure in a slightly different situation, and less equipped to understand subsequent explanations. Teaching materials that can be understood and teaching methods that foster understanding are needed if learning is to transfer." [3] Perhaps this explains why B-A students who only memorize and do not understand or relate principles to their experience are potential failures in the field. Business offices in this thinking age have limited use for those whose only development has been in the area of rote memory.

Learning and Action

The subject of personal budgeting is probably taught in some course in every high school in the United States. There is plenty of information available on the topic. A teacher teaching it assigns readings about it; has the students talk about it in the classroom; presents audio-visual materials; has problems solved; gives tests; awards grades. Yet how many young people have really related themselves to the subject personally and use budgeting in their personal lives? How many of the teachers teaching it have made budgeting a "discovery of personal meaning"? Has learning really taken place? Was the time spent on budgeting wasted? What *was* learned? Has behavior or thinking changed in any way because of the teaching?

Arthur Combs in his writing has said, "Education, as we have known it, has done pretty well in two of its phases. It has been quite successful in gathering information and in making information available to people. These problems we have pretty well solved. Our greatest failures are those connected with the problem

---

[3] *Ibid.,* p. 347.

of helping people to behave differently as a result of the information we have provided them."[4]

Have we in bookkeeping-accounting been overly concerned with subject matter and neglectful of looking to see if students have applied their learning in personal ways and in vocational activities? This is a question which needs answering if our teaching of this subject is to result in real learning.

The Teacher—a Key to Learning

The teacher, of course, is the key to learning since he designs the methods, points the way to the discovery and understanding of subject matter, and thereby colors the whole process.

There is a wealth of information concerning the elements that make a good teacher and the methods that are available to him in fostering learning. It is assumed that the reader will have been exposed to some of this general information or have access to it through courses and reading. Therefore, the space here will be limited to a discussion of several important concepts and newer ideas about teaching and learning which are vital if we are to be effective and up-to-date in bookkeeping instruction.

The teacher has a responsibility for helping to make democracy work. The teacher fulfills this responsibility by developing desirable attitudes toward the kind of work in which he is training students to earn their livings. Private business enterprise is one of the prime factors of our democratic way of life, and a respect for the values of endeavors in business should be basic to our education for business.

The teacher also fulfills this responsibility through developing thinking workers and not just a group of nonthinkers trained only to follow directions and take orders. In bookkeeping-accounting it is easy to subordinate the students to the subject matter, and insist that all be uniformly cast into the same pattern of action. But students bring differing abilities to a class. While, of necessity, there is uniformity in the subject matter, somewhere an opportunity

---

[4] Arthur W. Combs, "Personality Theory and Its Implications for Curriculum Development," *Learning More About Learning* (Washington: Papers and Reports from Third Association for Supervision and Curriculum Development Research Institute, National Education Association, 1959), p. 9.

should be given to individuals for some small show of independent, creative effort, or we are not going to develop leaders and initiators—just followers and order-takers.

The teacher can be most influential in this direction by using methods which encourage thinking and which take account of individual differences. Moreover, if a teacher regards his students as human beings he wants to help instead of just assorted I. Q.'s into which he must pour some subject matter, he will be more successful in developing leaders and initiators. A sixth grader summed it up when he said about a training teacher, "We had him figured out the first day. I don't see why he can't figure us out and treat us like human beings."

Enthusiasm for and confidence in the value of the subject matter lies at the heart of a satisfying teaching and learning experience. In Chapter 1, the importance of bookkeeping-accounting in the modern world was pointed out. When a teacher fully comprehends this importance, this feeling is conveyed one way or another to the students. When the value of a subject is felt, learning begins to take place. The foundation of our democratic way of life is strengthened when teachers develop alert, thinking business employees.

In contrast to this is the B-A teacher who would rather be teaching mathematics in a college preparatory course. His teaching is synthetic, rigid in method, limited in discovery of personal meaning, and produces a routine, frozen learning that might occur in spite of, rather than because of, his teaching.

The art of teaching lies partially in the ability to see the subject matter through the eyes of the students. Lesson plans, as will be seen in Chapter 6, usually contain motivation, presentation, application, summary, homework. Yet if the plan is to be successful, the teacher must go one step further, put himself on the students' side of the desk, think as the students are liable to think, and then ask, "Now what are they going to learn when I do this in my plan of teaching?" Too frequently the teacher sees only the subject matter to be taught and how it appears to him. He fails to consider the students' contribution to the situation and how he can specifically help them discover personal meaning in what he wishes to teach.

Student teachers more often than not plan their lessons for the eyes and ears of a critic teacher rather than for the learning of the students in a class, and thus begins a way of thinking in planning which neglects the students' point of view. Those whose responsibility it is to train teachers should evaluate the work of their teachers-in-training so that the highest values will be placed on meeting the challenge of producing learning rather than following a rigid list of lesson plan requirements to impress a critic.

High expectations are a prerequisite for achievement. It has been said that "the universe cooperates with your expectations." What does the teacher expect from his students? Too many teachers say apologetically, "Of course, we can't do very much in bookkeeping—so *many* low-ability students, you know." Then they return to the same old methods, same old assignments, same old tests and sink once more into the rut of no expectations. And what learning takes place in their classes? Exactly what they expected!

One of the exciting ideas in modern psychology is its view of the problem of intelligence. We are told now that how a person behaves is a function of his perceptions. The psychologist says, "If his perceptions are extensive, rich, and highly available when he needs them, then he will be likely to behave in effective, efficient, 'intelligent ways.' " [5] This notion has many implications for us. It means that what our students can do may not be as limited as we think. It may be the teacher who has been limited by the methods he has been using. Combs continues his discussion of this subject by saying, "If human capacities for intelligent behavior are dependent on perception, then they are far more open to change than we have ever supposed. Indeed, human perceptions are so much within our capacities that we may even be able *to create* intelligence by helping people to perceive more extensively and more richly and by creating situations that make it possible for these perceptions to be available when needed." [6] What a refreshing thought! How wonderful for students to have the idea presented that the educational straightjacket of an I. Q. might eventually be removed!

[5] *Ibid.*, p. 13.
[6] *Ibid.*

There will be no overnight changes resulting from this thinking. Combs continues, "That perceptual psychology puts the capacity for intelligent behavior within our grasp does not mean that we can make modifications quickly, easily, or at will. It does, however, open great new vistas down which we can now only dimly peer. It means that perhaps we are not so much the victims of circumstances as we have been led to believe. . . . It means we teachers need not feel defeated, that there are many things we can do, even with the most limited child." [7] To detail what these things may be and to try them out is the next step for the educator.

The next step for the B-A teacher is to delve more deeply into this newer idea which the field of psychology offers us and define its application to the subject. What perceptions about figures are of value to bookkeepers? What perceptions of relationships between accounts are necessary to an understanding of basic B-A principles? Can we study the perceptions of successful on-the-job bookkeepers and translate these into better methods of teaching?

In B-A teaching, then, it can be seen that taking a methods course, or reading a methods text, does not complete one's knowledge of how to teach bookkeeping-accounting or how one learns bookkeeping-accounting. These are ongoing, open-end subjects, always in a state of improving change, and the teacher is the motivating force at the heart of the change. We need to experiment with new experiences and new goals. Mackenzie points up this need when he says: "There appears to be tremendous public pressure that seems to imply that we will go forward in education by moving backwards and by picking up old solutions and old answers. We rush to grouping; we rush to tracking systems; we rush to more of the same things—greater quantities, making it harder—as though these are necessarily the best solutions for our problem." [8] And he concludes, "The visionary way of thinking is the only way left to us. We need to think of changing with the world." [9]

---

[7] *Ibid.*

[8] Gordon N. Mackenzie, "Freeing Capacity to Learn: Implications for Curriculum and Instruction," *Freeing Capacity to Learn*, ed. Alexander Frazier (Washington: Development Research Institute, National Education Association, 1960), p. 4.

[9] *Ibid.*, p. 9.

STUDY QUESTIONS

1. Why should a teacher use a variety of teaching methods rather than just one which he may personally prefer?

2. What are the seven concepts "central to the learning process" as listed by Cronbach?

3. How is learning currently defined by psychologists?

4. What are the steps in the suggested learning cycle?

5. For each step in the learning cycle, give at least one basic principle of learning.

6. When can we assume B-A learning has taken place?

7. Why is the understanding of basic principles of bookkeeping-accounting, as opposed to memorization of procedures alone, essential in the preparation of users of bookkeeping-accounting?

8. According to Arthur Combs, in what two phases has education done the best work? What is its greatest failure?

9. In what general way is the teacher a key to learning?

10. Indicate two ways in which the B-A teacher can fulfill his responsibility for helping to make democracy work.

11. How does enthusiasm for a subject come into being?

12. What is your understanding of the phrase "being able to see the subject matter through the eyes of the students"?

13. Explain how psychologists are encouraging us to have greater expectations of our students' achievement through their newer ideas about intelligence.

14. What should the B-A teacher do about the newer thoughts in psychology about perception and intelligent behavior?

DISCUSSION QUESTIONS

1. Give specific examples of learning as the discovery of personal meaning in the B-A teaching field.

2. For each of the seven concepts basic to the learning process give an illustration of its specific functioning in the teaching of bookkeeping-accounting.

3. Combs says our greatest failures are those connected with the problem of helping people to behave differently as a result of the

information we have provided them. Discuss the application of this statement to bookkeeping-accounting, including the following questions: What is desirable "behavior" in bookkeeping-accounting? How should we expect the "behavior" of B-A students to change as a result of our teaching? Do we have any measure of the change in behavior in bookkeeping-accounting? What kinds of studies might be helpful in this area?

4. Give specific examples of how a B-A teacher can help to make democracy work.

5. Discuss ways in which creative effort can be fostered in a B-A class.

6. How does a teacher "figure out" students? What constitutes being "treated as a human being"?

7. Discuss how enthusiasm for a subject may be conveyed to a student group.

8. Psychology offers the idea that we might create intelligence by developing perceptual ability in students. What does this mean to you? Can you illustrate how the idea is functioning or might function in the teaching of bookkeeping-accounting?

PROJECTS

1. Using the seven concepts of learning, observe a B-A lesson and specifically identify how each concept was present in the lesson.

2. Pick a topic in bookkeeping-accounting and list specific classroom procedures you can use which require thinking on the part of the student as opposed to rote memory.

3. Write a paper on (a) The value of bookkeeping-accounting to business, or (b) The importance of bookkeeping-accounting to an individual's personal life.

4. Pick a subject in bookkeeping-accounting and list all the experiences (work, recreational, educational) a young person might have which would have some relationship to the subject—its details and its basic principles.

SELECTED REFERENCES

Bruner, Jerome S. *Toward a Theory of Instruction.* Cambridge, Massachusetts: The Belknap Press of Harvard University Press, 1966.

Combs, Arthur W. "Personality Theory and Its Implications for Curriculum Development," *Learning More About Learning*, Papers and Reports from the Third Association for Supervision and Curriculum Development Research Institute. Washington: National Education Association, 1959. pp. 5-20.

Cronbach, Lee J. *Educational Psychology*, 2d ed. New York: Harcourt, Brace and World, Inc., 1963.

Mackenzie, Gordon N. "Freeing Capacity to Learn: Implications for Curriculum and Instruction," *Freeing Capacity to Learn*, Papers and Reports from the Fourth Association for Supervision and Curriculum Development Research Institute. Washington: National Education Association, 1960. pp. 1-9.

Stephens, John M. *The Psychology of Classroom Learning*. New York: Holt, Rinehart and Winston, Inc., 1966.

The Importance of Planning

No phase of learning to teach or of improving teaching can do more to contribute to the teacher's success than can effective planning for instruction. Good teaching and steady progress in learning are not possible without plans for reaching the objectives of the course.

The larger objectives of bookkeeping-accounting were stated in Chapter 3. It is the teacher's responsibility to plan his daily teaching so that these objectives are reached in the time alloted to him. Therefore, the teacher must plan day-to-day classroom objectives through which the student will finally achieve the major course objectives. For example, a class for a particular day may have the objective, "To reach an understanding of the meaning of depreciation and its importance to bookkeeping-accounting." This objective could have been determined as a result of forethought and systematic planning after seeing its proper relationship and place in supporting the major objectives of the course. It might best be reached if the teacher prepares and follows a daily lesson plan. This plan might be so developed and taught that students leaving the class could feel and say, "Today I learned something new in bookkeeping,"—a reaction that should follow each day's B-A class.

Unfortunately, all teachers do not plan so wisely and so well. Another teacher with a similar class might have arrived at the objective, "To keep the class quiet this period." To meet this objective, he might extemporaneously evolve a plan to give the class a reading assignment or a problem to work out at their desks—almost any reading assignment and almost any problem that might or might not have a relationship to the larger objectives of the course. In this case, some student might learn something, but probably for the majority of the class it would mean only the passing of another bookkeeping-accounting period.

All teachers have objectives and all teachers plan, but these two illustrations show that it is the level of the objective and the caliber of planning which are all-important. The relationship among objectives, achieving objectives, and the quality of planning is inseparable.

Many factors are involved in a teacher's success. Some of these, such as the teacher's personality, his regard for young people, and his feeling for the subject of bookkeeping-accounting, are difficult to change in a methods course. But methods and techniques of teaching center around plans that can be learned by all who have been properly selected for the teaching profession. The saying "Teachers are born, not made" is false. Some may have greater aptitudes, interests, and "gifts" for teaching than others, but teaching is a skill that can be learned; and planning is an important factor in this skill. A teacher—any teacher—regardless of his experience can improve his teaching in proportion to the planning he does.

The Advantages of Instructional Planning

Common questions that student teachers and beginning teachers ask are: How fast should you teach? How much time should be spent teaching the work sheet? How does one space the coverage of a semester or a year course? How should discipline problems be handled? What can be done with students in the class who seem disinterested? How are pupil respect and cooperation secured? A common, yet the least helpful, reply to these questions is, "You will learn from experience." True, experience will help solve these problems for some beginning teachers, but good planning could eliminate or minimize them from the beginning. Experience, coupled with good reasoning and continued thoughtful planning, will answer the questions in the best manner possible. Leave planning out of the solution of these and other problems and a hit-or-miss teaching situation results.

Thoughtful planning contributes the following advantages to the learning situation:

1. Helps set course and daily goals or objectives of learning.
2. Gives the teacher the opportunity of forethought in considering and applying sound educational principles of learning.
3. Organizes the learning. Saves time by teaching the right thing at the right time. Sets a steady progress in daily assignments and coverage. Keeps the teacher and the class on the subject and headed in the right direction.
4. Improves class management. Gives businesslike atmosphere to the class. Cuts down on disciplinary problems. Gains respect and cooperation of more students who feel that they are learning something—getting somewhere.
5. Makes classroom teaching easier as a result of the above advantages.
6. Lends confidence and gives assurance to beginning teachers.

Planning is not an open sesame for teaching success. One could plan long, hard, and conscientiously and still be a weak or ineffectual teacher. But planning can be and often is the difference between success and failure, between master teaching and mediocrity, between enjoyment and dislike of teaching. Planning is necessary for good teaching, for improving instruction, for becoming a better teacher.

Essentials for Effective Planning to Teach Bookkeeping-Accounting

Before a bookkeeping teacher can plan for teaching so that effective learning takes place in his class, he must have a thorough knowledge of the following and be able to apply such knowledge in planning and in teaching.

1. He must have a sound knowledge of B-A subject matter and practices and know the character of good job performance.
2. He must have sound and well-established goals toward which he and his pupils are working.
3. He must know the various approaches to the teaching of bookkeeping-accounting and the order of subject-matter presentation, and he must select those which will be the best for his pupils.
4. He must know and make use of what we know about learning and methods of teaching that effectively help his students to learn.

5. He must be familiar with the available teaching materials, and how and when to use them.
6. He must be able to evaluate learning progress, to know the standards of a good performance, and to use such evaluation to optimum advantage in his teaching.

To divorce general educational principles, general methods of teaching, and reference to subject matter from a special methods text in bookkeeping-accounting is not feasible. This text assumes that the reader has a background in the B-A subject matter—item 1 above. While it also assumes that the reader has some knowledge of educational concepts and general methods of teaching (see item 4), Chapter 4 did deal briefly with fundamental concepts of learning, and Appendix II summarizes some general methods of teaching. Otherwise, items 1 and 4 above will not be discussed in this book except as they relate to special problems or difficult areas of B-A instruction.

With this observation in mind, and because item 2 above—the objectives of B-A instruction—was discussed in a previous chapter, the problem of choosing an approach and an order of presentation (item 3) is the next question demanding attention by the B-A teacher who plans for good instruction.

Approaches and Orders of Presentation

The term "approach" in the teaching of bookkeeping-accounting is used variously in the writings on B-A instruction. Some claim that what is called an approach to the teaching of bookkeeping should be referred to as the order of presentation. Others use the term "approach" to describe the daily start, the daily approach, that a teacher makes in his day-to-day presentation of new learnings. The most common usage, however, refers to the means by which the class, the first week or so, is introduced to the study of bookkeeping-accounting. This approach will usually have a definite bearing on the order of presentation of subsequent topics or areas of B-A instruction. Because the initial approach and the order of presentation are interrelated, the following discussion handles them concurrently.

More than twenty approaches to the teaching of bookkeeping-accounting have been developed by business educators. Those which are mentioned most frequently in the writings on B-A instruction and appear to be most widely used are subject-matter approaches that lead in quickly to a coverage of the bookkeeping cycle.

The normal, on-the-job progress of B-A activities passes through a cycle from journal entries to posting to the ledger, to a trial balance, to a work sheet with adjustments, to a balance sheet and an income statement, and then to closing, balancing, and ruling the books. When the books are closed and a post-closing trial balance is taken at the end of the fiscal period, the bookkeeping cycle begins again.

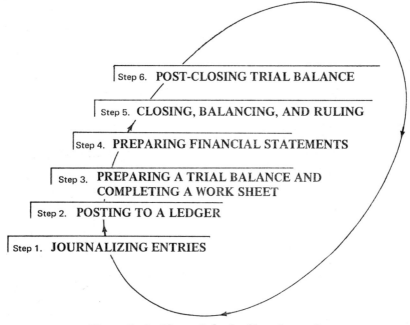

| Step 6. POST-CLOSING TRIAL BALANCE
| Step 5. CLOSING, BALANCING, AND RULING
| Step 4. PREPARING FINANCIAL STATEMENTS
| Step 3. PREPARING A TRIAL BALANCE AND COMPLETING A WORK SHEET
| Step 2. POSTING TO A LEDGER
| Step 1. JOURNALIZING ENTRIES

Figure 5—1. Chart of the bookkeeping cycle

Three of these six steps obviously require a prerequisite of B-A knowledge—the trial balance and work sheet, the closing phase, and the post-closing trial balance. This eliminates them as good focal points to introduce the study of bookkeeping. The remaining steps, however, do not necessarily require a previous knowledge of bookkeeping, and the study of bookkeeping can be introduced at any of these points in the cycle. From these steps, therefore, have been developed the three most common subject-matter approaches to B-A teaching: the journal approach, the ledger approach, the balance sheet approach. The income statement is rarely used to introduce students to bookkeeping, although it has occasionally been used as the next step in the order of presentation following the balance sheet.

The Journal Approach

The journal method of approach has the logic of teaching the steps in a bookkeeping cycle in the order in which they are generally practiced on the job. The student first learns how to journalize and to record business transactions in a book of original entry—usually the general journal. Next he learns the form of an account, how to post and to use the ledger; then a trial balance and the work sheet; and so on to complete the simplest of steps in a cycle. This approach and correct on-the-job order of presentation through the cycle have logic and B-A practice to support them.

Some teachers have taught bookkeeping-accounting successfully for years with the journal approach. There is, however, a major argument against it. The student who is introduced to bookkeeping through this approach often works and studies for weeks learning to journalize and to post, without knowing or seeing very clearly where he is headed. He frequently does not know how these routine duties are related to the total bookkeeping picture. He often must accept a certain amount of learning and practice on faith—on the teacher's word alone. This approach can be like a dull introduction to the study of history, starting at the "logical" beginning—sometime B. C.—and having the student learn facts and figures as he comes along through the ages without relating them to a major purpose for studying history—to understand better where we are now headed as a people and as a nation.

The Ledger Approach

The ledger or account method of approach has the logic of starting with basic, fundamental concepts of bookkeeping-accounting—the account, the book of secondary entry but of primary importance; the why and how of account balances, their debits and credits. Advocates of this approach point out that the account is the central figure around which all B-A duties revolve. The most common order of presentation following this approach is to move ahead to proving the equality of debits and credits by taking a trial balance, then journalizing, posting, and proceeding to the preparation of financial statements.

Major opponents of this approach make the same criticism that they level at the journal approach—it is a mechanical, routine approach which fails to share with the student the purpose, the use to which the routine work of keeping accounts will be put. Opponents also point out that such an approach starts in the middle of the cycle and lends confusion by moving back to the journal and then ahead to culminating steps in the cycle.

The Balance Sheet Approach

The balance sheet method of approach, along with its variations as described later, is by far the most common and popular approach to the teaching of bookkeeping in high school today. The balance sheet approach has the logic of first showing the student where he is going—to what use B-A records will be put and why they are needed. It shares an important objective, an important reason for keeping books, with the student before starting him upon the pathway for reaching such a goal. It can be said, perhaps at the expense of making an oversimplified statement, that there are two major purposes of bookkeeping-accounting: (1) to show what a business or person has or owns—the balance sheet; (2) to show how the business or person got that way—the income statement. It can be, and usually is, more stimulating for the average student to give him this broader, more intellectual approach so that he can see relationships. In contrast, the student who is introduced to bookkeeping by the journal or the ledger approach is most generally given what might be called a routine posting clerk's introduction to the subject.

In Chapter 3, when the importance of the interpretive objective was discussed, it was mentioned that a major criticism of B-A instruction was the overemphasis given to teaching the repetitive and routine work of the bookkeeper—that too much of the *how* of bookkeeping-accounting and not enough of the *why* was being taught. While there is much merit to this criticism, it does seem worth mentioning at this point that the balance sheet approach is a *why* approach, whereas the journal and ledger approaches are both *how* approaches. Thus, as long ago as the third and fourth decades of this century, when the balance sheet approach started to receive favorable attention, educators even then were aware of the need for a better balance in their courses between the *why* and the *how* of bookkeeping-accounting.

One common order of presentation following the balance sheet approach is to proceed to an understanding of the need for accounts, the meaning of debit and credit, and the use of the ledger. This is then followed by the use of the journal for recording transactions, posting transactions, taking a trial balance, preparing a work sheet, preparing financial statements, and finally the closing of the books and taking a post-closing trial balance at the end of the fiscal period. While such an order of presentation does not follow exactly the order of the steps in the cycle, it currently seems to be the most successful order for introducing students to their first trip through the simple bookkeeping cycle.

The balance sheet approach has always been challenged on the basis that it starts at the finish of a bookkeeper's normal duties and not with the beginning or more common duties. Originally the balance sheet approach was unsuccessful when too technical or too formal types of balance sheets were used to introduce students to bookkeeping. Then as the use of simpler forms came into prominence, this approach far outdistanced the journal and ledger approaches in popularity.

More recently the balance sheet approach is being challenged on other counts. Some claim that many bookkeepers never prepare a balance sheet, that accountants do such work. Some point out that the determination of income (the income statement) is more important than the determination of capital (the balance sheet). Some point out that the amounts of many accounts on a balance sheet are, at most, estimates of value and are not exact. For example, estimates of depreciation can never be exact to the penny or even to the dollar; thus all fixed assets that depreciate are either overstated or understated. Critics who use this as a reason for opposing the balance sheet approach then claim that giving the balance sheet the prominence of an approach usually results in the students' misconception that it is a correct, infallible statement of values and that such a prominence overemphasizes the true status of the balance sheet.

Any challenge that is accompanied with good supporting reasons and offers sound ways for improvement will advance B-A teaching. However, evidence seems to support the point of view that the balance sheet method of approach has proved its merit as a clear, helpful means of introducing students to bookkeeping-accounting. Therefore, until its critics can do better than recommend a return to former methods, the balance sheet method will probably continue to outrank other approaches in popularity.

Variations of the Approaches

Over the years the three basic approaches for teaching the subject matter of bookkeeping have been modified to overcome various teaching difficulties that have arisen. For many learners the balance sheet with its technical names for accounts, the equation "assets = liabilities + proprietorship," and the need to comprehend its significance in the total picture of bookkeeping offered too many complicated abstract concepts for a completely successful introduction to the study of bookkeeping-accounting. As a result, this technical balance sheet approach was soon pushed into the background of popularity by evolving modifications or variations. The first of these variations was to simplify the learning by introducing the bookkeeping or balance sheet equation first before leading students more gradually to the balance sheet as a whole. This then became known as *the equation,* or *the balance sheet equation,* or *the bookkeeping equation approach.*

Even this more simplified approach, however, left the student with technical terms and abstract concepts to master during his first day or two in the course. So the equation approach, an evolution of the initial balance sheet approach, was further simplified and improved by substituting simple everyday words for the technical terms. The word "owns" was used instead of assets, "owes" instead of liabilities, and "net worth" or "ownership" instead of proprietorship or capital. Thus, the student first learned to use everyday words in the equation. He learned that when no debts exist, what a persons *owns* = his financial *worth.* Next he learned the equation "owns — owes = net worth." After the concept of the equation using simple, everyday words to determine the net worth of an individual was mastered, then a personal balance sheet of an individual was examined before proceeding to the use of technical bookkeeping terms, and eventually to a simple balance sheet of a small business.

Because of the B-A teacher's ability to relate such initial material to the net worth of students or other individuals rather than to business enterprises, some of the many teachers who use this approach label it a *personal approach* to the study of bookkeeping. Regardless of what it is called—either a personal approach or a variation of the balance sheet or the bookkeeping equation approach—it is a popular approach in the high schools today. The work starts with the clear and simple method for determining what a person is worth financially and how such information can be clearly listed. When the skill and the information in this easy step is learned, the student is then shown its relationship to a simple business enterprise and balance sheet. The balance sheet is now presented as a point of beginning rather than as a final goal in bookkeeping work. This is based on the premise that, if a person is going to keep books, he must first note what he owns, what he owes, and what he is worth. In the development of this approach the balance sheet provides the reasoning behind *debit* and *credit* as they are used in the journal and the ledger. These emphases meet the criticism noted previously of the balance sheet approach and thus make it the most popular and successful method of introducing the study of bookkeeping-accounting to high school students today.

As modifications have been made with the balance sheet approach, so comparable modifications have been made with the other approaches. Some teachers who start off by introducing their students to accounts without first mentioning the ledger, refer to this modification of the ledger approach as *the account approach.*

It is also common, even when teachers say they start with one of the above approaches or their variations, to begin the first day or so of teaching by dealing with the place of bookkeeping in business or the reasons for keeping books. While this is not an approach dealing with specific subject matter, it nevertheless can be classified as an approach as it is defined on page 100. This motivational approach is discussed below.

The Motivational Approach

In the survey made to secure from experienced and outstanding successful B-A teachers suggestions for the content of the first edition of this text, many teachers expressed concern over the problem of creating and holding the interest of their students— the problem of motivation, of getting students interested, and of holding their interest. Part of the solution to this problem lies in proper selection of students, or, better still, a more considered judgment by students in *their* selection of a B-A course, as was discussed in Chapter 4. Even a more satisfactory pupil selection, however, would not eliminate students with short spans of interest, students with weak motives, students with different primary goals than those of the course. It is essential, therefore, to consider these students in determining teaching method.

What can we do in bookkeeping to help these students and to give them a higher level of aspiration, to improve or lend strength to their motives and their goals? Perhaps an approach that begins with B-A records is not the best introduction to classes containing students who possess low or mediocre levels of aspiration. Teachers who make a quick plunge with their classes into the new vocabulary, new phrases, new forms of technical bookkeeping may give a permanent chill to the interest of some students and drown the aspirations of others. Perhaps what is needed in B-A instruction is a *motivational approach* that will strengthen and bring the motives of the pupils in the course more into line with the objectives of the course. This approach would be compatible with the motivational objective previously discussed.

This approach could center around the study of such types of problems or units as the following:

1. What good will B-A knowledge and skill be to me?
2. What do bookkeepers do in their work?
3. Who should study bookkeeping-accounting?

These are not offered as prescribed units for initial study, but are considered guesses as to some student needs. Meeting these needs would be helpful in motivating and sustaining higher levels of aspiration.

Some traditional teachers will say that such an approach to the learning of bookkeeping-accounting is a soft, nonvocational, non-businesslike approach—a waste of time. A few common reactions could be: "Why let students become confused and waste time on such questions when we know what knowledges and skills they need to know and the best ways to teach them? They are in class to learn bookkeeping; therefore start teaching it to them the first day. If they dillydally around with that kind of stuff the first week, we'll never complete the course." Teachers who might say such things also appear to be saying to their students, "Don't think about anything in this class except in those areas and on those topics about which I tell you to think. Yours is not to reason why, yours is to journalize, post, or try." Furthermore, they are ignoring a means of improving student interest and subsequent student effort; they are killing off motivational interests that may reinforce existing interests and speed up later bookkeeping learning; they are going counter to basic psychological principles of learning.

Use of a motivational approach, leading up and into an introduction of one of the steps in the cycle, could result in the following benefits:

1. The teacher could, at the start of the semester, get to know the reasons why students enrolled in the course and discover early in the course some of their needs.
2. Misconceptions about bookkeeping-accounting could be corrected.
3. Through classroom discussions of such topics students could have their beliefs about bookkeeping-accounting confirmed or corrected by other students rather than being told by the teacher.
4. Levels of aspiration could, where necessary and possible, be changed.
5. Goals for the course could be shared with the pupils.
6. Pupil-teacher planning could be introduced.
7. Confidence at the start of a new and strange study could be instilled or reinforced.
8. Early and lasting rapport between the teacher (who sees and shows interest and concern about why individual students are studying bookkeeping-accounting) and pupil can be established.
9. The students can start the course by thinking for themselves, not just doing as they are told.

This is not a new idea. Some teachers have been using it successfully for years. It just has not earned a name or been labeled as yet and has been submerged by the popularity of writing about subject-matter approaches.

The success of the motivational approach, as the success of any approach, depends primarily upon the teacher's confidence in its value and his ability to plan and use it effectively. Sometimes the preface of the students' textbook contains information about the importance of bookkeeping-accounting that can prove helpful for getting the students off to a good motivational start. The first two sample lesson plans in Chapter 14, *Getting Started—The First Week's Work*, illustrate in detail one way a class could be started with the motivational approach.

It should be noted at this point that this motivational approach is not limited to the first week or so of a course with the expectation that the interest of the students will be maintained through the remainder of the semester. It is not meant to replace day-to-day motivational techniques for introducing and reinforcing new learnings. It is meant to be an initial, interest-getting, head start for the learning of "bookkeeping." It is to be expected, however, that the teacher will plan to introduce each new technical topic in as clear, interesting, and stimulating a manner as possible.

Adapting the approach to the situation. Students today are learning bookkeeping-accounting under all three of these previously mentioned subject matter approaches and the various orders of presentation following the approaches. All have some logic to support them. Perhaps the amount of writing and the degree of textbook advertising on the topic of approach has given too much importance and confusion to the topic. Still an approach must be made, and the beginning teacher asks, "Which is best?" The most practical answer is—the approach that the teacher can use to best advantage for having his students learn bookkeeping-accounting. A teacher who does not see the advantage of nor possess confidence in the balance sheet approach will probably do better with another approach in which he feels more secure and confident. Beginning teachers, however, may not know nor have an opinion as to which approach they can use best. Teachers confronted with such a dilemma might do well to consider the following:

1. The popular success of the balance sheet approach and the psychological advantages it possesses in sharing goals with students give strong support to its use.
2. Any beginning teacher who uses a different subject-matter approach than that followed by the textbook put into the hands of his students should realize that he is taking away their anchor, going against their source of ready reference.

Relative to the second item above, it should be pointed out that considerable confusion and frustration could result if students listen to a teacher's presentation in class and then cannot find supporting or clarifying material in the text. In any major change or deviation from textbook material, the teacher should be careful not to confuse the student. This is not meant to be an argument for textbook teaching; it is merely a caution to the teacher who deviates from material in the textbook in use to be sure that the variation is clearly presented, that the students understand it as a variation, and, where necessary, supplementary material is put into the hands of the students for current and future reference. Similarly, it seems best, because of the time element and objectives of a first-year B-A course, to teach one way of doing a thing well rather than to have students learn several ways uncertainly. For example, it seems better for a student to understand thoroughly and to be able to adjust the merchandise inventory account one way rather than to have a hazy or confused understanding of several of the half-dozen ways that this can be done. The latter level of understanding and practice is more suited to the professional accounting course.

The Spiral Development in Bookkeeping-Accounting Instruction

Regardless of the approach used, it is rather generally agreed that the student should be taken through the first cycle as early in the course as is feasible. After this, in most first-year courses, the cycle is repeated several times. Each time the cycle is repeated some new learnings are added. Because part of the cycle is expanded on each subsequent time through it, a *spiral development* is said to evolve. For example, the first time through the cycle, the general ledger is the only book of secondary entry used, and only a dozen accounts might be learned. The adjusting entries and the eight- or ten-column work sheet might be omitted. The second time through the cycle, one or more subsidiary ledgers could be introduced, and more accounts and simple adjustments could be added. Thus, as new learnings are added each time through a cycle, the student is being introduced throughout the school year to a constantly expanding bookkeeping cycle.

Just as the authors of different textbooks use different approaches and orders of presentation to introduce B-A pupils to their first simple cycle, so textbooks vary somewhat as to which new topics are presented in each subsequent expanding cycle. For example, some texts introduce the adjusting of accounts the first time through the cycle, others delay adjustments until the second cycle is presented. Some mention controlling accounts early in a first-year course—the second time the cycle is covered; others introduce them during the third cycle. Some texts, particularly record-keeping texts, present material for taking the students through only one cycle, and this near the end of the text and at the option of the teacher. Others more commonly present material for as many as four or five expanding experiences through the cycle. Three such experiences for first-year bookkeeping students seem most common. Regardless of when or in which expanding cycle various texts introduce specific new steps, by the end of first-year bookkeeping the cycle as pictured by steps usually looks something like the diagram presented below. The few minutes that it would take a

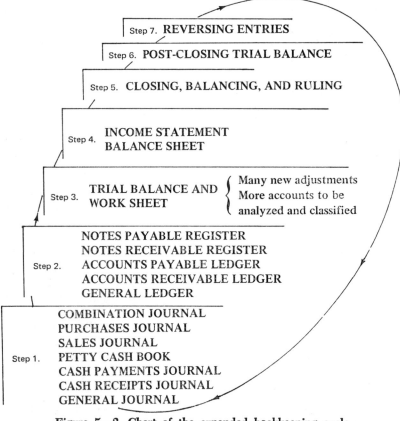

Step 7. REVERSING ENTRIES

Step 6. POST-CLOSING TRIAL BALANCE

Step 5. CLOSING, BALANCING, AND RULING

Step 4. INCOME STATEMENT
BALANCE SHEET

Step 3. TRIAL BALANCE AND WORK SHEET ⎰ Many new adjustments
More accounts to be
analyzed and classified

Step 2. NOTES PAYABLE REGISTER
NOTES RECEIVABLE REGISTER
ACCOUNTS PAYABLE LEDGER
ACCOUNTS RECEIVABLE LEDGER
GENERAL LEDGER

Step 1. COMBINATION JOURNAL
PURCHASES JOURNAL
SALES JOURNAL
PETTY CASH BOOK
CASH PAYMENTS JOURNAL
CASH RECEIPTS JOURNAL
GENERAL JOURNAL

Figure 5—2. Chart of the expanded bookkeeping cycle

teacher to draw such an illustration on the board or project on a screen to show the students what steps they will take and what steps they have covered each time through an expanding cycle would seem to be one simple and profitable way to relate what they are doing to the concept of the complete cycle. Practice sets are commonly available at the completion of each new expanding cycle for the major purpose of giving practice and drill, and to show the relationships of the steps in the cycle.

Teacher opinion regarding the importance of teaching the bookkeeping cycle ranges from not teaching it at all to the claim that it should be taught the first day of the course. Teachers who would not teach it at all are probably not only in the minority, but dealing predominately with students of low ability or interest who should be in some course other than bookkeeping. An excellent reply to such teachers, as good today as when it was written, is contained in a report by a state bookkeeping committee. They say:

> This simplification trend has made itself felt in bookkeeping. There are many, for instance, who would strip the course of all its basic characteristics and include only journalizing and posting. That would be a pure distortion of the subject. In bookkeeping you do not understand the parts unless you understand the whole. Let us simplify the whole, if we must, but let us not maim the subject. It is true that some students will never understand adjusting entries. A more practical solution here is to have a system of student selection and place this group in a more simplified course called record keeping. [This writer believes it should be clerical practice.] It is folly to argue that in most offices the bookkeeper does not go beyond the trial balance. Car producers do not manufacture cars to go the speed limit, but much more. The potential reserve facilitates the ordinary operation of the car. Likewise, in bookkeeping, if we know more than our present job demands, the potential reserve will facilitate our work and give us more confidence and satisfaction.[1]

Vocational Practices Versus Teaching Practices

Good B-A teachers are striving constantly to bring their students to a vocational level of B-A practice. An ultimate objective is to see their students perform activities in the way they are done

---

[1] "Report of the Bookkeeping Committee," *The Balance Sheet* (March, 1951), p. 297.

on the job. The road to this goal is rarely an easy one. It requires planning, ingenuity, step-by-step learning—in short, good teaching. To be successful in achieving this goal, some teachers, at times, teach things or permit their students to do things that are not done by the on-the-job bookkeeper. For example, some teachers permit their students to use pencil at the start of a course, some first teach students to credit the depreciation expense directly against the asset rather than teaching them first to credit an allowance account. When they do these things, they are sometimes criticized or told by supervisors and colleagues, "You are not following vocational practice. They don't do it that way vocationally."

The implication in such criticism is that a B-A teacher should never teach anything or permit students to do anything in class that is not vocational, on-the-job procedure. Such an attitude is absurd. Would these critics say the same to a professional or varsity football coach who has his charges jumping hurdles, playing touch-football, or pushing weighted objects around the gridiron during weekdays? They don't do these things when a Saturday's game is under way! Topflight, vocational skills and understanding are reached in stages and sometimes achieved in various ways. Teachers not only have a right but also an obligation to help students in every way that is reasonable and educationally sound to achieve vocational skills and understanding.

When teachers use procedures and techniques that the students have to *unlearn*, however, then they open themselves up to justifiable criticism. They are not helping their students achieve vocational competence in as short a time as possible. It takes time to unlearn.

There is considerable difference between unlearning and additive learning. In the first case the student is taught something that is easier, probably distantly related, but different than the ultimate objective. Then he is told, "But that is not the way the book-keeper does it." So he has to learn to forget to do something the way he was first taught. Additive learning is proceeding from the simple to the complex in reasonable, related steps or stages. For example, the student learns first that a balance sheet has assets on the left and liabilities and capital on the right. Then, later, he learns that these major classifications of balance sheet accounts can be broken down further into subclassifications, such as current and fixed. He does not have to unlearn anything. Assets still remain on the left and liabilities and capital on the right. He has merely added to his learning that accounts are subclassified on balance sheets.

Topflight bookkeepers and accountants take trial balances on adding machine tapes. Some prepare adjusting and closing entries, balance sheets, and income statements without listing all the account names on a trial balance and without extending the amounts onto a work sheet. Yet how silly it would be to attempt to teach the final phases and steps in a bookkeeping cycle by eliminating current teaching practices in this area—and try to jump students ahead to these topflight vocational procedures without first learning how to list trial balances and use work sheets.

Teachers, therefore, should not be too quick to accept criticism of their bookkeeping *teaching practices* that are not exactly in accord with *vocational practices*. In reality, it is the difference between these two practices that makes the difference between a bookkeeper and a bookkeeping teacher. If a teaching practice requires no unlearning by students, but rather is a simpler, additive learning step that helps students achieve more quickly a more complex skill or understanding, then a teacher is on safe educational ground.

STUDY QUESTIONS

1. Why does every teacher need to plan his work—his teaching?

2. What are five or six advantages that thoughtful planning contributes to the learning situation?

3. Name six essentials that a B-A teacher must know and be able to apply before he can effectively plan his teaching.

4. Why would the initial approach by which students are introduced to the B-A subject matter have a subsequent effect upon the order in which major B-A topics are dealt with in the course?

5. What are the six simple steps in a bookkeeping cycle?

6. Which of these six steps in the bookkeeping cycle have been used most commonly as initial approaches for introducing students to bookkeeping?

7. What are the names of these three most common approaches for introducing students to B-A subject matter?

8. Which approach, along with its numerous variations, is most commonly used today? What are the logical or psychological reasons that support its popularity?

9. What "new" approach is recommended for consideration in this chapter?

10. (a) When could this "new" approach for introducing students to a B-A course be used most effectively? (b) When would there be no need for its use? (c) What benefits could result from its proper use?

11. What is meant by the spiral development in B-A instruction?

12. What are some sound arguments for the necessity of teaching *all* of the steps in the B-A cycle to high school B-A students?

13. When and how can a teacher justify the teaching of or the practice of certain B-A activities that are not strictly vocational, on-the-job B-A procedures?

14. What is the difference between unlearning and additive learning?

DISCUSSION QUESTIONS

1. Comment on the following statement, giving specific examples: "A teacher, any teacher, regardless of his experience, can improve his teaching in proportion to the planning he does."

2. Which subject-matter approach for introducing students to bookkeeping-accounting would you choose to use? Why? What psychological arguments can be cited to support your choice?

3. Should students who do not possess the potential for understanding and mastering within one year all of the steps in a simple bookkeeping cycle be encouraged or permitted to enroll in a first-year course? Discuss.

4. Can a teacher who does not know the character of a good, on-the-job B-A performance be a good teacher of bookkeeping-accounting? If so, how?

5. If you were asked to list in the order of their importance the six essentials for effective planning to teach bookkeeping-accounting, in what order would you list them? Justify your answer.

6. Which of the following two types of persons do you believe has the greatest chance of becoming a successful teacher: (a) a glib talker with an outgoing personality who has not learned to discipline himself to the routine of planning, or (b) a less personable individual who plans his teaching carefully and truly likes and understands the work of a bookkeeper? Why?

PROJECTS

1. Analyze several recent first-year B-A textbooks and compare: (a) the approach and order of presentation that each uses in the first cycle; (b) how quickly the first cycle is presented (number of pages or chapters); (c) the number of cycles covered by each text.

2. Prepare a paper in support of the approach to teaching bookkeeping-accounting which you believe is best. Explain how this approach differs from the way you were introduced to the study of bookkeeping or accounting.

3. Observe a high school bookkeeping class being taught and submit a critique on the planning or any apparent lack of planning by the teacher.

4. Interview an experienced B-A teacher as to: (a) the importance he places on the planning he gives to his teaching; (b) the extent to which he plans now as compared with the time he devoted to planning when he first started to teach; (c) which approach he uses for introducing his students to bookkeeping-accounting, and why.

The Importance of Planning

Planning Organizes Professional Knowledge

When the prospective teacher enters a B-A methods course, he is ready to consider specific plans for day-to-day teaching. He has a wealth of professional knowledge that he learned in compartments—bookkeeping and accounting in one set of courses, educational psychology in another, general methods of teaching in another. Now, in the special methods course, he has considered bookkeeping objectives, common approaches to the teaching of bookkeeping, and related orders of presentation. How will he organize this related professional knowledge, which was learned separately, for its most effective daily use in teaching? Will he use the unit method? The project method? The developmental daily lesson plan? Or will he just stand in front of his class and tell them—lecture? What method or methods will he or should he consider in his day-to-day plans for teaching?

All Do Not Learn Best in the Same Way

The basic method of learning is doing. As stated by the philosopher John Dewey, "We learn to do by doing." The teacher's job, therefore, is to plan his teaching so as to get his students doing the things that best help them to learn the skills and knowledges that fall within the objectives of the course. The way the teacher does this is called a *method of teaching.* But all students do not learn best in the same way. As a result, the teacher cannot limit his planning to a single method of teaching, but must plan to use all methods that will be the most effective for the learning of bookkeeping-accounting.

Common Methods of Teaching

Students can learn by discussion, by listening, by reading, by writing, by being shown or having concepts and ways of doing things illustrated or demonstrated, by proper thoughtful developmental questioning, by being led or guided into proper channels—by trying, doing, succeeding. From these rather common ways of classroom learning have evolved methods of teaching. The simpler of these, which are nearly always present in a few more complex methods that will be discussed later, include:

The discussion method—where a group explores a topic, question, or problem, and individual opinions are expressed and heard.

The lecture method   —where the teacher talks and tells and the students listen.

The textbook-recitation method   —where the teacher assigns readings in a textbook and the students recite what they have read.

The demonstration method   —where the teacher shows how to do something and the students watch him do it.

The Socratic method   —where the teacher develops concepts and thinking by students through developmental questioning.

With the exception of the textbook method, which needed the invention of the printing press and mass production of books to bring it into prominence, these methods have been used for centuries and will undoubtedly be used for centuries to come. They might be termed basic methods of teaching. They are used to help students learn concepts, learn facts, acquire knowledge. They are helpful and indispensable to B-A instruction. Yet through none of these can the skill of bookkeeping be acquired. The demonstration can show how; the lecture, the discussion, the textbook, the Socratic method, each or collectively, can develop intellectual understanding of B-A principles and tell or explain how to perform B-A duties. But none, in themselves, causes the student to achieve skill in bookkeeping-accounting. Thus, whatever method is used to teach the facts, knowledge, or principles of bookkeeping-accounting, the pragmatic philosophy, the pragmatic method that "we learn to do by doing" must be included if we are to develop the skills which are an indispensable part of a bookkeeper's stock in trade. Students learn not what was in a lecture or in a book but only what the lecture or book causes them to do.

A loose use of the term "method" has developed in education whereby only slight variation in a way of teaching, or the unique application of common methods, results in the name of a new method. For example, in business law when legal cases are used to illustrate, explore, and discuss a principle of law, the *case method* is said to be used. Yet reading, telling, discussing, questioning might be the only basic methods used. When students work out an experiment in a physics laboratory, they are said to be using the *laboratory method*. In schools where double bookkeeping periods are in practice and the second period is used for doing what normally might be a homework assignment, the title *laboratory method* is also given to such teaching. When the same practice is followed in an art class, the term *studio method* is sometimes used. Similarly, team teaching and programmed instruction, which are discussed in Chapter 13, "Developing Trends Affecting Bookkeeping-Accounting Instruction," are two of the newer methods of teaching. Yet, when analyzed, they too are related to or make use of one or more of the common methods of teaching mentioned above.

The method that a teacher uses is sometimes determined by the school administration requiring all teachers to adhere to the pattern in common use throughout all classes. In other schools, the teacher is permitted a free choice and encouraged to move into newer fields of methodology. In considering method, therefore, it is necessary for the teacher to be familiar with the old as well as the new.

There are two basic facts that bookkeeping teachers need to be aware of in their choice and use of method. First, bookkeeping-accounting is comprised of both knowledge and skill. These are not learned in the same way. Knowledge of facts can be acquired by hearing, seeing, feeling, tasting, smelling, and associating or reasoning. Skill in bookkeeping requires actual practice, drill, and repetition. Second, no one single or exclusive method of teaching as mentioned above is best for all students. Methods must vary or be a composite of simple ways of teaching. Some students learn best by reading, some by listening, some by watching. None learn bookkeeping-accounting without performing related activities.

One might wonder if the preceding statement detracts from an earlier appeal to give more emphasis to the *why* and less to the *how* in B-A instruction. Such is not the case. The appeal is to take some of the time now used for drilling students excessively on the routine and repetitive work of a bookkeeper or accounting clerk and devote it to emphasizing more of the *why* of bookkeeping-accounting. Eliminating the *how* would be eliminating much of the students' ability to understand and appreciate the *why* of bookkeeping-accounting.

Day-to-Day Formal Lesson Plan Teaching

All good, successful methods of teaching require a daily plan for teaching. Therefore, the title of this one way of teaching— "Day-to-Day Formal Lesson Plan Teaching" or "Daily Developmental Lesson Plan Teaching"—is misleading and unsatisfactory. Yet the usual formality, the rigidity of prescribed teaching steps, and the adherence to a rather inflexible, predetermined daily plan for teaching that will be described lends credence to this title or classification of a teaching method.

One of the first organized plans for teaching that took into consideration ways for stimulating and reinforcing learning was evolved by Johann Friedrich Herbart, a German philosopher of the early part of the last century who today would also be classed as a psychologist. The five formal steps of the Herbartian method marked an early and important milestone in educational psychology and educational planning for instruction. In brief, these five steps included: (1) *preparation* for learning, (2) *presentation* of the new material to be learned, (3) *comparison* of the new learnings with old ones, (4) *generalization*, and, finally, (5) *application* of what was taught. Evolving from these five formal teaching steps came the steps found in some of the more popular formal daily lesson plans that are still in wide use today.

Day-to-day lesson plan teaching has been used so widely and for so long that it can be safely classed as a traditional way of teaching. It is a way that possesses clear-cut organization easily discernible by a beginning teacher. It centers itself principally in subject matter to be taught, and its presentation is clear, orderly, and moving toward a goal. It meets some of the psychological theories or laws of learning. When properly handled, students as well as the teacher can usually see daily progress. It provides for an easily administered course and thus contributes to the confidence of some beginning teachers. It has been a successful way of teaching and is today probably the most common way of teaching bookkeeping-accounting.

This method also has some disadvantages. Some of these can be overcome or minimized by an awareness of them and by providing for them; others cannot. Perhaps the eight criticisms leveled at the daily assignment-recitation procedure are equally applicable to the formal daily lesson plan method of teaching:

> [It] (1) is inconsistent with the new psychology of learning, (2) does not provide adequately for individual differences, (3) is destructive of student and teacher initiative, (4) is inadequate for purposes of achieving democratic values, (5) does not lend itself to cooperative teaching, (6) discourages the unifying of subject fields or learning experiences, (7) perpetuates the ground-to-be-covered conception of education, and (8) lends support to the slavish use of the textbook.[1]

It would be unwise for business educators who like lesson-plan teaching to depreciate or minimize these disadvantages. They exist, and if beginning B-A teachers are to be shown this method of teaching, they should be aware of these disadvantages so they can either minimize them or overcome them. At the same time, business educators would be correct in pointing out that educational theories which are applicable to academic or general teaching may not be fully applicable to special phases of vocational business education such as bookkeeping-accounting. For example, the lesson-plan method is objected to on the basis that it "perpetuates the ground-to-be-covered conception of education." That

---

[1] Harold B. Alberty and Elsie J. Alberty, *Reorganizing the High-School Curriculum*, 3d ed. (New York: The Macmillan Co., 1962), p. 332.

is true, but the vocational student who does not cover the ground necessary for achieving vocational competence has been denied a major objective of the course. Job competency for these students sets a minimum scope of ground to be covered. The fact that it helps perpetuate "courses" and "discourages the unifying of subject fields or learning experiences" is also true.

As the reader considers these disadvantages and measures their importance, he might wonder why so much space is subsequently devoted to a method of teaching about which some modern methodologists are critical. There are several reasons for this:

1. The day-to-day formal lesson-plan method of teaching still appears to be the most widely used method of teaching bookkeeping.
2. It has been a successful method even though advocates of newer methods offer greater promises.
3. Some teachers will be obliged to use it.
4. Some of its techniques can and should be used, regardless of the name of the method.
5. Educational theories applicable to academic or general teaching, which prospective B-A teachers hear about in general methods courses, may not be fully applicable to special phases of vocational business education, such as bookkeeping-accounting.

The Lesson Plan

Lesson Plan Outline

The formal lesson plan contains certain common steps, each step having a clear purpose in the accomplishment of the daily aim. The steps and their purposes are listed below.

COMMON STEPS IN THE OUTLINE OF A FORMAL DAILY LESSON PLAN, WITH EXPLANATORY REASONS FOR EACH DIVISION OR STEP IN THE PLAN *

Step or *Division*	*Purpose*
1. **Title of Lesson** (Topic)	For reference or filing purposes.

---

* Alternate names for steps or divisions are given in parentheses.

2. Aim of Lesson (Objective) (Goal) (Purpose)

To require teacher to state in simple, concise sentences what is to be accomplished this day. Helps keep teacher on track in the planning that follows, and can help him during lesson presentation from straying or letting students wander too far from the day's objective.

3. Preclass Preparation (Materials Needed)

To be sure that necessary materials are on hand before the lesson starts. Student interest and attention can be lost and class time wasted if the teacher must stop during the lesson to hunt for illustrative material, paper, books, or other materials and supplies that he or his students need.

4. Preparation (Motivation) (Connection with previous learning) (Introduction) (Review)

To arouse student interest and get student attention. Such opening remarks, questions, or classroom activity must have a relationship and lead into the presentation that follows.

5. Presentation

To present the new knowledges or skills to be learned. This is the heart of the lesson. All remarks, all questions, all activity should be outlined or planned so that the aim of the lesson is completed. No new subject matter should be included in the *presentation* that does not contribute to the *aim* of the lesson.

6. Application or Drill

Testing

To help reinforce or fix the new learnings that were taught in the presentation. To enable the teacher to find out (test informally) whether the students understand and can apply what was taught. Drill is application, but application is not always drill. Application could accompany presentation.

7. Summary

To organize and clinch the teaching. This could be a brief oral summary by the teacher, or, in order to test understanding and application, the students could do the summarizing.

8. Assignment Usually to give the students opportunity for further application of what was learned or further drill on the skill involved in the new learnings. Students should realize that such is the case, and the teacher should find time to point this out for each assignment. Assignments should not, however, always follow the same pattern. Some assignments should require students to delve into new material before the teacher presents it in class. A teacher who *always* introduces new learnings in class before giving students a chance to study new material on their own is cheating some students of a way of learning at which they may be best, or which will have to be acquired later for college use.

9. Teacher's Remarks For immediate reference as to shortcomings or omissions in today's presentation that should be corrected or covered tomorrow. For future reference when this lesson is again presented. Such remarks should include the strong and the weak points of the plan as used and should be written down immediately after the lesson plan has been used.

Sample Lesson Plans

The lesson plan outline on the previous pages shows the steps or divisions in a common form of daily lesson plan and explains the psychological reasons for some of the major divisions in such a plan. The following two sample lesson plans show the form that such planning can take when used for teaching bookkeeping-accounting.

The major method of teaching in both of these lessons is by showing. Both, therefore, would be called demonstration lessons. Note, however, that the methods of questioning and discussion also play important parts, and that, while present, the telling or lecturing phase is kept to a minimum—as it generally should be on the high school level.

Note also a structural difference between the outline of these two plans. In the first plan the application, the real test to see if the students can do (apply) what they were taught, follows the complete presentation by the teacher. This is the best location for the application in most lessons. The second sample lesson plan, however, illustrates how the application can be included along with the presentation. (Additional samples of detailed formal lesson plans will be found in Chapters 14 and 22.)

SAMPLE DAILY LESSON PLAN No. 1

1. Title:	The trial balance
2. Aim:	To teach students (1) how to prepare a trial balance, and (2) what a trial balance does and does not prove.
3. Materials Needed:	On board a diagram of a two-column journal, two sheets of two-column journal paper for each student, and one stenciled "ledger" in T account form for each student. See page 129. (An overhead projector with similarly appropriate materials could be used instead of a chalkboard.)
4. Preparation:	*"Yesterday we learned how to (1) foot and balance an account and (2) how to prove the accuracy of the cash account."*

"Let us check your memories:
What is meant by footing a column? Pencil footing a column?
What are the steps in balancing an account?"
       Ans. (a) Foot debit column.
           (b) Foot credit column.
           (c) Subtract the smaller footing from the larger and place the difference in the Items column on the side of the account that has the larger total.

(Note: The beginning teacher who is not confident of the correct answers to questions he plans to ask, will write the answers on his plan.)

"How is the accuracy of the cash account proved?"
"Now that we know how to balance an account and

how to prove the accuracy of the cash account, let us see how we can check on the accuracy of all of the accounts in the ledger."

5. Presentation:
(Salient points to be covered)

"The procedure of proving the equality of the debits and the credits in the ledger is called taking a trial balance."

Write the term "trial balance" on the board, or use an overhead projector to project on a screen.

(Note: With the *related vocational objective*, discussed in Chapter 3, in mind, the B-A teacher who can write shorthand could also write the shorthand outline for this new business term—thus relating the study of bookkeeping-accounting to the interests of some of the non-bookkeeping majors in the class.)

Distribute the two-column journal paper and stenciled sheets containing the simulated ledger with accounts footed and balanced.

(Note: If the students have workbooks, these could be used along with a textbook problem instead of a teacher-prepared problem.)

Tell class that as you demonstrate the preparing of a trial balance, all are to work along with you at their seats.

Take class through the following five steps in demonstrating the preparation of a trial balance.

Step 1. Write the heading. (a) Name of business, (b) the word "trial balance," and (c) the date.

Ask how this compares with the three items in the heading of a balance sheet. (Association in teaching helps fix the learning.)

Step 2. Enter on the trial balance each account in the ledger: its name, number, and balance.

After demonstrating the entering of several accounts properly, with the class following along at their seats, (a) call on students to tell you how and where to record certain accounts and their balances, and (b) call on several class members to come to the board (or to the overhead projector) and complete the entering of accounts and balances. (Tell class that the use of the income and expense summary account will be explained at another time.)

Step 3. Rule a single line across both amount columns under the last amount listed.

Step 4. Add each amount column.

Explain that when the two totals of the trial balance are equal, the trial balance is said to be in balance and that the bookkeeper can then assume that all of the debit amounts in the ledger equal all of the credit amounts.

Step 5. Rule a double line under the totals across the amount columns.

Explain that such a double ruling in bookkeeping-accounting work indicates that the work above the double lines is correct and complete.

Tell class that when a trial balance is in balance it proves only that the debits in the ledger equal the credits—that it does not prove the complete accuracy of the bookkeeping records.

Challenge class to tell what two kinds of errors are not disclosed by a trial balance that is in balance.

Ans. 1. When an amount is posted to the correct side but to the wrong account. Give example.

Ans. 2. If a transaction is omitted entirely. <u>Give example.</u>

6. Application: Have class work out one of the end-of-chapter problems contained in the textbook similar to the one done in class.

Teacher circulates around the classroom observing progress of the students and accuracy of their work and helping those in need.

Teacher erases the board or turns off the overhead projector.

7. Summary: *"Let us now see what we remember about our work today."*

Ask questions similar to the following:

(Note: Some of the end-of-chapter questions of the textbook being used should be helpful here.)

1. What is the purpose of a trial balance?
2. What is the first step in preparing a trial balance?
3. What are the three parts of the heading of a trial balance?
4. After writing the heading, what is done next?
5. How do you know in which column of the trial balance to place account balances?
6. When is the trial balance said to be in balance?
7. What one thing and one thing only does a trial balance in balance prove?
8. What does a trial balance in balance not prove?
9. Give an example of one kind of error not disclosed by a trial balance. Another kind?

8. Homework: Assign an end-of-chapter problem that is similar to the work done in today's class.

9. Teacher's Remarks:

For Use With Lesson Plan: THE TRIAL BALANCE

A LEDGER WITH ACCOUNTS FOOTED

CASH	11
371.00	723.93
1087.67 1440.60	
1811.60	

J. M. GREENE, CAPITAL	31
	2900.00

AUTOMOBILE	12
3170.00	

INCOME AND EXPENSE SUMMARY	32

OFFICE FURNITURE	13
745.60	20.00
37.50	18.00
39.00	10.00
774.10 *822.10*	*48.00*

COMMISSIONS INCOME	41
	1377.60

OFFICE MACHINES	14
254.40	15.00
76.00	
175.00	
490.40 *505.40*	

ADVERTISING EXPENSE	51
7.64	
9.77	
17.41	

ADAMS COMPANY	21
25.00	91.00
	66.00

AUTOMOBILE EXPENSE	52
25.00	

ENTERTAINMENT EXPENSE	53
5.00	

DANIELS COMPANY	22
100.00	300.00
	200.00

MISCELLANEOUS EXPENSE	54
4.50	
7.52	
12.02	

STAR GARAGE	23
42.00	1250.00
50.00 *1158.00*	
92.00	

RENT EXPENSE	55
120.00	

Sample Lesson Plan No. 2 which follows could be taught early in the course, several days after the students were introduced to a trial balance, or it could be delayed until after trial balances were encountered the second time through the expanding spiral of bookkeeping-accounting learning.

SAMPLE DAILY LESSON PLAN No. 2

1. Title:	Locating common errors that sometimes appear in a trial balance.
2. Aim:	To bring students to an understanding of a systematic approach for locating errors that sometimes appear in a trial balance.
3. Materials Needed:	On the board diagram of city streets, two-color chalk, eraser, stenciled problems, duplicated homework material. An overhead projector with appropriate materials could be used instead of a chalkboard.
4. Preparation:	Tell story of brother parking his car and not remembering on which street he left it.
	Trace hit-and-miss route taken to find it.
	"What would have been a better way to find his car?"
	Have student trace suggestion on the board.
	"What is the advantage of this suggestion over the hit-and-miss method my brother and I used?"
	"This is what I want to do for you today—save you time and effort on homework."
	Cite typical story of students who claim they spend a half hour doing a problem and another half hour finding an error.
	"How many in class have had a similar experience?"
	Tell class that you are now going to show them how to save time and energy on homework when an error is disclosed in the trial balance.

5. Presentation:
(Salient points
to be covered)

Pass out problem sheets. Tell class to add each column in trial balance #1 once only—insert totals —and turn paper face down.

When all or most class members have finished, call for hands as to number in class who did not find columns in balance.

"If I had not stopped you, what would you have done when you saw that the columns were not in balance?" Ans. Re-add the columns. *"All right— do this."*

Actually this first problem is in balance, yet some students in a large class will not arrive at a balance the first time they add the columns.

Place on the board the heading and Step 1:

STEPS FOR LOCATING SOME COMMON ERRORS DISCLOSED BY TRIAL BALANCE

Step 1. Re-add to check accuracy of addition.

Tell class to add each column in trial balance #2 once only—insert totals—and turn paper face down.

"How many did not get a balance in #2?"
"What is your first step for locating errors?"

Have class re-add to check accuracy of addition.

"What are some of the errors that may have occurred?"

List on the board:

1. Entered amount on wrong side of trial balance.
2. May have copied amount incorrectly.
3. Amount of balance in ledger may have been computed incorrectly.
4. An amount posted to ledger may have been incorrect.
5. May have made error in original journal entry.

Place on the board:

Step 2. <u>Find difference of totals in trial balance and divide by two.</u>

This may help disclose an amount on the trial balance that has been entered in the wrong column.

"Why do we divide by two?"

Tell class to add each column in trial balance #3 once only—insert totals—and turn paper face down.
Have class members repeat rules #1 and #2.
Refer to common trial balance errors already listed on the board.

Place on the board:

Step 3. <u>Find difference of the totals in trial balance and divide by 9.</u>

(a) Explain transposition of numbers.

If time remaining in class period seems sufficient, use trial balance #4 for teaching sliding numbers.

(b) Explain sliding numbers.

"What errors on a trial balance will these steps fail to disclose?"

Stress point that these steps give opportunity for a quick systematic approach for finding many errors. Refer to original story about trying to find auto.

6. Application:　　There was a constant application of learning as this lesson was being presented. After each step for locating an error had been taught, the students were required to apply their learning of that step by performing it each subsequent time a trial balance failed to balance. Further application is called for in the homework assignment.

7. Summary:　　*"Now let us see what we have learned."*

Ask questions similar to the following:

1. What is the first step you would take if a trial balance didn't balance when you added it?

    2. If it still doesn't balance, what is the second step?

    3. If you still haven't found your error, what is the third step?

    4. What would you do next?

    5. What step have we previously learned to follow so as to eliminate a certain type of error before we even start to total the trial balance?

    6. Do these suggestions cover the finding of all errors on a trial balance?

(Note: This summary could be handled in a 2-3 minute written quiz.)

8. Homework: Assign the completion of several trial balances containing errors similar to those covered in this lesson.

9. Teacher's Remarks:

How necessary are detailed, written lesson plans? When student or beginning teachers first learn about lesson plans and start preparing formal daily plans in the manner illustrated, some of their reactions are as follows:

"I didn't think a teacher did all that planning."
"I wouldn't need to include so much detail in my plans—I can remember."
"Should I use the same plans again next year?"

To leave a beginning teacher under the impression that, in schools which subscribe to this method of teaching and for teachers who follow it, such a detailed daily plan is required for each classroom period would be discouraging. It is true that some student teachers require two or more hours to develop and write down the plan of a good developmental lesson. Others require less time. With practice in writing such plans and with experience in teaching, the new teacher will learn how brief he can be and still teach well. As the beginning teacher prepares one, three, five, or a dozen extremely detailed plans and uses them in his teaching, he should find himself falling into these steps, seeing their advantage, and getting the feel of successful teaching under this method. Then, with a good knowledge of subject matter, formal lesson planning will take minutes instead of hours.

There are always some beginning teachers who are confident that they can teach without planning, or do not need to write out a plan in order to teach their best. Anyone entering the teaching profession with such a belief is mistaken. True—sometimes a new teacher will work out a detailed written plan and then not need to refer to it for help. But this is usually the result of the forethought, the organizing, the preparation that came from working out the plan. Then, too, circumstances may sometimes cause a teacher to conduct a class or to present a lesson without previous preparation. Occasionally he may find himself doing an excellent impromptu job. As a general rule, however, his best teaching will result from preplanning.

The beginning teacher as well as the experienced teacher who might question the need for even the briefest of written plans for teaching is asked to face up to the following challenge. Suppose, for example, he is called upon to teach 100, or 200, or more B-A students at one time over closed-circuit television instead of several classes of 30 students over a desk in a classroom. Would he face the TV camera without notes?—without a plan?—with nothing on the hidden prompter board? None but a fool would choose to improvise his teaching in such a situation, so how could any teacher defend the position that his 30 or 60 students in several classes were less important and deserved less of his thought and attention than the 100 or more taking the course through the less personal medium of TV?

The minimum of brevity for any teacher in the planned steps for a lesson plan for any classroom presentation might be compared to the minimum steps in a good sales-promotion letter—the introduction, the body, and the close. The introduction aims at getting the reader's attention and interest. The body covers the objective, the salient points. The close summarizes, appeals for action, rounds off or clinches what has been covered in a manner that does not leave the reader confused, dangling, or uncertain.

Another brief and commonly used outline for a teaching plan is the following four-step plan:

Step 1. Prepare the learner.
Step 2. Present the materal to be learned.
Step 3. Practice and apply the learning.
Step 4. Test on understanding and ability to do what was taught—what was presented.

The most effective teaching plans are those the teacher prepares for himself. All teaching plans, even the formal ones being discussed, should be individual and distinctive—the teacher's own. Ideas and suggestions can be gleaned from another's plans. But it is the mental process, the forethought, and the organization that go into the written plan which make planning most valuable, not the completed product that lies on the desk for an occasional glance.

The Review Lesson

The beginning teacher who is concerned over the time required for planning should realize that all lessons are not introductory lessons, such as those illustrated. There are review lessons, and there are other class periods spent on drill and application of what was taught in an introductory lesson on a previous day. Thus all lessons are not aimed at teaching new knowledge or new skill.

The quick summary near the end of an introductory lesson is helpful for emphasizing and for fixing the salient points of the period's teaching. Similarly, when review lessons are planned at the end of a chapter, the end of a marking period, or near the close of a semester, the students' grasp of the subject matter can be strengthened by such summarizing and reteaching.

Special weaknesses disclosed by classroom observation, by the students' homework, by short quizzes, as well as comments under the "Teacher's Remarks" section of his lesson plans can serve as valuable clues for knowing where to place the emphasis in the review. Furthermore, when students do poorly on an examination it is a good practice to review immediately the weak areas disclosed by the examination and thus not limit review teaching to a time immediately preceding an examination. After all, an examination can also be used as an aid to teaching and learning and need not be relegated to the sole function of sorting out levels of students and grading them.

The Repeated Use of Lesson Plans

Still another factor related to the time devoted to planning is the possibility for repeated use of good plans. It is true, however, that some supervisors and administrators have the rule that their teachers are not to use a lesson plan more than once. Such a rule is an attempt to overcome one of the shortcomings of this method of teaching—that once a teacher has prepared a set of daily lesson plans for a course, he might stagnate or fall into a teaching rut by using such plans over and over again, year after year. Such teachers are like the little boy who, when asked how he happened to fall out of bed the night before, replied, "I guess I slept too close to where I got in." Some teachers go to sleep very close to where they enter the profession.

This rule of not permitting a teacher to reuse a good plan seems as unwise as telling a teacher he cannot use the same textbook in his class for more than one year regardless of how good it is. An excellently planned and taught lesson this year could be just as worthwhile taught from the same plan the next year. Teachers have good and bad days. Why should plans for the good days be discarded? A more sensible approach to eliminating this danger would seem to be to encourage teachers to discard their weak plans and improve others. Thus the suggestion for "Teacher's Remarks" at the close of each plan.

The Element of "Time" in a Lesson Plan

Judging accurately the amount of time that it will take to teach a lesson is difficult. A good procedure for beginning teachers is to plan for presenting more material than they think they can cover. Then they need not be concerned that they will "run out" of material. If there is time left over following the complete presentation of the lesson, start the students on the homework assignment. This is usually further application of the day's learning and is educationally sound. It can also be an encouraging technique for getting homework done.

Beginning teachers are sometimes concerned about how much of the daily lesson time should be spent on motivation—on presentation. The long-legged, statuesque President Lincoln was once asked, "How long should a man's legs be?" He replied, "Long enough to reach the ground." Similarly the best answer to teachers asking about time is, "Long enough to do the job effectively." There should be no set rule such as three minutes for preparation, and thirty minutes for presentation. Lessons vary. Students vary within a class, between classes, between schools. Some motivational introductions can be effective with a sentence or two. Others might require half the period. Some lessons need only a few minutes to make the presentation and maybe a half hour or several periods to complete the drill necessary for acquiring the skill being taught. Generally, however, the presentation is the step requiring the major portion of a class period.

Variations of Formal Lesson Plans

There are numerous variations in the outline of the formal written daily lesson plans as illustrated on pages 125-133. Some teachers find it helpful to state the aim of the lesson in two ways—the teacher's aim, as was done in the illustrations, then the student's aim. This is an additional step aimed at helping to keep the lesson and the teacher activity centered on pupil need, pupil activity, and pupil viewpoint. Since, in this method of teaching, both aims are usually teacher-determined, there seems to be little advantage in it.

Some plans subdivide the "preparation" into teacher preparation and student preparation. Teacher preparation includes all the things the teacher should do before he starts the lesson, such as getting the materials and supplies he needs and preparing chalkboard rulings. Student preparation is synonymous with the terms "preparation" or "motivation" as previously illustrated—getting the student interested and receptive for the new learnings to come. Sometimes when "student preparation," "motivation," or "connection with previous knowledge" is B-A knowledge that the students acquired previously in the course, the term "review" is used. In fact, some teachers believe that all new lessons should start with a review of former learnings in bookkeeping-accounting and always label this step "review." Such an introduction to new learnings has merit. It is supported by the psychological principle: ". . . proceed from the known to the unknown." It could help reinforce previous learnings as well as relate new learnings to those that went before.

Because some B-A knowledge is only related to other B-A knowledge and practice, some new learnings can be introduced only in this manner. However, by going outside of the students' realm of previously learned subject matter and into the realm of their more common experiences for introductory material, the course can be made more interesting and meaningful for many students. Bookkeeping-accounting can be a less formidable subject for many students when they see some of its relationships to things they learned outside of school, rather than have new B-A learnings always related to previous B-A knowledge.

For example, the preparation or motivational section (Item 4) of Sample Daily Lesson No. 1 on page 125, aims at capturing student interest and attention for learning about the trial balance by challenging them to remember what was taught in the previous day's class. The following start for the same lesson goes outside of the classroom for interest-getting material to introduce them to the preparation of and the reasons for a trial balance.

ALTERNATE START FOR SAMPLE DAILY LESSON PLAN No. 1

---

4. Preparation:
(Motivation)
"Yesterday we learned a method of checking the accuracy of our records. What was that method?"

Ans. How to prove the accuracy of the cash account.

"Today we are going to learn an additional way of checking the accuracy of our records. We are going to prepare a trial balance."

Write the term "Trial Balance" on the board, or use the overhead projector.

"What does the word trial mean?"

Ans. Putting something to a test or a proof.

"With what kinds of trials are you familiar?"

Ans. Olympic trials, court trials such as Perry Mason on T.V., purchasing an item on trial, etc.

"Why do we have trials?"

Ans. To test a product or a person and to prevent making mistakes.

Ask the following leading questions to clinch reason for having trials.

"Would you put an athlete on the team before he gave a trial performance?"

"Should a judge sentence someone to jail without first giving him a trial to see if he was guilty?"

"Should a bookkeeper tell his employer how much profit the business made before first checking his records for accuracy?"

"The purpose of a trial balance (pointing to term on board or screen) is to establish proof of the equality of the debits and credits in the ledger."

"Today we are going to see how this is done. First, we will see how a trial balance is prepared. Second, we shall see what this trial balance proves and what it does not prove."

Another common variation in the form of a daily lesson plan is to divide the page of the plan in half, the left side being devoted to the teacher's activities, the right to students' activities. Under "Teacher Activities" the questions the teacher is going to ask and the things he is going to do or ask the students to do are listed. Dovetailing these teacher activities, on the right side of the page he lists the "Student Activities" that he plans or anticipates as a result of each of his own listed activities. Such a plan has the advantage of indicating to some degree what proportion of the period will be taken up by teacher activity or domination, and how much or what kind of a part the students will be playing in the learning. For example, when the left-hand column shows that he is telling the class something, the right-hand column would reflect the activity "listening." When the left-hand column shows the teacher's questions, the right-hand column shows the correct or anticipated student answers. This two-column breakdown of activities does not, however, eliminate the use of the formal steps commonly used and previously illustrated.

Capturing and Sustaining Pupil Interest

The most challenging section of any teaching plan is the intro-duction—the attention getting, the interest getting, the motivational phase of the daily work of teaching. How can the teacher rekindle the interest or enthusiasm that was present in yesterday's or last week's class for a quick start of today's 45-minute session? How can the teacher associate or relate what is eventually to be learned in the day's presentation with what is already known by the students? Learning is easier when we can quickly associate the new learning with something that we already know.

Arousing interest, sustaining it, and getting the students to see and do the things that will best help them to learn calls for creativeness in teaching. Because individual pupils, classes, and teachers differ, creativeness in teaching must take different forms.

A common plea by beginning teachers is, "How do you intro-duce or motivate your class to learn the journal, the work sheet," and so on. Experienced B-A teachers would, of course, supply many different answers to such questions. It is also probably true that the most successful of such techniques are the ones which the teacher himself developed. Perhaps, however, it would be helpful to teachers in training to see illustrated a few of the various interest-getting approaches that a teacher might use in introducing one common bookkeeping topic, such as the journal. The following four brief illustrations do this:

SAMPLE INTRODUCTIONS FOR A FORMAL DAILY LESSON PLAN

Title:	Introducing the journal
Aim:	To help students understand the initial use and form of a journal.
Supplies Needed:	Journal paper for student use, one bound and one loose-leaf journal for illustrative purposes.

ILLUSTRATION 1

Motivation:	Ask questions similar to the following:

1. How many of you have ever kept a diary?
2. What does the word "diary" mean?
3. Why do people keep diaries?

4. What reasons can you give for a business or a businessman keeping a diary?

Teacher to add to and summarize these reasons.

The teacher then moves into the *presentation* by stating that it is the bookkeeper who keeps the diary of a business; that there is a special name and form for keeping the chronological record of business transactions. He then proceeds to illustrate and develop the new learnings to be acquired.

ILLUSTRATION 2

(Provided one teaches in a town or a city where the local newspaper has the word "JOURNAL" in its title.)

Motivation: Ask questions similar to the following:

1. What is the name of our local paper?
2. How often is it published?
3. What does the word "journal" mean?
4. What is recorded in it?
5. What reasons can you give for a business or a businessman keeping a journal, a daily or chronological record of business transactions?

ILLUSTRATION 3

(Provided one teaches in a small seaport town where most, if not all, students are already familiar with the term "ship's log.")

Motivation: Ask questions similar to the following:

1. How many of you know what a ship's log is?
2. Will you please tell us what it is, John?
3. What goes into it?
4. Why is it kept?
5. What reasons can you give for a business or businessman keeping a daily record of business transactions?

The above three illustrations take the student out of the classroom and out of the subject of bookkeeping-accounting to show the relationship between a daily, chronological business record of important business transactions with a daily chronological record of other means. This is not *always* possible, feasible, or preferable.

The following additional illustration shows a start of the same lesson whereby the teacher makes the connection of what is to come with previous in-the-class learning. In this latter instance the students would have learned about the ledger and the accounts before being introduced to the journal.

ILLUSTRATION 4

Motivation: *"Let us start this morning with a game."*

"Everybody please turn to page —, where you will see a series of accounts showing entries of business transactions recorded for the month of January."

"Let us assume that you were the bookkeeper who recorded these transactions. Your employer comes to your desk and says, 'Please make a list, according to your records, of everything that happened to the business on January 12.'"

Give directions similar to the following:

1. Do this now by listing this information on a piece of blank paper.

2. As soon as you can tell me everything that occurred on January 12, raise your hand.

3. Let us see who can finish first.

Teacher watches clock and as soon as a number of students have raised their hands says, *"Mary Smith was first. It took her six minutes. Most of the rest of you took from seven to ten minutes. You did this fairly quickly."*

"If your employer asked you this question frequently, however, how could you arrange to tell him more promptly—say within a few seconds—while he waits for the answer?"

After the class is led to see the advantages of daily and chronological records, the teacher leads them into the presentation of the lesson.

When students are properly motivated, their energies are easily channelled into activities that help them solve the current problem.

There is probably no better way for cutting down on student discipline problems than through careful and successful planning to capture and hold student attention. The task is not an easy one. The teacher must know his students and how best to *create* and *sustain* their interest. Hilgard and Russell, in writing about motivation, make the strong statement: "If there is any conclusion from recent research of which a teacher may be sure, it is that there is no known formula or infallible set of procedures to motivate all pupils at all times." [2]

This should prove comforting to the overly conscientious teachers who reach depths of frustration when they cannot keep all students interested and motivated at all times. Any teacher, however, who permits such knowledge to throw him into a lethargic, do-nothing attitude about motivation, who does not use every brain cell at his command to incorporate plans, ideas, and techniques that will help motivate and sustain the interest of his pupils, is certainly not a teacher in the true sense of the word.

Homework

The right homework, properly assigned and properly handled, is an important part of the teacher's plan for learning. Homework should usually be assigned in a manner that relates it to the learning of the period. B-A students need further practice or drill to clinch what was taught in class. As a result, most B-A homework assignments consist of end-of-chapter drill or application problems that give the students the opportunity to apply their understandings and to fix such learnings.

At the start of this chapter it was said, ". . . all students do not learn best in the same way." For this reason homework assignments should not always be further application of the day's teachings. Occasionally they should call for students to bore in and learn new concepts and new procedures for themselves. The practice of study should be learned before students leave high school. Such study assignments will give some students the opportunity to learn in a way which is best for them—by reading. Therefore, just as it

---

[2] Ernest R. Hilgard and David H. Russsell, "Motivation in School Learning," *Learning and Instruction*, Forty-Ninth Yearbook of the National Society for the Study of Education, Part I (Chicago: University of Chicago Press, 1950), p. 37.

is important to vary one's method of teaching, so it is important to vary the homework assignments.

What should be done with homework assignments after they have been completed? The ideal solution from a learning standpoint is to collect all assignments, correct and mark them, and return them. But this is not practical for teachers who teach five or more classes a day and who may give homework assignments to as many as 100 to 200 pupils daily. One compromise is to start off the course by collecting, marking, and returning all homework. While even a week of this can be burdensome, it impresses most students with the importance the teacher places on homework and will help to get some off to a better start—"as the twig is bent so grows the tree." After this kind of a start, the teacher who continues to overload himself correcting homework can easily become dissipated with work and turn into a dull grind instead of a stimulating teacher. But here, too, thoughtful planning can solve the problem. Plan not to collect homework for certain assignments. Occasionally have the students self-check their own. This can be done quickly by using an overhead projector to show on a screen the correct solution for all to see and compare with their own solution of the homework assignment. Sometimes turn each class member into an "auditor" and have each of them, with teacher guidance, check the homework of a classmate. On other days spot-check the work of a limited number of students; on Monday, rows A, C, and E; on Tuesday, all boys in the class; on Wednesday, all who got less than a "B" grade at midterm; on Thursday, rows B, D, and E; and so on whereby only a "reasonable" amount of the teacher's time is spent correcting homework.

If homework is important, it must be treated with importance. If it is collected, it should be marked and returned. Teachers who collect homework and then throw it into the wastebasket are excellent examples of how to lose friends and alienate students.

Finally, how much homework should be given—how long should the assignment take? Most high school students carry at least four major subjects. If each teacher of a major subject made not more than a half-hour homework assignment, and if there were no study-hall periods available, this would mean a two-hour stint each evening for the student. After six hours or so per day in school, should adolescents be expected to do more?

The Project Method

The project method accomplishes learning by having students complete a plan or course of action related to the subject matter being studied. For example, a group of boys in a shop course may undertake the building of a set of bookcases for the school library, or an individual student may set out to construct a radio or a table for himself. In a home economics course, all or part of a class might prepare and serve food for a school banquet, or one student might make a set of slip covers, curtains, a dress, or the like. The project selected can be a class project, a group project, or an individual project. It may take a short period of time or extend over the length of a course. It may involve one segment of subject matter or include the whole sequence.

This method is not new. Its widest use was first in vocational and skill subjects, particularly agriculture, and was later adopted quite generally in the high school curriculum. This is one traditional method of teaching which, when handled judiciously, was never under serious attack by advocates of newer methods. In fact, although the term "project method" is no longer used very extensively, projects themselves are an essential phase of the modern unit method of teaching.

Bookkeeping teachers have used it with success for years, and should continue to use it. There are various ways in which it is used in the learning of bookkeeping-accounting. Probably the most common way is through the construction or working out of practice sets. (The use of practice sets is discussed on pages 176-179.) If a B-A class, or a group, or a student, under the guidance of the teacher undertakes to keep the books of the school cafeteria; operate a school bank; manage the sale of tickets, the advertising, and the financial records of school football or basketball teams, the school play, the Red Cross drive, and so on; each could be a project and the project method of teaching could come into play.

The use of this method, like all others, depends upon the forethought, planning, and use of good teaching principles practiced by the teacher. A daily plan, not necessarily the formal type discussed previously, is essential. The success of a project and the learning that can accompany it is certainly affected by the manner in which students are introduced to it and the attitude with which they undertake the project. Here the motivational approach can again come into the teaching picture, and goal sharing and pupil-teacher planning techniques can be used. Students who are merely told that they are going to do a practice set, keep school records, and so on, are certainly not going to be as interested and enthusiastic, nor profit as much, as if they had a voice in the decision or an understanding of the advantages of such projects. A student should feel that it is *his* project, not the teacher's.

When a school or service project, such as keeping cafeteria records or running a school bank, is undertaken, the learning results should equal or surpass what could be learned in the classroom. Once students have derived the optimum learning or skill development from handling school records, they should not be exploited and kept doing such work. B-A teachers must be alert to the law of diminishing learning returns in connection with the choice of the kind and the length of the project.

Care should be taken not to confuse *any* kind of in-school work experiences with the project method of teaching. The project connotes the finishing of a job undertaken, accomplishing a task, completing a unit of work. Thus, completing a practice set, keeping the cafeteria books for a fiscal month, handling the entire financial records for a school play—all could be projects undertaken by a student, a group of students, or a class. However, posting a few school records occasionally, having students rotate in acting as cashier in the cafeteria, and the like, could be good in-school work experiences; but such piecemeal, scattered undertakings by students cannot be classed under the project method.

The project method offers an opportunity for learning skills that cannot be learned from textbooks. It can give students an immeasurable feeling of satisfaction, of accomplishment. It is a method which in bookkeeping-accounting would seem best to interpose between other methods of teaching. It is difficult to imagine a good B-A course being organized only along the lines of a series of projects. Its best use in bookkeeping-accounting is for the major purpose of applying previous knowledge and skill, for clarifying and knitting together relationships, for clinching previous learnings.

Simulated Office Plan Teaching

A principle of vocational education involving the teaching of skills is that learning is more effective when it is presented as nearly as possible in the setting in which it will eventually be used. The shop arrangements in some vocational schools teaching auto mechanics, carpentry, dental mechanics, beauty culture, and the like, resemble so closely on-the-job working conditions of these various occupations that they meet or come very close to meeting this educational principle. Because bookkeeping-accounting has for years been presented in the traditional type classroom, and because it has been done in this kind of a setting with a fair degree of success, it would be difficult for many B-A teachers to arrange to get the modern equipment necessary to turn their rooms into simulated offices. The "setting" referred to in this principle, however, encompasses more than layout and equipment. It is also concerned with the vocational procedures and practices, the vocational atmosphere. Teachers who have been able to secure very little, if any, office equipment for their rooms may still be able to provide the setting "as nearly as possible" through a method called "The Simulated Office Plan."

This plan operates along the following lines. A type of office, common to the local community, which the subsequent work in the classroom is to represent and simulate, is decided upon. The firm that this "office" represents is given a name. All necessary blank and completed business forms, such as requisitions, purchase orders, office memoranda, checks, invoices, and bills of lading, are prepared in advance. Office positions and work stations, such as office manager, head accountant, chief bookkeeper, cashier, requisition clerk, purchase order clerk, posting clerks, and accounts payable clerks, are established. Before the plan is put into operation and the flow of work begins in the "office," the students are shown by diagram the various work stations and how each fits into the picture.

From the first day's work, each student takes his assigned position, the flow of work proceeds, and each student carries out his assignment using the same materials that he would use in a real office. Since this is a learning situation and students are not thoroughly, if at all, prepared in advance for handling the duties of each station, they must be given instructions to help them. It would be impossible for the teacher to do this orally without a considerable waste of time. Therefore, this is usually done in the form of a master office manual or instruction book supplied to each student so that he has a ready reference to find out what his duties are on particular days that he is assigned to particular positions. This crucial phase could also be handled by supplying the students with daily instruction or job sheets.

After they have had sufficient time in one position to understand and perform duties of that position, students rotate to a new position. Thus, after a month, two months, or a semester of this practice, each student will have had the opportunity of serving in and performing all the common duties in a bookkeeping office.

This type of plan for teaching bookkeeping-accounting lends itself to improvising. In a large class, two students could be assigned to each work station. When students rotate into new positions, they can be introduced to their new position by the student who has just previously learned it and is ready to move on to another position. A floating or flying squad of two or three students can be set up to fill in for absentees. The teacher can discontinue the plan for a day or two when he needs to teach new material or review and reinforce old learnings.

This method, since it is concerned almost entirely with the vocational objectives of bookkeeping instruction, would seem most feasible for use at some time in the second-year course, perhaps near the close of the second year, immediately before the student goes to work in a real office.

In spite of its obvious merits, this plan is not a popular one for teaching bookkeeping. Some major reasons for this lack of popularity are contained in the following facts:

1. No tailor-made teaching materials—business forms, job or instruction sheets, teacher's manuals or guides—are available for immediate use applying to such a plan.
2. The time required of the teacher for preplanning—getting forms prepared, working out a balanced set of business transactions that will be a reasonable load for each student each day in each of the various positions—is, *initially*, a monumental task.
3. Some teachers are not sufficiently familiar with modern office and bookkeeping practices to be able to formulate such a plan.

Two important suggestions seem pertinent for teachers considering the use of this method. First, the entire plan should be worked out to the last detail, from the first to the last day that the plan will be in operation. Second, regardless of how perfectly the teacher has planned the activities and progress of the students during the first try-out of the simulated office plan, he should not be discouraged nor condemn it merely because some snags or faults show up in the plan during its initial use. It is difficult to imagine any teacher being able to evolve a completely perfect plan at first trial. Sincere teachers who use this method successfully admit that it requires revising to bring it close to perfection. As one teacher remarked, "I've used it for over twelve years and I'm still improving." The need for important revisions or improvements are sometimes discernible only after the plan has been tried—a fact true of all new teaching plans.

Laboratory Teaching

A laboratory is a room fitted for conducting scientific experiments, analyses, or similar work. Thus the kind of teaching that is carried on in a laboratory—directing experiments or analytical work—would to some extent describe the laboratory method of teaching. In high school this method is most commonly found in chemistry and the physics courses. It is sometimes a part of college instruction in accounting. In such instances, the room is usually fitted with office machines, and students are assigned to analyze accounting and auditing problems. For example, one set of supplies in such a laboratory could consist of an actual or facsimile set of books of a firm that went bankrupt. The accounting student could be assigned to analyze these books for such purposes as determining why bankruptcy occurred, or how bankruptcy might have been avoided, or, for purposes of learning, how to prepare a legal auditing report for presentation in court. Such a procedure in college accounting courses is rightly entitled to the term "laboratory method."

In the teaching of high school bookkeeping-accounting, actual laboratory work in which experimentation or analysis is carried on is rare. Perhaps the choice of the term in high school bookkeeping-accounting is chiefly to glamorize or give status to a class period.

Some of the few remaining high schools that offer a double period in B-A instruction refer to the second of these periods as the "laboratory period"—the first being devoted to instruction in new knowledges of bookkeeping-accounting. The usual pupil activity in this second so-called laboratory period is to apply what was learned during the first period or to secure practice in skill development. Frequently this period develops into a homework-doing time for schools or teachers who do not subscribe to homework for students.

The term "laboratory period" is also sometimes given to that period in schools during which weak or failing students are required or encouraged to return to their B-A instructor for additional daily or weekly periods of tutorial guidance. Thus in high school bookkeeping-accounting, the term would seem to apply more to the name of the period than a method of teaching. So-called B-A laboratory instruction has a long way to go in most high schools before it earns the right to be called the laboratory method of teaching.

Coordinated Work-Experience Teaching

Work experience, *in itself,* is a means of learning, not teaching. When work experience is coordinated with instruction, it then becomes a teaching as well as a learning situation. Then the teacher is responsible for using ways of teaching that will help the student-worker acquire increased benefits from both the work experience and the formal instruction. Each should compliment the other so that each contributes to increased learning from the other. When this results, coordinated work-experience teaching is taking place.

After a student has studied, tried, and learned some of the basic principles and techniques of bookkeeping-accounting, one of the most satisfying, encouraging, and stimulating experiences he can have is to apply his knowledge and ability successfully to a lifelike, office-like, on-the-job experience. The conscientious teacher realizes this and tries to give his students B-A experiences that are as close as possible to on-the-job experiences. The use of practice sets or other projects and the use of the simulated office plan are examples of how teachers bring lifelike office procedures into the classroom.

These might be called in-class work experiences. They are excellent ways of teaching bookkeeping-accounting.

The ultimate step in this direction, however, is for the student to perform duties in a real situation where he is not just practicing but performing usable productive B-A work, where he is engaged in a real job and having a true vocational experience. There are two places where he might get such experiences. One is in school, but out of class, performing vocational work in the school office, cafeteria, school store, and the like. The other is working in a part-time B-A job in a local business office while still studying bookkeeping-accounting in school.

When students in a B-A class have such opportunities, the class-room teaching and learning opportunities are broadened in scope and made easier and more effective. To take advantage of these opportunities the teacher must coordinate the classroom instruction with the on-the-job experiences of his pupils. This requires no new teaching method. It does require the teacher to know:

1. the kind of duties his students are performing;
2. the strength and weaknesses of his students in the performance of these duties;
3. employers' impressions of his students—what they are looking for in part-time work experience students, and in B-A graduates;
4. areas of B-A instruction that were omitted, weak, or ineffective.

Knowing these things, he should then be able to plan his teaching to (1) include necessary knowledge and skills previously omitted; (2) strengthen the weaknesses and overcome shortcomings of present work experience students; (3) use student experiences to stimulate, to encourage, to teach nonwork experience students or other work experience students; (4) relate instruction to experiences of the students so that it is more meaningful and more easily understood by them. Planning of this kind results in coordinating his teaching with the interests, the needs, and the problems of his working as well as his nonworking students. This kind of teacher planning, if done thoroughly and properly, can be more helpful, or more effective, or more conducive to learning than most other planning. Office occupation programs, in which either coordination or the project method must be present, are discussed on page 326.

Unit Teaching

All teachers teach units of knowledge, but all do not thereby use the unit method of teaching. Teaching units of knowledge or units of skill is not necessarily synonymous with the unit method of teaching. The term "unit teaching" is frequently misused and misinterpreted. Many teachers claim they use the unit method when in reality they only break the subject matter down into convenient units and proceed to use the formal daily lesson plan method or some other formal plan.

A recent summary of this method as it exists in its best form today is described as follows:

> . . . a learning unit involves (1) a broad comprehensive problem or project which is a common concern of the group, (2) a series of related activities so selected and organized as to provide common learnings for the entire group and individual learning in terms of the specific needs, abilities, and interests of students, and (3) a program of continuous cooperative evaluation of outcomes.
>
> Usually unit teaching involves three stages as follows: (1) the *planning stage* in which problems are clarified, alternate plans of work considered, and decisions reached as to how the group shall proceed; (2) an extended *working stage* in which there is much group discussion, library research, investigations, experimentation, individual and committee work, and the like; and (3) a *culminating stage*, in which results are brought together, conclusions are reached, and results evaluated.[3]

It should be obvious that unit teaching is not only concerned with units of subject matter, but is equally concerned with *a process* of teaching which takes into account modern psychological principles of learning dealing with individual differences, goal-sharing, pupil-teacher planning, and pupil self-evaluation. While these characteristics cannot be claimed as the sole property of the unit method, this method requires the inclusion of these characteristics in its plan and operation before true unit teaching can be achieved or claimed.

The Morrison Plan [4] for teaching gave rise to unit teaching. Morrison, like Herbart (page 120), had five teaching or learning

---

[3] Harold B. Alberty and Elsie J. Alberty, op. cit., pp. 332-33.
[4] Henry C. Morrison, *The Practice of Teaching in the Secondary School*, rev. ed. (Chicago: University of Chicago Press, 1931).

steps in his plan. The names of Morrison's five steps—(1) exploration, (2) presentation, (3) assimilation, (4) organization, and (5) recitation—were similar in terminology to those of Herbart's. The reader, however, should not infer from this that their plans were similar. Some major distinctions between the Morrison Plan and the Herbartian method include the following:

1. Herbart's steps were for a single recitation or classroom period, while the Morrison Plan was intended for use over several or numerous periods.
2. The Herbartian steps were to fit all kinds of learning, while Morrison claimed that attitudes of understanding, attitudes of appreciation, special abilities, and skills were different products of learning and thus required different teaching techniques.
3. The Herbartian method presented learning in fragments, while the Morrison Plan recognized that learning was most effective in terms of wholes.

The Morrison Plan, with its psychological improvements over the Herbartian method, holds important implications for all teachers. Morrison, like Herbart, however, seems open to criticism on the basis of prescribing five fixed, invariable steps in the teaching process. It would appear, therefore, that the B-A teacher contemplating unit teaching would find it more profitable to move directly into the more modern practices of such teaching and prepare his plans in accordance with the three major general stages that have evolved from Morrison's earlier prescribed unit plan—the planning stage, the working stage, the culminating phase.

Such a broad area as financial statements can be developed in bookkeeping-accounting under the unit method by:

(1) The students becoming aware of the need for such statements in the recording of business events.

(2) The students planning *with* the teacher how to discover what such statements are, the principles upon which they are built, and how they are prepared in business offices by bookkeepers. This might be done by readings, by visiting business offices in the community, by having experienced bookkeepers talk to the class, by showing filmstrips or films, by planning an exhibit of the financial statements of various business houses in the community.

(3) After the decisions are made as to the best procedures to follow, the working stage is entered and the individuals or groups

of individuals proceed to carry out the plans. After the plans have been fulfilled—the visits made, the speaker heard, the references consulted, and so on—the results are consolidated, conclusions are formed, and decisions made again by the class as to the effectiveness of their actions in informing themselves concerning financial statements. It is worthwhile to repeat here that much of the value in developing such a unit in bookkeeping-accounting lies in the learnings attained through the methods by which the students acquire that learning—the planning, the group work, the visits, the visual materials, the pupil evaluation, and so on.

Modern unit teaching, as briefly described here, gives promise of developing into one of the most common teaching methods of the future. It seems, however, that it can be better applied by teachers of social business subjects and of social studies than by teachers of bookkeeping-accounting, shorthand, or typewriting. How successfully it can or will be adopted by B-A teachers remains to be seen. Experimentation is needed to support the claim for its effectiveness in teaching the skills and the knowledges required by the vocational bookkeeper within the time and the space limitations at present in force within the average high school.

Pupil-Teacher Planning

Cooperative planning of learning activities by the teacher and the students has been practiced in the best classrooms under the guidance of the topflight teachers for many years. The educational value of such planning has been recognized and strongly advocated by psychologists and curriculum experts. It is a frontier topic in education and a controversial issue in secondary school curriculum reorganization.

The very life of a democracy is dependent upon the ability of its citizens to plan and work together toward commonly established goals. This fact alone is a strong reason for considering with real seriousness the place of pupil-teacher planning in any subject-matter field. Too frequently curricular trends developing in general areas are disregarded in the specialized subject-matter courses. This slows down education's forward movement and is confusing to students who are forced to adjust their actions many times a day from autocratic to democratic classroom administration and to the many degrees of each that exist.

Students are more interested in doing things in which they have had some voice in the planning, and the planning itself is a real learning experience. A class that has helped plan a visit to a business office by choosing the office, phoning or writing for an appointment, arranging for the transportation, planning just what is to be observed, writing a letter of appreciation after the visit, and so on, has a far richer experience than the class that is merely informed that it is to take a trip and to meet under the clock at 2:00 p.m.

Pupil-teacher planning does not imply a blank-check procedure whereby the pupil fills in such a check for any activity in a harum-scarum manner. The teacher also plans, and his voice still carries the wisdom of knowledge and experience. B-A teachers know the psychological methods of skill building. They know how to take students from one difficult area up to the next step at a minimum waste of time and application. Therefore, if students who are studying a subject such as bookkeeping are given the opportunity to do some of their own planning, they, it would seem, will soon arrive at the conclusion that the teacher might carry them along faster and better than they can carry themselves through doing what they think they want to do.

Someone at this point might say, "But here you are giving sanction to autocratic teaching." This is not quite true. If the student has progressed to the point, through deliberative action, where he sees the value of teacher help, teacher guidance—in short, the teacher telling and teaching certain techniques, skills, and knowledges—he is *not* back at the old autocratic atmosphere where he works *for* the teacher. He is now working *with* the teacher to learn certain things—things that can best be taught by the teacher.

This same trend in cooperation is to be found in business and industry when the employees and employers meet to discuss improvement of working organization, procedures, methods, surroundings, and other conditions.

Pupil-teacher planning takes no time away from the hours a teacher must spend on planning. It may even increase the time necessary, since guiding a group toward cooperative decision is a more difficult task than autocratically directing action. The reward for the time spent in such planning, however, is the development of a pupil-teacher relationship that stimulates pupil thinking, pupil suggestion, respectful pupil criticism, and thus develops a thinking, socially cooperative bookkeeper as well as a well-trained technician.

Pupil-Teacher Planning Activities

What are some of the pupil-teacher planning activities that will fit into a B-A course?

1. **Choosing the course.** The most important planning in which a pupil should participate is that of freely and wisely choosing to study bookkeeping-accounting. Before enrollment in the business education curriculum, students interested in choosing a business career should be given the opportunity to study with unbiased help and guidance *about* the subject so that they determine for themselves whether technical training in bookkeeping-accounting is a need of theirs which should be met. Students learn best that which they want to learn—that which they feel they need to learn. Such a study might occur in the general business course, or in special vocational study groups or classes, or it might be organized as a volunteer after-school activity or assembly program series.

2. **Planning the distribution of various responsibilities of classroom management.** This is discussed later.

3. **Planning practice and use of materials.** Not all students require the same amount or kind of practice to learn the various bookkeeping knowledges and skills. Students are challenged to learn more if they can adjust their practice in and out of class to suit their own ability. Such planning would include an analysis of their own weaknesses and decision as to what practice and how much is needed to accomplish the goal in mind. This kind of cooperative planning with the teacher for individual practice might well be extended to planning with the class for the use of practice sets, workbooks, tests, and other materials.

4. **Discussing and planning the solution of real school bookkeeping problems.** There are many real problems in bookkeeping right in the school community, and the solution of these problems offers realistic experiences not to be found in doing any specific textbook problem. Wherever possible, then, the teacher should offer to the class the opportunity to plan records to be kept for the cafeteria, athletic events, class dances and plays, and so on. Keeping such records naturally follows and contributes to the welfare of the school as well as to the student.

5. **Having former pupils now on the job suggest course modifications to better help meet needs.** Former students are in a good position to tell teachers what can be done within the B-A classroom to make the course more effective for on-the-job needs. Former students returning to the classroom as successful bookkeepers or accounting clerks are also an excellent motivating experience for present students. Inviting former students and present students to sit down with the teacher in a round-table meeting to discuss the course and its improvement is another satisfying pupil-teacher planning occasion and one effective technique that is often neglected.

These suggestions are indicative of the potentialities of the use of pupil-teacher planning in the improvement of B-A instruction. The wealth of experiences available through such cooperative planning is great. Such wealth is available to the teacher as well as to the students, since through cooperative planning the teacher comes to know his students as he can never know them in autocratic domination. The wealth available to the student lies in the variety of experiences obtainable, the opportunities to reason and to decide and act upon decisions; the chance to work with people not only in the immediate classroom but in the school and in the community; and, above all, the chance to see the result of his action upon himself and others. These are cogent reasons for the inclusion of pupil-teacher planning in the B-A classroom.

Long-Range Planning

Up to this point, emphasis has been given to the need for daily planning in the methods described. In addition to this short-range planning, long-range planning is essential. It is common practice for a department head or a principal to ask a teacher for a *course outline* of the subject he is teaching. The course outline, frequently called a *syllabus*, or a *course of study*, is the long-range plan of the teacher for his subject and should be prepared whether requested or not. It is not only essential for the teacher to plan his course and to know what route he intends to take for the entire year; the course outline can be of vital help when made available to the substitute teacher who is called upon to fill in for a regular teacher with a prolonged absence.

A complete course of study usually includes:

1. A foreword—an introductory statement expressing the value and necessity for offering the course, its relationship to other courses, and how it fits into the overall program of the school.
2. The objectives to be achieved.
3. An outline of the subject matter to be covered.
4. A list of the teaching materials to be used.
5. A suggested list of major student activities and projects.
6. An up-to-date bibliography of helpful references for the teacher.

Before the teacher can plan well the *"outline of the subject matter to be covered"* in the course of study, he must take into account, along with the course objectives, the following basic factors:

1. The needs of the pupils—What related courses and past experiences have they had in the curriculum? Why are they taking the course? How are they selected for the bookkeeping course? What is the caliber of the bookkeeping students?
2. The needs of the community—What are the number, and what are the kind of bookkeeping and accounting job opportunities in the employing community?
3. The time available for teaching the course—How long are the class periods? How many class periods per week? per month? per year?
4. The extent of bookkeeping and accounting offered in the curriculum—Does the school limit its offerings to a one-year course, or are two years offered?
5. The size of the classes—What is the average number of students in a first-year B-A class? in a second-year B-A class?
6. The teaching materials and community resources available—Does the school make available such equipment as overhead projectors, calculating and bookkeeping machines, bookkeeping charts, a photo-copy machine, unit record equipment, flip charts, bulletin boards, tape recorders, and so on? Does the school supply such items as textbooks, working papers and study guides, film strips, practice sets, supplies for making transparencies and other forms of visual aids?

The answers to these questions give the teacher specific guidance in deciding what should be taught, why it should be taught, and how it can best be taught under the existing circumstances.

Knowing that only one year of bookkeeping-accounting is to be offered to a small group in a rural area with few audio-visual materials available will require a different approach to the development of a course outline than if one knows that two years of study are available in a school with large classes, a wealth of audio-visual materials, and an immediate employment market for bookkeeping-trained high school people.

Course outlines have been prepared by a number of state departments. In some instances, the state requires that they be followed rather closely. Other states offer them as a statement of minimum essentials. Some large cities follow the same practice, and many individual schools have their own course outlines on file.

When the teacher prepares a course outline, these sources should be consulted to be sure that school, city, and state requirements are being met. The textbook to be used in the classroom is a source of help, also, but it should be noted that textbooks may fail to include all the subject matter that should be offered to students in the local community. In this day and age of rapid change, it is necessary for all teachers to constantly update the textual materials they are using. For example, changes in tax laws occur frequently and differ from state to state, and automated data processing procedures may modify business record procedures to some degree.

After consulting these suggested sources, the content of the individual's course outline depends upon the teacher, his breadth of knowledge, his ingenuity, and the depth of his desire to meet the needs of his students and his community.

STUDY QUESTIONS

1. Why is planning essential for one's best teaching?

2. What is the basic method of learning? Is there any method of teaching that does not take into account this basic method of learning? Support your answer with illustrations.

3. How can the statement "No one, single, exclusive method of teaching is best for all students" be justified?

4. What names have been given to some common, traditional methods of teaching?

5. Why has it been said that a loose use of the term *method* has developed in education?

6. Why is it of paramount importance for the B-A teacher to understand that the teaching of bookkeeping-accounting is concerned with both knowledge learnings and skill learnings?

7. Who was Johann Friedrich Herbart, and what was his contribution to planning for teaching?

8. What are the advantages of the daily developmental lesson plan method of teaching? What are the disadvantages leveled against this way of teaching?

9. Why is it of paramount importance for teachers to understand the disadvantages or weaknesses of a method of teaching?

10. What are the common steps and their purposes in the formal daily lesson plan?

11. How necessary are detailed, written lesson plans for beginning teachers?

12. What are the three minimum steps to look for in any form of daily lesson presentation?

13. How can a teacher know what is best to emphasize in a review lesson?

14. Why is it claimed that the daily attention- or interest-getting phase of teaching is the most challenging?

15. Why should a B-A teacher who assigns homework regularly not be expected to collect and mark all such assignments?

16. What is meant by the project method of teaching? Illustrate with an example from a B-A class.

17. Describe the simulated office plan method of teaching bookkeeping-accounting. What special cautions should the teacher keep in mind when introducing this method?

18. Why has the laboratory method of teaching bookkeeping-accounting on the high school level been criticized?

19. What is the difference between ordinary work experience and coordinated work experience?

20. Differentiate between in-school work experience and out-of-school work experience.

21. What are the three major stages involved in the unit method of teaching?

22. Besides a large block or topic of subject matter, what is involved in the broader educational concept of the unit method of teaching?

23. What are some of the educational advantages of cooperative planning of learning activities by teacher and pupils?

24. Why should it be clear to both a student and teacher that pupil-teacher planning is not a blank-check procedure whereby the pupil does all the deciding of what is to be done in and out of the classroom?

25. What are some learning activities in a B-A class that lend themselves readily to pupil-teacher planning?

26. What are the six major divisions suggested for a course outline or syllabus?

DISCUSSION QUESTIONS

1. If you were a *methods* teacher of bookkeeping-accounting and one of your most able students told you that he thought it a waste of time to prepare written lesson plans, how would you react to this situation?

2. For each of the common methods of teaching, give a specific example of B-A subject matter which would appropriately be taught by using that method.

3. If all learning can be classified under two major classifications, i.e., knowledges and skills, should not methods courses be limited to preparing teachers (1) to teach knowledge, and (2) to teach skills—thus eliminating special methods courses that deal with how to teach typewriting, how to teach bookkeeping-accounting, and so on?

4. Choose five topics that would be taught in a B-A class and briefly outline for each a motivation which could be used.

5. What would you include in an itemized list of all the factors that must be considered in (1) keeping books for the school cafeteria; (2) selling tickets for the football games; (3) operating a school bank.

6. "The unit method of teaching has no limitations for teaching any skill or any academic subject." What supporting evidence or reasons can you give to back up whichever stand you take, for or against, this statement?

7. How essential and useful are teacher-prepared syllabi for high school B-A courses? What should be included in them?

8. Discuss the advantages and the disadvantages to the students and to the teacher of the use of (1) the project method and (2) the simulated office plan method.

9. What is the best and the most practical way for a B-A teacher to handle the students' completed homework assignments?

10. The principles of bookkeeping and accounting are said to be essentially the same from Maine to California. Why, therefore, should there be differences in the course outlines used by high schools across the country in first-year B-A courses?

PROJECTS

1. Prepare six different introductory daily lesson plans for use in introducing students to major topical areas in bookkeeping-accounting.

2. Prepare a series of five lesson plans for use in teaching one week of bookkeeping-accounting.

3. Prepare teaching plans for the topics or areas of bookkeeping-accounting that you have found most difficult to teach.

4. Outline in lesson plan form several different motivational introductions to a topic of your choice.

5. Choose three topics in bookkeeping-accounting and outline motivational introductions to them.

6. Come to class prepared to demonstrate how you would apply or teach one of the teaching plans developed in Projects #1, 2, 3, 4, or 5, above. Your methods instructor will give specific directions for this assignment.

7. Prepare a teaching plan for a unit of instruction reflecting the characteristics of the *unit process* of teaching.

8. Prepare a paper offering suggestions and showing the extent to which pupil-teacher planning can be practiced in the teaching of bookkeeping-accounting.

9. Prepare a course syllabus for a first- or second-year B-A course containing all six of the divisions of a course outline suggested in this chapter.

10. Prepare a course syllabus showing the objectives, B-A content, and bibliographical references for use when teaching slow learners.

11. Prepare a course syllabus showing the objectives, B-A content, and bibliographical references for use when teaching fast learners.

12. Observe a B-A class and note the various methods of teaching used during one class meeting.

13. Observe a lesson being taught and see how many of the five steps usually included in a formal lesson plan you can identify.

14. Choose three topics in bookkeeping-accounting and prepare a motivational introduction for each to show how the subject matter can be directly related to students and their interests.

15. Prepare a paper dealing with the basic factors that should be taken into account when planning the subject matter content for a course outline of a first-year B-A course.

SELECTED REFERENCES

Abarbanell, Frank. "Teach Bookkeeping by Asking Questions," *The Balance Sheet.* XLVII (March, 1966), 297-298, 335.

Alberty, Harold B., and Elsie J. Alberty. *Reorganizing the High School Curriculum,* 3d ed. New York: The Macmillan Company, 1962.

Archer, Fred C. "Resources for Motivation," *Business Teacher.* XLI (November-December, 1963), 11.

Brady, Mary M., and Ethel Hale Blackledge. "Ten Ways to Motivate Bookkeeping Students," *Business Education World.* XLII (February, 1962), 23-24.

Gibson, Harry L. "Listening, a Competency Needed by All Business Students," *The Journal of Business Education.* XLIV (October, 1968), 27-29.

Guthrie, E. R. "Conditioning: A Theory of Learning in Terms of Stimulus, Response, and Association," *The Psychology of Learning,* Chapter 1, p. 55. Forty-First Yearbook of the National Society for the Study of Education, Part II. Chicago: University of Chicago Press, 1942.

Harris, E. Edward. *Requirements for Office and Distributive Education Teacher-Coordinators,* Monograph 115. Cincinnati: South-Western Publishing Co., 1967.

Hilgard, Ernest R., and David H. Russell. "Motivation in School Learning," *Learning and Instruction,* Chapter 2, p. 37. Forty-Ninth Yearbook of the National Society for the Study of Education, Part I. Chicago: University of Chiago Press, 1950.

Krause, Ruthetta. "Paper Grading and Checking: What About Student Attitudes and Responsibilities?" *Business Education World.* XLVII (October, 1966), 36, 43-45.

Morrison, Henry C. *The Practice of Teaching in the Secondary School,* Revised Edition. Chicago: University of Chicago Press, 1931.

Myers, Alden. "Project Bookkeeping—An Effective Means to Understanding," *The Balance Sheet*. XLVII (April, 1967), 347-349, 381.

Pancrazio, Sally, and James J. Pancrazio. "Class Recitation Needs Resuscitation," *The Balance Sheet*. XLIX (March, 1968), 297-298, 336.

Redinbaugh, Donna H. "The Beginning Teacher: In the Beginning . . .," *Business Education Forum*. XXII (March, 1968), 24-26.

Satlow, I. David. "Getting Students to Reason in Bookkeeping," *Business Education Forum*. XXI (October, 1966), 20-23.

—————. "How Do You Go About Preparing a Daily Bookkeeping Lesson?" *Business Education Forum*. XIX (March, 1965), 21, 28.

Stewart, Jeffery R. Jr. "Improving Instruction in Bookkeeping Through the Systems Approach." *Business Education Forum*. XXI (December, 1966), 14-16.

Wilson, Elinor S. "Teaching Bookkeeping by the 'Ear' Method," *The Balance Sheet*. XLVII (September, 1965), 17-18.

Chapter 7

MATERIALS AND DEVICES USED IN THE TEACHING OF BOOKKEEPING-ACCOUNTING

The good B-A teacher uses the educational tools and devices that are necessary to perform his teaching most effectively. A wise use of a variety of devices can clarify, expand, and speed his students' learning. The following observation is worth consideration.

> . . . in 1912 both industry and education devoted 75% of their expenditures for the construction of buildings and 25% of the expenditures were for tools used in those buildings. Fifty years later we find that industry is now devoting 25% of its expenditures for buildings and 75% for tools, while education in this country still devotes 75% of its funds to the construction of buildings and 25% for tools. In other words, we are living in a technological society but we are teaching as if we were still in the Industrial Revolution. Until this ratio is reversed for education we cannot expect to do the job that we dream about, because we will not have the tools to do the job.[1]

The Bookkeeping-Accounting Textbook

The B-A textbook is the teacher's fundamental teaching tool for helping students acquire their B-A knowledge and skill. A basic textbook, a sort of home base in the hands of the students, gives them a certain sense of security, lends an element of organization to their learning, and gives them an easily available source of reference so necessary in mastering the details of B-A procedure. Therefore, a well-chosen textbook can enhance both the teaching and the learning of bookkeeping-accounting.

---

[1] John D. Bardwell, "The Newer Media in the Teaching of Business Subjects," *Proceedings of the Thirty-seventh International Course in Business and Economic Education* (New York University, 1965), p. 21.

The Importance of Textbook Selection

Varying degrees of freedom are permitted the B-A teacher in his choice of a textbook. Some states and schools offer an approved list of textbooks from which the teacher may choose the one he wishes to use. Some teachers inherit a textbook already in use in the school. Many teachers, however, face the sole responsibility for the choice of the book that in most instances is the basis for the bookkeeping practices and procedures their students will carry into the business offices of their community. A carelessly chosen textbook can be a great handicap, perhaps for a long time, since textbooks frequently are used for many years and, in some instances, changing one after it is adopted is a difficult task.

How to choose a textbook. Books have been written on the choice and evaluation of textbooks; comprehensive and complicated rating forms have been established; and methods of choosing textbooks have been thoroughly explored. The average high school teacher, unfortunately, does not always have the time or is not given the incentive to read the books or master the techniques of the use of the rating forms. The large majority of the teachers who have a free choice of textbooks tend to use a more informal method.

There are simple, practical procedures that teachers can follow which will improve their choice of a textbook so that it is a help, not a hindrance, in their teaching. A list of minimum essentials that the textbook should supply to the teacher is the first consideration.

1. The text should have at least some of the same *objectives* that the teacher has for his course. The objectives of a textbook are usually briefly stated in the preface. Therefore, reading the preface, together with a list of the course objectives, and checking off the objectives that the book and the course of study have in common is one simple step a teacher can take. Another step is reading the teacher's manual with thoughtful consideration. The manual commonly offers a detailed presentation of the philosophy and methodology of the text and should be a familiar source of reference for all teachers.

2. The text should contain most of the *subject matter* that has been determined as desirable for the students, and should possess

CRITERIA FOR EVALUATING
BUSINESS EDUCATION TEXTBOOKS

A check in the first column of these criteria should be considered a positive response and a check in the second column a negative response. It is conceivable that a teacher might want to give some items more weight than others. For instance, the positive responses in items 1 to 4 might be given 5 points each, the responses in items 5 to 8 be given 3 points, and the responses in items 9 to 14 be given 1 point. Then, too, it is possible that a teacher may wish to add comments after some items indicating the reason for a response.

1. ORGANIZATION OF CONTENT MATTER (GENERAL)

a. Covers necessary areas	☐ Yes	☐ No
b. Covers these areas satisfactorily	☐ Yes	☐ No
c. Covers additional areas	☐ Yes	☐ No
d. Additional areas will be	☐ Helpful	☐ Distracting

2. ORGANIZATION OF CONTENT MATTER (SPECIFIC)

a. Content	☐ Stated clearly	☐ Not clear
b. Sequence of material	☐ Satisfactory	☐ Unsatisfactory
c. Terms and vocabulary	☐ Satisfactory	☐ Unsatisfactory
d. Up to date	☐ Yes	☐ No

3. END OF CHAPTER AND/OR UNIT ACTIVITIES

a. Meaningful	☐ Yes	☐ No
b. Varied	☐ Yes	☐ No
c. Thought provoking questions	☐ Included	☐ Not included
d. Organization	☐ Satisfactory	☐ Unsatisfactory

4. ILLUSTRATIONS

a. Size	☐ Satisfactory	☐ Unsatisfactory
b. Relation to subject matter	☐ Satisfactory	☐ Unsatisfactory
c. Captions	☐ Satisfactory	☐ Unsatisfactory
d. Number	☐ Enough	☐ Too many or too few
e. Recent	☐ Yes	☐ No

5. PHYSICAL MAKE UP

a. Binding	☐ Durable	☐ Not durable
b. Cover	☐ Attractive	☐ Unattractive
c. Paper	☐ High quality	☐ Inferior quality
d. Type	☐ Clear and readable	☐ Difficult to read

6. PREFACE

a. Importance of subject	☐ Stated	☐ Not stated
b. Objectives	☐ Stated	☐ Not stated
c. Explanation of content	☐ Stated	☐ Not stated

7. TABLE OF CONTENTS

a. Completeness	☐ Very complete	☐ Incomplete
b. Organization	☐ Satisfactory	☐ Unsatisfactory

8. INDEX

a. Subject	☐ Yes	☐ No
b. Alphabetic	☐ Yes	☐ No
c. Complete	☐ Yes	☐ No

9. COPYRIGHT

a. Date	☐ Three years or less	☐ More than three years
b. Revision frequency	☐ Five years or less	☐ More than five years

10. INSTRUCTIONAL AIDS

a. Teacher's Manual	☐ Available	☐ Not available
b. Workbook	☐ Available	☐ Not available
c. Printed Tests	☐ Available	☐ Not available

11. COMPARISON OF COST (ON QUALITATIVE AND QUANTITATIVE BASIS) WITH OTHER PUBLICATIONS

a. Textbook	☐ About the same	☐ More expensive
b. Workbook	☐ About the same	☐ More expensive
c. Printed Tests	☐ About the same	☐ More expensive

12. PUBLISHER

a. Reputation	☐ Good	☐ Poor
b. Service to schools	☐ Satisfactory	☐ Unsatisfactory

13. AUTHORS

a. Education and experience	☐ Broad	☐ Limited
b. Professional field	☐ Business education	☐ Other
c. Professional standing	☐ Good	☐ Poor

14. OTHER

a. Appropriate title	☐ Yes	☐ No
b. Usage by other schools	☐ Extensive	☐ Limited

Business Education Facilities, Supplies, and Aids, Eastern Business Teachers Association Yearbook, 1963, ed. William Selden (The Eastern Business Teachers Association, 1963), Vol. 36, p. 275.

Figure 7—1.

the subject matter approach and order of presentation which is in accord with the teacher's convictions. Checking the table of contents with the course outline is a simple way to determine whether or not this requirement is met.

3. The *problems* designed to give practice in the application of the principles explained in the text should be clear in their application and instructions and understandable in the subject matter to be used. A number of problems of varying degrees of difficulty would be desirable to help the teacher provide for individual differences and interests. Sampling one or two areas of subject matter and studying quite carefully the problems, questions, instructions, and suggestions for student activity will indicate to the teacher the quality of the materials for practice and development.

4. The written, explanatory *textual material* should be clear, with the technical vocabulary built up gradually throughout the text. Naturally, the *print* should be easy to read and the *illustrations* should support the written text and challenge the student's interest. Reading thoroughly one chapter and three or four pages chosen at random will give some estimate of these elements in the text.

5. The instructional and *learning materials* that correlate with the book are valuable enriching elements and timesavers for the teacher. For some books, such items usually include the teacher's manual, the solutions booklet, a workbook, projects, wall charts, film strips, transparencies and practice sets for the application of the principles being studied.

6. The *cost* of a book is an important factor because school boards operate on budgets which are sometimes limited. Cost must be considered, but it should be considered in relationship to the ability of a text to aid the teacher and his students.

In spite of careful examination and analysis, in spite of rating forms and evaluation, a book is not known until it has been used. A teacher may prepare himself for choosing a textbook by using several B-A textbooks as he plans and teaches, evaluating them gradually day by day in relationship to his class and its needs. Within a short time, the texts most helpful in any particular situation will become apparent, and when the time comes for a new text to be chosen, such a choice will be based upon use and experience.

Use of textbooks. The manner in which the teacher introduces the textbook to his students, refers to it in his instruction, and recommends its use largely determines the students' attitude toward it. He may make it a problem book containing the chores to be performed before they can "get through" the course; or a Bible of bookkeeping—an "ever-present help in time of trouble." He may make it a book containing daily reading assignments—"pages 16-20, no more and no less"; or it may be a book that is intriguing to browse through, constantly promising exciting and important things to come.

In planning the use of a B-A textbook and introducing it to students, it should be held in mind that it is an aid to learning; that to the degree that it successfully promotes the doing of activities common to on-the-job bookkeeping, to that degree is it a good teaching aid. As stated before, B-A skill and knowledge are acquired by doing bookkeeping, not just reading about it.

With this in mind, several suggestions for the improvement of the use and status of the textbook in the B-A class are made below.

1. In the initial presentation of the book, examine the entire book. Start with the class at the title page and point out the authors, their positions, their backgrounds and qualifications for writing the book. Note the table of contents, the preface, the index, the summaries, the glossary, and any other items with which one using the book should be familiar. Indicating the price of a book tends also to give it value. Explain how the book is to be used in the course and its place in the learning of bookkeeping-accounting. Never introduce students to a textbook by saying, "This is the book we are going to use. Read pages 1-6 for tomorrow."

2. Motivate textbook assignments. One simple way to do this is to relate in a few words the homework assignment with the classroom work just completed. Sometimes assign students the reading of material not yet covered in class, thus giving them a chance to explore, to master ideas on their own. Have them read for a purpose—to be able to explain accounts receivable, to locate terms they do not understand, to determine what routines are followed in posting, and so on. Turn to the book in class and illustrate how one can read with a specific purpose in mind instead of just covering the words on the page.

3. Refer to the book in the class to reinforce the facts or ideas being presented. A great respect for the authority of the printed word is in many students' minds, and frequently the printed word takes precedence over the spoken words of the teacher.

4. Give some in-class practice in finding given subject matter in the book. Show the students how to use the index and the table of contents to find material rapidly. Drill the class by calling out topics to be located in the book.

5. Do not feel that everything in the text must be used, every problem completed. Use problems judiciously—to give sufficient practice to master the skills and the knowledges of bookkeeping, to care for individual abilities and interest. Omit topics or chapters that have no relationship to the interests or needs of the class. Remember the textbook is supposed to be an aid to teaching and not a straight jacket in which to enclose student activity.

BOOKKEEPING TEXTBOOKS PUBLISHED SINCE 1960

Boynton, Lewis D.; Carlson, Paul A.; Forkner, Hamden L.; and Swanson, Robert M. *20th Century Bookkeeping and Accounting; First-Year Course,* 23rd Edition. Cincinnati: South-Western Publishing Co., 1967.

Boynton, Lewis D.; Carlson, Paul A.; Forkner, Hamden L.; and Swanson, Robert M. *20th Century Bookkeeping and Accounting; Advanced Course,* 23rd Edition. Cincinnati: South-Western Publishing Co., 1968.

Clow, Cletus; MacDonald, Douglas; Blanford, James; Freeman, M. Herbert; Hanna, J. Marshall; and Kahn, Gilbert. *Gregg Accounting, Advanced Course,* Second Edition. New York: Gregg Publishing Division, McGraw-Hill Book Co., Inc., 1969.

Freeman, M. Herbert; Hanna, J. Marshall; and Kahn, Gilbert. *Accounting 10/12.* New York: Gregg Publishing Division, McGraw-Hill Book Co., Inc., 1968.

Janis, Arthur and Miller, Morris. *Fundamentals of Modern Bookkeeping; First Course.* New York: Pitnam Publishing Corporation, 1965.

Olson, Milton C.; Zelliot, Ernest A.; and Leidner, Walter E. *Introductory Bookkeeping,* 3rd Edition. Englewood Cliffs, New Jersey: Prentice-Hall, Inc., 1961.

Wolpert, Saul. *Bookkeeping and Accounting; Introductory Course,* 7th Edition. Englewood Cliffs. New Jersey: Prentice-Hall, Inc., 1960.

In addition to the preceding regular high school bookkeeping text-books, the following programmed book [2] is available:

General Programmed Teaching Corporation, *Beginning Bookkeeping*, Chicago: Encyclopaedia Britannica Press, Inc., 1964.

Teachers' Manuals and Solutions Booklets

A *teachers' manual* is a small booklet supplied by publishing companies to teachers to accompany the textbook in use. Its purpose is threefold: (1) to explain and justify the organization and the use of the material in the textbook, (2) to assist the teacher in planning and making what the authors believe to be the most effective use of the textbook, and (3) to make the textbook more easily understood, used, and liked by the teacher. Manuals are usually prepared by the authors and are available for most textbooks.

Manuals are helpful to beginning teachers and to experienced teachers whose pupils are using the textbook for the first time. Some of them contain suggested time schedules or weekly calendars indicating average progress through the text. Beginning teachers who have not learned how fast they can proceed through a course often find these very helpful and comforting—although there is always the possibility that they could do better if they did not limit themselves to such a schedule.

Teachers' manuals should not be ignored by teachers. A slavish use of them, however, can result in their becoming a poor substitute for the thinking that a teacher might otherwise put into his planning and teaching.

A *solutions booklet* is another aid that is supplied to the teacher whose students are using the textbook in his class. Sometimes it is a part of the teachers' manual, but usually it is a separate booklet. It is the teachers' key and contains the correct answers to questions at the end of chapters, the completed solutions and final answers to all problems in the text, and usually shows the transactions and the solutions to practice sets worked out in complete detail.

Some publishing companies, in order to cut down the bulkiness of the solutions booklet and thus make both the manual and the solutions booklet more serviceable for teachers, will list the answers

---

[2] Programmed instruction is discussed on pages 337-342.

to end-of-chapter discussion questions in the teachers' manual and list only the answers to problems and practice sets in the solutions booklet.

The latest improvement in solutions booklets is to print them in a manner which enables the teacher to reproduce on a photocopy machine any of their pages as transparencies for use on an overhead projector. (Overhead projectors and transparencies are described later in this chapter.) This enables the teacher to have the class quickly check the accuracy of their previous day's homework assignment against the correct answer projected on the screen in front of them. Some teachers might also use such transparencies for giving the students a brief preview of the solution to occasional homework assignments—pointing out and cautioning them about difficult areas or possible stumbling blocks. Regardless of the form in which these solutions booklets are made available, they are great timesavers for B-A teachers, particularly when the teacher does the auditing and marking of practice sets and other written problem work assigned for homework.

Three cautions, however, seem in order. First, teachers should not let this timesaving aid bind them so closely to the exclusive use of textbook assignments that they fail to construct and assign helpful types of problems which may not be in the text, which are not effectively handled by the text, or which more directly fulfill objectives of the course. For example, the type of lesson illustrated in the sample plan on page 130 gives students practice in the technique of locating errors. Some B-A texts do not offer practice problems in these techniques. Teachers who subscribe to the importance of such learning in the teaching of bookkeeping-accounting should not be loath to plan and work out practice problems just because the text and solutions booklet fail to supply them with ready teaching and testing material.

A second caution is that the teacher who never works out or carefully studies the assigned homework problems because they are all worked out for him in the solutions booklet is sometimes unable to judge the difficulty and the length of the assignment by just a glance at its solution in the key. Furthermore, such rather "blind" assignments deny him the opportunity of occasionally preparing students, at the time of assignment, for some of the difficult steps in the problem.

A third caution is that some teachers, particularly beginning teachers, might use them so constantly in class that students start to wonder just how well their teacher understands the subject. Their confidence in him becomes undermined. An illustration of this occurred in a high school where a student fad started the mentioning of a teacher's name and accompanying it with the letters of the college degrees that he held—"Mr. Jones, B.S.," or "Miss Smith, B.S., M.A." One teacher's name was always followed by "B.S., A.B.R." Judicious inquiry brought to light that "A.B.R." stood for "Answer Book Reader."

Workbooks

Workbooks are valuable teaching aids that are available with most high school B-A textbooks. The form and make-up of workbooks vary with the different textbooks for which they are prepared. While some contain working papers only, usually B-A workbooks contain both working papers and study guides.

Working papers consist of facsimile bookkeeping papers—various kinds of journal paper, ledger paper, work sheet paper, payroll registers, and the like—that have been specifically designed to supply sufficient and correct space for working out the end-of-chapter problems contained in the accompanying text.

The use of working papers offers many advantages to both the students and the teacher of bookkeeping. When problems are assigned from the textbook, the teacher does not have to take the time to select and distribute the sheets of different kinds of B-A paper that the students are to use—the workbook contains just what is needed. When the workbook material is turned over to the teacher for evaluation, there is uniformity of paper and identical location of the work on each page—all of which makes it easier and quicker to inspect and mark. Since only the right forms or kinds of paper are contained in the workbook, students can use only the right forms in their work and thus do not adopt bad habits of improvising and turning in work on paper of all sizes, shapes, and rulings. As the students' work from this booklet accumulates, they can derive the satisfaction of feeling and seeing progress. Pride in their work is thus enhanced, and this can stimulate neatness—an important element in the keeping of books. Working papers might be classed as motivating devices since most students seem to prefer them to the use of loose B-A paper supplied by the teacher.

Some working papers save much routine repetition in student work by presenting some of the problems partially completed. This enables the student to concentrate on the new learning that is required in completing the problems.

Most schools use workbooks in bookkeeping-accounting because they are economical and increase the effectiveness of the instruction. The forms in the bound workbooks are arranged in the most efficient manner to avoid waste of paper. In each case the proper number of lines required for the solution of the problem is provided. If, on the other hand, the student were to work the problem on loose sheets of paper, he would use a greater amount of paper and thus, in the long run, increase the cost of supplies in the B-A course.

Study guides in a workbook consist of one or more pages of objective questions to help the student determine whether or not he comprehends the content of a chapter or unit in the accompanying textbook. Whereas working papers are used to see how well a student can *do* B-A work, study guides are used to help the student (and teacher) find out whether or not he *understands* the work described in a chapter, and to "test" his *knowledge* of such understanding.

Study guides can be put to various uses and should not be used in exactly the same manner throughout the year.

One common use of study guides is as a homework assignment, when the student completes the answers as he studies the chapter. The teacher then either collects the study guides, marks and returns them, or goes over the correct answers in class for the students to self-check the accuracy of their work.

Study guides also serve as tests for students after the study of the chapter has been completed. When this is done, most teachers will arrange to have the study-guide pages designated for such testing detached from the bound workbook and handed in at the beginning of the year. (Other teachers have all study-guide pages detached and handed in at the beginning of the year in order to have better control of the materials.)

Occasionally a study guide might be used as a pretest: that is, before the student has read the chapter. This would enable the teacher to determine how much of the information in the chapter the students already know.

Some teachers claim that workbooks encourage copying. Teachers who make such a claim could be challenged to explain why assignments in workbooks lend themselves to copying any more than nonworkbook assignments. The major evidence they offer on this claim is that completed workbooks are passed on to students in subsequent years' classes. The answer to the problem of passed-on completed solutions to the workbook lies in the hands of each individual teacher. It can be eradicated by a thoughtful and skillful teacher who has demonstrated his real desire to help each of his students acquire success in the B-A course. For example, some teachers collect and destroy all workbooks (and practice sets) each year. Others introduce a few additional or different entries in the problems each year so that the solutions will vary from year to year.

Let us consider this matter of copying. Much of the work that a vocational bookkeeper does is copying—taking numbers from one form and copying them onto another. Copying is not cheating. The two words are not synonymous. Copying becomes cheating only when the teacher has established the rule that students must not copy from one another's work. This is a good rule, a necessary rule in certain instances where it can be enforced, such as during examinations. It is a rule that has never successfully been enforced regarding homework. Students who break such unenforceable rules are learning to cheat. They are also learning to copy—a major bookkeeping function. Why not eliminate the rule that causes some students to establish the cheating habit? It can be done to everyone's advantage and without subscribing to or encouraging the copying of homework.

Some students complete a B-A course and still cannot recognize readily different kinds of bookkeeping paper or cannot remember simple columnar headings. The teacher, therefore, should plan to give opportunity, aside from that given at examination time, for students to learn columnar headings and acquire some judgment in the choice of bookkeeping paper and forms. Workbooks should not be a substitute for thinking and planning by the teacher. For example, a few teachers feel obliged to see that all pages in the workbook are used up and assign every problem in the workbook.

This results all too frequently in subjecting some students to a certain amount of "busy work."

The manner in which a teacher uses a workbook and the character of that workbook will determine the value of such a teaching or learning device. When a teacher makes sure that a good workbook is used wisely in his classes, the best student and teacher work will result.

Practice Sets

B-A practice sets consist of miniature or facsimile books of record that a bookkeeper uses in recording common business transactions. Most practice sets are accompanied by complete facsimile business forms, such as invoices, sales receipts, checks, and notes, from which the student can secure his information in the same manner as on-the-job bookkeepers receive their information for journalizing and recording. These sets can also be secured without business papers. In this instance the students obtain their information for working out the set from the transactions printed in narrative form in the text. When the latter practice is followed, students do not usually require as much time to complete the set and the expense is less, but they are denied the job-like experience of working with business forms. Practice sets vary in length and difficulty—ranging from covering the most simple of transactions in the simplest of B-A cycles and requiring only a few days to complete, to fairly complex sets requiring four or more weeks to complete.

There are two major purposes for using practice sets in the teaching of bookkeeping-accounting: (1) to provide an opportunity for students and teacher to integrate the principles and techniques of bookkeeping-accounting and thereby to clarify the relationships of the principles, the techniques, and the steps of bookkeeping-accounting in the whole picture—the cycle—and (2) to provide a review of B-A knowledge and skill.

The most common way that practice sets are used is for each student to possess his own set and complete it himself. Another way, requiring fewer sets for the class, is to have separate groups of four or five students working on one set. For example, one keeps the general journal, one the general ledger, one or more the special ledgers, and so on. Students are rotated in their positions after a certain number of transactions have been recorded so that each has an opportunity to perform all of the common B-A functions in the set and in the cycle. In essence, this way of using a practice set is a miniature or pocket edition copy of the simulated office plan of teaching.

This rotation method possesses some obvious advantages to recommend it—it is less expensive; it offers experiences in working with and getting along with others; it could result in team competition; it permits brighter students to help the slower ones in their group; and it more closely follows the breakdown of duties as carried out in large offices. All practice sets, however, do not lend themselves to an equal or even fairly equal distribution of daily assignments to each of the students in the group. Therefore, until practice sets are specifically designed for this purpose, it is improbable that this use will become very popular.

Practice sets have several strong advantages to recommend their use. (1) They give students an opportunity to apply B-A principles and skill in a unifying manner that pulls the segments of bookkeeping-accounting together and aids them to see and understand the entire cycle. (2) Practice sets help bring students close to vocational practice, particularly if business forms are used. Their successful use (3) instills confidence and (4) stimulates interest. Like workbooks, they can (5) engender pride and (6) initiative, leading to a (7) feeling of satisfaction of accomplishment.

There are three major criticisms leveled against practice sets: (1) they cost money; (2) if students have been told that they must do all of the work themselves, practice sets breed cheaters; (3) because some sets are rather lengthy, some teachers feel that the weeks spent completing such sets might more profitably be spent on new phases of bookkeeping-accounting.

Teachers who object to the amount of student time spent on practice sets may be trying to use too many sets in the year. Some publishers make as many as five different sets available with a single text. It is the teacher's choice to decide which of these would be best to reinforce his pupils' learning. Many teachers prefer to use a practice set immediately after the students have covered all the steps in the text that takes them through the first simple cycle. Such a practice set helps the students comprehend the cycle early in the course. If the class secures this early grasp of the cycle, a delay until the end of the year before using a final and more lengthy practice set might be desirable. Some teachers find one set sufficient, and some use three. In a second-year course, a practice set early in the course can act as a good review to take care of summertime forgetting, and then one near the end of the course is a good culminating experience.

One study that surveyed the use of practice sets by 130 business teachers in the state of North Dakota summarized some of the findings as follows:

> (a) Practice sets were used by 97 percent of the teachers. (b) Almost 50 percent used two practice sets; no teacher reported using more than three sets. . . . (d) Students were generally permitted to progress at their own rates. (e) Completion of sets, however, was required by specified dates.[3]

When starting a class on a practice set, it is generally best to keep the class working together for a day or so to be sure that all understand the work. Then, after seeing that the students start correctly, the teacher should encourage them to proceed at their own speed. When such a sound educational procedure is followed, it is helpful for each student to know what minimum progress he should be making on the practice set by certain dates.

Teachers who do not permit students to progress at their own rates of speed on practice sets—who require students to limit their work on practice sets to the classroom—are overlooking one of the best opportunities that they have for recognizing and catering to individual student differences. Many an experienced teacher can recall how some of their students had their interest in bookkeeping catch fire for the first time when the first practice set was tackled. If students, however, are required to proceed in lockstep unison through the practice set and are not encouraged or permitted to proceed at a faster than average pace, there is less likelihood of students being stimulated by practice set work.

Teachers will find it helpful to subsequent instruction if they work out or examine practice sets in advance of their first use in

---

[3] Le Roy Swenson, *A Study of Procedures Used in the Administration of Practice Sets in First-Year Bookkeeping in the State of North Dakota* (M.S. thesis, University of North Dakota, Grand Forks), pp. 97. As reported in *The National Business Education Quarterly*, Vol. 30, No. 1 (Fall, 1961), p. 54.

class. This will enable them to spot possible stumbling blocks, difficult areas, new transactions or materials, etc. With such information available, they can guide their class more smoothly through the working out of the set. Time may be taken in class to reinforce or prepare students for new or difficult steps which may be in the offing for that night, or in a week-end's homework assignment.

Teachers should not overlook the real value of testing students for comprehension as they proceed through the practice set. In the early stages of bookkeeping-accounting, in spite of good teaching, some students may learn to perform B-A duties by rote rather than by understanding. Such students often lack the comprehension to interpret data and records. Occasionally, brief short-answer quizzes requiring interpretation of results will disclose to both student and teacher how well the students understand what they have done and what the books reflect at different stages in the practice set. Thus the testing procedure can be valuable as a learning experience for the students.

Finally, a comprehensive, objective, "audit" test of the students' understanding of the entire practice set is a good procedure on the day that all sets are to be completed. Such a procedure has two major advantages. First, since students should know about this at the time the practice set is started, it encourages student effort at understanding and discourages copying. Second, it cuts down on the amount of time that the teacher would normally take for examining the sets. For example, the audit test will show the student's ability to understand and interpret the set, and will also show if he had right answers to key amounts in the set. As a result, the teacher could then limit his examination of the set to items readily seen at a glance; its neatness, legibility, proper ruling and balancing, and so on.

Notebooks

Undergraduate students preparing to be B-A teachers frequently ask the question, "Should we have our high school students keep notebooks in class?" Some good, experienced teachers require notebooks, others do not. It is a moot question. The right answer must rest with the individual teacher—the procedures he uses in teaching, and the help the students gain by keeping notebooks.

There are two major reasons for requiring students to keep notebooks in a B-A class. First, if workbooks or study guides are not being used by the class, a summary accumulation and source of the student's work can be helpful for reference and for instilling pride of achievement in the work completed and accumulated. Second, if no textbook is being used or if the teacher includes material in the course not covered by the textbook, students could use notebooks for necessary reference, study, and review. Aside from these limited reasons, there seems little justification for requiring students to perform the task of keeping notebooks.

Exceptions, of course, do exist. Some teachers find it worthwhile to have students collect common business forms used in the community and accumulate their collection in a notebook. Teachers who use practice sets *with business forms* would probably find this less rewarding. Other teachers might claim it is an advantage to require students to keep a glossary of terms in a notebook. This latter reason in not as valid nor as rewarding in a B-A class as it is in a business law class. Once the student is presented with a new term in bookkeeping-accounting, he is usually bombarded with it so constantly in class and in the text for the next few days, as well as the rest of the course, that the need for listing it in a notebook is questionable. For example, the day that the term *asset*, or *liability*, or *depreciation*, or *ledger*, or almost any B-A term is introduced to the student, it is usually new and strange to him. But from then on he not only uses it himself time and time again, but he also hears it repeated frequently by the teacher and students in the class. He learns it quickly and best through repetitive use and practice, not through writing it down and memorizing its meaning. Because terms are learned rapidly and easily through repetition, a notebook of B-A terms could be considered busy work. In learning business law terms, the same situation is not true to the same extent. While this subject is also replete with new terms for students, many law terms are touched upon once rather briefly and then do not appear again until a review or examination is encountered.

Notebooks, even on the high school level, sometimes develop into a cut-out, scissors-and-paste affair of pictures dealing with the subject. When this occurs, they should not be considered a requirement for average students in any high school class. In classes where notebook assignments require thought and judgment dealing with the subject, they have merit. For example, after studying the different kinds of appeals that advertising uses, a salesmanship class could be required to obtain magazine illustrations demonstrating such appeals. These illustrations could then be labeled, explained, and justified in their notebooks. The application of this practice in a B-A class hardly seems worthwhile when related to other more valuable activities and the allotted teaching time involved.

Short-Answer or Objective Tests

Most companies publishing B-A texts, in addition to supplying teachers' manuals, solutions booklets, workbooks, and practice sets, also supply objective achievement tests with keys. These tests are discussed in Chapter 10.

The Use of Other Audio-Visual Materials in Bookkeeping-Accounting

The Use of Basic Audio-Visual Materials

The chalkboard. No visual aid is or should be more frequently used in the teaching of bookkeeping-accounting than the old (or modern) reliable chalkboard. Aside from the general rules dealing with stance, legibility (including large and heavy writing), and neatness, there are some special tips for its easier and more effective and frequent use by B-A teachers.

The two-column journal, plain T account, or ruled ledger account are forms that a good bookkeeping teacher uses constantly on the chalkboard. In schools where a classroom is used only for B-A instruction, the teacher could consider ruling these forms on various front or side classroom boards in a permanent manner. Then he would not have to draw the forms several times during a class period or hundreds of times during a year. The most effective way to make permanent rulings is to use a sharp steel point and etch the lines into the chalkboard. While the result will not immediately appear distinctly, chalk dust will soon settle into the etched lines and neat, permanent, white lines will result.

Permanent rulings are usually not feasible when other classes use the same room. The B-A teacher might then consider semipermanent rulings that will remain on the board even though erasers pass over them a half-dozen times or more. These can be eradicated at will with a damp cloth. There are three common ways for making semipermanent rulings. One way is to use a wax crayon called "tailor's chalk"—the same kind the tailor uses to mark suitings. If "tailor's chalk" is not readily available, a "ditto" correction pencil will produce similar results. Another way to make semipermanent rulings is to thoroughly wet the board and, while it is still wet, use an ordinary piece of chalk to draw the lines of the forms. This last method would have to be a before-class procedure so that the board and wet lines have a chance to dry, which normally takes only a few minutes.

Timesavers for temporary rulings include holding two or more pieces of chalk in one hand so that the writing points are far enough apart to draw two or three parallel lines at one stroke. Also, B-A teachers could secure the same five-pronged chalk holder with which music teachers draw in a single stroke the five parallel lines to represent a staff of music. Some teachers prepare master headings of journals, accounts, the work sheet, and the like on large pieces of cardboard. When in use, these are hung on the top frame of the chalkboard. They save time and give well-spaced starting places for the vertical lines to be extended on the chalkboard below.

A quick, unique, and practical way to illustrate entries using the desired bookkeeping form is to project the image of the complete form onto the chalkboard by use of an overhead projector. Teachers who do this have available transparencies of various blank bookkeeping and business forms. These include such forms as a journal page, a ledger account, a blank check, or a work sheet. Then, when they want to teach the recording or posting of entries, the preparation of a work sheet, or the writing of a check, they project the desired form directly onto the board and use chalk for writing on the chalkboard within the projected rulings. This practice eliminates the time that would otherwise be taken for ruling the form on the board. Although the projected images are usually black being projected on a black chalkboard, the rulings are easily discernible by both students and the teacher. Additional uses of the overhead projector are discussed starting on page 189.

The use of various colored chalk helps make complementary entries in T accounts or in the adjustments column of the work sheets stand out when illustrating such techniques as adjusting the merchandise inventory account.

All good B-A teachers insist on neat, legible work. Most insist that students use a ruler for drawing lines. To be consistent, teachers are obliged to set a good example. This is why many use a yardstick for ruling their demonstration work at the board. A yardstick made at home or in the school workshop can be better than the thin, narrow commercial ones. If it is about four inches wide with a grip or a handle screwed on one side, it can be held more firmly with one hand while ruling with the other. These few tips illustrate some of the more common improvisations that bookkeeping teachers devise to save time and expedite chalkboard work in the teaching of bookkeeping-accounting.

The bulletin board. The bulletin board as a teaching or learning medium is frequently neglected in B-A classrooms. Its success as a teaching device centers on the teacher's attitude and his willingness and ability to see it put to good use. In general it should be kept alive by changing it frequently so it will draw student interest and attention. It must have reader appeal.

The bulletin board can be used for displaying business forms and papers under use and discussion—invoices, vouchers, the correct and alternate forms of balance sheets, income statements, and the like. It can be used effectively for displaying students' work and student progress charts that might be used when working on lengthy practice sets. It can be a motivating device by displaying occupational information and current news notes relating to B-A practices and procedures.

By displaying exemplary student work on the bulletin board, it can be used as a means of encouraging students to write neatly and legibly. However, teachers need not limit such displays to outstandingly fine examples of student work. If, for example, students with poor or illegible handwriting have shown some improvement, an encouraging reward can be to display such progress beneath BEFORE and AFTER signs on the bulletin board.

It is true that keeping a bulletin board constantly alive—constantly changing—is one more teaching task. Some teachers, however, overlook the learning potential in having students help plan and maintain a functioning bulletin board. Other teachers include such responsibility in classroom planning and organization so that students rotate in having the responsibility for this assignment.

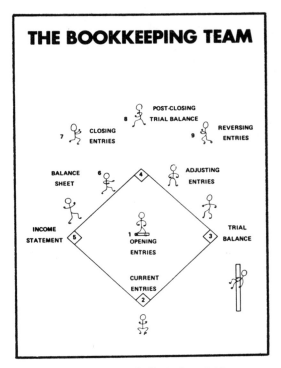

Figure 7—2. A bulletin board idea

The illustration above is an example of the use of a bulletin board. The figures are made of pipe cleaners, and the ball diamond and bases are made of yarn. The booklet in which this idea appears is *Bulletin Board Ideas*, 1963, prepared by Alpha Alpha Chapter, Delta Pi Epsilon, Colorado State College, Greely, Colorado.

The flannel board. Little has been written about the use of the flannel board in bookkeeping-accounting. Seldom, if ever, does one see it demonstrated or hear it referred to in talks on the teaching of bookkeeping-accounting. It seems fair, therefore, to assume that the flannel board is seldom used in the B-A classroom. Maybe this is because its use would first require the teacher to spend considerable time preparing his own materials for the board. Maybe it is because the methods courses that help to prepare B-A teachers slight or ignore the flannel board. Whatever the reason for its rare utilization, a flannel board can be an effective device for occasional use in the teaching of bookkeeping-accounting. The teacher who will take the time to prepare materials that will fit into his teaching could strengthen, and at the same time shorten, many a lesson presentation by illustrating some of his teachings with a flannel board.

A chalkboard is more flexible than a flannel board and as versatile, but the flannel board presents displays quicker, neater, and in a more interesting manner. Furthermore, its use does vary the presentation, and such occasional variation can improve the interest and attention of the students.

Motion pictures. Motion picture films that the B-A teacher can use are principally vocational guidance or motivational films, which are effective when presented at the start of a bookkeeping course. Except for the film, "Accounting, Basic Procedures," [4] there are few motion picture films available that have been specifically prepared for use in the teaching of the technical phases or procedures in bookkeeping-accounting. Other types of films, prepared principally for use in social business courses, such as "Fred Meets a Bank," second edition, from Coronet Films, and "How Banks Serve" and "How to Use Your Bank," [5] include a relationship to B-A knowledge. Thus, they are not out of place in a first-year B-A course, provided they were not first seen in other business courses. As a means of motivation and instructing students on good handwriting, the Coronet film, "Improve Your Handwriting," could be shown.

International Business Machines Corporation has produced an excellent color film which explains the basic elements in automated data processing. Its title is "Man and Computer: A Perspective." Another IBM movie, "A Computer Glossary," discusses some of the common data processing terms.[6]

Current films may be listed in catalogs available in the school's audio-visual office, such as the *Catalog of Modern Talking Picture Service, Coronet Instructional Films,* and *Business Education Films,* as well as professional journals (discussed on pages 225-226). Reviews of films are frequently included in the professional journals.

---

[4] For more information, write Coronet Instructional Films, 65 East South Water Street, Chicago, IL   60601.
[5] Obtain film through your local bank, American Bankers Association.
[6] The nearest IBM branch office has information concerning these films.

Any film which is chosen to be shown to a B-A class or to any other class should be done so for the purpose of making a contribution which will help meet the objectives of the course. The teacher should be just as alert to his teaching responsibilities on the day that a motion picture is assisting him as on the day that he alone is doing the teaching. Generally, there are three instructional steps that he should consider in his planning for the period during which the film will be shown. Although these steps require extra effort on the part of the teacher, the results normally warrant such attention to details.

1. Preparation.
    The teacher should know the film (a preview may be necessary), and prepare his students for salient points for which to look.
2. Presentation—the showing of the film.
3. Follow up.

Through discussion or oral quizzing the teacher should find out what the students saw and learned from the film. Such a procedure acts as a summary and sometimes discloses the need for showing the film a second time. Activities resulting from the viewing of the films may also be planned.

The showing of a film should have an instructional objective, and steps should be taken to see that the showing does not develop into a "period off." The students, however, should not be subjected to such a formal and detailed introduction and such a rigid or formal quiz period after the showing that the viewing satisfaction which should be present is removed. Some films might be shown for the purpose of creating discussion. When the teacher has this aim in mind, the film could be shown without any more of an introduction than a statement such as, "We are going to see a film today. I shall be curious to hear what you think of it."

In addition to the sources for films indicated in the footnotes of the previous page, all teachers should be familiar with the rental or lending services of three other principal sources. These are:

1. Local board of education film libraries.
2. State education department film libraries.
3. College or university film libraries.

Filmstrips. *Silent filmstrips* available for use in the B-A class, in contrast to sound motion picture films, deal almost entirely with the technical phases of bookkeeping-accounting. There are a number of these now available dealing with each of the steps in a simple cycle as well as such other titles as "Bank Reconciliation," "Bookkeeping and Accounting Errors," "Petty Cash Systems," and the like. Some teachers find filmstrips helpful in the teaching of bookkeeping-accounting—others do not.

Most bookkeeping filmstrips do not show anything new or different from what is illustrated or explained in a good textbook. Their major asset is that they picture B-A procedures through a different medium, and their occasional use can make them more appealing and interest-getting than the usual classroom presentation. Coupled with this advantage is the fact that the teacher can readily turn back the filmstrip to a previously shown illustration and can pause for discussion at will on any frame or illustration. Then, too, all students are looking at the same illustration at the same time. Filmstrips, most of which are now being produced in color, are rather commonly priced at about $6 a roll, whereas a 12- to 15-minute black-and-white motion picture costs about $60, and a color motion picture costs about $120. Because of their relatively low selling price, filmstrips are sometimes not available for rent. A reel of motion picture film, however, can usually be rented for a day or two at a moderate charge.

A major disadvantage of filmstrips is that the room must be darkened in order to show them, and students should not be required nor permitted to do written work in a darkened room. Another disadvantage can be the letdown that students feel as a result of their conditioning to the moving, animated picture they see at the movies or on the television screen.

Since all current filmstrips in bookkeeping-accounting are silent, not accompanied with a synchronized running commentary on a record dealing with the frames or illustrations, it is essential for the teacher to supply the running commentary. Thus, the teacher must, before showing the filmstrip to the class for the first time, preview it and prepare what he is going to say and teach as the filmstrip is used in class. Teachers who object to filmstrips on the score that "they fall flat" or lack interest are generally those who failed to prepare for this necessary kind of presentation.

Society for Visual Education

Figure 7—3. Examples of frames from bookkeeping filmstrips

Major sources of filmstrips for use in the B-A classroom are:

Business Education Films, 5113 16th Avenue, Brooklyn, NY 11204.

Business Education Visual Aids, 104 West 61st Street, New York, NY 10023.

McGraw-Hill Book Company, Text-Film Department, 330 West 42nd Street, New York, NY 10036.

Society for Visual Education, 1345 Diversey Parkway, Chicago, IL 60614.

South-Western Publishing Co., 5101 Madison Road, Cincinnati, OH 45227.

The filmstrips which the Text-Film Department of McGraw-Hill Book Company produces correlate with the textbook *Accounting 10/12*, published by the Gregg Division of the McGraw-Hill Book Company.

The filmstrips which the Society for Visual Education produces are based on the textbook *20th Century Bookkeeping and Accounting*, published by the South-Western Publishing Co. and are the same filmstrips available from the publishing company of the textbook.

The opaque projector. The opaque projector can occasionally be put to good use in class by showing and explaining various B-A problems and concepts. It can be used for enlarging textbook and other illustrations for the students. For example, during or at the completion of an assigned problem or practice set the teacher could project upon the screen the correct solution as shown in the solutions booklet. Students' homework could be similarly projected and left on the screen for class discussion.

The most unsatisfactory element of the opaque projector in a B-A class is the necessity for a darkened room while it is in use. This makes it inadvisable for students to do any written work or reading at their seats while the room is kept dark. Even to keep the room in semidarkness and permit students to perform written work in such light is a poor teaching practice.

The overhead projector. The overhead projector projects over the head of the teacher onto a screen or wall in back of him the writing, drawing, or picture that he wants the students to see.

This projector has several major advantages. It can be used effectively in a fully lighted room. Thus the student is able to read and do written work without any danger of eyestrain while the projector is in use. The teacher faces the class as he demonstrates the work. He has better control over the class than when he turns his back to write on the chalkboard. Because there are commercially prepared transparencies readily available for use with this projector, the teacher can demonstrate the use of all of the common bookkeeping forms (1) without having to take the time to rule the chalkboard, and (2) in a manner which can be neater than work done at the board. Furthermore, the transparencies can be used over and over again.

In addition to using the overhead projector to demonstrate anything that might otherwise be developed at the chalkboard, teachers can, with the use of a photocopy machine, prepare transparencies from their solutions booklet showing the answers to the homework problems. Then when the previous day's homework assignment is gone over and discussed in class, students can effectively and speedily compare their solutions with the perfect solution on the screen.

Figure 7—4a. Draw or rule diagram, picture or lettering on a plain sheet of paper, marking dark, clear and sharp images with soft pencil.

Figure 7—4b. Place sheet of transparency film over the original and pass them through an infra-red office copier.

Steps in preparing and using a transparency

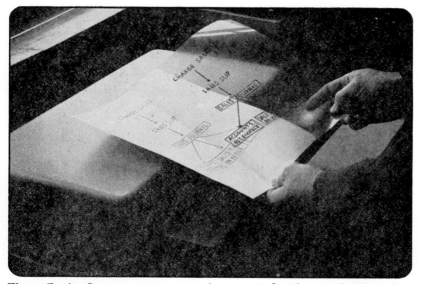

Figure 7—4c. Separate transparency from original. Film can be framed in cardboard if frequent use is expected. Save original for future use if desired.

Figure 7—4d. The projected visual has magnetism and attention-getting power which establishes an ideal setting for effective teaching and learning.

While the overhead projector has been in use for more than a quarter of a century and has had wide use by industrial and commercial firms in their in-service training programs, it is only recently that it has been given the attention that it deserves in teaching bookkeeping-accounting and other business education subjects. One of the reasons for this delayed educational response is the fact that when it was first introduced to the B-A teacher the writing tool supplied was a special wax crayon. This crayon wrote legibly enough, but the size or thickness of its writing was more similar to that of a marking pencil than to the neat, precise figures of a bookkeeper. As a result, teachers found it almost impossible to squeeze numerals into the columns and rulings provided on commercially prepared transparencies of bookkeeping and accounting forms. Now this situation is changed. The old, soft, special wax crayons have been replaced with harder wax pencils of different colors that can be sharpened to a reasonably fine point. Equally if not more important to the B-A teacher is the fact that ink is now being used. One way this is done is to use acetate ink in a special pen. Another way is to use a regular fountain pen with a medium point, containing Higgins black ink to which Pakon, an ink and opaque additive, has been added. The use of this ink produces a fine quality of reproduction that is easily erased from the transparency with a damp cloth.

If bookkeeping-accounting must be taught in a classroom that is short on chalkboard space, an overhead projector can readily be used to solve this problem. B-A teachers with plenty of board space available also have come to like the overhead projector as a helpful tool which permits them to vary and improve their teaching. Furthermore, teachers of bookkeeping and accounting who may be called upon to teach via open or closed circuit television will find the use of the overhead projector and the transparencies as described below most helpful if not essential.

Transparencies for use with the overhead projector. The overhead projector will not project material in textbooks or illustrations printed or written on paper, as does the opaque projector. Only transparencies can be used effectively with this machine. The transparent material that is used for preparing transparencies consists of sheets or pieces of acetate. It can also be secured in a roll.

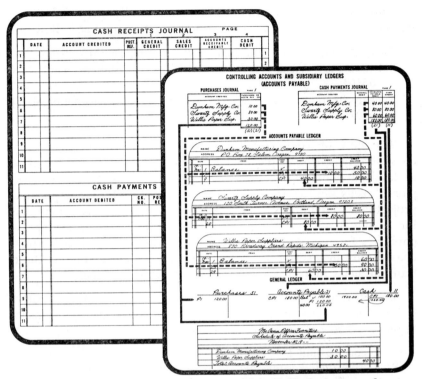

Figure 7—5. Bookkeeping transparencies of blank forms and relationship charts

Transparencies can be teacher-made and are also available commercially. They can be used over and over again.

Three of six major sources of commercially prepared transparencies for use on an overhead projector are the following publishers of high school B-A textbooks.

Gregg Division, McGraw-Hill Book Company, 330 West 42nd Street, New York, NY 10036.

Pitman Publishing Corporation, 20 East 46th Street, New York, NY 10017.

South-Western Publishing Co., 5101 Madison Road, Cincinnati, OH 45227.

Each of the sets of transparencies which the above companies make available relates to the first-year B-A textbook published by that company and listed on page 170.

Three other major suppliers of commercially prepared transparencies for use in high school B-A instruction are the following:

Tecnifax Corporation, 195 Appleton Street, Holyoke, MA 01042.

3M Company, Visual Products Division, Box 3100, St. Paul, MN 55101.

Tweedy Transparencies, 208 Hollywood Avenue, East Orange, NJ 07018.

The cost of commercially prepared transparencies can vary considerably. For example, a simple black and white projectual of a standard bookkeeping form such as a T account or a general journal sells for as little as $1.50 or $2.00. More complicated projectuals containing several colors and several overlays may sell for as much as $5.00 to $10.00 each. Furthermore, some transparencies for use in teaching bookkeeping-accounting can be purchased only in a set or a series. These range from as few as three transparencies in a set to as many as over 200 in a series.

Bookkeeping-accounting wall charts. Commercially prepared B-A wall charts are available. One company produces these charts in mounted sets of eight. They include:

1. Recording and Posting the Opening Entry
2. Journalizing, Posting, and Preparing a Trial Balance
3. Work Sheet and Financial Statements
4. Closing the Ledger (For a service business)
5. Adjusting the Ledger
6. The Bookkeeping Cycle
7. The Data Processing Cycle
8. Automated Processing of an Order.[7]

The cost of these charts varies with the type of mounting and ranges between approximately $84 and $120 for the set of eight. Those that have roll mountings can be fastened permanently above the chalkboard at the front of the room and can be pulled down for instant use. Each has its own function to introduce, illustrate, review, and teach various steps in the cycle. Since they are readily available for quick reference when "permanently" mounted at the

---

[7] A descriptive brochure may be obtained from the George F. Cram Co., 130 E. Washington St., Indianapolis, IN 46202. These charts are also available from South-Western Publishing Co., 5101 Madison Road, Cincinnati, OH 45227.

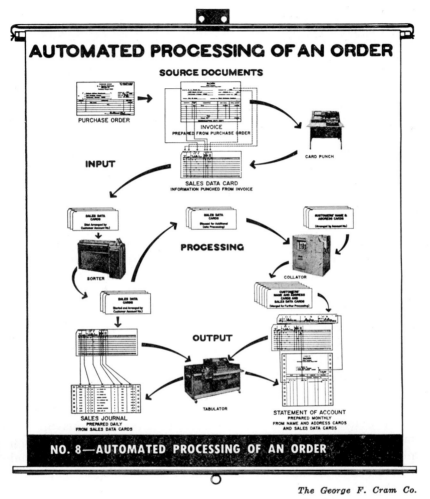

The George F. Cram Co.

Figure 7—6. Bookkeeping-accounting wall chart

front of the room, they can be used frequently during the course for illustration, review, recall, and as reminders in answering students' questions referring to previously covered material. They would be a good educational investment for the teacher who uses them well and in this manner. For the teacher who would use each one only once or twice in helping introduce new material, and then would not refer to them again until the next year, the investment hardly seems justified.

The Gregg Division of the McGraw-Hill Book Company publishes a series of wall charts [8] correlated with its accounting textbook. This series includes:

Side A	Side B
1. Balance Sheet, account form	Flowchart symbols
2. Income Statement	Flowchart of a cash payments systems
3. Flowchart of a cash receipts system	Worksheet
	Schedule of Cost of Goods Sold and Income Statement
4. Flowchart of a purchasing system	Statement of Owner's Equity and Balance Sheet (report form)
5. Flowchart of a sales system	

Bookkeeping-accounting tapes. Commercially prepared audio tapes [9] are available for use in the teaching of B-A concepts. These tapes, containing 96 lessons, each lasting 30 minutes, are correlated with the 23d Edition of the textbook, *20th Century Bookkeeping and Accounting.*

This is a new medium for teaching bookkeeping-accounting and will probably be of greatest value when used to provide individual or small-group instruction to students whose abilities either require or enable them to learn bookkeeping-accounting at a pace different than the average.

Individual head sets lend themselves to screening out distractions and concentrating upon the specific facts being presented on the tapes. As a result, attention and learning should be expected to be better where head sets are used, rather than playing the tapes openly in a classroom. In addition, logically the instruction placed on commercial tapes is planned more meticulously and edited more carefully than the remarks stemming from individual teacher's lesson plans.

B-A instruction by tapes seems to hold the greatest promise for success when one or more of the following factors is present:

1. When bookkeeping-accounting can be taught in a room equipped as a listening laboratory, or where equipment is available for two or more students to listen to different lessons at the same time.

---

[8] These wall charts may be ordered from the Gregg Division, McGraw-Hill Book Co., 330 W. 42nd St., New York, NY   10036.

[9] For information about these tapes, contact Educational Research Associates, 1119 West Park Avenue, Portland, OR   97205.

2. When teachers are searching for help in providing for individual student differences.
3. When schools operate under a system of modular scheduling (see pages 342-345) and students are in the properly equipped B-A classroom for varying lengths of time.

Flow charts. A diagram that shows all the steps involved in a particular activity or procedure is called a flow chart. The simple diagram of the steps in the B-A cycle on page 101 is a flow chart. For years, B-A teachers have been using flow charts in their teaching. For example, many a teacher has helped students learn the steps for closing the ledger by showing those steps diagrammed on the chalkboard, or on the overhead projector, or on a teacher-made visual aid. Similarly, many a teacher has helped students learn the order and procedure of posting with the use of a diagram.

These facts are cited for three reasons. First, to remind teachers of the importance of diagramming and visualizing procedures— even simple procedures—for students. Second, to point out that flow charting did not first enter the B-A class along with the rather recent advent of automated data processing. Third, to alert teachers to the advantage of giving emphasis early in the B-A course to the use and understanding of simple flow charts. Then later, if the more detailed and formal charts are encountered in a study of the relationship of automated data processing to manual data processing, the learning is easier for the students.

A flow chart as a teaching device can help the student learn the order of a particular activity or procedure in bookkeeping-accounting. It can also help him see and understand the relationship between a procedure in manual bookkeeping as compared with the same operation performed with automated data processing equipment. With such use, flow charts have an important place in the B-A course.

A caution, however, seems in order. The construction of flow charts is not the work of the bookkeeper or accounting clerk. The B-A student should not necessarily be assigned the same amount of drill and application in the preparation of flow charts as he is assigned to learning the vocational activities of the bookkeeper. In other words, the teacher needs to keep a proper perspective on this new type of student assignment that has come to the B-A course along with the teaching of automation. Teachers need to make sure that the time and the effort required to work on flow charts does not become excessive and thus extraneous to the objectives of the course. When this happens, the assignments become busy-work assignments rather than learning assignments. (The teaching of automated data processing in the B-A course is discussed in Chapter 24.)

Use of Other Audio-Visual Devices

Federal Income Tax teaching kit. The United States Treasury Department through its Internal Revenue Service has been supplying Federal Income Tax Teaching Kits to high schools since the early 1950's. These kits are revised each year. They are supplied free of charge and are usually mailed during January to the schools that have requested them.

The following partial description of the U. S. Government Teaching Taxes Program material for 1968 is taken from a pamphlet, Document No. 5172 (Revised May, 1967) of the United States Treasury Department.

First, there is the student text called *Understanding Taxes* (Publication 21). This text is a large colorful pamphlet like the magazine section of your Sunday newspaper. Its 28 pages contain sections on preparing income tax forms, illustrated tax problems, a Federal budget summary, a history of U.S. taxations and sample tax forms for student use.

Second, there is a student text called *Understanding Taxes—Farm Edition* (Publication 22). This text contains the same material as Publication 21 plus eight pages devoted to farmer tax problems and how to fill out farm income tax returns.

Third, there is the *Teacher's Guide* (Publication 19) containing solutions to problems from *both* student texts plus enlargements of tax forms. It also contains background information on the teaching materials, instructions for obtaining additional teaching aids, and sample questions to be used in a Teaching Taxes unit.

Your Internal Revenue district office has available, on a very limited basis, 16-millimeter sound movie films, which you may want to use to introduce or to supplement the Teaching Taxes Program. You may order these materials by letter or by a telephone call to the Teaching Taxes Coordinator for your Internal Revenue district office.

Social Security Tax teaching kit. The Social Security Administration of the Department of Health, Education, and Welfare makes available a kit of teaching and learning materials which is similar to the Federal Income Tax Kit. In many schools, these kits are more often used in social studies and general business classes than in B-A classes. Some teachers, however, wish to teach more about how our social security program operates than is covered in their B-A textbooks. These teachers can request copies of the kit, "Teaching Aids on Social Security" from their local social security offices.

Awards and contests. Earlier in this century, annual state-wide contests for high school students of bookkeeping, shorthand, and typewriting were quite popular. This kind of competition, where one student or one school won a prize for finishing first, second, or third in the contest, is no longer found in most states. In March of 1968 a total of only 13 such contests in bookkeeping were reported,[10] and most of these were not state-wide contests. These contests lost their popularity because some educators frowned on this kind of competition--where there is only one winner and so many losers.

There are, however, desirable fields of competition—in self-reliance, in personal effort, in cooperation with others. A number of schools give awards or other special forms of recognition to their B-A students who attain certain standards of achievement. Some publishing companies provide such awards as pins, certificates of credit, certificates of proficiency, and rolls of honor. The pins are supplied at a nominal cost. The certificates and rolls of honor are usually free. When a B-A class or a school participates in such an awards program, the standards for winning awards or for achieving special recognition is entirely in the hands of the teacher. Thus, it is possible that all successful B-A students can acquire some form of award or recognition. The problem in teaching is not to eliminate competition but to preserve the courage and hope of those who do not win.

---

[10] "Commercial Contests, Spring, 1968," *The Balance Sheet* (March, 1968), pp. 320-323, 335.

Teacher-constructed audio-visual materials. Many teachers prepare their own bookkeeping and accounting audio-visual materials. They do it because the specific type of material they want is often not otherwise available. They do it because they see that it improves their teaching and makes the job of teaching and learning easier. One should not hesitate to illustrate a teaching point just because the idea for a teaching aid that might flash through the individual teacher's mind is not already available in commercial form. No commercial materials, regardless of how extensive, will ever satisfy all teachers. Each teacher can come up with ideas and self-made materials that will best fit his own teaching. Therefore, the B-A teacher should be prepared to construct or prepare teaching materials he wants and needs and cannot get otherwise. A few of the more common materials that teachers have constructed for their own use include posters, diagrams, transparencies, flow charts, enlarged illustrations, flash cards, cartoons, tape scripts, slide films, filmstrips, and 8 mm. movie films.

Mnemonic devices. All good B-A teachers strive to teach in ways that will best help their students to remember what has been taught. From a past generation, B-A teachers have been given the mnemonic device—an artificial association aimed at helping one's memory.

For example, when the students are learning the accounts that are reported on the balance sheet, some teachers will show the class a large teacher-made poster or some other picture of several tall, ice-capped mountains. The teacher then asks the class to tell the names of the tall mountains in Switzerland. When the word "ALP" is mentioned, it is written on the board in a manner to show how the word "ALP" is made up of the first letter of those accounts that appear on the balance sheet. The teacher then stresses that all will now remember that "ALP" accounts are the only kind of accounts that appear on the balance sheet.

A ssets
L iabilities
P roprietorship

Carrying this a step further, the teacher asks what is on the top of the mountains in the picture. When the word "ICE" is forthcoming, the teacher points out that just as "ALP" accounts appear on the balance sheet, the "ICE" accounts are those that are reported on the income statement.

I ncome
C ost
E xpense

Figure 7—7. Bookkeeping cartoons

A mnemonic device is a form of gadgetry in teaching. It might be interest-getting for the moment and appealing to the elementary or the low ability student. But for the average young person in an electronic age, it may seem childish and elementary. The time spent on teaching such a device could better be spent on developing more personal and natural associations with the B-A content. This more natural approach would probably evoke more productive learning and greater retention of the subject matter.

One study in the use of mnemonic devices stated, "There is little about mnemonics in modern psychological literature. Most of that little is hostile." [11] This study further indicated that mnemonic devices used in the teaching of a unit of subject matter in psychology did not appear to help either rote or meaningful learning any more than teaching without such devices. The author of this research found in his reading and study that, ". . . mnemonic devices have been most used in learning lists, outlines, bare-boned rather than rich content," [12] and, "Mnemonic devices particularly suggested themselves for forced rote learning." [13]

It might be well, then, for the B-A teacher to weigh carefully any extensive use of mnemonic devices.

The Bookkeeping-Accounting Room, Equipment, and Supplies

When new schools are to be built, when new or different classrooms are to be assigned for B-A instruction, or when old rooms are to be renovated, it is common and correct practice to ask the B-A teacher to help determine what layout and equipment is best for achieving the aims of the course.

The B-A teacher, therefore, should be prepared to offer the best possible assistance in planning the surroundings in which B-A learning is to take place. These surroundings should assist the learning process. A well-lighted, well-supplied, orderly room with inviting working space can be an inducement to effort in contrast to a dingy, cramped, disorderly area that may seem to breed dingy, cramped, disorderly learning.

---

[11] S. Adams. "How Good is a Prescribed Mnemonic Device in Learning Textbook Content?" *Journal of Educational Research*, Vol. LV (March, 1962), pp. 268-269.
[12] *Ibid.*
[13] *Ibid.*

Bookkeeping-accounting is a specialized subject and can well require a schoolroom especially equipped for the subject. Not all schools, however, are so fortunate in the possession of space and finances that they can afford such a special room. The B-A teacher, therefore, will have to base his recommendations for the improvement of his teaching surroundings upon what it is possible to achieve in his own particular school.

If the school is a small one with a limited business curriculum, probably the classroom must be used by other classes. When this occurs, the room and its arrangement should be planned in cooperation with the other subject-matter teachers in order that its multiple uses may best be achieved.

If the curriculum of the school is a broad and varied one with a number of separate classes in bookkeeping-accounting, possibly a special classroom may be set aside for use only by the B-A students. Then the contents and arrangement of the room can be planned more freely to promote the best learning.

The Room

A room with sufficient windows to provide good natural light, without long hours of direct sunlight glare, is desirable. Working in rooms with the bright sunlight falling on bookkeeping paper may provoke eyestrain. A north room is preferable.

Research in business offices has indicated that light colors for walls, ceilings, and floors favorably affect office workers and the work they do. Light greens and grays seem to be the most desirable from both a psychological and a physical point of view. White may be applied to the wall receiving the least amount of natural light since white has the highest reflection capacity.

Experimentation in the kind of lighting that is most beneficial to the different types of office work is constantly being conducted in modern business offices. Where carefully balanced artificial light is essential in schools, it is wise to consult a local lighting engineer who can make a study of the existing lighting system and prepare some professional recommendations for improvements based on his findings.

Modern teaching methodology emphasizes the use of audio-visual materials. The B-A room should be equipped for the use of these materials. Electrical outlets, space for use and storage of visual machines, screens, and exhibits, bulletin board space, and chalkboard areas are necessary.

MATH-U-MATIC, INC.

Figure 7—8. Bookkeeping-accounting classroom.

Desks and Chairs

A basic requirement for desks and chairs in a B-A room is that they provide a nonfatiguing and adequate working space. In providing such space, constant and heavy use by many classes should be anticipated and sturdy furniture supplied. Flat-topped desks with light-colored surfaces have proved to be the most efficient and the least fatiguing to the eyes. Book compartments and other storage space within the desks simplify the handling of supplies in the classroom and provide the opportunity for the class to practice neatness and organization of materials—desirable abilities on the job. The height of a desk should be such that when a person sits at it, assumes a comfortably erect position, bends his arms at the elbow to assume a writing position, and raises them slightly, the arms will rest on the desk's surface. The shoulders should not have to hunch because the desk is too high, nor should the back have to bend because it is too low. Fatigue from these poor positions causes errors and slows down efficient work production.

It is difficult to provide accurate seating heights for all students. Probably the best way to take care of most of the students is to have desks thirty inches high and chairs of varying heights. Several low platform stools upon which short people can place their feet and thus support their weight correctly will be helpful.

The most basic consideration in the choice of chairs for the B-A room is that they provide the proper back support and allow the student to rest his weight on his feet rather than on his arms with which he must do so much writing. The stools mentioned above will help correct this deficiency if it exists.

All desks, chairs, and other equipment should be free to be moved into various classroom arrangements as desired. The noise level of moving furniture should be kept at a minimum by noise-reducing glides on the legs of the equipment.

Machines

Adding-listing machines and calculating machines are common office tools for the bookkeeper or accounting clerk. It is not unusual for a bookkeeper to have a calculator on his desk to eliminate the labor, the time, and the element of human error involved in the calculations of bookkeeping-accounting. It is desirable, therefore, for a classroom to be equipped with at least one full-bank adding-listing machine, one ten-key adding-listing machine, and one rotary calculator. Naturally, if the budget permits, and the number of students justifies, more than one machine of each type would be advantageous. The machines should be placed along the walls of the room, convenient for students to use in completing problems.

In schools that are serving large industrial or commercial areas, a course in posting machines or bookkeeping machines might be justified. A survey of the business needs in the community will determine the advisability of including these more expensive and specialized machines in the course of instruction.

A limited school budget may prohibit the purchase of machines for a B-A class if such machines are to be found in an office machines room. If this is so, arrangements should be made for the B-A class to borrow the machines for a time or use the office machines room until familiarity with the common office machines has been accomplished. The teaching of machines in a B-A course is discussed starting on page 305.

Reference Table, Magazine Rack, and Bookcase

A reference table with a magazine rack behind it encourages the reading of current materials by the students. The following professional magazines and bulletins, particularly apropos for the advanced B-A students, can be considered for the B-A teacher and pupil.

The Journal of Accountancy (monthly), American Institute of Certified Public Accountants, 666 Fifth Ave., New York, NY   10019.

The Accounting Review (quarterly), American Accounting Association, School of Commerce, University of Wisconsin, Madison, WI   53706.

The Accountant's Digest (quarterly), 13 Bay View St., Burlington, VT   05401.

Yearbook of American Institute of Certified Public Accountants, 666 Fifth Ave., New York, NY   10019.

Financial pages of daily newspapers.

The magazine rack and reference table are good places to display pamphlets and booklets describing careers in bookkeeping, accounting, and other office work.

The reference table may also be used to display illustrations of forms, statements, etc. that are appropriate to the topic being studied.

The bookcase should contain B-A texts other than the one used in class, a standard dictionary, an accounting dictionary,[14] *Accountants' Handbook*,[15] and any material that will contribute to the study of bookkeeping-accounting for the specific community.[16]

Room Arrangement

The arrangement of equipment in a B-A room must be solved keeping in mind the advantages and limitations of the specific room

---

[14] Eric L. Kohler, *A Dictionary for Accountants* (3d ed.; Englewood Cliffs, NJ: Prentice-Hall, Inc., 1963).

[15] R. Wixon (ed.), *Accountants' Handbook* (4th ed.; New York: The Ronald Press Company, 1956).

[16] Teachers wishing to consider additional reference materials should refer to *The High School Business Library*, American Business Education (Quarterly), Special Issue, Vol. XVI, No. 4, May, 1960. pp. 264-270.

and the immediate instructional needs. Room arrangements will probably vary as the kind of work being done in the B-A class varies. If the students are to view a film, it will be necessary to have a traditional classroom arrangement with the seats facing front. If the class, however, is working in groups on practice sets, a group arrangement of desks would be desirable. If the simulated office plan is being used, the equipment will be arranged in the best manner to handle the flow of work. The desk arrangement in a B-A classroom should not be static.

The placement of machines, bookcases, reference tables, and so on will depend upon space available, electrical outlets, and convenience for use. Arrangement of the room may be cooperatively planned with students, studied while in use to locate defects, and corrected by wise rearrangement. Doorway areas should be clear, and students should be able to move around the room to the various study points without disturbing others.

It is commonly recommended that a bookkeeping-room layout be like an office layout. An office layout tends to be rigid and has usually been based upon the work flow through that particular office. The B-A learning situation requires flexibility. Thus, an office layout is recommended only during the time when a simulated office plan is in use.

In addition to the teaching materials and equipment that have been discussed, supplies—pens, pencils, paper, pencil sharpener, etc.—are needed for the operation of a B-A class. Workbooks may be used by the students, but additional problems should also be solved. For this reason, the various kinds of journal, ledger, and work sheet or analysis paper should be available.

A variety of pens and pencils are available on the market from which to choose according to personal preference. Ball-point pens have eliminated the inkwells in the desks of bookkeeping classes of a generation ago. Their improved manufacture and moderate price make them a popular tool for the B-A student as well as the bookkeeper or accounting clerk.

The presence of adequate supplies, well-chosen and of good quality, handled with efficiency, and used judiciously, contributes to satisfactory learning in bookkeeping-accounting.

STUDY QUESTIONS

1. Why is the careful choice of a textbook for student use important?

2. What are some of the minimum essentials that a teacher should consider in choosing a textbook?

3. What are some suggestions for the use of a textbook which, if put to practice, will improve its use and status?

4. What are the purposes of a teacher's manual?

5. What are the three cautions suggested to teachers regarding their use of solutions booklets or keys?

6. In what ways do workbooks or study guides provide advantages to both students and teacher?

7. What are the disadvantages in the use of workbooks or study guides?

8. Why do so many teachers require their students to use practice sets?

9. If your high school principal asked you to explain the uses and advantages of practice sets, what would you tell him?

10. Why do some educators object to the use of practice sets?

11. What advantages do some teachers see in the use of notebooks by their bookkeeping students? Why is it that perhaps only a small minority of B-A teachers require the use of notebooks by their students?

12. What are some of the special tips to B-A teachers on the use of the chalkboard?

13. What three different devices were mentioned for use in ruling straight lines on the chalkboard?

14. How can a bulletin board be used to improve interest and instruction in the bookkeeping classroom?

15. What reasons were given as to why flannel boards are perhaps rarely used in B-A instruction?

16. What kinds of projection machines are of value in the teaching of bookkeeping-accounting? Evaluate and compare their uses in the teaching of bookkeeping-accounting.

17. What materials for use in projection machines are available for B-A instruction? Compare the teaching advantages of the various kinds of such materials.

18. Under what circumstances could a teacher justify the purchase of commercial B-A charts?

19. What is a major teaching disadvantage and caution to which all teachers should be alert when using projectors in a darkened room?

20. Why should students become familiar with simple flow charts early in a B-A course?

21. What materials does the Internal Revenue Service make available for use in teaching federal income taxes?

22. Why is caution advocated in the use of mnemonic devices?

23. Why should a B-A teacher be prepared to prescribe the best location and the best layout and equipment for a B-A room?

24. When a classroom must be used by other than B-A classes during the school day, what effect does this have on the teacher's drawing up plans for its layout and its equipment as a B-A classroom?

25. What are some factors that help to determine the best location in a school building for a B-A room?

26. What provision should be made in a B-A room for the use and storage of audio-visual materials?

27. What are the factors to be considered in the choice and location of desks and chairs for a B-A room?

28. On what grounds can a B-A teacher justify his equipment requisition for certain kinds of office machines for his classroom?

29. What reference materals, for use by students and teacher, should be made available in B-A classrooms?

30. Why is it said that the arrangement of desks and chairs in a B-A room should not be static?

31. What essential supplies should all good teachers have readily available for use in their B-A classroom?

32. What effect should the use of workbooks or study guides have upon the need for supplying B-A students with various kinds of journal, ledger, and analysis paper?

DISCUSSION QUESTIONS

1. Which five of the teaching aids discussed in this chapter are the most valuable for helping students to learn bookkeeping-accounting? In what order of importance do you believe they should be rated?

2. A B-A methods textbook, such as this one, and a teachers' manual are both aimed at helping the teacher do a better job of teaching. How do they or how should they differ primarily in content and

objectives? When should the teacher look to the manual for suggestions and guidance? When should he look to the methods textbook?

3. How many different practice sets should a first-year class complete? At what time(s) in the school year is it best to have students work on practice sets?

4. Choose one of the following statements and support it:
   (a) I believe that the learning in my B-A class will be enhanced by my requirement that each student keep a notebook.
   (b) I do not believe that the required use of notebooks in a B-A class results in the best use of the students' time and effort for learning bookkeeping-accounting.

5. Why is it that a common weakness in many beginning B-A teachers is inadequate and poor use of the chalkboard?

6. Why do you suppose that motion picture films dealing with the technical phases or procedures in bookkeeping-accounting have not been produced in quantity?

7. Why is it desirable to consult and use several B-A textbooks in your teaching rather than to limit yourself to the textbook your students have?

8. The use of the various teaching materials should be well-balanced in time and emphasis. Discuss how an overuse of any teaching material can throw a course out of balance and cause the material itself to lose its value. Illustrate.

9. Discuss the advantages of a B-A teacher's being assigned to a classroom that he will use exclusively in his school.

10. Some B-A teachers do not want adding or calculating machines in their room on the grounds that the use of such machines would detract from their students improving their mental and manual arithmetic skills in addition, subtraction, multiplication and division. Do you agree or disagree with these teachers? Why?

11. Since on-the-job bookkeepers use office machines in their work, what is the teacher's responsibility to see that his students have the opportunity to use office machines in their assignments and work?

12. Some B-A teachers believe it is good and necessary training to require students to use pen and ink, rather than ball-point or fountain pens, for their classroom work and assignments. What reasons would you give in support of this requirement or in opposition to this belief?

13. It *is* said that Socrates, one of the greatest of all teachers, never had a school building nor a room to teach in, nor equipment to teach with. Another famous educator is credited with the remark that all he needed for teaching was a student at the other end of a log. People opposed to financial requests for new or improved school buildings and equipment have been known to cite these illustrations in response to such requests. How do you believe B-A teachers should respond to such remarks?

14. Is a special room and special equipment really necessary for B-A instruction?

15. When is student competition in a class good for students and when is it bad for them?

16. How do you feel about the practice of giving special awards, such as gold and silver pins, to the better students in a B-A class?

PROJECTS

1. Choose a B-A textbook and prepare in lesson-plan form exactly what you would do and say in introducing it to your class.

2. Analyze scientifically and completely several high school B-A textbooks and prepare a written report of your procedures and conclusions.

3. Choose three topical areas in bookkeeping-accounting and prepare visual materials that you can use in teaching these areas.

4. Prepare an annotated list of audio-visual materials, showing their up-to-date prices, available to the B-A teacher.

5. Plan and write on the chalkboard an illustration helpful to the teaching of some phase of bookkeeping-accounting.

6. Plan and set up a bulletin board display on some theme or topic in bookkeeping-accounting that would be interesting and helpful to students.

7. Preview a film that might be used in a B-A class. (1) Outline the introduction you would make in presenting the film; (2) list the questions you would ask to be sure the class comprehended the content of the film; (3) list several discussion questions that might be given to your group to start discussion on the film.

8. Prepare a series of transparencies for use on the overhead projector in teaching a bookkeeping lesson.

9. Prepare a paper evaluating the use of the chalkboard as compared with the use of the overhead projector in a B-A class.

10. Prepare a blueprint or diagram showing the layout and equipment for an "ideal" B-A room and a brief paper supporting the proposals shown on the plan. Indicate the kinds of equipment, location of lights, color of room, storage space, etc. This could also be documented with suppliers' literature giving descriptions, specifications, and prices of the equipment recommended. Estimate the cost of such a room fully equipped.

11. Prepare a list of supplies that should be available in all B-A rooms. Justify the items on the list and indicate in what quantity they would be needed.

SELECTED REFERENCES

Adams, S. "How Good Is a Prescribed Mnemonic Device in Learning Textbook Content?" *Journal of Educational Research*. LV (March, 1962), 268-269.

Alleva, Francis P. "Transparencies and the Overhead Projector," *Business Education Forum*. XXI (February, 1967), 20-21.

Alston, Wayne A. *Successful Devices in Teaching Bookkeeping*. Portland, Maine: J. Weston Walch, Publisher, 1955.

Bardwell, John D. "The Newer Media in the Teaching of Business Subjects," *Proceedings of the Thirty-Seventh International Course in Business and Economic Education*. New York: New York University, 1965, p. 21.

Barker, Phyllis Ann. "Federal Income Tax Instruction Belongs in Bookkeeping Courses," *Business Education Forum*. XXII (December, 1968), 7-10.

Burton, John R. "The Matrix: An Aid to Understanding Bookkeeping," *The EBTA Journal*. VI (Spring, 1968), 50-53.

"Business Classroom Equipment Guide," *Business Education World*. XLVIII (March, 1968).

Business Education Facilities, Supplies and Aids, Eastern Business Teachers Association Yearbook, Vol. 36 (New York: New York University Bookstore, 1963).

Caldwell, J. Edward. "Projected Instructional Techniques," *Developing Vocational Competency in Bookkeeping and Accounting*, Eastern Business Teachers Assn. Yearbook, Vol. 40, Chapter 14 (New York: New York University Bookstore, 1967).

Clayton, Dean, and Ray Stearns. "The Purpose, Selection, and Evaluation of Bookkeeping Practice Sets," *The Journal of Business Education.* XLIV (October, 1968), 19-20.

Duarte, Daniel. "The Value of a Practice Set in First-Year Bookkeeping," *Business Education Forum.* XXII (November, 1967), 16-17.

Educational Media Index, Vol. 4, Business Education and Training. New York: McGraw-Hill Book Co., Inc., 1964.

Faux, M. Charles. "A New Matrix Approach to Accounting Training," *The Accounting Review.* XLI (January, 1966), 129-132.

Fesmire, Walker, and R. W. Partridge. "Accounting Made Easy—by the Matrix," *Journal of Business Education.* XLII (January, 1968), 147-149.

Forkner, Hamden L. "Textbook Illustrations Can Illuminate Bookkeeping Instruction," *Business Education Forum.* XVII (May, 1963), 22.

Gilmer, Larry L. "Bookkeeping Practice Sets—Useful Review Device," *The Balance Sheet.* XLIX (April, 1968), 352.

Hanna, J. Marshall. "Reading Bookkeeping Illustrations," *Business Teacher.* XLI (May-June, 1964), 18, 33.

Madsen, Russell. "Ask Your High School Bookkeeping Class to Solve a Bookkeeping Crossword Puzzle," *The Journal of Business Education.* XLIII (January, 1968), 157, 163.

Malsbary, Dean R. "Using the Matrix in Teaching Bookkeeping," *The Journal of Business Education.* XLIII (November, 1967), 54-56.

McCormick, Frank L. "Improving Instruction in Bookkeeping Through the Visual Dimensions of Accounting Instruction," *Business Education Forum.* XXI (December, 1966), 7-9.

Miller, Morris. "Improving Teaching Effectiveness in Bookkeeping," *The Journal of Business Education.* XXXIX (April, 1964), 280-281.

Murray, Samuel. "Draw It Once Only," *The Journal of Business Education.* XXXVII (November, 1961), 57-58.

Musselman, Vernon A., and Russell A. Johnston. "New Media for Teaching Bookkeeping and Accounting," *New Media in Teaching the Business Subjects,* National Business Education Yearbook, No. 3, Chapter 8 (Washington, D.C.: National Business Education Association, 1965).

Palmer, Elise D. "Overhead Projector Eliminates Your Blackboard Jumble," *The Balance Sheet.* XLIX (March, 1968), 299, 335.

Programmed Learning: A Bibliography of Programs and Presentation Devices, 4th ed. 1967-68. Carl H. Hendershot, 4114 Ridgewood Drive, Bay City, MI 48707.

Ruff, Raymond. "Guides for the Use of Guest Lecturers," *Journal of Business Education.* XXXIX (February, 1964), 218.

Satlow, I. David. "Using the Textbook in the Bookkeeping Class," *The EBTA Journal.* IV (Fall, 1965), 8, 10, 12, 23.

Selden, William. "Assessing Classroom Facilities and Equipment," *Developing Vocational Competency in Bookkeeping and Accounting,* Eastern Business Teachers Association Yearbook, Vol. 40, Chapter 16 (New York: New York University Bookstore, 1967).

"Study Compares Overhead Projection with Chalkboard Instruction," *Business Education World.* XLVIII (September, 1967), 16-17.

Swenson, LeRoy. "A Study of Procedures Used in the Administration of Practice Sets in First-Year Bookkeeping in the State of North Dakota." Master's thesis. University of North Dakota, Grand Forks, 1960.

Visual Aids for Business and Economic Education, Monograph 92, (Revised), Cincinnati: South-Western Publishing Co., 1968.

Wunsch, Michael R. "The Use of Study Guides in Bookkeeping Instruction," *Business Education Forum.* XXIII (March, 1969), 21-22.

Resources Available to the Bookkeeping-Accounting Teacher

The previous chapter dealt with the "tools" of teaching—the common teaching materials and devices available to the B-A teacher. However, the teacher who limits his teaching to the use of these previously mentioned materials and devices is ignoring opportunities for stimulating, broadening, and improving the learning of his pupils. Many resources for use in improving B-A instruction are available. These include: (1) in-school (but out-of-class) resources, (2) local community resources, (3) state community resources, (4) national community resources, and (5) international community resources.

Utilization of School Resources

The program of a school includes not only the formal schedule of subject matter classes, but also the many extracurricular activities of the students. It is generally expected that all teachers will assume the responsibility for conducting an extracurricular activity. In some schools they may choose or initiate the activity themselves. In others the responsibility is assigned. In general, school superintendents and principals try to distribute extracurricular assignments among the faculty in an equitable manner. The two most common kinds of extracurricular responsibilities that fall to the bookkeeping teacher are (1) the keeping of certain school financial records and (2) sponsoring a commercial club.

Keeping school financial records. Some school financial records for which business teachers may be made responsible include

215

school banks, the athletic budget or some other segment of the budget, cafeteria records, and special fund drives, such as the Red Cross or Community Chest. Usually only one of these activities is assigned to a teacher.

If such an assignment is given to the teacher, a thorough study of the situation is first necessary. Make a list of all the recording factors, the people who are involved, the responsibilities of each person concerned, the time it will take, the final reports necessary, what has been done before, and any other elements present in the situation. With all of these in writing before the teacher, the procedures—bookkeeping and otherwise—can be planned that will give smooth operation and efficient results.

The keeping of financial records as an extracurricular activity for the B-A teacher has many advantages. First of all, it is a real challenge for the teacher to demonstrate his mastery of practical bookkeeping, and it is an opportunity to illustrate to the school community the real worth of business knowledge and of a business-like approach to the work of the school.

Second, it offers an opportunity for students to see bookkeeping-accounting in action. It might be possible for the teacher to plan the keeping of financial records with student help from the B-A classes. Students doing the work under guidance can profit greatly from such in-school work experience. The values of B-A knowledge become realistic, and the personal experience of such values is a strong motivating factor for studying bookkeeping-accounting. According to the school situation, individual students may take turns keeping the records, or groups of two or three may be assigned. Such work also makes an excellent project for a commercial club.

Some words of caution should be given. The work given to the students should be within the realm of what they have studied, and all their work should be guided and checked constantly. Then the students will find the work experience a learning one, and the teacher will eliminate the chance of criticism because of inaccuracies. Furthermore, when such learning experiences in this type of work have been fully achieved by the participating students, the teacher should not exploit his helpers by prolonging the work assignment.

The keeping of meaningful financial records upon which a successful school activity is based, and also making the activity more successful as a result of the records, is a satisfying experience for the teacher and the students who may participate in the work.

Sponsoring a commercial club. A commercial club helps knit together students and teachers with common interests, and its advantages are immeasurable if it is properly and skillfully organized and effective and active in achieving social or service objectives. The question most often asked by teachers is "What do you do in a commercial club?" That, of course, is more or less up to the group and its sponsoring teacher. The most successful, happy group is the one that has some definite, worthwhile goal toward which to work and that spices its work with occasional, simple social activity or celebrates the achievement of its goal by a large social event.

A commercial club may take over the responsibility of keeping certain financial records. Other suggestions for club activity include making a continuing study of the employment needs of business offices in the community; making a follow-up study of business graduates and keeping a bulletin board and file record of their jobs for present students to see; making a study of the different kinds of business and industrial work in the community and publishing a manual to describe the various kinds of employment opportunities available in business and industry; sponsoring and planning a business show in cooperation with businessmen of the community.

The process of planning for the work and the social activity of the group is just as important as planning for the teaching of subject matter in a class, and the kinds of good planning in the club are the same as good planning for the classroom. This is a student club, and therefore students should do the planning. It is up to the teacher, however, to check and gently guide the planning being done so that its purpose will be accomplished, so that all students can participate to their best advantage, and so that no offense may be taken with the activities planned. This applies to the social as well as to the business end of the club. Nothing is so dull and disheartening as a group congregated for a social time where no plans for entertainment have been laid. And nothing can knit a group closer together than to work hard and then to have a deserved good time at a well-planned social event.

The largest national organization of high school business students is the Future Business Leaders of America.[1] The FBLA is sponsored by the National Business Education Association and also has college chapters. Most of the college chapters use the name Phi Beta Lambda instead of FBLA.

Another national organization of high school business students which has been expanding since the passage of the Vocational Education Act of 1963 is the Office Education Association.[2] Membership in the OEA is open only to business students with a career objective. The OEA also has a post-secondary division in its organization.

A third national business student organization is the National Business Honor Society.[3] This organization limits its membership to, "A student who has demonstrated his ability to do high quality work in all the subjects in which he is enrolled; particularly, the business subjects." The National Business Honor Society is approved and sponsored by the Catholic Business Education Association.

A national organization tends to knit together the business students all over the country and can give more meaning and effectiveness to club work. Regional and national conferences also add incentive to the work of local chapters.

Utilization of Community Resources

There is an increasing awareness today of the oneness of the school and the community, and a well-trained teacher must be informed not only in subject matter and methodology, but also in the utilization of community resources to enrich the learnings of his students.

"Bridging the gap" was a popular expression some years ago to describe activities that presumably brought the school and the community closer together. It is no longer an apt phrase since an open-door policy in many communities has made the school an integral part of community life if not the heart of its existence.

The B-A teacher must become aware of this and know that he can no longer close the doors to his classroom and establish a

---

[1] Future Business Leaders of America, National Business Education Association, 1201 Sixteenth Street, N.W., Washington, DC   20036.

[2] Office Education Association, P. O. Box 4287, Madison, WI   53711.

[3] National Business Honor Society, P. O. Box 4900, Pittsburgh, PA   15206.

junior ivory tower in which he trains workers for a nebulous outside world. Instead he must establish a two-way communication system that will permit educational opportunities to come into the classroom from the community, and permit educational service to go into the community. The utilization of community resources is not all a "getting" situation for the school. The school should be one of the most "giving" resources in the entire community.

Unfortunately, some teachers are reluctant to call on the community to help with their teaching, feeling that to do so reflects on their ability and lowers their status in the eyes of others. This attitude reflects a narrowness of educational vision that is to be decried. Learning goes on forever, and education is a continuing living process.

The speed of communication and transportation in today's world has extended the boundaries of the community, and the teacher considering community resources must not include only the local community, but the state, national, and perhaps the international communities as well. A teacher in constructing a list of the community resources available to him for use in teaching bookkeeping-accounting must of necessity consider all these communities.

A cooperative pupil-teacher planning procedure is valuable in determining what community resources would be of greatest help to the B-A students. The students come directly from the community, their parents are community members, and from both students and parents can come valuable timesaving information concerning the appropriateness of various community resources under consideration.

Local Community Resources

What are some of the resources available to the B-A teacher in the local community?

1. **Business forms and papers.** Bookkeeping should be taught as nearly as possible in the manner in which it is to be used. Bringing into the classroom some of the more common forms and papers in use in the local community offices is one way of doing this. If sufficient copies are not available for use by whole classes, they at least could form the basis for a bulletin board display, and similar forms could be duplicated to supply the need. Such forms could also be used in constructing the type of homework assignment and

drill problems that give practice in doing the kinds of work that future employers might require. In large metropolitan areas, however, the numerous forms in use would vary so greatly from one business to another that a project studying the similarities of commonly used forms could be a more practical assignment.

There are some instances in which a large firm in the locality will each year employ a sizeable number of the graduating students. In such instances it would be wise to develop units of work in bookkeeping-accounting utilizing not only the business forms and papers used by that concern, but also the practices and the procedures followed, provided, of course, they follow up-to-date practices.

2. **Field trips.** Field trips to a local bank, an accounting office, the bookkeeping office of a local concern, a data processing center, and so on would be of value to B-A students. The bookkeeping process, however, is complex and hard to see through the eyes alone. Relationships need to be understood, and this is a mental process. Therefore, if a field trip is undertaken, the teacher, the students, and the business representative need to plan well for the achievement of optimum benefits. Planning is necessary also for economy of time since it is expensive to the business to have a group in its offices for a long time. A plan that has proved desirable in some concerns is to go through an office, starting with the receipt of a purchase order and continuing through all the various processes until it is filled. In visiting offices that do not permit this type of observation, it is well for the students with the teacher to plan questions so that specific information as well as general values are attained.

3. **Guest speakers.** The office manager, the personnel director, the public accountant, the programmer, the former bookkeeping student working as a bookkeeper—these are some of the people within the community who as guest speakers can be of help in answering specific bookkeeping questions and in bringing the work of the business office closer to the classroom. Businessmen, however, are not trained teachers and do not always know how to impart their knowledge and experience to others. When such speakers are needed and are chosen, it is well to indicate what questions should be answered or what topic is to be covered.

GUEST SPEAKER'S GUIDE FOR _____ SCHOOL

Your name and organization _____

General topic of talk _____

Date and time for your appearance _____

Exact location of the class _____

Instructions concerning who will meet you and where you will be

met _____

Parking instructions _____

School policies regarding guests _____

Length of time you are to talk _____

Age, sex, and number of students _____

Vocational objectives of students _____

Suggested handouts, aids, or supplementary materials you might

make available to the class _____

Specific suggestions concerning the topic of your talk and how it

fits into the day's lesson plan _____

_____

_____

_____

Figure 8—1. Guest speaker's guide

The results will then usually be more helpful to the B-A class than inviting a speaker to talk on some general topic.

Filling out a form similar to the one illustrated in Figure 8-1 and forwarding it to the guest speaker some time in advance of his presentation would indicate the forethought the teacher has given to the event. Furthermore, it would generally be appreciated by most speakers and would prove helpful to the guest in preparing his talk.

4. **Community surveys.** One of the best ways to be sure that a high school business program, including the bookkeeping-accounting program, is providing adequate preparation and is meeting the needs of the community as well as the graduates is to (a) conduct a survey of business offices, and (b) conduct a follow-up study of former students. Studies of this nature help determine if the instruction is adequate. They can also help disclose strengths and weaknesses in the preparation of former students as well as finding out the kind of office jobs available.

The major steps in any successful survey include the following:

(a) State clearly and concisely the purpose or aims of the survey.

(b) Determine what facts are needed in order to achieve the aim.

(c) Know how, where, and when to get these facts.

(d) Use the facts and information to fullest advantage.

5. **Advisory committee.** Many high school business departments have a committee of respected townspeople to act in an advisory capacity on problems facing the department. In many states, such committees are a requirement for securing federal funds under the Vocational Education Act of 1963, which is discussed starting on page 324.

Members of the advisory committee should be selected on the basis of their background, position in the community, interest in business education, and their willingness to serve in an active and constructive manner. It could include one or more representatives from such local groups as the following:

Public bookkeepers and/or public accountants

American Management Society

National Secretaries Association

Data Processing Management Association

Parents Association

Office Workers (Where office workers are unionized, a union representative may be advisable.)

In addition to representatives from the community, the advisory committee should include such school personnel as the department chairman and the principal or superintendent.

The status of the committee would be that of advisers only. It would offer suggestions and counsel on important problems dealing with the training of office workers. When necessary, such a committee could be helpful in convincing the school administration of the need for keeping office machines and other equipment updated. In addition to supplying advice, a well-selected and functioning advisory committee helps maintain necessary rapport with the business community.

6. **Service organizations.** The Chamber of Commerce, Kiwanis, Rotary, Lions, and other service organizations are also potential sources of educational help. The Chamber of Commerce has information that is available to those who ask for it concerning the size and status of businesses in town. The service clubs are sources of cooperative help in a community survey to determine the bookkeeping needs or plan a school business exhibit or similar projects. A discussion with the educational committees of these organizations might also open up other areas of cooperation.

7. **Part-time business experience.** Because they are specialists in their field, numerous high school B-A teachers, particularly in smaller communities, have been approached by local businessmen to help solve an accounting problem or to keep their books on a part-time basis. Sometimes they are singled out to be a treasurer of a local service club or social organization, and frequently fellow faculty members and local townspeople approach the B-A teacher for help or advice in preparing their personal income tax reports.

Such requests offer opportunity for the teacher to add to his bookkeeping experiences, to become better acquainted with his community, and perhaps to receive compensation for this additional work. The teacher should take every reasonable opportunity to so profit educationally, financially, and socially, provided, of course, that the work does not interfere with the satisfactory performance of his teaching position. The individual teacher taking advantage of such opportunities can also be one factor out of many that serves to bring school and community closer together and lends status to both the teacher and the school.

These, then, are suggestive of the local community resources available to the B-A teacher. Each community varies, naturally, and some teachers may find some of these resources not available, while others may find these plus many more not mentioned.

State Community Resources

In addition to the resources that are to be found within the local community, the state offers assistance to the teacher if he will seek it. The State Board of Education should be the main source of information and help to teachers throughout the state. Some states have well-developed state departments of business education with regularly published bulletins in business education and suggested courses of study and instruction. A list of audio-visual materials may also be available for use upon request. Some states have a library not only of educational books and magazines, but also of films, filmstrips, recordings, and the like that can be used by the teachers throughout the state. Field advisers or consultants are sometimes available. If called upon, they will visit the teacher in his school and assist in whatever way they can in the improvement of instruction. Each teacher should inform himself of the service that his state department offers.

State teachers colleges and state teachers associations publish bulletins and conduct meetings and conferences from which B-A teachers can receive teaching suggestions and participate in discussions of B-A problems. Unaffiliated regional teachers associations such as the Eastern Business Teachers Association and the New England Business Educator's Association as well as the regional affiliates of the National Business Education Association all perform helpful services for the business teachers in the specific regions represented. Most have an annual convention. Some publish such items as a journal or newsletters.

National Community Resources

1. **The United States Office of Education** maintains a business education service that is a potential source of great help on a national scale to all business teachers. The service rendered by this office depends to a great extent upon the requests that are made by teachers. If such requests are numerous enough and strong

enough, almost any educational service is available. In general, the services available at the moment lie in the field of the collection of school statistics, the development of research projects, and the publishing of various bibliographies and references in booklet form. A list of available pamphlets put out by this office is available upon request.

2. **The United States Government Printing Office** is a rich source of government-published materials upon many subjects that are pertinent to the study of bookkeeping-accounting—for example, budget booklets and information on bookkeeping for small business firms. A list of these publications is available upon request. Also upon request a teacher will be placed on the mailing list of this office and will then receive a notification of the new publications of the government as they appear.

3. **National Public School Business Teacher Associations**

(a) *The National Business Education Association,*[4] a department of the National Education Association, is a national organization of business teachers. It maintains an office and staff in Washington that is headed by its executive secretary. The National Business Education Association is not only comprised of the individual memberships of business teachers but is also made up of the five regional associations (Eastern, Southern, North-Central, Mountain-Plains, and Western Business Education Associations), the National Association for Business Teacher Education, and three divisions—an administrators division, a research division, and an international division.

The National Business Education Association publishes the *Business Education Forum* monthly, except during June, July, August, and September. The *Forum* offers a monthly "column" on the teaching of bookkeeping, and once a year an entire issue is devoted to this subject. While this resource is national in scope, it is applicable to the everyday teaching of bookkeeping-accounting. This association also supplies a yearbook to all of its members and publishes a quarterly magazine for those who subscribe and pay a slightly higher comprehensive membership fee.

---

[4] National Business Education Association, 1201 Sixteenth St., N. W. Washington, DC 20036.

(b) *The American Vocational Association* [5] has a division of Business and Office Education which is national in scope. As its name implies, the focus of the AVA is on vocational education and on helping people enter the world of work. Every month during the school year it publishes the *American Vocational Journal*. This professional publication goes to all AVA members. In addition to containing items of interest to vocational business teachers, the *Journal* includes articles of interest to the members of such other divisions of the AVA as Home Economics, Trade and Industry, Distributive Education, Agriculture, and Industrial Arts.

4. **Other professional publications.** One such periodical is the *Journal of Business Education.*[6] While not the product of any professional organization, it is also national in scope and contains articles of interest to the B-A teacher.

5. **Publishing companies.** Publishers of B-A texts make available to teachers not only the special teaching aids for their textbooks, but also publications containing articles of current interest. The *Balance Sheet* [7] and the *Business Education World* [8] are the most notable of these.

6. **Office management associations.** During the past several decades, there has been a close relationship between the Administrative Management Society (frequently referred to as AMS, and formerly known as the National Office Management Association) and the field of business education. National programs of cooperation have been established, and joint educational projects have been undertaken and successfully completed. Teachers may write to AMS for copies of publications of interest to business educators.

The American Management Association has an active research department, and its research bulletins are available to teachers. A mimeographed list of publications is available upon request, and the price is indicated thereon. Both the American Management

---

[5] American Vocational Association, Inc., 1510 H Street, N. W., Washington, DC   20005.

[6] *The Journal of Business Education*, 34 North Crystal St., East Stroudsburg, PA   18301.

[7] *The Balance Sheet*, South-Western Publishing Co., 5101 Madison Rd., Cincinnati, OH   45227.

[8] *Business Education World*, Gregg Division of the McGraw-Hill Book Co., 330 W. 42d St., New York, NY   10036.

Association and the Administrative Management Society have national and regional meetings. Quite frequently these meetings deal with problems that are specifically related to bookkeeping practices and procedures. Both organizations welcome the attendance of educators at their meetings.

International Community Resources

The International Society for Business Education. ISBE, a division of the National Business Education Association, promotes international cooperation in the field of business education. It publishes semiannually the magazine *International Review for Business Education* and annually holds two-week economic conferences on a rotation basis in various countries. The United States was the host country in 1952 and 1965. There are three official languages of the Society: English, French, and German. The United States chapter holds a yearly meeting for its members, many of whom are high school business teachers. This meeting is usually held at the annual convention of the National Association for Business Teacher Education (NABTE).

The United National Educational Scientific and Cultural Organization. UNESCO is the best known international educational organization. The B-A teacher may feel that he is far removed from the interests and efforts of this world organization. This should not be so. If UNESCO is to attain its goals, it must have the support and cooperation of all educators. Every teacher, of every subject, even in our most remote schools, should be alert to the objective: "Encouragement of exchange between teachers, students, and children of different countries."[9] Every B-A teacher can and should help in achieving its stated aim: "Cultivate an attitude of mind at home, at school, at the university, in business, in our professions, and in our leisure, which is inclusive not exclusive, which says 'yes' and not 'no' to all creative activity of whatever nationality, class, race, color, or religion."[10]

The Professional Teacher Contributes to Resources

The purpose of this chapter has been to identify sources to which a teacher can go for help to improve his students' learning.

---

[9] James Henderson, *UNESCO in Focus* (A Freedom Pamphlet, Antidefamation League of B'nai B'rith, 1949), p. 25.
[10] *Ibid.*, p. 45.

But the teacher who approaches these sources solely with a "getting" or "what's-in-it-for-me" attitude is not going to measure up to the role of a professional person.

One of the criteria for evaluating a teacher is, "How professional is he?" This, in part, is measured by the extent of his membership in professional organizations; the extent of his activity in professional organizations; the publications to which he subscribes and reads for keeping up to date; the professional meetings he attends and the extent of his professional contributions outside as well as inside the classroom.

STUDY QUESTIONS

1. Name five principal out-of-class resources that are available to the B-A teacher.

2. What advantages can accrue to the B-A teacher who has the extra-classroom assignment of keeping some of the school's financial records?

3. What are some of the advantages that a good commercial club offers to both students and the school?

4. Describe some worthwhile activities of a commercial club.

5. What responsibilities should the faculty adviser of a commercial club be ready, willing, and able to assume?

6. Why should a teacher know what community resources are available to him and his students?

7. Why do some teachers avoid using local community resources?

8. How can the "communities" that possess resources for use by a B-A teacher or class be classified in relation to size?

9. What are five common local resources found in most towns or cities where the high school offers a B-A course?

10. What plans should be formulated before utilizing certain kinds of resources?

11. In what kinds of bookkeeping activities are teachers sometimes invited to participate by individuals or groups in a local community?

12. What are some state and regional resources available to the B-A teacher?

13. What are five resources, national in scope, that can be helpful to the B-A teacher?

14. What do the initials ISBE and UNESCO stand for? In what ways can these organizations have any relationship to what goes on in a bookkeeping classroom?

DISCUSSION QUESTIONS

1. What should be the attitude of a teacher regarding the assignment to or the sponsoring of extracurricular activities?

2. What are some of the reasons why B-A teachers do not make full use of community resources? Which of these reasons, if any, are justifiable?

3. Discuss the various ways in which pupil-teacher planning can be utilized in the development of the community resources for bookkeeping-accounting.

4. What is your opinion as to the ethics and professional status of a B-A teacher who performs bookkeeping work in his community? What could be the advantages? the dangers?

5. Why is it important to the individual teacher and to the teaching profession that teachers become members of professional organizations and subscribers to professional magazines?

6. To what professional organizations should B-A teachers belong? Why? How would you list these in the order of importance?

7. To what professional publications should B-A teachers subscribe? How would you list these in the order of their value to B-A teachers?

PROJECTS

1. Prepare a one year's plan of suggested activities for a high school commercial club.

2. Prepare a detailed outline and plan showing the different kinds of community resources available to a B-A teacher. Indicate how and when these resources could be put to the best use. This project could be developed for a teacher's particular community or, for students who have not yet started to teach, a hypothetical community.

3. Using the four major steps suggested on page 222, outline a complete plan to survey your local community for one of the following reasons:

   (a) To determine the kind of bookkeeping forms and procedures that are common to small businesses.

(b) To determine the kind of bookkeeping forms and procedures that are common to large businesses.

(c) To determine the kind and extent of office machines used by local bookkeepers.

(d) To determine the kind and extent of bookkeeping work that is handled by automatic data processing machines.

4. Outline a plan for establishing and using an advisory committee for your high school business department.

5. Prepare a detailed plan for conducting a follow-up study of your high school B-A students who graduated.

6. Write a paper on the topic, "The Bookkeeping-Accounting Teacher as a Professional Person."

7. Prepare a paper evaluating all of the possible field trips that you would recommend for a first-year B-A class in the community where you teach or would like to teach.

8. List the topics in a B-A course for which you would recommend securing guest speakers. For each topic, explain the kind of background you would look for in the guest speaker, and why you would expect him to handle this topic better than you, the teacher.

SELECTED REFERENCES

Dabkowski, Elaine. "Business Teacher Work Experience," *The Balance Sheet.* Vol. XLVI (October, 1964).

Henderson, James. *UNESCO in Focus.* A Freedom Pamphlet, Anti-defamation League of B'nai B'rith, 1949.

King, Sam W. U. S. Department of Health, Education, and Welfare. *Organization and Effective Use of Advisory Committees,* Vocational Division Bulletin No. 288, Trade and Industrial Education Series No. 71. Washington: U. S. Government Printing Office, 1960.

Nolan, C. A., Carlos K. Hayden, and Dean R. Malsbary. "Effective Public Relations," *Principles and Problems of Business Education,* 3d ed., Chapter 18. Cincinnati: South-Western Publishing Co., 1967.

Weaver, David H. "Assessing Practices Through Community Resources," *Developing Vocational Competency in Bookkeeping and Accounting.* Eastern Business Teachers Association Yearbook, Vol. 40, Chapter 12. (New York: New York University Bookstore, 1967).

Chapter 9

A discussion of individual differences in any teaching field is one-sided if it considers only the differences occurring among students. Teachers have their individualities, too, and before considering how to work with student differences, it is appropriate to turn the spotlight on the teacher. Looking at the individuality of teachers *and* students may help in developing a better and more meaningful understanding of both.

The Teacher as an Individual

Each teacher has an impact on his classes as a person and as a teacher. One almost always can recall someone he knows whose entry into a field of work was specifically inspired by an individual teacher who sparked the fire of enthusiasm.

Everyone remembers certain teachers for their personal characteristics—the sense of humor; the tyrannical nature; the human understanding or lack of it; the dramatic ability; the warmth; the choice of clothes; the strictness in discipline. Other teachers are remembered for their mastery of the subject or lack of it; their precise plans of action or confused directions; their enthusiasm for teaching or obvious lack of interest; their fair demands for high standards or no standards at all; their stimulating teaching methods or boring habits.

Teachers develop different styles of teaching. They vary in their abilities to lead discussion skillfully, to explain abstract ideas clearly, to do long-range planning effectively, to use community resources wisely. They should try at one time or another as many of the varied procedures in teaching as possible in order to bring out possible talent which they may possess unknowingly. When a talent or interest is disclosed through experience, it can become an area of concentration toward more effective instruction and greater teacher satisfaction.

In discussing teachers, Stephens classified teacher types ". . . as the kindly, interested adult; the businesslike director of instruction; the lively forceful teacher; the master of subject matter." [1] These do not seem to be mutually exclusive characteristics. Hopefully, the B-A teacher, and all others, too, will aspire to the possession of all these qualities in as great a degree as possible.

The B-A teacher has a variety of roles to play—as a teacher and guidance counselor to his students; as a member of the teaching profession; as a member of a community; as a consultant with the parents of his students; as a bridging contact between business and the school. As he moves from role to role, he must work to retain his individuality, to evaluate his own abilities and shortcomings, and to concentrate on developing his strengths and lessening the effects of his weaknesses. He should keep from slipping into dullness and laxity by remembering that he influences his students just by being in the classroom, and that he can be a stronger influence for good by being there with something of value to offer.

Grouping Individuals for Teaching

The teacher meets the individuals he is to teach in groups or classes. Within the class the wide range of student ability and interest creates challenge both in teaching and in learning. How to group students for the most effective teaching has been the subject of study and experimentation for years. In a report on the education of adolescents from the Association for Supervision and Curriculum it is stated that, "Students should be grouped in various ways in different phases of their high school experience." [2] The report suggests that, ". . . the general education phase of an individual's schedule should be in classes that are heterogeneously

---

[1] John M. Stephens, *The Psychology of Classroom Learning* (New York: Holt, Rinehart and Winston, Inc., 1966), p. 16.

[2] Kimball Wiles and Franklin Patterson, *The High School We Need*, (Washington: Association for Supervision and Curriculum Development, a Department of the National Education Association, 1959), p. 14.

grouped." [3] This is suggested as one way to achieve the major purpose of general education for students—working with many different kinds of people and coming to understand the purposes, points of view, and values held by others.

However, the report goes on, "In the portion of the student's program that is elective, the grouping should be homogeneous in terms of two factors: the pupil's intensity of purpose and his level of achievement. Most people are familiar with kinds of grouping based on levels of achievement, e.g., such activities as varsity athletics, special music groups, and advanced typing. Not as much use is made, however, of the intensity of purpose factor in grouping. Yet intensity of purpose may be fully as important as the person's level of achievement. Intensity of purpose determines the amount of effort that an individual will exert. Some pupils who do not appear to have reached a level of skill equal to others will perform as well because of their great desire to be successful in a particular activity or field of study." [4]

> A recent advancement toward a flexible, school-wide plan of helping to provide for individual pupil differences is the use of computerized *modular scheduling*. Modular scheduling is discussed in Chapter 13, *Developing Trends Affecting Bookkeeping-Accounting Instruction*, starting on page 342.

The size of the school and the area of instruction determine what can be done in grouping. Large schools and specialized areas, such as business education, can easily narrow the range of differences in classes by grouping according to academic achievement and degree of interest.

In school systems where the smaller numbers of students make it difficult to schedule people of like ability into separate classes, the teacher must make the adjustment within his classes. Variations in the work may then be provided for groups of differing ability.

Where no attempt is made to group people of similar abilities either by classes or within the class, shortcomings and imbalances in teaching tend to occur. The teacher may first try to gear his

---

[3] *Ibid.*, p. 14.
[4] *Ibid.*, pp. 14-15.

teaching for the average student. Since the large majority of students in a class fall into this "average" classification, it is understandable that most of the teacher's attention should be directed to this group. This results in the slighting of both the slower and the more capable students.

The teacher may then begin to spot the poorer students, the potential failures, and start teaching specifically to help them, ignoring and boring the more capable. Or, he may be inclined by personal preference to teach to the more capable and leave the rest of the class floundering.

However, grouping students according to ability and interest does not eliminate the need for a teacher to provide for individual differences. For example, grouping all tall boys together doesn't automatically make a good basketball team. Interest, physical ability, drive, and self-discipline will differ. Nor does grouping people with high academic achievement and interest in the subject guarantee a group of easily taught potential bookkeepers and accounting clerks. A sense of purpose, a mind for detail and analysis may vary radically even in a selected group, and homogeneity and easy teaching can elude one's grasp like quicksilver.

It is obvious that the B-A teacher, regardless of whether his classes are grouped according to ability and interest or not, must specifically plan his classroom teaching to offer help and challenge to a variety of individuals.

Following are suggested procedures and activities which may be used to put emphasis on the student as an individual. They are planned to vary the experiences available to the student in developing his individual potentiality.

The Student as an Individual

In these days of large classes the teacher must wage a constant battle to keep the students as individuals uppermost in his mind. It is easy to submerge and drown them in routines designed to handle crowds. While the B-A teacher is dedicated to imparting the knowledges and skills of bookkeeping and accounting, his larger goal as a motivated educator is to receive students willingly, seek out their potentialities, and develop them (students *and* potentialities) to whatever degree possible within the time given to him.

Administrative Procedures

Student-information form. The first step the teacher can take is to find out early in the course something about his students as individuals. A quick way to do this is to have each person fill in a personal information blank on the first day. Such a form, illustrated in Figure 9–1, could include:

1. Name
2. Address
3. Telephone number
4. Grade in school (junior, senior, etc.)
5. Homeroom
6. Schedule of subjects being taken
7. Clubs and other activities in and out of school
8. Hobbies and other recreational interests
9. Past work experience
10. Part-time or full-time jobs being held now
11. Reasons for taking bookkeeping-accounting.

To the teacher reading this information after the first class, each student starts to become a person instead of a name and a seat number. This information also provides the teacher with teaching material. He can immediately start using illustrations and references from the students' work experiences and personal interests to explain the B-A concepts being taught. For example, a boy who has a part-time job in a supermarket can be helped to define assets, liabilities, and merchandise in terms of what he sees on his job. For a farm boy, when illustrating transactions through the use of T accounts, account names common to the farm can be used.

When references are made to the students' interests, the students become people rather than just names, not only to the teacher but also to the other members of the class. Establishing relationships between the students' interests and experiences begins the educational process. By weaving together the B-A knowledges and skills, the students' experiences and interests, and the chemistry of personal relationships in the classroom, the teacher gives color and pattern to the effort.

The disadvantaged, the average, and the gifted students all benefit from this kind of teaching. Kemp lists the disadvantaged child's characteristics for learning in the brochure subtitled "A

STUDENT INFORMATION FORM

YOUR NAME: (Last) _____ (First) _____

GUIDANCE COUNSELLOR: _____ YOUR GRADE: 10   11   12

                                                                    (Circle one)

YOUR STREET ADDRESS: _____ Zip _____ HOMEROOM NO. _____

NAME OF SCHOOL ATTENDED LAST YEAR? □ Here □ Other: _____ TELEPHONE NO. _____

                               (City)   (State)

HAVE YOU HAD PREVIOUS BUSINESS COURSES? (Place a check mark after the courses you have completed; circle the courses you are taking now.)

TYPEWRITING _____   SALESMANSHIP _____   BUSINESS MATH. _____

RECORD KEEPING _____   SHORTHAND _____   CONSUMER ECONOMICS _____

OFFICE PRACTICE _____   BUSINESS LAW _____   OTHERS? _____

HAVE YOU HAD ANY WORK EXPERIENCE?   YES _____   NO _____

IF "YES"   EMPLOYER'S NAME   KIND OF JOB   LENGTH OF TIME

   1. _____

   2. _____

   3. _____

ARE YOU WORKING NOW?   YES _____   NO _____

IF "YES"   EMPLOYER'S NAME   KIND OF JOB   HOURS OF WORK

_____

TO WHAT SCHOOL CLUBS DO YOU BELONG? _____

TO WHAT OUT-OF-SCHOOL ORGANIZATIONS DO YOU BELONG? _____

WHAT SPECIAL HOBBIES OR INTERESTS DO YOU HAVE? _____

WHAT IS YOUR SCHEDULE THIS YEAR?   PERIOD 1. _____   PERIOD 5. _____

                                        PERIOD 2. _____   PERIOD 6. _____

                                        PERIOD 3. _____   PERIOD 7. _____

                                        PERIOD 4. _____   PERIOD 8. _____

Figure 9—1.

Challenge to Vocational Learning." These characteristics seem directly applicable to most other learners regardless of ability, pointing out the need for personal reference, specific purpose, and vital experiences. Kemp says, "They are capable of working well and hard on a specific task or assignment which has a purpose for them; for example, taking courses which will result in a job or scholarship leading to a career." [5] The gifted appreciate purpose and direction as well as the disadvantaged.

After initial contact with the students and securing information during the first class meeting, the teacher should begin to organize his class for the greatest efficiency of learning and teaching.

Seating. Seating arrangements should be arrived at gradually with students having freedom to choose where they will sit. As the class progresses and the teacher has a chance to observe and discover the physical differences of the students, necessary changes can be made to achieve a good working organization.

Such physical deficiencies as eyesight, hearing, height, and the personal desires of the students should decide where they sit in the classroom—not alphabetical arrangement. A long time ago in the dark educational ages, students were seated according to the alphabetical arrangement of their last names regardless of any other factor. This simplified the clerical work of the teacher. Classes, however, should be seated for the comfort and best learning of the students instead of the clerical convenience of the teacher.

Classroom clerical procedures. The details of taking attendance, reading notices, collecting homework, passing out and collecting supplies, attending to windows and shades, and so on can be organized into specific areas of responsibility handled by student committees. Regardless of ability, most students can participate in this work at some time. The more capable students can develop the organizational plan into a classroom handbook and have it duplicated for use in their class and future classes. This experience is not unlike the preparation of an office manual which sets forth the rules for efficiency of operation.

---

[5] Barbara Kemp, *The Youth We Haven't Served, A Challenge to Vocational Education* (Washington: U.S. Department of Health, Education, and Welfare, Office of Education; U.S. Government Printing Office, 1966), p. 5.

The plan should be reviewed by the students at least once a year to determine whether or not it can be improved. Students change, relationships change, and classroom organizational procedures should change, too. In discussing with the students the organizational and personnel problems within the classroom, comparisons might be made to similar problems in an office situation.

All students of whatever ability should be encouraged to take on responsibilities which give them challenge and experience in working cooperatively with others. It is hoped that the membership of committees could be rotated so students would not be frozen into doing the same job all year while others do nothing.

If the teacher does some preliminary planning, class organization can be accomplished quickly and easily. A class period, or part thereof, devoted to organizing a system for handling clerical details is worthwhile. A businesslike classroom provides students with experiences they will meet in working in an organized office group. Educationally this experience is more productive than assembling individuals in a room to do as the teacher tells them.

Teaching Procedures

Explaining. Every student, regardless of his ability, appreciates and benefits by a clear explanation of a procedure or principle. For the student of lesser ability, simple language, chalkboard illustrations, and available multi-media instructional materials are necessary. For the more capable students such teaching techniques provide for a more rapid learning experience.

Questioning. In asking questions during the class period, ask questions of students that, in general, they can answer successfully. Rarely will it do any good to ask a student a question that the teacher knows he cannot answer. To ask questions beyond a student's ability just to prove to him or the class how little he knows wastes class time and acts as punishment. Punishment is like poison—in small doses it might cure, but constant use generally kills. On the other hand, challenge and the tough question are necessary for growth. Easy success all the time is mollycoddling and weakening. Strong mental exercise is needed to move to higher levels of learning. The skill of the teacher is displayed in the way he questions individuals in a classroom group so as to build the confidence of the unsure, challenge the sharp and quick mind, and keep the middle-of-the-roader on his toes. To be able to do this well takes practice—years of it—and a sincere interest in people and their development.

Homework. After a basic principle or procedure of bookkeeping and accounting has been explained and developed in class, homework assignments can be varied to offer individual students a choice and a challenge. Textbooks already offer problems of varying difficulty and complexity. Appropriate problems may be suggested by the teacher for challenge or to reinforce the classroom teaching.

Problems in line with the different interests and purposes of major groups in the class might be offered. Girls planning to become typists or stenographers could be assigned problems relating to the balance sheet and income statement, the solutions of which could be typed in proper form. If machines are available, some assignments could call for the use of posting and billing machines, or perhaps some data processing equipment. Boys interested in becoming service-station managers or farmers could have their group and individual interests enlivened by working problems and practice sets for such types of businesses.

In planning varying homework assignments to help individuals learn better, it is important that the high-ability student be given challenging problems and not just a double assignment—more of the same—because he works fast. Honors work should not be determined by quantity but by quality and challenge.

Overloading in homework is also discouraging to the slow learner, since his problem is one of time. It is better for him to do one problem well than six in a confused state because of pressure of time.

In providing for individual differences in homework, it is obvious that the teacher needs a working file of many types of B-A problems to supplement the basic instructional material. It is suggested that a prospective B-A teacher begin now to collect interesting and challenging problems to form a base for that file.

Many textbook problems vary in their degree of difficulty. The challenge of such problems can easily be changed by merely adding or deleting certain transactions and instructions. Furthermore, the types of mini problems discussed and illustrated on pages

261 through 265 can be tailor-made to possess varying degrees of difficulty.

In some community situations, small groups could be established for homework practice. Membership in such groups could vary over a period of time thus extending the relationship experience. For example, students at a particular level of instruction who live in the same neighborhood could meet and work together on new material or long problems. Advanced students might work with beginning students which would be a realistic experience since assistance is generally available in most offices. If a democratic atmosphere prevails in the homework group a more basic interest in learning might well overcome the "copying" desire since any unreasonable competitive element would diminish.

Field trips. Field trips to business offices, banks, and data processing centers where students can see and hear about what goes on in such fields of work provide learning experiences for everybody, including the teacher. Because individual differences must be considered, field trips need to be expertly planned. Students must be prepared for them—what to do, what to look for, what to wear, and how to express their gratitude for the opportunity. These trips should be followed by class-evaluation sessions, and formal "thank-you letters" should be sent to cooperating businesses.

If a whole class cannot go, a selected student group could go, then report back to the class. A more capable student can head a group which includes representative class members.

Community surveys. The entire class or a small committee can, through questionnaires or visits, study the immediate community to determine what is happening in B-A work—the jobs available, the salaries paid, the use of machines, the use of automation. Chapter 8 discusses community surveys in more detail.

Community service work experience. Individuals or groups within the B-A class can contribute their services by keeping records and collecting money and pledges for the Red Cross, the Community Chest, and other organizations. Such experiences extend the concepts of service, cooperation, and community interrelationships. It gives experience in working with adults, and since there are routine jobs as well as more creative ones, all levels of student ability can be accommodated. This experience also puts B-A skills into a real situation while showing students the need for knowledge and ability to work with people.

Work experience in the school. The same values that accrue from community service are available through in-school work experience. Where possible, students may assist in the following:

1. Selling tickets and keeping records of basketball, football and other athletic games as well as plays and dances.
2. Taking care of school banking programs.
3. Handling of school cafeteria books and accounts or student-operated stores.

A substitute for out-of-school work experience could be the establishment of a simulated office within the classroom. Small groups might be established to find out the duties performed and the flow in a large office. That particular type of business office could be simulated in the classroom. The students would then open the books, be assigned positions within their level of competency, and complete the B-A work through a fiscal period.

Work experience in business. Work-experience programs have existed for some time. Now, these programs are increasing because of the Vocational Education Act of 1963 as discussed in Chapter 13. Through the cooperation of businessmen in the community, students can be placed in an office for a predetermined period of time. The time and conditions under which the work should be undertaken may be determined in cooperation with business personnel.

Because there are all kinds of office jobs and varying levels of B-A work, the teacher-coordinator of the work-experience program must know his students well. Only then can he arrange for the right student to be placed in an appropriate position. While a work-experience position continues to be a learning experience for the student, he is usually paid for his work. Better relations with the participating employers are maintained when some screening process is used and some minimum standards met before students are eligible to participate.

Classroom or assembly programs. Additional experiences to broaden the scope of the class and help provide for individual student differences may include:

1. Student work exhibits, such as at Future Business Leaders of America chapter meetings.
2. Business machine exhibits and demonstrations.
3. Guest speakers, including former students who are successfully employed in B-A jobs; personnel officers of local businesses; employment-bureau representatives; representative producers or users of automated data processing equipment.

Out-of-class-tutoring sessions. A fairly common practice is to provide after-school help to students who have fallen behind the class because of absence, or who ask for special help, or who are not working up to their capacity. Such sessions are in the nature of special tutoring and should be open to students who want to attend because of their desire to improve. Usually such sessions become an informal class with the teacher going over work already covered in the regular class period.

Special tutoring favors the slower student. To balance this favor, an occasional after-class session could be planned when some advanced bit of B-A practice relative to current studies might be shown or discussed. Such a session could be for the special benefit of the more advanced and capable students.

Other out-of-class sessions should be devoted to individuals to determine the root of their trouble in mastering B-A knowledges and skills. This involves sitting down and working through a typical problem with the student. The teacher must analyze what the student does, thinks, and how he works until the source of the particular difficulty is apparent. When this diagnosis is made, plans for correcting the situation can be made. Just giving more work to a student who is having trouble is no solution at all. Diagnosing the difficulty first, then giving practice in the weak area is a more satisfactory method of handling individual differences.

Suggested experiences for the more capable students. The more capable student, having indicated his mastery of the basic B-A knowledges presented, may be given the opportunity to extend his learning and interests within the framework of the class by:

1. Studying in college-level textbooks and reading business magazine articles pertinent to discussions in class.
2. Being assigned challenging problems of a more difficult nature in the area studied.

3. Being assigned challenging problems which require original decisons and creative effort in the solutions. For example, a case or problem could be supplied calling for an analysis of (a) why the net income of a business started to decrease, (b) when to employ more help, (c) when and to what extent it would be profitable to move toward automated data processing.
4. Using such learning media as programmed instruction, B-A tapes, and filmstrips for self-instruction and speedier learning progress.
5. Working practice sets with more advanced application.
6. Acting as student tutors or student teachers.
7. Auditing other students' work.
8. Assisting the teacher in putting material on the chalkboard, making charts and other visual aids, or developing and maintaining an attractive bulletin board.
9. Studying income taxes and doing more advanced income tax problems.
10. Doing correspondence school work in elementary college accounting.

In planning these experiences, the teacher must be sure they are for the benefit of the students and not for the convenience of the teacher. It is very easy for a teacher to fall into the habit of using the more capable students as personal assistants to check homework, correct objective tests, and so on. As long as these activities enrich and enhance the student's knowledge and experience in bookkeeping and accounting, it is a desirable use of the student's time. But the value of such activities diminishes rapidly, and honest teachers eventually recognize they should provide more meaningful experiences than test correction and errand running. They will free their capable helpers for more educationally-rewarding activities. Teachers should always be on their guard against exploiting the capable, willing worker.

Acceleration. A number of schools are providing accelerated B-A programs for capable students. While these programs take different forms, there are two which seem most common.

One type of accelerated program is aimed at the more capable students who plan to terminate their formal education upon graduation from high school. They are placed in special classes in which the work found in high-school-level textbooks is presented rapidly and is supplemented with more advanced and difficult applications.

Another type of accelerated program gaining attention is the offering of a special honors course in college-level accounting enabling the college-bound student to receive credit for courses taken while still in high school. This program is certainly not new for many high schools. For years such honors courses have been offered in English, mathematics, and science.

Schools contemplating such a program for college-bound accounting or business administration students should take the following factors into consideration:

1. They will need agreements with one or more colleges regarding the credit to be granted.
2. They will need to select students of college caliber for the course.
3. They will need to bring their students to at least the same minimum standards demanded of introductory-accounting students at the institutions granting advanced credit.
4. They will be obliged to provide their students with learning materials (textbook, practice set, etc.) equal to college-level quality. (If they do not, their students will be at a disadvantage when they face for the first time the more sophisticated college materials.)

Suggested experiences for the less capable students. All too frequently the less-capable or disadvantaged young persons have their problems intensified by watered-down subject matter and exclusion from interesting experiences to a point where they are forced to concentrate even more on their narrow range of ability. It is this group which especially needs exposure to the possibilities in the community and the world through field trips, guest speakers, demonstrations, etc. Every effort must be made to broaden their horizons, not narrow them.

As stated before, with the slower student, learning is a matter of time. Therefore, his individual difference can first be taken care of by placement in a group which is working at a slower pace. Within the time available, most of the same basic B-A knowledges and skills should be presented as in any other class training bookkeeping and accounting personnel. Slower students who do not plan to become bookkeepers or accounting clerks may cover a smaller amount of the subject matter. For example, the student in the course for related vocational help as a future typist, store clerk, stenographer, or general clerical worker might be permitted to pass a first-year course without reaching an understanding and vocational competency in more advanced and technical areas such as accruals and reversing entries.

For learners obliged to progress at a more varied rate of speed than the average in the class, programmed devices—both textbooks and machines—seem, in theory at least, to offer some solution. Little has been accomplished in this respect for bookkeeping and accounting. However, the individual teacher may be able to devise programs for various levels of achievement. Programmed instruction is discussed in detail in Chapter 13.

Other experiences which may be offered to the less-capable student include the following. (These could well be supplemented by the individual teacher's imaginative thinking in this direction.)

1. Participating in field trips, class committees, and other activities offered to the entire class.
2. Making tapes, programmed materials, and filmstrips available for self-instruction by the student who has been absent or has fallen behind in class.
3. Arranging with employment agencies to give practice interviews and information on available positions in the B-A field.
4. Setting up simple personal or family records to encourage more effective money management.
5. Supplying imaginative assignments such as looking about the classroom and noting all the items which require the keeping of records. Doing the same thing at home or in a business block in town.
6. Providing large and colorful pictures (which hopefully will be changed periodically) of B-A records, B-A machines, B-A offices, and businesses in operation. (A brief discussion of these pictures assist the slower learner to understand in more detail just what is being portrayed.)
7. Providing other high school B-A textbooks and business magazines for browsing or specific assignment.

Personal conferences. There are students who do not fit into the group, who do not get along with the teachers, or who are disciplinary cases. Trying to solve their problems in the classroom, with an audience present, is in poor taste and may lead to all kinds of complications. A conference, therefore, should be held privately. At the conference, a friendly tone is established and an appeal made to the student to help discover the real reason for the trouble. If the teacher sits down with the student away from the desk (the desk emphasizes teacher vs. student), it may help to establish the friendly atmosphere necessary for a satisfactory conversation. The teacher will have to use all his powers of objectivity to rise above his personal feelings. Usually a frank and friendly talk about the situation starts the problem on its way to a solution. However, sometimes personalities continue to conflict in spite of every effort. The simplest solution then is to arrange for a transfer of the student to another class and teacher.

Conflict between a teacher and a student should not be allowed to disrupt a class and affect the learning of the rest of the members of that class. On the other hand, only after the teacher has made every effort to solve the differences should he, as a last resort, refer the situation to a higher authority. A teacher should make an honest attempt to get at the root of a difficult behavior problem. Merely doling out detention punishment or sending a student to the principal's office will not solve future problems with that student, and involving the principal and other staff members may only complicate the situation. The more people who become involved, the more difficult it is to reestablish a feeling of goodwill between the student and the teacher. The teacher who can successfully handle his own problems arising out of the individual differences of his students gains the respect of his students as well as that of the school administration and staff.

On occasion, however, the problem may be so serious and of such a nature that the only thing to do is to refer the student to a higher authority for help—the school psychologist, a psychiatrist, the principal, or some other person designated to handle such cases.

Conclusion

In conclusion, it might be wise to reiterate that the aim of the teacher in handling individual differences is not to mold every student to the same pattern, but rather to assay the assets and liabilities of each student. Then work with the individuals and the groups so that the members of the class both individually and collectively show a net gain at the end of the school year.

The individuals in a high school class are a pulsating, developing, growing group of young people, each with his own inimitable personality. Some of their characteristics may irk, but those characteristics may be just the ones that eventually bring success in future life. Most of their potentialities may be hidden beneath the varying exteriors and problems of emotional and physical growth being experienced. The successful teacher realizes that he has in every class a group of alive and different individuals, and that his professional responsibility is to help each one grow and make the most of his differences.

STUDY QUESTIONS

1. What are some traits and characteristics of teachers we have had which cause us to remember them favorably? Unfavorably?

2. Why should all teachers at one time or another try varied procedures in teaching?

3. What are some of the different roles that a B-A teacher must play?

4. When planning to deal with pupil differences, in what ways can a teacher quickly find out some important things about a student early in the course?

5. Why is it suggested that, "Students should be grouped in various ways in different phases of their high school experience."?

6. What two major factors should be taken into account when grouping B-A students homogenously?

7. What shortcomings in teaching tend to occur when no attempt is made to group students with similar abilities?

8. What information is commonly called for on a student-information form?

9. Describe the use a B-A teacher can make of the information furnished on a student-information form.

10. How can the seating of pupils in a B-A class play an important role in providing for certain kinds of individual differences?

11. What are some easy, sensible, and important ways in which a teacher can deal directly with single-pupil differences?

12. Describe how homework assignments can be used as a means of providing for individual differences.

13. What three kinds of work experience can be used to deal with individual pupil differences?

14. What experiences were suggested for challenging the more capable students?

15. What experiences were suggested for use with less-capable students?

DISCUSSION QUESTIONS

1. What is the possibility of finding one or more unfavorable characteristics in an outstanding teacher? Explain.

2. In what ways does a B-A teacher influence his students, "just by being there"?

3. Which kind of student grouping, homogeneous or heterogeneous, will result in the best learning for B-A pupils? Which of these groupings will make the teacher's job easier? The answer to which of these questions should decide the issue?

4. Explain why you would prefer to teach a class that was grouped homogeneously or hetergeneously.

5. Explain why you would prefer to teach a B-A class that was, itself, grouped homeogeneously or a class in which several groups had been identified homogeneously?

6. Assuming that a class has some average, some above average, and some below average students in it, which caliber of student do you believe gets the most attention from the teacher? The least attention? What should be done to arrive at a more balanced situation?

7. Brilliant or gifted students should be given as much teacher help and attention as any other group of students in the class. Do you agree or disagree with this statement? Why?

8. It has been said that, "A teacher should be a teacher of children first and a teacher of subject matter second." What relationship do you see between this statement and the philosophy which calls for teachers to provide for individual pupil differences?

9. Do high school teachers need a lighter teaching load in order to give *some* attention to pupil differences? in order to give *more* attention to pupil differences? in order to give *adequate* attention to pupil differences?

10. Under what circumstances might a student-information form be impractical and superfluous?

11. Under what circumstances, if any, might it be justified to ask a student questions that are perhaps too difficult for him to answer?

12. Many colleges and universities offering business-administration programs require their freshmen to concentrate on non-business courses. To what extent, therefore, do you believe that high schools can justify teaching college-level accounting courses for advance-placement credit?

13. In what areas of bookkeeping and accounting can small group work be used effectively?

14. How can both slow students and high-level students be given work suitable to their abilities within the same class?

PROJECTS

1. Write a paper describing in detail two of your most unforgettable teachers. (a) Describe one teacher that you remember because of his favorable traits and characteristics. (b) Describe the other teacher you remember because of his unfavorable traits and characteristics.

2. Assume that you have a student who is uncooperative and unsuccessful in your class. Make a list of all the things you could do to find and remove the reason for the difficulty.

3. Prepare a paper outlining procedures and methods of broadening the experiences and knowledges of the higher-ability B-A student.

4. Choose a class with which you are familiar and plan several groups for small group work.

SELECTED REFERENCES

Boynton, Lewis D. "Identifying and Teaching the More Capable Bookkeeping Student," *Business Education Forum.* XVI (April, 1962), 25.

Clippinger, Ray L. "Meeting the Need of the Slow Learner in Business Education," *American Vocational Journal.* XXXVIII (November, 1963), 26-27.

Enterline, H. G. (ed.). *Helping the Slow Learner,* a special issue of *American Business Education.* X (May, 1954).

Humphrey, Frederick. "The Low-Ability Student in Bookkeeping—One School's Solution," *Business Education Forum*. XXII (October, 1967), 16-17.

Johnson, William E. "Improving Instruction in Bookkeeping Through Meeting the Individual Needs of Students," *Business Education Forum*. XXI (December, 1966), 12-14.

Kemp, Barbara. *The Youth We Haven't Served: A Challenge to Vocational Education*. Washington: Superintendent of Documents, 1966.

Malsbary, Dean R. (ed.). *Providing for the Fast Learner*, a special issue of *American Business Education*. XIV (May, 1958).

Miller, Kevin G., Paul R. Long, and Richard W. Byrd. "Center Bookkeeping Around the Individual," *Business Education Forum*. XV (December, 1960), 11-13.

Price, A. I. "Recognizing the Need of the Slow Learner in Bookkeeping," *The Journal of Business Education*. XXXV (February 1960), 211-212.

Rothchild, Thomas A. "Business Education and the Slow Learner—An Awakening Giant," *The Balance Sheet*. XLVII (November, 1965), 106.

Schultheis, Robert A. "Business Education and the Slow Learner," *Journal of Business Education*. XLIII (November, 1967), 67-70.

Stephens, John M. *The Psychology of Classroom Learning*. New York: Holt, Rinehart and Winston, Inc., 1966.

Wiles, Kimball, and Franklin Patterson. *The High School We Need*. Washington: Association for Supervision and Curriculum Development, a Department of the National Education Association, 1959.

Appraising the learning accomplishments in the B-A class is a vital part of the teacher's work. Appraisal tells the students and the teacher how they are progressing toward their goals. It shows the learner the areas where he is weak, and it tells the teacher where he needs to improve his teaching. Evaluation is an educational feedback that determines behavioral changes necessary to improve learning.

The Responsibility in Evaluation

In evaluating the work of his students, the B-A teacher should recognize that he has a responsibility to each student, to parents, employers, society in general, and to himself.

To Each Student

Every student is entitled to help in understanding his strengths and weaknesses, his potentialities and limitations, and to the encouragement provided by knowing what direction to take for personal growth and development.

To Parents, Future Employers, and Society in General

Parents are educators, too, and appraisal of their children helps them direct home educational efforts. Employers want workers who will contribute to the efficiency of their organization, and a teacher's evaluation of a student is one indication of the potential efficiency of a future office worker. Evaluation in vocational preparation can also act as an accrediting function. It gives the stamp of approval from the educational institution to certain students planning to enter various vocations. In a broader sense, constant evaluation of students' work with resulting improvement of effort assures society that its members are growing.

To the Individual Teacher

How well pupils learn is one indication of how well they are being taught. A teacher discovers his own strengths and weaknesses by evaluating how well his pupils are learning and in what areas and by what means they are learning best.

In schools, evaluation has always been an assigned task. Teachers are called upon to give marks, write letters of recommendation, fill out employment rating forms, and give oral statements to prospective employers or parents. Recently educators have recognized the values of helping students appraise themselves, and self-evaluation techniques are being developed and improved.

The majority of B-A teachers probably report their evaluation in the traditional manner through the marks they give on report cards. The effectiveness of these marks is dependent on the teacher's purpose and point of view. Most teachers make a sincere effort to have marks reflect the best judgment possible, but there are some who use marks to punish or overpraise.

Basic Considerations for Appraising Students' Work

Evaluation is subject to a wide variety of opinion and controversy, but there are a few basic considerations that may help a B-A teacher improve evaluation, even within the bounds of a traditional marking system. They are as follows:

The Objectives of the Course Should Be Clear to Both the Teacher and the Students

Both teacher and students should have from early in the course a common understanding of the specific objectives toward which they are working. Both should also clearly understand that the purpose of evaluation is to measure growth toward these goals as opposed to "getting a mark."

The objectives of bookkeeping-accounting are discussed in detail in Chapter 3. It seems desirable, however, to emphasize here the need to evaluate students' achievements in the personal realm—ability to get along well with others, initiative, responsibility, neatness, punctuality, speed of work and the like—as well as the knowledge of subject matter.

The Students Should Know What Is Currently Being Appraised

Students should know what will be taken into account for arriving at a final grade—the concluding appraisal of how well they have achieved the objectives of the course.

The small day-to-day activities of the classroom—homework, tests, drills, practice sets, recitations—build up over the school year to accomplish the objectives of bookkeeping and accounting. These objectives are attained more effectively if the procedures of the evaluation process are clear—if students know how and for what purpose they are being evaluated each day or week. For example, if a test is to be given, the purpose of the test should be clear to the students. Testing becomes trickery if students are kept in the dark and simply told, "Tomorrow, a test." It becomes a device to get a mark rather than the learning experience it should be. Students should be informed about the objectives and methods of the test and the elements to be considered in marking—neatness, arithmetical accuracy, and knowledge of principles. Thus the test is an incentive for mastering certain knowledge and skills.

The Results of Appraisal Should Be Made Known
as Quickly as Possible

A knowledge of how well things are going is a strong motivation for improved effort on the part of both student and teacher. The value of knowing immediately whether a response is right or wrong is apparent in oral answers and in programmed instruction. (See Chapter 13.) When a student answers incorrectly in class, he knows at once. The correct response is usually arrived at quickly. Likewise, students using teaching machines and programmed instruction seem to work eagerly on the basis of finding out almost immediately whether or not their response is correct.

Unfortunately, teachers, being human beings, do not always provide immediate feedback of written work. If marking tests and evaluating projects is put off for days or weeks, the results may become meaningless. The mark on the paper then becomes the primary interest, the time lapse eliminating the value of knowing what errors were made. A teacher habitually late in marking papers is killing motivation for real learning that comes from immediate correction.

Knowing How Individual Students React to Appraisal Can Assist the Teacher in Future Appraising

For years psychologists have been saying that success and praise are incentives to effort. In the past they have said:

> "Success reinforces performance, releases further energy, and engenders favorable attitudes toward learning. Repeated failure, on the other hand, puts a drag on learning. Constant frustration discourages effort, gnaws viciously at interest, and begets indifference, resistance, or even severe inferiority." [1]

Modern psychologists are saying:

> ". . . success or hope of success nearly always increases interest and effort. This has importance beyond moment-to-moment motivation. One of the important objectives of education is to develop liking for learning so that the pupil will eagerly respond to opportunities for intellectual growth throughout his life. This, indeed, may be the greatest difference between the excellently educated man and the one who is merely trained. . . ." [2]

What implication do these facts have for the B-A teacher in the process of evaluation? Their practical application simply means that in class the habit should be established of commending what can be commended in a student's work and then indicating where improvement can take place; that the B-A problems done in class and assigned for homework should be within the scope and comprehension of the class so that success is assured; that the teacher be aware of individual differences and see to it that success is more often experienced than failure by most of the students by varying

[1] Arthur I. Gates, Arthur T. Jersild, T. R. McConnell, and Robert C. Challman, *Educational Psychology* (3d ed.; New York: The Macmillan Co., 1948), p. 381.

[2] Lee J. Cronbach, *Educational Psychology* (2d ed.; New York: Harcourt, Brace and World, Inc., 1963), p. 479.

the work to be done so that the least apt will be encouraged and the capable challenged and stimulated.

Testing in Bookkeeping

All B-A teachers are concerned with how well their pupils are learning bookkeeping-accounting and how well they are teaching. Beginning teachers are also particularly concerned with their speed of progress in teaching. "How fast shall I teach? How long shall I spend on adjusting entries? the journal? etc.?" The students supply answers to these legitimate teacher concerns in various ways: by the frequency and caliber of their oral responses in class, by their ability to perform classroom assignments, by their homework, by their ability to work out a practice set, by their attitude and show of interest. All such responses, and others, can help the teacher who is able to feel the pulse of the class and through these means tell the progress and condition of the "patient."

In general, however, most teachers feel more confident of analyzing student progress and more confident of the correctness in the grades they assign if they test their students more formally for their understanding and degree of achievement. This they do through the use of achievement tests. There are three kinds of achievement tests in bookkeeping-accounting.

Achievement Tests

1. Short-answer, objective tests. One common means of examining B-A students is through short-answer objective tests. Many such published tests are available. The ones teachers undoubtedly use most frequently are prepared to accompany the class textbook. They are supplied, usually at nominal or no cost, by the publishing company of the text. These tests are prepared for use following the class's coverage of certain sections of the textbook, usually every three or four chapters. Included in some test groups are special mid-term and final examinations as well as audit tests for practice sets the students have completed. (Practice set tests are discussed in Chapter 7.) It should be obvious that tests accompanying textbooks are geared to the material in the textbooks. They do not, therefore, test supplementary bookkeeping knowledge or skill that the teacher has taught from other sources.

Most teachers at some time or other prepare their own objective tests. Teachers who do this should be alert to and capable of practicing rules of good objective test construction. A summary of these techniques is found in "Testing and Evaluation in Business Education" by Hardaway. Chapters 3 and 4 are devoted to Construction of Tests for Classroom Use.[3] Also see Chapter 17 of this text for a discussion on testing students on the work sheet.

Some major advantages in using short-answer objective tests include:

(a) Good ones are readily available.
(b) They are easy and relatively quick to score.
(c) They lend themselves to objective scoring and grading rather than subjective teacher judgment or opinion.
(d) Students seem to prefer them to essay or other problem-type examinations.
(e) They are a quick way of testing much knowledge and understanding in a short time.

For these reasons, it is recommended that objective tests be used as one method of testing in bookkeeping and accounting. Teachers should realize that, although short-answer tests can be an excellent means for measuring student achievement in B-A knowledges, they usually do not fully test the student's skill. Nor do they show the student's achievement in applying his knowledge to specific practices and problems. Therefore, to secure a more accurate appraisal, the teacher must also use tests that measure ability to apply knowledge and understanding.

2. Problem-situation tests. In bookkeeping-accounting problem-situation tests measure not only the student's knowledge and understanding of B-A practices and principles, but they also test whether he has the skill and ability to apply what he knows—whether or not he can perform bookkeeping duties. An example of a problem-situation test in bookkeeping could be to supply the student with a list of the account balances of a particular firm (fictitious or otherwise) and information necessary for making the periodic adjustments and ask him to solve the problem of finding the net income or loss for the financial period.

A student who might be able on a short-answer, objective test to answer correctly all the questions about a work sheet and indicate

---

[3] Mathilde Hardaway, *Testing and Evaluation in Business Education* (3d ed.; Cincinnati: South-Western Publishing Co., 1966), pp. 77-134.

where amounts or certain accounts would appear, might be thousands of dollars in error if asked to complete the work sheet problem. Similarly, some students who might find the requirement of placing check marks in columns of the short-answer test on the work sheet a bit abstract for them, could work out a similar problem correctly when using real amounts for the various accounts. This is not to deny that a high correlation of success would be expected between students' successes on short-answer tests and their successes on problem situation tests. It is merely to claim that some students will show up to better advantage in one or the other, and that short-answer tests do not fully test B-A skill and the ability to apply B-A knowledge and principles. If this is true, teachers who restrict their achievement testing to the exclusive use of short-answer tests are not securing an accurate picture of student achievement in bookkeeping-accounting. Therefore, it is recommended that several types of achievement tests be used in the process of evaluation.

Some teachers do not include sufficient problem tests in their program because printed problem tests have not been available. Such a reason is indefensible. Since, however, at least one B-A textbook publisher has made available a series of printed problem tests along with objective tests, it is likely more students will be exposed to both types of tests.

3. Essay-type tests. The essay test is used less frequently in the B-A class than either the short-answer or problem test. While the short-answer test does measure comprehension, a better proof of knowledge is the students' ability to express meaning in their own words. For example, without an understanding of basic concepts, what student can answer the following question?

  (a) Explain the differences between the terms *income* and *cash*.
  (b) What is the relationship between the terms *liability, proprietorship*, and *equity?*
  (c) Explain the relationship between a manual payroll system and an automated data processing payroll system.

Essay-type tests are used less than short-answer and problem tests in part because it takes longer to correct them. Teachers who avoid using essay-type tests are cheating their students of the opportunity to practice organizing and expressing their thoughts.

In summary, a balanced testing program in bookkeeping and accounting demonstrates student *understanding* and *ability to perform*. Problem-situation tests as well as essay and short-answer objective tests are used in a balanced program. Because short-answer, objective tests (a) can test much understanding in a short time, and (b) are easy to score, their continued use needs no urging. But, to enrich and balance his testing program the teacher is urged to use problem tests and, occasionally at least, essay-type questions.

Comprehensive Tests

National business entrance tests. In a previous chapter the cooperation between the American Management Society and business education was mentioned. The National Business Entrance Tests [4] is one result of that cooperation. These tests are designed to fulfill the purpose indicated by the name—to measure the ability of students to work in an office.

The following excerpts are from a folder describing the tests:

> Tests in the Official Testing Series are available solely for administration at National Business Entrance Testing Centers, which could easily be your school. (Complete information about the Centers follows.) Testing Center sponsors usually administer tests in April, May, or June of each year; however, testing throughout the year is also possible. The costs for the tests in this series are:
>
> | | |
> |---|---|
> | Business Fundamentals and General Information .... | * |
> | Bookkeeping .... | $1.00 |
> | General Office Clerical .... | 1.25 |
> | Machine Calculation .... | 1.00 |
> | Stenography .... | 1.25 |
> | Typewriting .... | 1.00 |
>
> ---
>
> * One complimentary Business Fundamentals and General Information Test is furnished for each examinee taking one or more skill tests. Each examinee MUST take and pass this test to be eligible for a Proficiency Certificate.
>
> Included at no extra charge are the scoring, reporting, and consultation services; administrator's manual; prepaid delivery of tests to the Testing Center; and Proficiency Certificates for the students who pass the tests.

---

[4] *The National Business Entrance Tests* (Washington: United Business Education Association. Published by National Business Education, 1201 16th Street, N.W., Washington, D.C. 20036).

Certificates of Proficency are awarded to students who satisfactorily pass the tests. Certificates of Superior Proficiency are awarded to students who demonstrate outstanding achievement. These Certificates are recognized by hundreds of employers who give preference to their holders when selecting new employees.

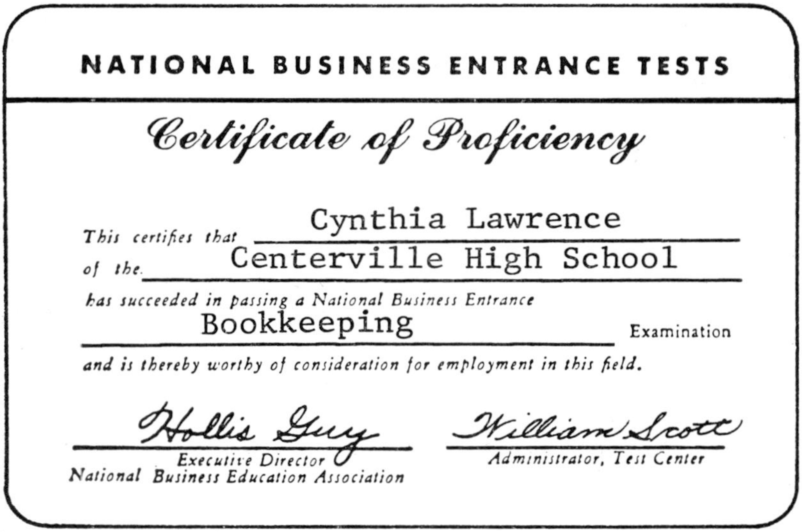

NATIONAL BUSINESS ENTRANCE TESTS

Certificate of Proficiency

This certifies that **Cynthia Lawrence**

of the **Centerville High School**

has succeeded in passing a National Business Entrance

Bookkeeping Examination

and is thereby worthy of consideration for employment in this field.

Hollis Guy
Executive Director
National Business Education Association

William Scott
Administrator, Test Center

Figure 10—1. Certificate of Proficiency

National Business Entrance Tests are prepared by testing specialists and business educators. Each test is reviewed by qualified office executives; in addition, the Joint Committee on Tests employs the services of a consultant who is a nationally recognized expert in test construction and measurement.

Students are tested for two hours. They are told just what will determine their score. The items included are: "(a) understanding of principles and practice, (b) ability to follow instructions, (c) neatness." The two-hour allotment of time is more than sufficient, and speed of work is credited by a bonus for each minute saved. Students are sometimes required to choose the right kind of paper from the materials supplied to them. The test is usually a series of practical B-A problems, and may include filling out forms, making various kinds of entries, reconciling bank statements, preparing financial statements, and locating errors.

Joint Committee on Tests

National Business Entrance Tests

Certificate of Superior Proficiency

David Kalter

having demonstrated proficiency in

Bookkeeping

is awarded this certificate in recognition
for outstanding achievement.

Ray Tauchert

Chairman of Test Center

Presented this __5th__ day of
__June__ 19 __70__

Figure 10—2. Certificate of Superior Proficiency

Mini-Problems for testing and review. As students proceed in the course, it becomes more difficult to test them within the time limit of one class period on anything but a segment or two of the bookkeeping cycle. However, at times there is a need for testing the students' understanding and ability to perform several or all of the steps in the cycle.

One way of doing this is to give students teacher-prepared mini-problems. These are simplified problems which require a basic understanding of principles and an ability to apply the principles. For example, the following type mini-problem could be given to review and test all the steps in the B-A cycle.

Example No. 1

MINI-PROBLEM

The Complete B-A Cycle

Bell Realty Agency's transactions for the month of July are listed below:

July 1. Bill Bell invested the following in his new real estate business: Cash, $2,000; Office Equipment, $500.

1. Paid cash, $175, for July rent.

31. Purchased new typewriter on account from Allen Equipment Company, $350.

31. Paid cash, $25, for utilities bill.

31. Received cash, $800, for commission earned during July.

Instructions:

1. Record the transactions. Use a two-column general Journal. Omit explanations.
2. Post the journal. Use skeleton T accounts. Omit dates and posting references.
3. Prepare a trial balance. Use six-column work sheet paper.
4. Complete the work sheet.
5. Prepare (a) an income statement, and (b) a balance sheet.
6. (a) Record and post the closing entries; (b) balance and rule accounts, (c) prepare a post-closing trial balance.

The complete solution for this problem is shown on pages 262 and 263.

SOLUTION TO MINI-PROBLEM (EXAMPLE No. 1)

Circled Numbers Refer to Instructions' Numbers

(1) Journal

Date	General Journal	Debit	Credit
19— July 1	Cash	2,000	
	Office Equipment	500	
	Bill Bell, Cap.		2,500
1	Rent Expense	175	
	Cash		175
2	Office Equipment	350	
	Allen Equip. Co.		350
31	Utilities Expense	25	
	Cash		25
31	Cash	800	
	Commissions Income		800
	Closing Entries		
31	Commissions Income	800	
	Income & Exp. Summ.		800
31	Income & Exp. Summ.	200	
	Rent Expense		175
	Utilities Expense		25
31	Income & Exp. Summ.	600	
	Bill Bell, Cap.		600

(2), (6a), & (6b) General Ledger

Cash   11

2,000	175
800	25
2,600 *2,800* 2,800	Bal. 2,600
Bal. 2,600	2,800

Office Equip.   12

500	
350	
850	

Allen Equip. Co.   21

	350

Bill Bell, Cap.   31

	2,500
	600
	3,100

Income & Exp. Sum.   32

200	800
600	
800	

Commissions Income   41

800	800

Rent Expense   52

175	175

Utilities Expense   52

25	25

SOLUTION TO MINI-PROBLEM (EXAMPLE No. 1) (Continued)

Circled Numbers Refer to Instructions' Numbers

③ & ④

Bill Bell
Work Sheet
For Month Ended, July 31, 19—

Account Titles	Trial Balance Dr.	Cr.	Income State Dr.	Cr.	Bal. Sheet Dr.	Cr.
Cash	2,600				2,600	
Office Equip.	850				850	
Allen Equip. Co.		350				350
B. Bell, Cap.		2,500				2,500
Comm. Income		800		800		
Rent Expense	175		175			
Utilities Exp.	25		25			
	3,650	3,650	200	800	3,450	2,850
Net Income			600			600
			800	800	3,450	3,450

⑤b

Bill Bell
Balance Sheet
July 31, 19—

Assets		*Liabilities*	
Cash	2,600	Allen. Equip. Co.	350
Off. Equip.	850	*Capital*	
		Bill Bell, Cap.	3,100
Total Assets	3,450	Total Liab. & Cap.	3,450

⑥c

Bill Bell
Post-Closing Trial Balance
July 31, 19—

Cash	2,600	
Office Equipment	850	
Allen Equipment Co.		350
Bill Bell, Cap.		3,100
	3,450	3,450

⑤a

Bill Bell
Income Statement
For Month Ended, July 31, 19—

Income:		
Commissions Income		800
Expenses:		
Rent Expense	175	
Utilities Expense	25	
Total Expenses		200
Net Income		600

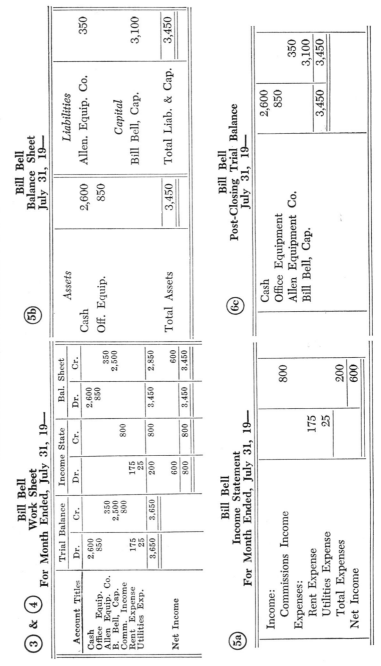

When students are assigned mini-problems, some tend to short-cut details and omit dates and posting references. A teacher's reaction to this is conditioned by his philosophy and objective in using the problems. Some teachers require dates and posting references and should so direct their students. Others are not concerned with details, particularly if the problem is a review assignment rather than a test. Still others direct their students to save time by eliminating repetitive practices that the students have already proved they know. In any case, teachers can easily condition students to their requirements and objectives.

The use of mini-problems supply a change of pace for students and teachers. They can be used as:

1. A pretest prior to a review.
2. A test or spot quiz.
3. A quick means of review.

Mini-problems prove especially useful when a school operating under a modular scheduling system assigns 15, 20, or 25-minute B-A modules. (See pages 342-345.)

Mini-problems challenging different levels of ability are easily constructed. They readily lend themselves to variation and change. For example, consider the following:

Example No. 2

MINI-PROBLEM

The transactions of the Four-Corner Service Station for the month of June are listed below:

June 1. Art Link invested $1,800 in cash in the Four-Corner Service Station.
2. Paid cash, $200, for June rent.
2. Paid cash, $500, for first shipment of gas to be marketed.
3. Purchased equipment on account from Carter Supply Company, $240.
15. Paid cash, $450, for second shipment of gas to be marketed.
29. Paid cash, $20, for utility bill.
30. The gas tank was empty and the cash register showed cash sales for the month totaled $1,500.

Some possibilities for varying the difficulty of this problem are as follows:

1. Use the same instructions as given for Example No. 1.
2. Eliminate the instructions for journalizing. Tell students to record the transactions directly into the T accounts.
3. Change the information in the June 30 transaction to show that $100 worth of gas remains in the tank—thus requiring (a) an eight-column work sheet, (b) an adjustment on the work sheet, and (c) an adjusting entry.
4. In addition to Suggestion #3 above, supply information calling for an adjustment of the equipment account.

Frequency of Testing

How often should tests be given in bookkeeping? Frequent tests seem to contribute most to learning. The teacher should keep in mind that tests are an integral part of his teaching program. Tests motivate the class to study. A controlled and wise use of this motivating power can increase the learning of a class. Testing everyday would quickly cause loss of motivating power, while testing only once a semester would have the same effect.

The frequency of tests should be related to the completion of a unit of work or the presentation of a basic concept. A test is given to measure a group's readiness to pass on to the next segment of learning. Testing every Friday regardless of class progress during the week is not an educationally sound practice. Frequent tests have value for weaker students since they help evaluate their efforts and strengthen their weaknesses before they get too far behind, and the rewards of good marks on frequent tests are encouraging to good students, too.

Surprise tests are not productive. They are a form of punishment to students. One psychologist states, "The results so far suggest that at the end of the term, the students working under a system of surprise tests learn less than those who know in adavnce when the test is to occur." [5]

In their position of classroom authority some teachers may easily and unconsciously slip into the attitude that tests and grades

---

[5] John M. Stephens, *The Psychology of Classroom Learning*, (New York: Holt, Rinehart and Winston, Inc., 1966), p. 87.

are their ultimate control over the actions of the class. This disciplinary point of view negates learning potentialities of tests. A superior teacher's point of view is expressed by Cronbach in concluding his comments on testing: "To summarize, tests motivate and direct learning by providing short range goals, by reducing broad objectives to definite aims, and by rewarding goods tries."[6]

Scoring and Grading Tests

A score is the number of points earned on the test. For example, on a test containing 70 true or false questions, if a student answered 55 correctly and each question was valued at one point, his score would be 55. Scoring a test can be done objectively.

Grades are symbols indicating the evaluation placed on the test work. Arriving at a grade necessitates judgment—teacher opinion. Grades are subject to inaccuracies resulting from the bias of the teacher, faults in the construction or directions of the tests, and the misuse of statistics. Grades have always been subject to human error and foible and probably always will be.

The B-A teacher should make every effort to improve his construction and his grading of tests. He can do this through experience, by reading the latest references, or by taking an educational course in this area. The following discussion gives the minimum essentials in scoring and grading and a starting place for the beginning teacher.

The starting point is to know the grading system of the school. Schools generally state their grades in numerals, zero to 100, or as letters, A, B, C, D, and F. One school considers 70 a passing grade; but in the next county 75 is the cutoff point for repeating a course. A "D" grade in one school requires a student to repeat the course; in another it is the lowest passable grade. Knowing the meaning of the grades starts building some concepts in the mind of the teacher.

One excellent list of criteria for defining letter grades is supplied by Schwartz and Tiedeman: [7]

---

[6] *Cronbach*, op. cit., p. 545.
[7] Alfred Schwartz and Stuart C. Tiedeman, *Evaluating Student Progress in the Secondary School* (New York: David McKay Company, Inc., 1957), pp. 393-394.

CRITERIA FOR DEFINING LETTER GRADES

The grade of A means
1. Objectives of the course are achieved.
2. Instructor has no reservations about the student's level of achievement.
3. Student is prepared for high-quality advanced work in the field.
4. Student is highly competent in the application of his learning in practical situations.

The grade of B means
1. Objectives of the course are achieved.
2. Instructor has minor reservations about the student's level of achievement.
3. Student is prepared for above-average quality of advanced work in the field.
4. Student is competent in application of his learning in practical situations.

The grade of C means
1. Objectives of the course achieved at a level which the instructor regards as minimum preparation for advanced work in the field.
   and/or
2. Student has average ability to apply his learning to practical situations.

The grade of D means
1. Objectives of the course achieved at a level which the instructor regards as submarginal as preparation for advanced work in the field.
   and/or
2. Student has low ability to apply his learning appropriately in practical situations and little learning to apply.

The grade of F means
1. Objectives of the course not achieved at a level which the instructor regards as the minimum preparation for advanced work in the field, i.e., the student should repeat the course if he plans to take further work.
   and/or
2. The student has not shown any significant learning from the course.
   or
3. The student has failed to complete the course without prearranging with his instructor for an incomplete.
   or
4. The student withdrew from the course after the last date for dropping a course.

Scoring and Grading Short-Answer, Objective Tests

Objective tests (true-false, multiple-choice, matching) are easy to score. In computer-equipped schools these tests can be scored for an entire class in minutes. The most work that objective tests can involve is laying a key beside the student's answers and comparing the student's paper with the key. The score is computed by adding up the number right, deducting a penalty for each error, subtracting the total of wrong answers from the total of right answers, or whatever way of scoring is decided upon.

Converting the score into a grade is the procedure that poses the problem. The answer to this problem depends on the teacher: his judgment as to what score constitutes an "average," "excellent," or "failing" performance on the test; his sense of fairness; his experience in previous tests; his comprehension of class differences each year; his awareness that the membership of some classes is highly selective and therefore not likely to follow a normal distribution of high and low grades.

If fixed standards are available, grades can be assigned relative to these. A teacher who has kept records for many previous classes, and has reasonable assurance that the standards fit most classes, can determine ahead of time what score equals each grade. Some city systems, textbook tests, and national testing programs have standards developed for specific tests.

Grading "on the curve"—applying the percentage distribution of the statistical normal curve—is a common procedure. This procedure is satisfactory if the test is proven valid and if distribution of ability in the class is normal. If there is any evidence distribution is not normal, humane adjustment must be made. One does not fail the lower percentage of *every* class just to accommodate the curve. In a highly selected group, it is conceivable that everyone could receive A's or B's.

Ways of Scoring Problem-Situation Tests

Scoring problem-situation tests is not as simple as scoring short-answer tests. However, objectivity can be reached through the use of a point-scoring technique. This centers around a master guide or key containing a list of penalties for various types of errors. The simplest type of point-scoring is a one-point deduction for each error. For example, if there were 186 possible errors on an assigned work-sheet problem and the student made 20 errors, his score would be 166.

Some teachers object to this method because certain errors deserve larger penalties. They point out that, if this method is followed, a student making a simple error in the transposition of numbers could have other errors that were merely a product of his first, original error. Thus he is penalized several times for his original error. Therefore, rules have evolved to improve on the system and at the same time to keep it objective.

Some teachers deduct only once for any one error regardless of how many subsequent errors are its direct product. Others give varying penalties to different errors. For example, one point may be deducted for an error in simple addition or subtraction; two points for the wrong account name or charging the amount to the wrong account; three points for another type of error; and so on, maybe up to ten points off for lack of neatness. Other suggestions prescribe decimal or fractional point-scoring of particular errors. An example of how complicated point-scoring can become is the multipage instruction booklet from the New York State Regents telling exactly how many points should be deducted for each type of error on the statewide Regents examination.

The price of objectivity in point-scoring is the feeling that the whole problem is not completely evaluated. Students and teachers get so bogged down in the details of the points that the major purpose of the problem is neglected.

If detailed analysis is used as a diagnostic procedure when presented to the students, it may have merit. A list of the details being penalized show both students and teachers the persistent errors, and evaluation can lead the pupil to practice for self-improvement.

Another evaluation process focuses on a sense of achievement not just on details. A record is kept of the number of problems correctly completed over a given period of instruction. These problems may be completed in class, on tests, or for homework. All problems incorrectly completed must be corrected. At the end of the instructional period, students having the largest number of initially correct solutions are awarded the high ratings, and those with only a few receive low ratings. If the teacher desires more weight be given certain problems, such as those on tests or particularly difficult homework assignments, he may increase their value to two or three instead of one. Thus if a student correctly completes four test problems valued twice as high as homework problems, he receives a score of eight for that test. A record of students' accomplishments kept over several semesters establishes minimum standards.

This procedure emphasizes the completed problems as business emphasizes completed records, and what constitutes an acceptable solution is important too. Accuracy of results, correctness of method, and neatness of appearance are basic requirements.

Because good work is recognized and rewarded, this method encourages the good student to do more. The slower student is less discouraged since his good work is recognized, and minimum standards assure his successful completion of the course.

Scoring and Grading Essay Tests

The first step in scoring an essay test is the preparation by the teacher of a written outline of necessary points to be covered in each complete answer. With this as a guiding checklist, four suggestions made by Ahmann and Glock listed below [8] will help teachers in securing a desirable degree of fairness in estimating achievement.

1. Score the pupils' responses anonymously. (Unfortunately, teachers, being human, tend to let the personalities of students affect them, and thus tend to give higher grades to well-behaved people, people they like personally, and those students who have already gotten high grades. Conversely, the weaker students and the less personable ones receive lower estimates of their ability. Numbers assigned to students' names can be substituted on the examination papers to avoid marking the name rather than the paper.)
2. Score all responses to each test item at one time.
3. Score penmanship, neatness, grammar, spelling, etc., independently of subject matter.
4. If possible, have another person score the responses independently. If not, do them a second time yourself. (The second reading often points up items the teacher missed the first time.)

The final grade on an essay test can be based on the points the teacher thinks necessary for completed answers, or it may be an A to F grade determined by the impression of the total paper. Obviously the former procedure seems fairer. As already pointed out, teachers are prone to give higher ratings to students who previously made good marks while assuming students with previoursly low grades could not possibly turn in good papers.

---

[8] J. Stanley Ahmann and Marvin D. Glock, *Evaluating Pupil Growth* (2nd ed.; Boston: Allyn and Bacon, Inc., 1963), p. 183.

Converting scores to grades is in the hands of the individual teacher and is dependent on his inherent sense of fairness, his knowledge of possible procedures, and his ordinary common sense.

Appraising Non-Subject Matter Traits

It has already been pointed out that part of a bookkeeper or accounting clerk's stock in trade is personal behavior characteristics, and through methods of teaching it is possible to develop these desirable traits. An estimate of achievement in the growth of desirable behavior calls largely for subjective judgment. The simplest way to judge improvement is to list the characteristics students are endeavoring to improve and then assign a rating to indicate the degree of improvement.

This area provides a place to develop pupil self-evaluation. A self-rating form may be completed by the pupils. The individual student may then confer with the teacher for a comparison with the teacher's ratings. During the comparison, the whys and wherefores of the ratings of both the teacher and the student should be discussed. This teacher-student exchange can be a real growing experience for the student and a clarifying one for the teacher.

Rating Form

A rating form evaluating personal behavior might include the following items:

1. Neatness of work
2. Legibility of handwriting
3. Oral contributions in class
4. Getting along with class members
5. Punctuality
6. Initiative
7. Cooperation
8. Ability to follow instructions
9. Personal appearance

Three or five classes or groups may be used in rating students. Evaluation may be in the form of a simple 1 to 5 indication, or letters A, B, C, D, E, or such words as "excellent," "good," "fair," and "poor." Space can be provided for the students' reasons why they did or did not give themselves a top rating. Self-evaluation has obvious advantages and is a rich learning experience for both students and teacher.

Standards of Production

Specific standards of production are found in individual businesses. In large offices where the bookkeeping and accounting processes are broken down into small segments that can be routinely performed, the amount of work completed in a time period is measured and standards of production established.

B-A standards are sometimes expressed in the number of postings per hour, and commonly refer to machine postings. No widespread agreement has been reached by business justifying a particular rate of B-A production as a school standard.

It is obvious that, if specific standards of production in accounting and bookkeeping skills are desired for a classroom, the teacher and the students will have to establish them cooperatively —and that is as it should be. The whole area of standards is needful of study, and it is a rich field for experimentation.

Conclusion

The teacher can end his cycle of teaching by asking, "What has come of all the marks I gave? What good have they done? What purpose have they served?" The answers to these questions lead to the realization that marks in and of themselves are sterile, end-of-road things.

A mark alone does not tell the student how to do better or aid in further learning; it does not regard the student as a person needing to know what to do. The computer age has depersonalized students to the point where the records show a name, a number, and grades.

The B-A teacher can help counteract this effect of the computer age by writing on tests and other papers a comment on something well done, a notation of ways to improve, or words such as *Good, Well Expressed, Much Better Than Last Time.* This helps evaluation become a human process leading students forward to higher degrees of learning.

STUDY QUESTIONS

1. What three responsibilities should the B-A teacher recognize in evaluating his students?

2. By what other ways than by giving grades or marks are teachers called upon to express an evaluation of their students?

3. Why should the objectives of a bookkeeping and accounting course have a bearing on the evaluation of the students in that course?

4. Why should students know what traits and performances of theirs are to be evaluated?

5. Why is it important for teachers to mark and return tests promptly?

6. By what various means do teachers determine how well their pupils are learning?

7. What are the advantages of using short-answer, objective tests?

8. Why should short-answer, objective tests not be used exclusively?

9. What does the problem-situation test usually measure better than does the short-answer, objective test? Why?

10. Why are essay tests used less frequently than short-answer tests?

11. What is the value of giving tests frequently?

12. What is the difference between a score and a grade on a test?

13. What means or techniques have been developed to score problem-situation bookkeeping and accounting tests as objectively and fairly as the short-answer tests?

14. What are some procedures for scoring essay questions fairly?

15. What are the National Business Entrance Tests? their purpose? their use? Who constructs them?

16. What personal traits or characteristics should be included in an evaluation program? Why?

17. Why is it difficult for teachers to acquire acceptable standards of bookkeeping and accounting production from business?

18. If teachers cannot secure acceptable standards of production from business, how can they arrive at acceptable standards for classroom use in measuring their students?

19. What, aside from a score or grade, should teachers write on pupils' tests and homework papers?

DISCUSSION QUESTIONS

1. Does the belief that, "Marks and other statements of evaluation should have a desirable effect on students," imply that a student should never be failed? Explain your answer.

2. Contrast the relative importance of evaluating technical ability with character traits essential to vocational success in an office.

3. A bookkeeper was once heard to remark, "I have to be 100% accurate with my records—not 90% or 75%. Yet while studying bookkeeping in high school I was praised for my grade of 85. There's something wrong here!" What implications do these remarks hold for the teacher?

4. Why should methods of evaluation vary from class to class? Illustrate.

5. Who should set standards for the bookkeeping and accounting class? How can they be established?

6. How and when should the minimum standards of achievement be made known to a class?

7. When should a student be failed in bookkeeping and accounting? How much consideration should be given to low I. Q., low interest level, social handicaps, etc.?

8. Should an outstanding student be denied an "A" in the course just because he does not write legibly?

9. What kind of test best measures bookkeeping and accounting learning?

10. What should the teacher do if everyone in a class does poorly on a test?

11. How frequently should short quizzes and period-long examinations be given?

12. How much weight should be given to (a) practice sets and to (b) homework in determining a student's final grade?

PROJECTS

1. Prepare a paper, based on sound principles of educational evaluation, that shows an ideal plan for arriving at the final grades of high school B-A students.

2. Prepare some short-answer, objective tests and some problem tests indicating the basic principles of test construction that you applied. Under certain circumstances, students performing this project could be asked to validate their tests.

3. Prepare a half-dozen essay examinations for use at different stages in (a) the first-year B-A course, (b) the second-year B-A course.

4. Prepare two essay questions for each of the first ten chapters of a modern high school B-A textbook.

5. Prepare a problem-type test on a topic of your choice to be given in a 45-minute class period. Explain the point-scoring system you would use for arriving at the grades.

6. Prepare mini-problems for testing the students' understanding and ability to perform:
   (a) Journalizing and posting
   (b) The preparing of work sheets, income statements, and balance sheets
   (c) All of the steps in the B-A cycle
   (d) Adjusting entries
   (e) Reversing entries

7. Prepare an objective test measuring students' understanding of a practice set they are working on or have just completed.

8. Prepare a paper on ideal procedures for evaluating classroom *behavior* only.

9. Prepare a paper on ideal procedures for evaluating student understanding, ability, and progress with the subject matter only.

10. Describe a B-A class with which you are familiar and list all the methods of evaluation that are used or could be used.

SELECTED REFERENCES

Ahmann, J. Stanley, and Marvin D. Glock. *Evaluating Pupil Growth*, 2d ed. Boston: Allyn and Bacon, Inc., 1963.

Boggs, Lohnie J. "Problem Testing in Bookkeeping: Some Guidelines," *Business Education Forum*. XVIII (December, 1963), 7-8.

Boynton, Lewis D. "Speed Standards in Bookkeeping," *The Balance Sheet*. XL (December, 1958), 160-161.

Cronbach, Lee J. *Educational Psychology*, 2d ed. New York: Harcourt, Brace and World, Inc., 1963.

Dryzga, Dennis E. "Evaluation of Bookkeeping Students," *The Balance Sheet*. XLIX (January, 1968), 204-205.

Ebel, Robert. *Measuring Educational Achievement*. Englewood Cliffs, New Jersey: Prentice-Hall, Inc., 1965.

"Evaluation of Pupil Progress in Business Education," *American Business Education Yearbook*, Vol. 17. New York: New York University Bookstore, 1960.

Forkner, Hamden. "Setting Realistic Standards in Vocational Bookkeeping," *Business Education Forum*. XX (May, 1966), 8-10, 13.

Garrison, Lloyd L. "Assessing Evaluation Techniques," *Developing Vocational Competency in Bookkeeping and Accounting,* Eastern Business Teachers Association Yearbook, Vol. 40, Chapter 15. New York: New York University Bookstore, 1967.

――――――. "Bookkeeping and Accounting," *The American Business Education Yearbook,* Vol. 17, Chapter 12. New York: New York University Bookstore, 1960.

Gates, Arthur I., Arthur T. Jersild, T. R. McConnell, and Robert C. Challman. Educational Psychology, Third Edition, New York: The Macmillan Company, 1948.

Hardaway, Mathilde. "Bookkeeping and Accounting," *Testing and Evaluation in Business Education,* Third Edition, Chapter 7. Cincinnati: South-Western Publishing Company, 1966.

Herman, David O. "Test Know-How for the Schools—1. Why Use Achievement Tests," *Business Education World.* XLIX (September, 1968), 11-12, 26.

――――――. "Test Know-How for the Schools—2. How Achievement Tests Are Made," *Business Education World.* XLIX (October, 1968), 22-25.

Langemo, Mark, and Gary Frandson. "Simplify Your Testing and Grading in Bookkeeping," *The Balance Sheet.* XLIX (November, 1967), 103-106.

Martineau, Errol James. "Bookkeeping Grading Folders," *The Balance Sheet.* XLVIII (May, 1967), 395-397.

"The National Business Entrance Tests," *Selected Readings in Business and Office Occupations—Designed Especially for the Classroom Teacher,* National Business Education Yearbook, No. 5. Washington: National Business Education Association, 1967.

Satlow, I. David. "Do's and Don'ts of Evaluation, Part I," *The Journal of Business Education.* XLII (April, 1967), 274-276.

――――――. "Do's and Dont's of Evaluation, Part II," *The Journal of Business Education.* XLII (May, 1967), 322-323.

Stephens, John M. *The Psychology of Classroom Learning.* New York: Holt, Rinehart and Winston, Inc., 1966.

Sydor, Alexandria. " 'Quickie' Quizzes for First Semester Bookkeeping," *The Journal of Business Education.* XXXIV (April, 1959), 287-289.

Thompson, Robert J. "Essay Testing of Business Information Related to Bookkeeping," *Business Education Forum.* XVIII (December, 1963), 11-12.

Travers, Robert M. W. *How to Make Achievement Tests.* New York: Odyssey Press, 1950.

The purpose of research is discovery—discovery of what the past has to teach; discovery of what is going on in the present; discovery of new trends, new ideas, new frontiers, new ways of doing things so that the future is better than the past.

The Meaning of Research

The word "research" through casual everyday use has lost its precise meaning. Second graders speak proudly of the minutes they spend looking for "Indians" in a big book as "research." High school students "do" research for several hours to get material for an English theme. Doctoral candidates measure their research time by the years it takes to complete a dissertation. Space scientists and medical researchers devote a lifetime to the discovery of new elements of life, new worlds, new instruments to combat disease. Thus it is evident that research means many things to many people.[1]

Research and the Bookkeeping-Accounting Teacher

What does research mean to the B-A teacher? A B-A teacher faces a problem which can be solved only through thorough study and experimentation. Or, he is a candidate for a master's or doctor's degree and is required to solve a problem using certain specific procedures. Or, he has a broader vision and wishes to contribute basic improvements to national and international

---

[1] Some of this chapter is based on Chapter 11, "Research in Bookkeeping," written by the author for the 1961 Yearbook of the Eastern Business Teachers Association.

bookkeeping-accounting and its teaching. This desire leads him to work in an organization whose objective is to raise the whole level of endeavor in both education and business through widespread study and research.

So the B-A teacher can meet research on three levels—informally in his classroom; at a graduate-collegiate level, with formal controls to meet institutional and degree requirements; and with a nation-wide organization or foundation devoted to basic research.

Action Research

Since bookkeeping-accounting is designed for practical and immediate application to both personal and vocational lives, it is important that what is taught is sound, current, and useful. How can one be certain that what he is teaching is understandable and useful to the student? What kind of research is most applicable to the discovery of truth? What kind of research is most useful to a classroom teacher?

The informal classroom study or experimentation by which teachers seek to improve their instruction is called "action research." Stephen Corey describes it thus:

> It is the argument of this Yearbook that whatever can be done to increase the quality of the attempts classroom teachers make to improve themselves results in activities that take on more and more of the characteristics of educational research. To the degree these attempts to improve become research oriented the chances are increased that the changes brought about in teaching procedures represent improvement as well.
>
> This kind of informal research or experimentation is often called "action research." The difference between it and the better-known kind of educational research is that *action research is undertaken by practitioners in order to improve their own practices.* The more conventional kind of research in education is conducted by experts with the expectation that the publication or dissemination by other means of their findings will cause *other people* to improve.[2]

The B-A teacher is in a unique and strategic position. When he seeks to improve his teaching, he can contribute a great deal

---

[2] Corey, Stephen M., "Research as a Methods of Self-Improvement," *Informal Research by the Classroom Business Teacher,* The American Business Education Yearbook (New York: New York University Bookstore, 1961), Vol. 18, pp. 11, 12.

to study and research in the B-A field, and do it as part of his daily work, not as an added time-consuming burden.

There was a time when research in business education was done by a select few, primarily doctoral candidates. But today it seems that doctoral students are economically unable to conduct comprehensive studies that take years to complete. Jobs are waiting, degrees must be had, and so doctoral studies are chosen, in part, on the basis of readily available data and the speed with which they can be utilized. Also, the results of formal doctoral studies just do not seem to get back to the teachers in the classrooms. The lines of communication are poor.

So the teacher in the classroom holds the key to real action study and basic research through seeking to improve his own work. How can this be done without a burdensome addition to an already full schedule?

The Teacher Begins with Well-Planned Records

A good place to start is by establishing easy-to-keep, easy-to-use, permanent records of what is done, what is used, and what the pupils achieve. Of all the teachers in a school, the B-A teacher should be especially appreciative of this need for simple, basic, continuing records. A businessman depends upon his records to show the direction toward successful operation of a business. Likewise the teacher needs records to guide the direction of his work and eventually to show the educational profit achieved.

Well-planned records take less time and are much easier on the nerves than a hodgepodge collection. They are also effective in making administrative reports and requests. A beginning teacher can easily keep records as good as experienced teachers, and such records can also be invaluable to curriculum builders, guidance counselors, and research workers.

Simple Records for Informal Daily Evaluation

The least a teacher can do to improve his teaching is to write simple notes on prepared lesson plans, tests, or other material telling what was good and what was not good. Then in another year unsuccessful procedures can be eliminated. When a businessman studying his records sees a department or a product not doing well, he finds out why and does something about it. So it should be in education.

If a test is given to measure success of teaching, the following questions should be answered.

1. What questions were commonly missed by the group?
2. Were those questions poorly stated or was the particular area poorly taught?
3. How can the teaching of this area be improved?
4. If the results were good, can this area be covered more rapidly in the future?
5. Were there certain individuals who did unsatisfactory work? Why?
6. Was there something wrong with the pupils, with the teaching, or with the test?

The same kind of questions can also be asked after presentation of new subject matter, audio-visual materials, work experience projects, and so on. The answers should be recorded for next year's class. Notes on the copies of the test, in the teacher's textbook, on lesson plans, or on a special evaluation form will change the teaching for the better the next time around.

This informal analysis is truly called *study.* When one goes deeply into a study, sets up control classes, constructs special tests, analyzes the scores, compares with other groups, and reports in a certain academic form, he is doing research. The typical teacher does not have time for specialized research. His interest is in the simple, informal study of his daily work to direct his action more effectively. However, he can still contribute to basic research by making his records available to research workers.

Records for Yearly Evaluation

Even though the businessman records transactions daily, there comes a time when a summary of all transactions and an analysis of their results is necessary. A balance sheet and income statement must be compiled to determine if the business is being operated profitably. The B-A teacher should do the same.

Almost every teacher has some record of what is done in his classes. These records range from detailed daily lesson plans, to course syllabi or the table of contents in the textbook. But most of them cannot be compared with what happened this time last year, what is to happen next year or five years from now; and it is comparison that shows how much progress is occurring.

The businessman figures his financial progress by preparing an income statement at the end of a day, week, month, year, or whatever time he wants. But the educator can work best in time units of years. He must discover how this year's class compares with last year's class in the amount of material covered, test scores, or employment.

Since all of us are conditioned by our modern way of life to want quick and immediate results, long-term records are sometimes hard to put into practice. But the teacher who recognizes his unique opportunity to accumulate helpful information will have the patience and vision to do his daily work so that it develops into a real contribution to business education.

A Record of Subject Matter Covered

In recording what is taught in class, a five-year form is desirable. Since the purpose of the form is to compare what is taught, the recording should be weekly units. Notations are made of textbook and supplementary materials covered, audio-visual materials used, tests given, work experience units used, and so on. Below is an example that could be drawn up on analysis paper:

BOOKKEEPING I

Week	1970-71	1971-72	1972-73	1973-74	1974-75
1 Textbook pages	——	——	——	——	——
Supplementary material used	——	——	——	——	——
Audio-visual aids used	——	——	——	——	——
Tests given	——	——	——	——	——
Teacher remarks	——	——	——	——	——
2 Textbook pages	——	——	——	——	——
Supplementary material used	——	——	——	——	——
Audio-visual aids used	——	——	——	——	——
Tests given	——	——	——	——	——
Teacher remarks	——	——	——	——	——
3 Textbook pages	——	——	——	——	——
Supplementary material used	——	——	——	——	——
Audio-visual aids used	——	——	——	——	——
Tests given	——	——	——	——	——
Teacher remarks	——	——	——	——	——

A code next to each item gives a quick indication of the value the teacher places on the materials. For example, using the numbers 1, 2, and 3, *one* placed after an item would indicate that it was excellent and should be used again; *two*, that the item had only fair value; and *three*, that the educational value was low or nil.

After a desirable form is developed, it would take only a few minutes a week to complete. Beginning with the second year, a picture of accomplishment would begin to develop. This picture together with records of student achievement encourages effort to equal, if not exceed, what has been done before. Thus study of what has been done gives impetus to try to improve.

Think of the unique contribution to vital research B-A teachers could offer if such records were kept by all the B-A teachers in one school, one city, or one state.

A Pupil-Information Record

A second useful form gives personal information and summarizes each pupil's achievement. This record need not increase the work of the teacher since it can be handled almost completely by the pupils.

A large card with one side for personal information and the other for achievement records will serve the purpose here. On the first day of class, the pupils can fill in the personal information. The cards can be arranged alphabetically by pupils during class. Quick examination of the cards gives the teacher immediate insight into the nature of the class group and a rough assessment of handwriting ability. Even in schools where the teacher knows his pupils well, having the information in writing makes it available to others and thus its value is shared.

An inexperienced teacher will find this a good procedure for the first moments of class. Any teacher obtaining this record the first day will find the class impressed by the businesslike methods of the B-A teacher.

The personal student information is useful in improving teaching and assisting research work. The forms vary according to the needs of the teacher. Listed below are items which appear on most forms and suggestions as to how the information may be used.

THE ITEM	ITS USE
Name Age	Study age range of those taking bookkeeping-accounting and relate to subsequent success.
Business subjects taken prior to this course	Study relationship between achievement in bookkeeping-accounting and achievement in business courses already completed. The results should be valuable in planning curriculum revision.
Other subjects taken this semester	This is useful to know if a student is having difficulty in his work. The teacher may also see ways to relate bookkeeping-accounting to other courses being taken, such as office machines, economics, and business law.
Membership in school clubs	The teacher may be able to refer to B-A activities in club work. For example, a simple question directed to a club member about receipts for club dues helps the entire class relate bookkeeping-accounting to their own experiences and gives a new zest to study. In-school work experience projects might be developed—keeping the records for school play productions, ticket sales, and cafeteria management.
Membership in out-of-school organizations	Similar to preceding.
Part-time employment —kind of work, place of work	Wherever possible relate the work in class to the experience of the students. Make a list of places where students are employed during their school years or after graduation. Use this list as a starting point in a study of bookkeeping-accounting practices in the community. Develop a student project with part-time workers to study business practices in the community.
After-graduation employment or college work	This information could be secured by the succeeding class. It opens the way to follow-up studies of teaching effectiveness and the success of students on the job. It is also useful in establishing a student placement file.

These items are suggestive and are not all inclusive.* Qualities of a good personal record form are simplicity, directness, and usefulness. Do not accumulate information for the sake of collecting, but cut ruthlessly anything which cannot or will not be used. Easily established and maintained, these records are ever after available for improving teaching and providing information for study.

Summary Record of Achievement in Bookkeeping-Accounting

A teacher has not completed his work until the student is on his way to placement in an office job. In many of the smaller

---

* An example of a comprehensive student information form is shown on page 236 of Chapter 9.

communities businessmen turn to the teacher for workers. In the large city, the school placement officers turn to the teacher. The teacher holds the key to successful job placement and, therefore, needs summary records for each reference.

An individual achievement form maintained on the reverse side of the personal-use record gives a permanent reference for job recommendations, and it also provides information necessary to summarize the group's achievements. This form includes:

1. Final semester grade in the subject.
2. Scores on National Business Entrance Tests and on city and state examinations.
3. The teacher's personal evaluation of the student's strengths and weaknesses. (Grades and test scores are cold, impersonal measurements of certain areas of knowledge. A teacher's statement gives more meaning to scores and makes the scholastic picture of the student more lifelike.)

Summary of Records

In business there comes a time when a summary of individual transactions and results is necessary to ascertain how business is progressing. So it is in education. Individual scores and pages of information about each student mean very little. Only when information is summarized and analyzed does the teacher get the whole picture—the educational profit of his teaching.

The records suggested here permit the teacher to summarize:

1. The subject matter covered in each class.
2. The ages and experiences of the pupils taught.
3. The scores and grades—an estimate of teaching success and learning achievements.

With these data and comparable data from previous years, a teacher begins to assess his educational profit for that year.

The Teacher Acts on the Records

Records are a waste of time unless some action is taken. If the teacher practices what he preaches, he reacts to the recorded data. Seeking inspiration, he reads methods books or current magazines, attends conventions, or studies at a college. Best of all, the teacher really thinks about improving teaching and tries new ideas particularly appropriate to his situation. New ways of doing things, new ideas are needed. The teacher solving problems with original thinking contributes more to business education than the teachers trying only what others are doing. There are artists who point out that true creativity comes when a child is given paint and brush and told to paint; that creativity is killed when he is shown how to hold the brush and told what colors to use. So it is hoped that after the "income statement" is taken, the teacher wanting to increase educational profit will be creatively active in his methods.

Formal Educational Research

Research performed under the direction of graduate educational institutions or research organizations must meet certain formal requirements and follow established patterns of development. Yet, behind the formal procedures and presentations are many of the same questions practicing teachers are asking.

Kinds of Educational Research

Formal educational research is classified according to the methods of the research. Naturally, the method used is determined by the question being asked. Listed here are formal educational classifications of research in bookkeeping-accounting. After each classification suggested techniques and questions are listed which might be answered by such research.

Experimental	Establishing control groups, constructing tests to measure learning, teaching under careful guidance to answer, "What kind of testing best measures learning derived from practice sets?" "What thought processes should be emphasized in teaching the mechanics of adjusting entries?" "How much routine practice is necessary to master concepts and mechanics?"
Follow-up	Using questionnaires or personal interviews to answer, "Where are our students getting jobs?" "What kinds of work are they doing?" "Is there anything we should have taught and didn't?" "What personal uses are made of B-A knowledge?"

Historical

Consulting original documents, people, and various kinds of written data to answer, "What is the story of B-A development?" "What has been the development of the responsibilities of book-keepers and accounting clerks over the years?" "What are the factors present in the development of office automation?"

Occupational Analysis

Using an occupational survey or job analysis technique to answer, "What new jobs are developing?" "What are the newest procedures in payroll work, in accounts receivable?" "What are the promotional patterns in the B-A area?"

Philosophical

Analyzing writing and thinking to answer, "What is the place of bookkeeping-accounting in management decisions?" "What are the ethics of bookkeeping-accounting?"

Prognosis

Analysis of the abilities which seem to be needed in bookkeeping-accounting, preparation of tests, tryout of tests and comparison of scores with some criterion of achievement or performance to answer, "Can we predict who will be successful?"

Survey

Using survey techniques (questionnaires, interviews, observation, testing, and analysis of literature or occupations) to answer, "What standards are being achieved?" "Are standards realistic?" "Are businesses changing their way of doing bookkeeping and accounting?"

Educational Research in Bookkeeping-Accounting

A look at the present status of B-A research shows the limitation of available studies. What kind of research has been done in this area?

Devine, in his study [3] classified 185 reports completed between 1950-1960 according to the type of research used. He reports results as follows:

---

[3] Devine, John William, *A Comprehensive Analysis, Classification, and Synthesis of Research Findings and Thought on the Teaching of Bookkeeping and Accounting, 1950-1960* (Ph.D. Thesis, Indiana University, September, 1962.)

	Total	Percent
Descriptive survey	157	84.9
Development growth	22	11.9
Experimental	3	1.6
Historical	3	1.6

Devine explained that the descriptive survey studies were generally made "to provide bases for determining course content, courses of study, supplementary materials, and for determining the adequacy of programs." [4]

The developmental-growth studies were described as "usually statistical in nature and were made to isolate factors on which success or failure in bookkeeping and accounting could be predicted." [5] This would seem to place these studies under the classification of "Prognosis" in the list presented on page 286.

The studies under the last two classifications were described thus: "The experimental studies were undertaken to provide a basis for determining the value of one instructional method as compared with another," and "The historical studies dealt with the development of bookkeeping and accounting courses, particularly the objectives and approaches." [6]

Devine further analyzed the 185 studies and classified them according to the problems with which they dealt and tabulated these findings: [7]

CLASSIFICATION OF PROBLEMS USED FOR RESEARCH

Major Classification	Number	Percent
History and status	22	11.9
Course content	27	14.6
Classroom management and instructional methods ...	16	8.6
Instructional materials and facilities	30	16.2
Prognosis, guidance and follow-up	27	14.6
Evaluation	36	19.5
Employment characteristics	27	14.6
Total	185	100.0

One concludes as a result of Devine's work that those studying the B-A field have been primarily focusing their attention on the

---

[4] *Ibid.*, p. 20.
[5] *Ibid.*, p. 21.
[6] *Ibid.*, p. 21.
[7] *Ibid.*, p. 18.

status quo. There is need for more investigation into the basic truths bared by carefully interpreting the historical events which have brought bookkeeping-accounting to where it is today. Nothing has been done about discovering any underlying philosophical consideration, defining the processes of thinking, or exploring the work ethics which affect the work of the world.

Probably because the average business teacher has not been adequately trained to perform occupational analysis, little is done by educators in this vital area. And experimental teaching, being a time-consuming procedure, is avoided by most degree candidates because they cannot afford the time required.

Devine's study indicated the large percentage of studies made between 1950-1960 were at the master's degree level as shown below.[8]

THE LEVELS OF THE RESEARCH

Level of Research	Number	Percent
Master's thesis	110	59.4
Master's project, report, paper, or seminar report	41	22.2
Doctor's thesis	31	16.8
Doctor's project	2	1.1
Independent study	1	.5

Most of the research reported in this study was done under the restrictions of college degree requirements. Furthermore at the master's degree level, it is safe to assume those doing the studies were beginners in professional research. It can also be implied that a basic interest in B-A research for its own value has yet to be evidenced. The lack of independent study is clearly indicated by Devine's figures. It is apparent that research in bookkeeping-accounting requires striking improvement before contributing realistically to B-A performance and teaching.

Tonne stated in one of his writings about research, "The elixir for the improvement of research in business education is not easy to discover."[9] He went on to suggest four steps toward improvement. (1) More funds must be made available. (2) Directors of

---

[8] *Ibid.*, p. 19.
[9] Tonne, Herbert A. "The Nature and Purpose of Research in Business Education." *National Association of Business Teacher Educators*, Bulletin 66, Guide to Research in Business Education, 1957, p. 11.

research must have a devout interest in research and the capacity to do good research themselves. (3) Research must be done for the sake of the achievement itself and not to achieve status or a degree. (4) Small studies should be coordinated through the use of a uniform pattern so that the sum total of many small studies will be more meaningful than the work of an individual.[10]

In spite of his criticisms of research, Tonne looks forward to a betterment of the situation when he says, "Nevertheless, there are many signs of hopeful interest and sufficient numbers of people concerned to argue well that in the future our research will improve and be more meaningful than it has been to date."[11]

Bookkeeping Follow-Up Study

Report of State-Wide, Follow-Up Study of Bookkeeping Students

A recent and comprehensive study of high school students is titled, "A Follow-Up of New York State High School Bookkeeping Students."[12] While this study was limited to the state of New York, its purpose and scope makes it worthy of special mention.

The excerpts [13] presented below from the summary of this study cannot do justice to the detail contained in the complete report of 477 typewritten pages. They do, however, indicate (1) the extent to which high school students make use of their bookkeeping knowledge, and, to some extent, (2) the validity of knowledges and skills taught.

> The study which has resulted in this report was designed to produce information that would be of particular benefit to the New York State Bookkeeping Syllabus Committee in their syllabus revision work. The major objective of the study was to determine what kinds and amounts of business, educational, and personal uses had been made of bookkeeping skills and knowledges by a sample of former students who had studied New York State syllabus-outlined courses in Bookkeeping I and Bookkeeping II. Within that major objective, the emphasis of the study was on determining the

---

[10] *Ibid.*, p. 23.
[11] *Ibid.*, p. 23.
[12] Fairbank, R. E., *A Follow-up of New York State High School Bookkeeping Students.* (Albany: State University of New York at Albany, 1967).
[13] *Ibid.*, pp. 455-463.

frequency with which certain *specific* skills, knowledges, and activities of bookkeeping had been used by those former students. The study was *not* designed to provide a descriptive analysis of the work of bookkeepers.

The data for this report were gathered by means of a specially designed questionnaire which was mailed to a selected sample of former high school bookkeeping students. Responses were received from 2,064 persons who had studied syllabus-outlined bookkeeping courses in 59 public schools of New York State during the 1960-61 school year. Of those respondents, about 31 percent had terminated their formal bookkeeping study with Bookkeeping I, about 27 percent had terminated their bookkeeping study with Bookkeeping II, and about 34 percent had studied some bookkeeping or accounting at the post-high school level in addition to their high school bookkeeping. Nearly 34 percent of respondents had studied bookkeeping in New York City schools, over 20 percent had studied in Large City schools, about 37 percent in Small City-Suburban schools, and over 8 percent in Rural schools . . . nearly 85 percent of the group had been out of high school for four or five years.

Summary

Concerning Uses of Bookkeeping in Business Life

1. Many former high school bookkeeping students had worked as bookkeepers or had used their bookkeeping in office-store, non-bookkeeping jobs since leaving high school; for those students, bookkeeping education had been vocational education.

   The data of this study indicate that approximately 66 percent of all respondents, all of whom had studied Bookkeeping I and many of whom had studied further high school or post-high school bookkeeping, had used their bookkeeping skills and knowledge for some period in office-store work since leaving high school. About 41 percent of all respondents had worked as bookkeepers; about 26 per cent had worked as bookkeepers for a year or more since leaving high school. Approximately 24 percent of all respondents had not worked as bookkeepers, but had held non-bookkeeping office-store positions using bookkeeping skills and knowledges. About 23 percent of all respondents had held bookkeeping positions and also had held non-bookkeeping positions in which they had used bookkeeping skills and knowledges. About 34 percent of all respondents had *never* held bookkeeping jobs or other office-store positions using bookkeeping.

2. Many former high school students whose only bookkeeping education was (New York State) syllabus-outlined courses in Bookkeeping I or Bookkeeping I and II had worked as bookkeepers or had held other office-store positions using their bookkeeping skills and knowledges; for those students, high school bookkeeping had been terminal, vocational education.

Many of the respondents in this study had completed only high school Bookkeeping I or Bookkeeping I and II, without further bookkeeping study at the high school or post-high school level. Nearly 30 percent of those Bookkeeping I students had worked as bookkeepers since leaving high school; more than 16 percent of the Bookkeeping I group had worked as bookkeepers for a year or more. About 22 percent of the Bookkeeping I group had not worked as bookkeepers but had worked in office-store positions in which they had used their bookkeeping skills and knowledges. Thus, about 52 percent of Bookkeeping I respondents had used their bookkeeping vocationally in office-store work.

Of the Bookkeeping II group, nearly 34 percent had worked as bookkeepers, with nearly 23 percent of the group having worked as bookkeepers for a year or more. An additional 25 percent of the group had not worked as bookkeepers but had worked in office-store positions using their bookkeeping. Thus, about 58 percent of Bookkeeping II respondents had used bookkeeping vocationally in office-store work since leaving high school.

3. The greater the amount of formal bookkeeping education, the greater was the probability that the student had used the bookkeeping vocationally . . .

4. For those respondents who had worked as bookkeepers, full-time bookkeeping work was more common than part-time bookkeeping work . . .

5. For those students who had worked as bookkeepers, employment in service businesses was more common than employment in manufacturing, merchandising, or other businesses . . .

6. The type of school in which students had studied bookkeeping had little, if any, relationship to subsequent uses of bookkeeping in business.

For all respondents of the New York City, Small City-Suburban, and Rural school categories, rate percent of employment as bookkeepers, the length of time worked in bookkeeping, and the nature of the job as part-time or full-time were very similar. The rates percent of Large City students in these three factors were slightly, but consistently, higher . . .

7. The uses of bookkeeping in business were similar for sub-groups of respondents who had been out of high school for three, four, and five years . . .

8. Nearly all former bookkeeping students had graduated from high school or had received high school equivalency diplomas . . .

9. Proportionally more females than males worked as bookkeepers.

    About 22 percent of all respondents were males, and about 78 percent were female. Thirty-seven percent of all male respondents had worked as bookkeepers, and slightly more than 42 percent of all females had worked as bookkeepers. Of the Bookkeeping I and Bookkeeping II groups, however, the rates percent for females who had worked as bookkeepers was about double the rate percent for males. The considerably higher employment rates of males in the All Respondents group, by comparison with males of the Bookkeeping I and Bookkeeping II groups, may indicate that proportionally more males continue their bookkeeping education beyond high school and then obtain work as bookkeepers. Other evidence in this study does indicate that proportionally more males than females continue bookkeeping study beyond high school.

10. Specific bookkeeping items had been used with highly variable frequency in office-store use. Some specific bookkeeping items had been used frequently or occasionally by many respondents; some items had never been used by many or nearly all respondents . . .

Concerning Uses of Bookkeeping in Personal Life

11. Many high school bookkeeping students had completed some kind of post-high school education, had studied post-high school bookkeeping, and had found knowledge of bookkeeping useful in their education beyond high school . . .

12. Specific bookkeeping items had been used with highly variable frequency in personal life and, generally, had been used less frequently in personal life than in business life.

Research Supported by Organizations or Foundations

Research in bookkeeping-accounting is practically nonexistent on a nationwide level through the auspices of a national organization or foundation. It may be that as educational research grows in general, interest will develop in business education research to seek truth instead of only to get a degree. As trained research people in business education emerge, research in bookkeeping-accounting will become significant and meaningful.

The National Business Education Association, the National Association for Business Teacher Education, Delta Pi Epsilon, and The International Society for Business Education are the types of existent educational organizations which could sponsor and spark research projects on a national and international level.

The finances needed to support research are available from the federal government and from foundations. Borg in his discussion of financial support for educational research points out that the major sources of federal support are the Cooperative Research Program and the Title VII Program of the United States Office of Education. In 1962, $5 million was appropriated to support research in all areas of education under the Cooperative Research Program. The Title VII Program is devoted to research in new educational media such as television and teaching machines. In the fiscal year 1962, $4.75 million was budgeted for this program.[14]

Research in business education could be eligible for support from these two programs if business educators were strongly enough interested in some vital phase of research necessary for the real improvement of business education throughout the United States.

Foundations are another source of funds for really vital research—a source as yet untapped by business education. In the United States there are over 12,000 foundations, and they have at their command assets of over $11½ billion. Nearly half of the money granted by these foundations has gone to education.[15]

Graduate fellowships, scholarships, and loans are available through educational institutions, in addition to the United States Office of Education and the foundations.

It seems when one looks at the sources available to help, that our greatest need in bookkeeping and accounting is the vision, insight, and knowledge necessary for the development of more vital problems in research.

---

[14] Walter R. Borg, *Educational Research—An Introduction* (New York: Dave McKay Company, Inc., 1963), p. 384.
[15] Ann D. Walton and S. E. Andrews (eds.), *The Foundation Directory* (New York: Russell Sage Foundation, 1960), p. 4.

Business Research

Business is constantly studying its own efficiency, and what it discovers has value for us. Large companies have their own research departments. Companies manufacturing and selling office machines are illustrative of this. Organizations such as The Administrative Management Society, The American Management Association, and the American Accounting Association sponsor research projects. Reports of this research are available to educators through business periodicals or as pamphlets issued by the various organizations.

The relationships and channels of communication between business and business education are not strong or direct. This is probably true because the interests of the two are basically different. The businessman is chiefly interested in his own particular company with its specific problems of production and efficiency. Educators are primarily interested in developing the capacities of people to the highest potential and preparing students for business opportunities. However, there are points where the interests of educators and businessmen overlap, and research could take place in these areas.

A prominent business educator of former years, Frederick G. Nichols of Harvard University, was the prime force in establishing a strong relationship between The Administrative Management Society and business education. This cooperation led to the establishment of tests for selecting the most qualified people available for placement in business offices. These National Business Entrance Tests are now administered through the National Business Education Association. Perhaps the future will produce similar constructive action.

Study or Research?

There are no clear-cut boundaries among the levels of research mentioned earlier in this chapter. Indeed, in practice there is much overlapping. This gives rise to the question, "When does a study become research?" There are two features common to studies which may justify their being called research. One is the matter of generalization, and the second is the degree of precision and control through scientific procedures.

For example, if a teacher in a Hartford, Connecticut, school studied questionnaires showing how many of his graduates used bookkeeping machines on their first job, he may conclude that in his particular high school, it is desirable to offer instruction on bookkeeping machines. His conclusions are of particular interest to him, but since his study was entirely local, it cannot be generalized that all the schools in the United States or even that any other single school should offer bookkeeping machine instruction. Until a study is comprehensive enough to permit generalizations applicable to a large number of schools, it cannot justifiably be classified as true professional research.

To raise this same problem to the level of professional research requires thorough, controlled, and meticulous development of the procedures and the sampling. Scientific procedures must be used in determining the number and types of communities and businesses to be studied. Questionnaires and interviews would have to be structured carefully with space-age precision and control before one could justifiably make generalizations. Only with this kind of precision and control is a study rightfully called "true research."

Borg, in his discussion of educational research, points out, however, that "The research worker in education is faced with a difficult dilemma. If he attempts to maintain close control on the research situation to obtain scientific precision, he usually must alter the conditions so greatly that there is very little similarity between the research situation and the related situation in the public schools. On the other hand, if he strives for reality in his research so that his findings may have direct application to the public schools, he must usually sacrifice much of his scientific control. Even at its most precise level, research in education cannot match the precision and control possible in the physical science laboratory." [16] Nevertheless, it behooves all of us to raise the level of our research closer to the precision of true research.

The First Step in Research

Before one embarks on any study or research, he must first look back and see what has been done. He must be sure no one

---

[16] Borg, *op. cit.*, p. 16.

else has already found a solution to the problems posed. He can also profit by experiences others have had in their attempts to solve problems.

The findings of research are not always easily available. The teacher interested in finding what research in the field has to offer for his use, must first learn to locate research completed and under way and where to procure reports on research.

In the future it may be possible to enter an automated library, press the button marked "bookkeeping-accounting research" and in a matter of minutes have a machine produce a listing of all the available references on the subject. In the meantime, the researcher must painstakingly consult the various indexes and ferret out the studies, articles, and books which might seem to contain what he wishes.

In each instance he starts with current publications' indexes and works back through the years until he uncovers all that is needed to satisfy his current intellectual curiosity and collegiate requirements or until he exhausts available sources.

The available references and indexes most appropriate for use by the B-A teacher are listed below. The list is not exhaustive, but rather an identification of the basic references—the starting point for research at all levels—the first step.

REFERENCES AND INDEXES FOR THE B-A TEACHER

ABSTRACTS OF RESEARCH AND RELATED MATERIALS IN VOCATIONAL AND TECHNICAL EDUCATION (ARM) and ABSTRACTS OF INSTRUCTIONAL MATERIALS IN VOCATIONAL AND TECHNICAL EDUCATION (AIM). 1900 Kenny Road, Columbus, OH: Educational Research Information Center (ERIC) Clearing House, Center for Vocational and Technical Education, Ohio State University, 1967 to date. These two quarterly publications contain comprehensive listings of documents processed by the Center.

Alexander, Carter, and Arvid J. Burke. HOW TO LOCATE EDUCATIONAL INFORMATION AND DATA, Fourth Edition, Revised. New York: Teachers College, Columbia University, 1958. This is a basic reference book for planning a study in education. It is invaluable for determining sources of information necessary to any level of research work.

BUSINESS EDUCATION INDEX. Louis C. Nanassy, editor. Delta Pi Epsilon Fraternity. New York: Gregg Publishing Division, McGraw-Hill Book Company, Inc., 1940 to date. An index of business education articles compiled from a selected list of periodicals and yearbooks.

BUSINESS PERIODICALS INDEX. New York: H. W. Wilson Company, January 1958 to date. A specialized index covering articles in business magazines.

DOCTORAL DISSERTATIONS ACCEPTED BY AMERICAN UNIVERSITIES. New York: H. W. Wilson Company, 1934 to date. Compiled by the National Research Council and the American Council of Learned Societies by the Association of Research Libraries.

EDUCATION ABSTRACTS. Paris: Educational Clearing House, UNESCO, 1949 to date. Lists research articles published in the professional journals in psychology and education.

EDUCATION INDEX. New York: H. W. Wilson Company, 1929 to date. A basic index of articles and books on education.

DISSERTATION ABSTRACTS. Ann Arbor, MI: University Microfilms, Inc., 1955 to date. A monthly compilation of abstracts of doctoral dissertations submitted by over 100 cooperating institutions.

ENCYCLOPEDIA OF EDUCATIONAL RESEARCH, Third Edition. Chester W. Harris, editor. New York: The Macmillan Company, 1960. Published every ten years.

Johnson, H. Webster. HOW TO USE THE BUSINESS LIBRARY, Third Edition. Cincinnati: South-Western Publishing Company, 1964. A manual providing sources of business information as well as a guide for training in the use of a business library.

MASTER'S THESES IN EDUCATION. H. M. Silvey, editor, Cedar Falls, IA, 1952 to date. Master's theses are listed under about forty major educational topics.

Rahe, Harves. ACCOUNTING-BOOKKEEPING-RECORDKEEPING RESEARCH INDEX. New York: Gregg Division, McGraw-Hill Book Company, Inc., 1967. A comprehensive list of: Research studies in the teaching of accounting, bookkeeping, and recordkeeping from 1923 to 1966, classified by author, subject, university (if thesis or dissertation), and date.

READER'S GUIDE TO PERIODICAL LITERATURE. New York: H. W. Wilson Company, 1900 to date. Author and subject index covering general and nontechnical periodicals published in the United States.

RESEARCH STUDIES IN EDUCATION. Bloomington, IN: Phi Delta Kappa, 1953 to date. A yearly compilation of doctoral dissertations completed and under way in education.

REVIEW OF EDUCATIONAL RESEARCH. Washington, DC: American Educational Research Association, 1931 to date. Published five times each year.

STANDARD EDUCATIONAL ALMANAC. Los Angeles: Academic Media, Inc., 1968 to date. A source of up-to-date information "on virtually every aspect of education." Published annually.

WHAT RESEARCH SAYS TO THE TEACHER. Washington, DC: Department of Classroom Teachers and American Educational Research Association. Published irregularly. A series of pamphlets, each discussing research in an area of interest to teachers. Latest issue lists topics covered in all previous issues.

PERIODICALS FOR THE B-A TEACHER

DELTA PI EPSILON JOURNAL. Irene Place, editor. St. Peter, MN: Gustavus Adolphus College, 1957 to date. A quarterly of the Delta Pi Epsilon Fraternity devoted to research, scholarship, and leadership in business education.

NATIONAL BUSINESS EDUCATIONAL QUARTERLY. Washington, DC: National Business Education Association, 1932 to date. The fall and spring issues are devoted to research. Each fall issue supplies brief abstracts of studies completed the previous year. The spring issue contains a listing of research studies in business education completed and under way, as well as articles dealing with research.

STUDY QUESTIONS

1. What is the purpose of research?
2. On what three levels may the B-A teacher come in contact with research?
3. What is meant by the term *action research*?

4. Why should a B-A teacher in particular be expected to keep basic and continuing records of his progress?

5. Give some examples of action research by the B-A teacher.

6. What use could a teacher make of a comparative year-to-year form showing his subject coverage in a B-A course?

7. What are the major items suggested for inclusion on a pupil-information record?

8. What use should the teacher make of the records he keeps?

9. What action studies are suggested in planning for individual differences?

10. Identify six different types of educational research and give examples of each.

11. What should be the first step in any kind of study or research?

DISCUSSION QUESTIONS

1. Are grade school students using the term *research* correctly when they claim that they have to do "research" for an English paper?

2. Is there any truth in the claim that some educational research is proving the obvious—proving what we already know to be true?

3. Is proving what we think we already know a waste of time?

4. Identify one or more of the teacher-kept records suggested in this chapter which you consider of real value, and indicate why you believe they are helpful.

5. If a B-A teacher were fortunate enough to be assigned a teacher-aid, which of the records suggested for action research might be kept by the aid instead of the teacher?

6. Should the B-A teacher or the school's placement office have the final say in meeting employers' requests for workers?

7. Should a teacher whose class is a week behind normal progress because he experimented with a new method of teaching be subject to administrative criticism?

8. Why has there been such a limited amount of experimental research in bookkeeping-accounting by educators?

9. Is it the fault of business educators or of businessmen that there is not a closer rapport between the two groups?

PROJECTS

1. Construct some forms as suggested in this chapter for keeping records of (a) subject matter coverage, and (b) pupil information.

2. List all of the information former students now working in local offices could supply that would help improve the bookkeeping course. Construct a questionnaire for a follow-up study to secure this.

3. Choose a problem about the teaching of bookkeeping-accounting and prepare a paper giving the research already done on this problem.

4. Outline a study to prove or disprove the need for a second-year B-A course in your local high school.

5. Outline the plan of a study to determine the B-A practices and procedures followed in the local community, but not included in the existing course of study.

6. Outline a plan for a student survey of the community to ascertain:
   (a) number and types of B-A machines in use
   (b) extent to which bookkeepers are called upon to perform all steps in the B-A cycle
   (c) kinds of non-B-A duties that the local bookkeepers and accounting clerks are called upon to do
   (d) the extent and use of automated data processing equipment in the community.

7. Complete a study to prove or disprove that the students enrolled in your first-year B-A classes are as bright as the average students attending your school.

SELECTED REFERENCES

Bangs, F. Kendrick, Principal Investigator. *Curriculum Implications of Automated Data Processing for Educational Institutions,* Boulder, CO: University of Colorado, 1968. (Available from Executive Secretary, Delta Pi Epsilon, Gustavus Adophus College, St. Peter, Minnesota 56082.)

Borg, Walter R. *Educational Research—An Introduction.* New York: David McKay Company, Inc., 1963.

Calhoun, Calfrey C., and Marjorie R. Calhoun. "Comparison of the Readability Level of High School Bookkeeping Textbooks with the Reading Achievement of Bookkeeping Students," *Business Education Forum.* XXII (April, 1968), 21-23.

Corey, Stephen M. "Research as a Method of Self-Improvement," *Informal Research by the Classroom Business Teacher*, American Business Education Yearbook, Vol. 18, pp. 5-16. New York: New York University Bookstore, 1961.

Devine, John W. *A Comprehensive Analysis, Classification and Synthesis of Research Findings and Thought on the Teaching of Bookkeeping and Accounting 1950–1961*. Doctoral dissertation, Indiana University, 1962; *Business Education Quarterly*. XXXII (October, 1963), 13; *Journal of Business Education*. XXXIX (October, 1963), 30.

Erickson, Lawrence W., and Mary Ellen Oliverio. *Evaluative Criteria for Survey Instruments in Business Education*, Monograph 111. Cincinnati: South-Western Publishing Co., 1964.

Fairbank, R. E., Project Director. *A Follow-up of New York State High School Bookkeeping Students*. Albany: The University of the State of New York, State Department of Education, 1967.

Gardner, William E. "Involving the Classroom Teacher in Research," *Delta Pi Epsilon Journal*. VI (May, 1964), 65-69.

Good, Carter V. *Introduction to Educational Research*, Second Edition. New York: Appleton-Century-Crofts, Division of Meredith Publishing Company, 1963.

House, Forest Wayne. *Factors Affecting Student Achievement in Bookkeeping in High School*. 1951 Delta Pi Epsilon Research Award. Oklahoma Agricultural and Mechanical College, 1953.

Informal Research by the Classroom Business Teacher, American Business Education Yearbook, Vol. 18. New York: New York University Bookstore, 1961.

Lanham, Frank W., and J. M. Trytten. *Review and Synthesis of Research in Business and Office Education*. Columbus, Ohio: The Center for Vocational and Technical Education, Ohio State University, 1966.

Lomax, Paul S., and W. Harmon Wilson. *Improving Research in Business Education*, Monograph 105. Cincinnati: South-Western Publishing Co., 1962.

McGrath, G. D., James J. Jelinek, and Raymond E. Wochner. *Educational Research Methods*. New York: The Ronald Press Company, 1963.

Moulton, Priscilla M. "Research Sources," *Business Education World*. XLIV (November, 1963), 20-21.

Poulsen, Roy G. "Research to Improve Classroom Teaching," *Journal of Business Education*. XLIII (January, 1968), 158-160.

Satlow, I. David. "Abstract of Significant Research in Bookkeeping and Accounting," *Developing Vocational Competency in Bookkeeping and Accounting*, Eastern Business Teachers Association Yearbook, Vol. 40, Chapter 22. New York: New York University Bookstore, 1967.

Spanswick, Ralph S. "Manual Bookkeeping Jobs for First-Year Bookkeeping Students," *Business Education Forum*. XXII (April, 1968), 15-16.

Verry, Dana Hedrick. "Action Research—What and How?" *Business Education Forum*. XXIII (November, 1968), 25-26.

Waterman, Roland C. "Improving Instruction in Bookkeeping Through Research and Action," *Business Education Forum*. XXI (December, 1966), 12-14.

Areas of Disagreement

B-A teachers are in general agreement on many aspects of a high school B-A course. However, it would be a sad day if they should agree on everything. Progress results from healthy and knowledgeable controversy. Progress is retarded by opinions derived without knowledge, by misunderstandings, and by purely emotional reactions. This chapter identifies some of the common controversies—differing opinions—and attempts to stimulate and challenge thought on these topics.

Teaching Related Economic and Business Law Concepts

The B-A teacher is in an excellent position to incorporate both economic and business law knowledge into his course. Some teachers do this. Others do not.

Those who bring economic principles into the B-A class argue with considerable justification that economic competency is the most slighted general education objective in the secondary curriculum. They might further point out that integration of economic concepts in bookkeeping-accounting not only falls under the general education objective of the B-A course but enriches it without detracting from the vocational objective. At appropriate places in the B-A course, these teachers take time to discuss such topics as the following: the types and functions of banks; the law of supply and demand and its effect in a free economy; formation of capital and its relation to savings and investment; the effects of taxation on incentive to work, to save, and to invest.

A similar case has been made for teaching business law concepts—bad debts, bailments, caveat emptor, sales, and employee-employer relationships.

If economic and business law concepts are taught, they should also be incorporated in tests and mastery of them required. As reported in an earlier study,[1] unless teachers give emphasis by including examination questions pertaining to these learnings, little or no value is derived in presenting them to the class.

The amount of *time* and emphasis given to related economics and business law concepts is a crucial problem. Any steps taken in the business education curriculum should strengthen rather than weaken. Under the pressure of time, adding an appreciable amount of teaching material in any course means cutting out some other subject matter or doing a superficial job on everything. This can weaken the vocational competency of the students preparing for business positions.

To have a competent business office force in the future, prospective workers must be given a comprehension of economic concepts and the law of the land. In schools where these subject matter areas are not a part of the business studies, teachers should work to have economics and business law included as courses in the curriculum rather than including these related concepts in bookkeeping-accounting and other vocational subjects. There is an old adage appropriate to the situation, "That which is everybody's business frequently becomes no one's responsibility."

The presence in the curriculum of specific courses in economics and law does not preclude mentioning economic concepts and business laws in the B-A class. If students are currently taking these subjects, cross references in bookkeeping-accounting can be made. The more capable people in the B-A class interested in these areas can be directed to further study and perhaps report to the class.

In making decisions about the inclusion of related business law and economic concepts in the B-A course, the teacher should review his objectives and the total situation. Then, in the light of his best judgment and others concerned, he may proceed to do that which is of the greatest value to the students.

---

[1] William C. Mickelson, *The Practicability of Introducing Economic Concepts in Bookkeeping* (Master's thesis, Mankato State College, Mankato, Minnesota, 1966), p. 36.

Teaching Automated Data Processing

The whole area of automated data processing is a new vocational field. People working in this new vocation are in jobs non-existent a few years ago. The automated data processing department in any institution works with information of *all* kinds, including B-A data. In hospitals, motor vehicle departments, space programs, steel mills, chemical factories, and other areas the information processed is widely varied. Since techniques of automated data processing are applicable to the handling of B-A data, some B-A procedures are affected. Because of this, elements of automated data processing must be considered in the B-A class.

As with economic and business law concepts, the amount of time and the depth one gives to the automation field is a crucial point of discussion. It is difficult to mark where one passes from the subject matter of bookkeeping-accounting to subject matter more appropriate to an automated data processing course. No matter how difficult, however, the teacher must make the attempt to define the boundaries. Both areas must be kept strong in preparing future business employees.

The treatment of automated data processing in the B-A class is discussed at length in Chapter 24.

The Use of Machines in the Bookkeeping-Accounting Class

While many B-A teachers favor the use of machines in their classes, others do not. Those who oppose the placing of adding and calculating machines in their classes usually claim that bookkeeping-accounting should improve arithmetic skill, and the use of machines diminishes this skill. Others object, claiming the machines create discipline problems. Since it is not economically practical to equip each student with a machine, twenty, thirty, or more students are obligated to share the few adding and calculating machines available. This, they say, causes trouble.

Teachers favoring machines answer these objections as follows:

1. Since adding and calculating machines are common items of equipment in today's offices, students should be given the opportunity of learning to use them.

2. Making machines available for adding long columns and as aids in computing problems, encourages students to complete assignments.
3. A teacher experiencing discipline problems created by machines is perhaps prone to discipline problems from other sources also.

In addition to adding and calculating machines, some teachers have bookkeeping and accounting machines (billing, posting, and all-purpose) in their classes. This is not feasible in all schools. If classes are large and machines so few that students lack proper instruction, the teacher is hard put to defend their use. In schools where classes are small and only one or two types of machines are common to the community, a better defense can be made for familiarizing students with their use.

Every high school should strive to give the vocational training needed most by business graduates. A majority of B-A personnel needs and uses skills on the common office machines—typewriter, adding machine, and calculator. Therefore, most high schools should offer training in their use before acquainting students with the specialized, advanced types of accounting machines. Furthermore, it is worth remembering that employers of machine operators prefer people who understand manual procedures and underlying principles of bookkeeping-accounting. Machine bookkeeping-accounting, including automated data processing, has not as yet eliminated the B-A steps in the business cycle or the need for people to understand principles. However all B-A teachers should keep abreast of trends in machine bookkeeping-accounting.

T Accounts Versus Two-Column General Journal for Analyzing Transactions

There are two principal ways which teachers and textbooks generally use throughout a bookkeeping course for illustrating the analysis of a business transaction:

1. How it would appear as a two-column general journal entry, OR
2. How it would appear in T accounts.

A third way that is used initially when *introducing* students to the analysis of business transactions is to illustrate the effect of the transaction on the bookkeeping or accounting equation. But after such an introduction, either the teacher, or the textbook, or both usually proceed through the rest of the course to short-cut the lengthy equation analysis by the use of T accounts or the form of the two-column general journal with its debit column and credit column.

A current examination of both introductory college accounting textbooks and high school bookkeeping textbooks shows that the use of the two-column journal illustrations is more popular in introductory college accounting textbooks than in high school book-keeping texts. Since it is a common practice to "teach as we have been taught" and since many high school B-A teachers were intro-duced to this field when they took the introductory college account-ing course, many are prone to continue to follow the procedure to which they were introduced at college. As a result, such teachers use the two-column general journal rather than T accounts for illustrating on the chalkboard or on the overhead projector an analysis of business transactions.

It should be made clear that both methods have been and are being used successfully. But is one better than the other? Based upon current high school textbook usage a trend appears to favor the use of T accounts. Those who are pleased with this trend can present the following arguments to support the use of T accounts.

1. *Debit* means one thing and one thing only—the left-hand side of a standard ruled account. *Credit* means one thing and one thing only—the right-hand side of a standard ruled account. Some stu-dents, therefore, who learn early in the course to always associate *debit* with a left-hand *column* and *credit* with a right-hand *column* of a journal are confused when they are called upon to use a com-bination journal for the first time with its multi-columns and no left nor right-hand columns.

2. Because of the increased popularity of special journals and combination journals, the two-column general journal is, in most businesses, rarely used except for such special entries as opening, closing, adjusting, reversing, correcting, and such miscellaneous entries as cannot be recorded in other journals. It is not, therefore, very realistic to analyze a transaction in a form of journal where the entry might never appear.

3. When T accounts are used, no ritual requires that the debit part of the entry be recorded before the credit part. Students called upon to demonstrate an analysis through the use of the

two-column general journal form are generally required to supply the debit entry first, whereas some students could sometimes get the "key" to understanding the transaction by being permitted or encouraged to give the credit part first.

Those who continue to favor the older use of the two-column general journal form for illustrating the analysis of new business transactions as they arise, claim that requiring students to write the *explanation* for each transaction is a helpful learning step not called for when T accounts are used.

Teaching Arithmetic

Arithmetic is a skill which can be quickly lost. High schools use various procedures for helping students retain their arithmetic skills. Some do this by offering a course in business arithmetic, while others integrate the teaching of arithmetic with such courses as general business, bookkeeping-accounting, and office practice.

B-A teachers are not in agreement as to which procedure is best. Some believe that a business arithmetic course should immediately precede the B-A course. Others believe this course should be taken concurrently with first-year bookkeeping-accounting. Still others believe arithmetic instruction should be integrated with bookkeeping-accounting. Then, too, occasionally a teacher is found who closes his eyes to the problem and takes the attitude, "I'm here to teach bookkeeping-accounting not arithmetic."

A student cannot learn certain skills in bookkeeping-accounting if he does not know how to perform the arithmetic computation that precedes the recording of a correct bookkeeping entry. If a teacher is conscientious about his responsibility for teaching bookkeeping and accounting, the conclusion seems simple. When the class has difficulty, the teacher will immediately explain the necessary arithmetical procedures. Even in schools where students have previously had or are taking concurrently a business arithmetic course, this teaching time is frequently necessary.

Support of the above statements is found in two recommendations from a study dealing with this topic:

1. Bookkeeping instructors should be more conscious of the arithmetic needs of their pupils. Arithmetic related to bookkeeping should be taught in the bookkeeping classes as the need arises.

2. Bookkeeping teachers need not be concerned about time spent in the bookkeeping classes on instruction and drill in arithmetic related to bookkeeping. Apparently success in arithmetic heightens the interest and motivates the pupils to do better in bookkeeping.[2]

The arithmetic involved in bookkeeping is simple—addition, subtraction, multiplication, and division. Because this arithmetic of the bookkeeper calls for computational skills only, and because the "new math" of recent years continues to emphasize these skills, today's bookkeeping students trained under this "new math" should be no less skillful in their ability to compute than students of previous years.

There are only a few arithmetic-problem areas in bookkeeping-accounting. In the main these center around:

1. Computing the terms of sales and purchases.
2. Computing valuation accounts—depreciation and bad debts.
3. Computing interest and discount.

In teaching arithmetic as in teaching bookkeeping-accounting the problem must first be clear. The teacher must illustrate the problem and the arithmetic concepts and procedures to be learned. Second, he must give sufficient time for repetitive practice.

Lack of understanding of common terms is often a source of confusion. For example, students should be helped to see that—

Rent is money paid for the use of another's nonmonetary property.
Interest is money paid for the use of another's money.
Both can be money paid out for expenses, or money received as income.

Money paid *in advance* of the use of another's property is prepaid rent.
Money paid *in advance* of the use of another's money is prepaid interest—discount.
Both can be money paid out for prepaid expenses, or money received as prepaid income.

This is reducing the problem of learning terms to its simplest form. This is where some students in a B-A class must start.

---

[2] William F. Sites, *The Effects of Integrating Arithmetic Instruction and Drill with First-Year, First-Semester Bookkeeping* (Master's thesis, Ohio State University, 1961), p. 81.

As the terms become more complex, continued assistance on the simplest level must be devised. Graphic description is frequently helpful if not essential. For example, suppose the students are being introduced to the following type of problem:

> On January 1, C. C. Rowe gave a 6% promissory note to R. Smith in exchange for the use of $100 for 30 days. On what date must this note be paid and how much will C. C. Rowe have to pay R. Smith?

The teacher could develop the following "outline" on the chalkboard or overhead projector and ask students to replace the question marks with the information supplied in the problem. After all the information is recorded, it becomes obvious to students what the problem involves. This procedure gives the student a key or a tool with which to work. It gives him an aid, or technique to follow. When such a procedure is used, it can be expanded and applied to more difficult problems dealing with discounting of interest-bearing notes.

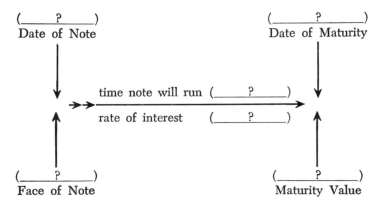

Every good B-A teacher uses this same technique for teaching bookkeeping and accounting. When asked to explain a transaction, one of the first things many teachers do is place three or four T accounts on the board, and, in cooperation with the students, develops the entries visually. This is exactly what was done with the above arithmetic problem. Furthermore, what teacher in his undergraduate days has not faced an examination question that forced him to "draw-it-out" before showing the final work on the examination paper? The suggestion here is to give equal and similar graphic, concrete help when teaching some of the arithmetic involved in bookkeeping-accounting.

Alertness by the teacher in examining test results and other student work determines when sufficient arithmetic practice has been given.

There is one skill in arithmetic that many students face for the first time in bookkeeping-accounting. This is horizontal addition and subtraction. Students are previously taught and conditioned to add and subtract vertical columns of figures. They enter the B-A class conditioned to this one way of adding and subtracting. When we consider, however, the number of times a bookkeeper or accounting clerk performs across-the-page addition or subtraction, it seems reasonable to suggest that students need to be helped and conditioned to this skill. An occasional classroom drill in horizontal addition and subtraction is desirable. The first such drill should be with one-or-two-digit figures on the chalkboard and should include a discussion on how to use the eyes and mental processes. Subsequent drills can be presented from paper, can increase in difficulty, can be oral or written, can be timed, and can follow the normal development from simple problems to complex problems.

Teachers themselves have to determine the penalty or scoring of arithmetic errors in bookkeeping. Those who inflict no penalty in their scoring and grading are in essence telling their students that bookkeeping and teachers of bookkeeping are not concerned with accuracy.

Pen Versus Pencil in the Bookkeeping-Accounting Class

Experienced teachers frequently enjoy a friendly squabble over whether students should be permitted to use a pencil in a B-A class. The use of the pencil at the beginning of the B-A course permits some students to get off to a happier, more successful, and more encouraging start. The mistakes they make are not so permanent and may be corrected more easily. However, vocational bookkeeping-accounting is done in ink if a machine has not taken over. For this reason, the use of pens on work completed for credit should be a requirement for every student after the first month or two. Most students today are at home with ball-point pens and can write as well with them as with pencils. The use of pens requires, of course, that approved methods of error correction be taught.

Method of Correcting Errors

Should erasing be permitted? Many bookkeepers and accountants correct simple errors by using an eraser or a fluid ink eradicator. This is common practice. It is not illegal. It is not, however, always good practice to make corrections this way. From both a legal and a practical standpoint, books that have errors changed in this manner can be subject to question and be more suspect. Such corrections do not stand up well in the eyes of a court, a jury, an examiner, or an auditor.

An error in an amount can be canceled by drawing a line through the incorrect figure. The correct number is then written immediately above the canceled amount. When a simple error is corrected in this manner, the bookkeeper is frankly stating he made a mistake.

Students should know these facts. They should not be misled as happens occasionally with the false statement, "Since it is illegal for bookkeepers to erase, it will not be permitted in this class." A student can learn the best way to make corrections without a harsh rule that forbids erasing ever. Teachers who insist on such a rule do not practice it themselves anyway. The author remembers observing a demonstration lesson on how to correct simple errors. The theme that ran through the lesson was "Bookkeepers don't erase, students in this class must not erase." The best way to make simple ruled-through corrections was excellently illustrated and taught. Yet twice during the blackboard demonstration the teacher inadvertently made mistakes which he *erased*.

Use of Abbreviations

Should abbreviating be permitted? B-A teachers have differing opinions concerning the abbreviating of account titles and business terms. This difference stems from the varying requirements (or lack of them) teachers encountered in their college courses or vocational experiences. Professors of college accounting center attention on understanding theory and some care little or even ignore the details of routine recording. Employers' requirements for bookkeeping details vary from office to office—some demand quality appearance with few abbreviations; others are willing to sacrifice appearance for the expediency of abbreviation.

What should the high school teacher do about this problem? Should he permit students to abbreviate when opening an account, journalizing, or preparing financial statements? If he permits them to abbreviate such lengthy account titles as *Purchases Returns and Allowances, Federal Unemployment Taxes Payable,* and *Accumulated Depreciation—Delivery Equipment,* should they also be permitted to abbreviate shorter accounts titles such as *Pur.* for *Purchases, Equip.* for *Equipment,* or *Adv. Ex.* for *Advertising Expense?* If the teacher does not permit abbreviations, does he take time to set a perfect example by never abbreviating when he uses the chalkboard or the overhead projector?

Abbreviations in this modern age seem to be the order of the day. NATO, UNICEF, OEO, etc. are familiar shortcuts in the American language. The print-outs of computers and tabulating machines are full of abbreviations. But, while abbreviations are speedier, they also carry the potentiality of error in incorrectly made or incorrectly read abbreviations. Since B-A records are the basis for the financial operation of a business, it is important that no error or misinterpretation occur.

There are two solutions to this problem. By tradition and by preference there are employers who ask their workers to use a minimum of abbreviations. A more common procedure in business is to abbreviate only when the space in the journal, the ledger, or a financial statement is not sufficient for writing the full account title or business term. Many teachers adopt this practice as a rule to be followed by their students—as a solution to this problem of abbreviating. Furthermore, textbooks supplying script illustrations usually follow this procedure, thus supplying excellent patterns for the students. It behooves the teacher, therefore, to be sure his requirements do not ignore the standards his students may be called upon to meet.

Teachers objecting to this rather fixed, single-system procedure point out that students will meet a variation of demands on the job. As a result, their solution is to vary scholastic requirements in the classroom. They frequently ask students to prove they are capable of producing the highest quality of work required in any office—no abbreviations, no misspelled words, entirely legible, neat, and errorless work. On the other hand, when the teacher believes the emphasis should be on mastery of a principle, the expediency of abbreviations would be accepted, if not encouraged. The teacher who prefers this solution will balance his requirements and the students' use of abbreviations throughout the course, thus preparing them to meet the test of quality production on the job.

Improving Handwriting

The teaching of handwriting in a B-A class is a debatable issue. But, in spite of machines and automated processes, writing by hand is still a required skill in business, and legible, neat handwriting is a prized possession and a marketable commodity. A bookkeeper or accounting clerk whose handwriting is not readily understood is not performing adequately, and a good B-A teacher will not slight or ignore handwriting problems. It can be discouraging, however, to have a number of students whose handwriting must be improved before they can qualify as average, good, or above average B-A students.

There are numerous techniques used to achieve legibility and neatness in student's work. *First,* the students must be helped to understand the essential need for legibility and neatness. *Next,* they must be made aware of the importance that it will be given in the course. *Finally,* the teacher must throughout the course (1) give recognition and status to this characteristic, and (2) give help and encouragement to students who need it.

It is essential that the class must first, near the start of the course, be made thoroughly aware of this cardinal characteristic of good bookkeepers or accounting clerks and thus good B-A students. This can be done in part by borrowing a set of well kept books from a local businessman for display in class.

When students understand this first essential, they are better prepared to understand why the teacher is frequently referring to neatness and legibility of handwriting; why the teacher requires some students to re-do their homework; why the teacher takes . three, five to ten points off for lack of neatness on homework or examination papers; why the teacher places samples of each student's work on the bulletin board as that student performs neat work or shows improvement; why the teacher might require some students to use pencil instead of ink or vice versa; why the teacher gives a "B" instead of an "A" to the brightest student in the class;

in total, why the teacher has given special attention and status to neatness and legibility. Judicious use throughout the course of these techniques should bring most students to a level of improved and satisfactory written work.

Laziness or indifference, rather than lack of handwriting ability is frequently a cause of sloppy work. Most students respond and improve under the above practices. However, there is a good way for teachers to discover at the start of a course which students can or cannot write neatly and legibly. Before discussing legibility in bookkeeping, the teacher can have the class copy "in your neatest and clearest handwriting, taking all the time you need," several complete journal entries from the text. Before they begin, stress again that it is not important how long they take to copy the work, but that the work is assumed to be their neatest, clearest possible production. Results of such a scheme can prove helpful in two ways. *First*, it discloses the students who possess weak or illegible handwriting, and whether this weakness involves writing words, figures, or both. *Second*, it can be filed away as a future reference to show the lazy, indifferent, or sloppy student proof that he can do neater work if he takes the time and wants to.

But what about the relatively few students who never acquired reasonably good handwriting skills and whose penmanship is abominable and seemingly hopeless? What can be done if they are unable to improve? Even they can be helped.

It has been proven that many students with handwriting difficulties can learn to print much quicker than they can be taught to correct their handwriting faults. Teachers who find "hopeless" handwriting cases might encourage these students to print. Printing is a frequent requirement for filling-in forms in many businesses.

A logical and important question to consider is "What amount of time should be taken to treat weaknesses in arithmetic, handwriting or other areas related to B-A success?" While there is no detailed or pat answer to this question, it would seem that where the majority of the class needs help, it would be logical to assist them as a group during class time. Frequently only a few students need special help. In such instances it is better not to steal classroom time from the majority to help the few. Here, special out-of-class sessions, special homework assignments, and the utilization of student teachers is in order.

"Bookkeeping" Versus "Accounting" as a High School Course Title

In Chapter 1 the distinctions between record keeping, book-keeping, and accounting were discussed. These same three terms are used as titles for high school business courses. There seems to be no controversy or misunderstanding as to the difference between a course labeled "record keeping" and a course labeled "bookkeeping." Record keeping is a low level, watered-down bookkeeping course for students with below average abilities. The fact that both a record keeping course and a bookkeeping course are, at times, found in the same school is proof that there is an understanding of the differences between the two.

The same clear distinction cannot be made between high school courses labeled "bookkeeping" and those named "accounting." The objectives and subject matter found in these courses are the same. The controversy, therefore, is which of these two titles is better, "accounting" or "bookkeeping"?

Those who prefer "accounting" offer the following major arguments to support this title:

1. The drawing of a sharp distinction or dividing line between bookkeeping and accounting cannot be done. High school students in first-year bookkeeping deal with many of the same principles and practices that college students deal with in a first-semester accounting course.
2. The term *accounting clerk* is increasing in popularity, and the better students who finish a one or two-year high school course qualify for some of these positions.
3. The term *accounting* carries more prestige than *bookkeeping* and thus has greater appeal for some teachers and students.

However, at present the great majority of high schools use the course title "bookkeeping" or "bookkeeping and accounting" for the following reasons:

1. Since the course first entered the high school curriculum it has been called *bookkeeping*. As a result, no one is confused about a course labeled *bookkeeping*. Guidance counselors, principals, parents, and employers all understand by tradition and usage the meaning of the term and the level of vocational preparation it offers.

2. Bookkeeping is an *occupation*; accounting is a *profession*. High schools can train and prepare bookkeepers—they cannot turn out accountants. Bookkeeping is concerned with computing, classifying, and recording business data. Accounting, on a higher plane, is concerned with examining, analyzing, and interpreting.

3. The *Dictionary of Occupational Titles* [3] lists bookkeepers as well as accounting clerks under a clerical classification while it lists accountants under an "Administrative and Specializations" grouping.

4. The *Occupational Outlook Handbook* [4] combines bookkeepers and accounting clerks under the major classification "Bookkeeping Workers."

5. Special publications assisting high school guidance counselors center their descriptive career information on such titles as "Bookkeeper and Bookkeeping Machine Operator," and "Bookkeeper I and II." Much of their information parallels the information in the *Occupational Outlook Handbook* and the *Dictionary of Occupational Titles.*

6. Teachers and research workers seeking high school level information in the *Business Education Index* or the *Education Index* will get their best help under the term "bookkeeping." Over the years, nearly all articles, studies, and books indexed under "accounting" refer to the teaching of post high school courses. Thus our present distinctive frame of reference would be lost if all high schools were to replace the term "bookkeeping" with the term "accounting."

This controversy does not have to be settled by a conclusion calling for either "Bookkeeping" or "Accounting" as the course title. In schools where this dispute exists, most, if not all, of the foregoing facts could be used to give some support to a compromise course title such as "Bookkeeping and Accounting" or the hyphenated title "Bookkeeping-Accounting." Either such title would acknowledge the reality of the existence of bookkeepers and the expanding opportunities for such workers, would recognize that some of these bookkeeping workers are accounting clerks who may be trained in high school, and would give the touch of prestige which some people need for work satisfaction.

---

[3] U. S. Department of Labor, *Dictionary of Occupational Titles, 1965, Volume I, Definitions of Titles* (3d ed.; Washington: U. S. Government Printing Office, 1965).

[4] U. S. Department of Labor, *Occupational Outlook Handbook, Career Information for Use In Guidance* (Washington: U. S. Government Printing Office, 1966).

Should All Terminal High School Business Students Be Required to Take an Introductory Course in Bookkeeping-Accounting?

Some schools require all terminal business education students of average ability to take an introductory bookkeeping course. Others do not.

Schools having this requirement maintain that all students planning to earn their livelihood in business should learn the language of business and how business operates. These schools believe introductory bookkeeping and accounting provides this background. It is their opinion that salespeople, typists, and stenographers should not be narrowly trained for business—that the typist is a better employee if she understands the contents of the letters and the reports she types—and the distributive-education student is a more satisfied and valuable employee if he understands the business records necessary in a retail business.

Some of the reasons other schools do not require terminal business students to take bookkeeping-accounting are:

1. They believe that some students could profit more by taking a course other than bookkeeping.
2. Their guidance system does not identify nor classify students as "College Preparatory," "General," "Business," or "Home Economics." Thus students have no "track" or special curriculum to follow. Instead, student programming and scheduling is worked out individually each year, based on the student's record and interests.

STUDY QUESTIONS

1. What are some of the arguments for and against the teaching of economic and business law concepts in a B-A class?
2. Why should automated data processing be given some attention and coverage in the B-A class?
3. Why do some teachers object to having office machines in their classes?
4. What reasons support the use of office machines in a B-A class?
5. Training on which types of business machines should be given priority for B-A students?

6. What are the two most common ways used throughout a B-A course for illustrating the analysis of business transactions?

7. What are the advantages of using T accounts to picture the analysis of a business transaction? of using the two-column general journal entry?

8. In what ways do high schools attempt to help business students retain their skill in arithmetic?

9. What new skill in arithmetic do many students face for the first time in bookkeeping-accounting?

10. Why should students be required to use pens for most if not all of their work?

11. What better way is there for correcting errors than by using an eraser or a fluid ink eradicator? Why is this considered a better way?

12. What are two solutions used by teachers for solving the problem of how much abbreviating students should be permitted in their written work?

13. What are some of the techniques teachers can use to help their students produce legible, neat handwriting?

14. What facts are available to support calling a high school course *accounting*? to support calling a similar course with the same subject matter *bookkeeping*?

15. What reasons can a high school give for (a) requiring all terminal business students of average ability or better to take an introductory B-A course, (b) not requiring these students to take such a course?

DISCUSSION QUESTIONS

1. Why do you believe that a teacher should, or should not, be expected to teach economic and business law concepts in a B-A course?

2. How much time, if any, should be devoted to teaching automated data processing in a first-year B-A course?

3. In your judgment what would be the ideal type and number of office machines to have in a first-year B-A class of 25 students? in a second-year class of 25 students?

4. Discuss the feasibility of making the training on all-purpose bookkeeping machines a part of a second-year course in bookkeeping-accounting?

5. Which is the soundest way to illustrate the debit and credit of a business transaction—by the use of T accounts or by following the form of a two-column general journal entry?

6. In which course and to what extent should B-A students be trained to operate each of the following machines: the ten-key and full bank adding-listing machines, printing calculator, key-driven calculator, rotary calculator, electronic calculator, posting-billing machine, general-purpose bookkeeping machine, cash register, typewriter, automatic typewriter, time clock, teletype, card punch, sorter, interpreter, collator, reproducing punch?

7. How much time should be devoted to teaching arithmetic in the B-A class?

8. What amount of classroom time do you believe should be taken to treat student weaknesses in handwriting?

9. To what extent should students be permitted to use a pencil for their B-A assignments?

10. To what extent should students be permitted to correct their written errors with erasers?

11. To what extent do you believe students should be permitted to abbreviate their written work? Justify your answer.

12. Present fully the logical arguments why you believe a high school course should be given one of the following course titles: *bookkeeping, bookkeeping and accounting,* or *accounting.* How many of your arguments are based on fact? on opinion?

13. Do you believe all terminal high school business students with average ability or better should, or should not, be required to take an introductory course in bookkeeping-accounting? Why?

PROJECTS

1. Prepare a paper identifying the major economic concepts that could be integrated with the teaching of a first-year bookkeeping course. Specify where in the course these concepts can best be introduced.

2. Prepare a paper identifying the major business law concepts that could be integrated with teaching of a first-year B-A course. Specify where in the course these concepts can best be introduced.

3. Prepare a layout for an ideal B-A classroom showing the kind and location of office machines recommended. Show the location of electrical outlets for all machines, including projectors.

4. Prepare a paper outlining the research needed to settle the question of the type and extent of office machine training necessary for the B-A students in a particular community.

5. Survey several dozen manual bookkeepers in your community to ascertain the extent to which (a) errors are corrected by erasing, and (b) abbreviating is practiced. Prepare a report of your survey indicating the implications that should be drawn for teaching B-A in your community.

6. Prepare a lesson plan which centers on teaching arithmetic for each of the following: straight line method of depreciation, interest, short-cut methods of computing interest, discount on interest-bearing notes, merchandise turnover, accounts receivable turnover.

7. If you teach in a high school where you believe the terminal business students are narrowly trained for a business career, prepare a paper for presentation to your principal or local curriculum committee outlining how this situation can be improved. Support your recommendations with sound educational principles.

SELECTED REFERENCES

Boynton, Lewis D. "Bookkeeping versus Accounting as a High School Course Title," *The Balance Sheet.* L (April, 1969), 340-342.

Cook, Fred S., and Eleanor Maliche. "Office Machines Used in Business," *The Delta Pi Epsilon Journal.* VIII (May, 1966), 1-15.

Enstrom, E. A. "High School Handwriting—A Challenge," *The Journal of Business Education.* XLIV (November, 1968), 73-75.

Darst, Marian. "Use of Small Machines in a Computer Era," *Business Education World.* IL (December, 1968), 6-8.

Gratz, Jerre E. *Major Issues in Business Education,* Monograph 106. Cincinnati: South-Western Publishing Company, 1962.

Griffith, Robert. "Integration of Economic Concepts in Beginning Bookkeeping Classes," *The Balance Sheet.* XLV (October, 1963), 63-64.

Guyton, Percy L. *A Teachers Guide to Economics in the Business Education Curriculum.* New York: Joint Council on Economic Education, 1963.

Mickelson, William C. "The Practicability of Introducing Economic Concepts in Bookkeeping." Unpublished Master's thesis. Mankato State College, Mankato, Minnesota, December, 1966.

Satlow, I. David. "Bookkeepers Never Erase," *The Balance Sheet.* XLIV (November, 1967), 113-116.

Sites, William F. "The Effects of Integrating Arithmetic Instruction and Drill with First-Year, First-Semester Bookkeeping." Unpublished Master's thesis. Ohio State University, 1961.

United States Department of Labor. *Dictionary of Occupational Titles*, Vol. I, Definition of Titles, Third Edition. Washington, D.C.: Superintendent of Documents, 1965.

————————, Bureau of Labor Statistics. *Occupational Outlook Handbook*, 1968-1969 Edition. Washington, D.C.: Superintendent of Documents, 1968.

Veterans Administration. "How to Improve Your Handwriting," V.A. Pamphlet 03-2. Washington, D.C.: Superintendent of Documents, 1960.

Chapter 13

DEVELOPING TRENDS AFFECTING BOOKKEEPING-ACCOUNTING INSTRUCTION

New developments in both education and in business affect the teaching of bookkeeping. No one has a greater responsibility for keeping up-to-date with such changes than do B-A teachers.

Consider the fact that B-A teachers of the 1950's had to learn *after they started teaching* the meaning and use of such terms as automation, team teaching, cycle billing, aging accounts, programmed instruction, and many, many new terms applicable to automated data processing. The quicker they updated their B-A courses with such appropriate information and learning, the more up-to-date was the preparation of their students for work in the modern office.

Consider also that it was not until *after* the passage of Public Law 88-210, Vocational Education Act of 1963, that federal funds were made available for the first time to aid with the training of personnel for office occupations, including bookkeeping. The quicker the B-A teachers learned of this development and of the extent to which such funds were available to them in their respective states and communities, the quicker those in need of such help were able to use it to improve their teaching and the learning of their students.

A good B-A teacher is an up-to-date business teacher. He is aware of current developments and maintains business and professional contacts as discussed in Chapter 8, "School and Community Resources." The responsibility for keeping up-to-date is great and immeasurable. Occasionally, what might look like a new development proves to be no more than a passing fad. Although some new trends are detrimental and should be stopped, most are advantageous and the natural outgrowth of progress. The role the

B-A teacher plays in their development is significant only when he:

1. is aware of existing and developing trends
2. understands the reasons for the actions that create trends
3. teaches in a way, or takes other action, that brings his opinion and influence to bear upon the trends.

Federal Legislation—A Recent Stimulant to Trends in Business Education Including the Bookkeeping-Accounting Program

While there were earlier federal acts having a small effect on business education in a few urban areas, it was not until 1963 that the first major act was passed making "business and office occupations" specifically eligible for government funds.

The Vocational Education Act of 1963 (Public Law 88-210)

According to the 1966 revision of *Vocational Educational Bulletin No. 1*, the Vocational Education Act of 1963 was designed, among other things:

> To maintain, extend, and improve existing programs of vocational education, to develop new programs, and to provide part-time employment for youths who need earnings to continue their vocational education on a full-time basis. For persons of all ages in all communities: those preparing to enter the labor market, those in the labor market who need to upgrade their skills or to learn new ones, and those with special educational handicaps. For construction of area vocational school facilities.[1]

The following definition supports the fact that high school B-A courses fall under the provisions of the Vocational Act of 1963.

> "Business and office occupations" means those occupations pursued by individuals in public or private enterprise or organizations which are related to the facilitating function of the office and includes such activities as recording and retrieval of data, supervision

---

[1] U. S. Department of Health, Education, and Welfare, *Administration of Vocational Education, Rules and Regulations, Vocational Education,* Bulletin No. 1. (Washington: U. S. Government Printing Office, 1967), p. ix.

and coordination of office activities, internal and external communication, and reporting of information.[2]

While the provisions of the Vocational Education Act of 1963 are too numerous and detailed to examine here, the following factors should be noted:

1. Each state must have a state board for administering the funds and an approved State Plan which outlines the policies and procedures for using its share of the funds. Since these State Plans vary from state to state, and since the act does not specify amounts of money for any one vocational field, such as for office occupations or for agriculture or for distributive education, the amounts of federal funds reaching and affecting business education departments and other vocational units will vary from state to state and from community to community.

2. To be eligible to receive funds, schools must come under the supervision of the state board of education. They must also offer vocational education leading to immediate employment but not leading to a baccalaureate degree. Thus public high schools, public technical and vocational schools, and such post-high school institutions as two-year community colleges offering training for "business and office occupations" are eligible.

3. The state must first make its expenditures for vocational education. These expenditures are then subject to reimbursement on a matching basis with federal funds. In other words, every dollar of federal funds must be matched with state or local funds.

4. Funds may be used for such broad vocational purposes as construction of vocational school facilities, instructional equipment, preparation of teaching guides and instructional materials, organization and utilization of advisory committees, staff salaries, teacher education, state administration and supervision, periodic evaluation, and research and development.

Predicted Educational Trends Stemming from the Vocational Educational Act of 1963

Because the first appropriation for the Vocational Educational Act of 1963 was not authorized until September of 1964 and funds did not affect vocational business education in many states until 1966 and 1967, it is still rather early to document nation-wide

---

[2] *Ibid.*, p. 5.

changes affecting B-A instruction. However, certain trends are being established. In fact, as federal funds continue under the 1963 Act, business education should change for the better in much the same way as vocational areas where federal educational funds have been available for years as in agriculture, distributive education, trade and industry, and home economics.

Increased and improved instructional equipment. Many high schools, community colleges, and business-teacher-preparing institutions have lacked audio-visual equipment and materials such as overhead and filmstrip projectors, copying equipment (for making transparencies), tape and record players, and video tape recorders. Now, with the help of federal funds, these items are obtainable.

B-A teachers in many schools are seeing their requests for adding machines, calculators, and bookkeeping machines being approved for the first time. Similarly, some schools that had little or no chance of offering automated data processing courses are now starting to secure equipment for use in these courses. In such schools, teaching the relationship between manual bookkeeping-accounting and automated data processing, as discussed in Chapter 24, should be eased considerably. Furthermore, when automated data processing equipment is available, B-A students may take a data processing course concurrently with second-semester or second-year bookkeeping-accounting or graduate into such a course after a year of B-A instruction.

More cooperative work-experience programs for bookkeeping-accounting students. The Vocational Act of 1963 requires participating schools to either provide a cooperative work-experience program for vocational students or have these students complete a suitable vocational *project.* A suitable vocational project for B-A students could be the successful completion of one or more practice sets. Some schools will elect to have their B-A students complete such a project, and other schools will establish a cooperative work-experience program. As a result, the number of cooperative work-experience programs for B-A students can be expected to increase.

This trend calls for more business teachers, including B-A teachers, to prepare to be teacher-coordinators of work-experience programs. Teachers coordinating the activities of students in a work-experience program teach bookkeeping-accounting as well as supervise the students on their respective jobs. This out-of-school work supervision calls for special preparation at teacher-training institutions.

Increased number of advisory committees. Many State Plans require that schools seeking funds appoint a lay advisory committee of local citizens. (Advisory committees are discussed starting on page 222.) The growing number of citizen-advisory committees which will result should help to bring high school training for office occupations closer to the practices desired by the local business community.

Strengthening the vocational stature of business education. Since the funds available under the Vocational Education Act of 1963 are to help states, "To maintain, extend, and improve existing programs of vocational education, to develop new programs (of vocational education), . . ." [3] it is understood that funds are not to be spent for purposes other than vocational education and its improvement.

This, among other things, requires that the schools applying for federal funds available under this Act must identify the students in the program and arrange to see that, "Vocational instruction will be designed to fit individuals for gainful employment in a recognized occupation." [4] The Act goes on to state, "All students receiving vocational instruction in preparatory classes under the State Plan will have an occupational objective which is a matter of record. This objective may either be a specific recognized occupation or a cluster of closely related occupations in an occupational field." [5]

The requirement of identifying—of making a matter of record—the occupational objectives of students preparing for office occupations should improve the educational as well as the vocational guidance of many high school students. High schools that permitted *terminal students* to make a narrow selection of a course or two in business will be obliged to consider the practice of programming these students into a sequence of courses aimed at improved vocational education. The vocational aspect of business education will certainly be strengthened provided this is done without returning

[3] *Ibid.*, p. ix.
[4] *Ibid.*, p. 15.
[5] *Ibid.*, p. 15.

to the evil of not permitting the program's college-caliber students to enroll in college-preparatory or honors courses.

Strengthening the vocational aspect of business education could also lead to more schools offering a second year of bookkeeping-accounting. The need for this advanced instruction is supported by the findings of a recent doctoral study.

> The majority of the firms advertising bookkeeping jobs were not willing to hire persons with only one year of high school bookkeeping *unless* those persons had experience in a previous bookkeeping job. As a result, there were very few opportunities for a person with only one year of high school bookkeeping and no on-the-job bookkeeping experience to secure a bookkeeping job immediately upon graduation from high school.
>
> Persons with a one-year course in high school bookkeeping who were successful in securing employment in manual bookkeeping jobs frequently performed activities related to banking procedures, use of special journals, payroll records, accounts receivable records, and bookkeeping machines.[6]

Changing requirements in the preparation of business teachers. The passage of the 1963 Act and the subsequent increased emphasis given to vocational education is affecting preparation requirements of high school business teachers in three ways.

First, more business-teacher trainees are required to have vocational office experience before graduation and certification to teach. *Second,* more college courses are being made available, and in some instances required, in the foundations and philosophy of vocational education and supervised work experience. *Third,* more financial assistance is available for business-teacher education programs. This is perhaps most obvious in those states and institutions offering reimbursable courses for undergraduate office education majors and "free" or reimbursable graduate courses and workshops to experienced, in-service teachers.

The following excerpts from a doctoral study of the effect of the Vocational Education Act of 1963 on business-teacher programs support the above.

---

[6] Ralph Sterling Spanswick, "An Investigation to Determine the Qualifications and Skills Desired, Accepted, and Actually Used in Manual Bookkeeping Jobs, *The Journal of Business Education,* Vol. XLIII (March, 1968), p. 252.

Thirty-four different courses were added to office education teacher education curriculums in the (141) institutions surveyed. Forty-seven percent added a course in vocational education: 35 percent added one in cooperative office education; and about 10 percent added a course in data processing and supervised work experience.

Approximately 40 percent of the institutions offering curriculums for office education coordinators in cooperative programs instituted these programs after the Vocational Education Act was approved.

Reimbursable courses offered for office education majors by about 25 percent of the institutions were vocational education, typewriting, methods of bookkeeping, methods in shorthand and transcription, and secretarial office practice.

About 30 percent of the office teacher educators thought that the greatest benefit to be derived from the Vocational Education Act of 1963 was the availability of funds for equipment and instructional materials.

Approximately 60 percent of the office teacher educators thought that the new emphasis upon the vocational objective of business education programs had greater stature than before.[7]

Increased research in business education. Some educators have predicted that research stimulated by funds from the 1963 Education Act could prove to be the Act's most significant contribution to business education. Whether or not this is realized, the fact that funds are available for research programs has increased needed activity in these areas. Recent significant research endeavors such as the nation-wide study, "Curriculum Implications of Automated Data Processing for Educational Institutions;"[8] the extensive New York State study; "A Follow-up of New York State High School Bookkeeping Student;"[9] and the comprehensive Connecticut study, "Business Education Curriculum Implications of the Effects of Technology on the Types of Office Machines Used by Selected

---

[7] R. Charles Long, "A Study to Determine the Effect of the Vocational Act of 1963 Upon Business Teacher Education Programs in Selected Colleges and Universities," *The Delta Pi Epsilon Journal,* Vol. X (February, 1968), pp. 15-17.

[8] F. Kendrick Bangs, Principal Investigator. *Curricular Implications of Automated Data Processing for Educational Institutions* (Boulder, Colrado: University of Colorado, 1968).

[9] R. E. Fairbank, Project Director. *A Follow-up of New York State High School Bookkeeping Students.* The University of the State of New York, The State Department of Education, Albany, September, 1967.

Connecticut Businesses;" [10] are only a few examples of studies stimulated by the availability of federal funds.

A further aid and stimulus to research in business education is the Center for Vocational and Technical Education [11] located on the campus of Ohio State University, but operating as an independent unit. This is one of the Educational Research Information Centers (ERIC) which makes up a comprehensive information system designed and funded by the U. S. Office of Education. This Ohio center serves as somewhat of a clearing house, a repository, and a reporting center for all research in the area of vocational and technical education, including business education.

Vocational Educational Amendments of 1968

Federal vocational education acts are frequently expanded and changed. Educators must keep abreast of legislation changes affecting vocational education and office occupations in particular. The first legislation to change some of the stipulations of the Vocational Education Act of 1963 is an act called the *Vocational Education Amendments of 1968*. This Act seeks to expand vocational education by increasing funds for similar programs authorized under the Vocational Act of 1963. This includes the previously mentioned areas of research, cooperative work programs, and advisory committees.

Other Educational Trends

Up-grading Bookkeeping and Accounting in the Curriculum to Post-High School Institutions

Teaching bookkeeping-accounting to older and more mature students of the junior college level is generally easier and the results are usually more successful than in high school. The subject matter can be upgraded and the students prepared for high grade initial positions. Employers often prefer to hire the more mature community or junior college graduate.

---

[10] Cletus A. Clow. *Business Education Curriculum Implications of the Effects of Technology on the Types of Office Machines Used by Selected Connecticut Businesses.* Connecticut State Department of Education, Hartford, April, 1967.

[11] Center for Vocational and Technical Education, Ohio State University, 980 Kinnear Road, Columbus, OH   43212.

The junior or community college movement (which until recently has been more prevalent in the Far West and Midwest than in the East) has resulted in thousands of young adults continuing their formal education through the 13th and 14th years. Students planning to enter a career in business after junior college are delaying their specialized vocational training until the last two years of their schooling. This is desirable since vocational skills are best taught just before they are put to use. Motivation is easier and loss of the skill from disuse is eliminated. The exception would be the student who can enroll in a college-level course in accounting (sometimes called an accounting "honors" course) in high school and receive advanced placement credit in the college of his choice.

Even in communities offering free education for the 13th and 14th years, the 12th or last year of high school will continue to be a popular time for many students to leave school. Until laws are written requiring longer attendance, there will continue to be a real need to offer bookkeeping in the 11th and 12th grades.

Downgrading the Subject Matter of Bookkeeping-Accounting

Shortly before the middle of this century, some high schools started to offer courses in record keeping that more or less were a low-level form of bookkeeping. These courses appear to have increased during the past several decades because of three developments.

First, in the late nineteen twenties and early thirties many states passed laws forcing more students to remain in school for a longer period of time. *Second,* the old ninth-year vocational junior-business-training course started to disappear, replaced by a general or basic business course. *Third,* business was breaking down office duties into an assembly-line type of organization—requiring less ability and different skills than those developed in stenography and B-A courses. Thus schools were eliminating the ninth-year *vocational* business training courses, which had a primary aim of preparing boys and girls for entrance into low-level office jobs, while business was increasing its need for general clerks and workers in simple types of office jobs.

Most schools took the position at this time that secretarial or B-A training was the best student preparation for vocational office positions, and since students were required to remain in school longer, why not give them a higher level of training? However, many of the students failing bookkeeping-accounting and shorthand, as well as those with no vocational business training, were securing clerical employment in offices—particularly in the large cities.

Two apparent solutions to this problem resulted in the practices now in evidence. One was to open up a general clerical course or sequence of courses to help such students. The other solution was to offer easier courses in bookkeeping; thus the course record keeping developed.

Evidence questioning the need for year long record-keeping courses is found in the following conclusions of a research study completed by Robert A. Schultheis.

> Because of the marginal nature of the slow learners' potential employability in record keeping positions and because of the clerical nature of these positions, a separate course in vocational record keeping for slow learners does not appear to be justifiable. An entire year spent in the preparation of slow learners for positions in which they can expect to be only marginal employees does not appear defensible use of their time or of educational resources.
>
> An analysis of related research, however, does indicate that slow learners appear to have some employment potential in some general office positions. A program of studies designed to provide slow learners with the general office skills, knowledge, experiences, and attitudes necessary for initial employment in general office positions would appear to be more justifiable than the preparation of slow learners for specific record keeping jobs, such as cash clerk or invoice clerk.[12]

This downgrading is evident today by the number of record-keeping textbooks available and by the many articles in professional periodicals suggesting elimination of steps normally taught in the bookkeeping cycle. Such practice limits the training of students to initial office positions only. For some students with low

---

[12] Schultheis, R. A., *The Potential Employability of Slow Learners in Recordkeeping Positions*, Unpublished doctor's thesis, Indiana University, Bloomington, 1966, 198 pp., as reported in *The Delta Pi Epsilon Journal*, August, 1968, pp. 27-32.

abilities, perhaps the most we can do is get them up to a minimum employable level. We must, however, be on guard against letting the needs of below-average students infringe upon the abilities and treatment of the average and the above average. The two situations where record-keeping courses have perhaps done their greatest harm are (1) where they take the place of a bookkeeping course, and (2) where they are used as try-out courses for all students interested in taking bookkeeping.

This is not to oppose the teaching of record keeping—low-level bookkeeping. Record keeping is a common function in larger offices, and low-ability pupils interested in becoming office workers should be offered training. Where we need to reexamine our philosophy is how long such training is offered. It seems a better allocation of the students' and the teacher's time to teach record keeping as a major unit in a general clerical course. Record keeping would then be taught for several months as opposed to a full school year.

Today with improved aids and teaching we should teach more in less time. In record keeping we teach less in more time. If these courses must be offered, let us make sure that students who could learn more in less time are not programmed into them.

Team Teaching

When two or more teachers cooperate in teaching a course or a unit of instruction, we have team teaching. While there is nothing new about one or more teachers cooperating with or helping others, the term "team teaching" is relatively new. The broader concept of team teaching goes beyond two or more teachers jointly or alternately teaching a course—

> Team teaching typically includes the following essential characteristics: (a) Students are arranged in classes of 70 or more for oral and visual presentations and in groups of 12 to 20 for discussion. (b) Team members take assignments according to their competencies and determine the sequence and manner in which the material is to be presented and the structural arrangement (large group, small group, or individual study) most effective for a particular purpose.[13]

---

[13] William Georgiades, "Team Teaching: A New Star, Not a Meteor," *NEA Journal*, Vol. LVI (November, 1967), pp. 14-15.

In addition to the above description, the following elements are found where team teaching is truly effective: (1) cooperative teacher planning and evaluation; (2) use of clerical or teacher aids; (3) availability and use of appropriate teaching materials and equipment for large and small group instruction; (4) the support and encouragement of the school's administration.

The extent to which business teachers have practiced and reported on team teaching in literature seems quite limited. Perhaps the vocational business education subjects do not lend themselves well to team teaching. A good B-A teacher or a good typewriting teacher seems more likely to be good at teaching all or nearly all phases of his subject rather than just certain topics. In elementary grades and in social studies on the secondary level, team teaching seems to have flourished. In these fields the specialties and individual competencies of teachers might be more applicable to team teaching.

However, B-A teachers should consider this newer trend. A beginning teacher could well team up with a master B-A teacher to the mutual advantage of students and staff. The B-A teacher with specialized and practical experience in banking, insurance, or travel should not shy away from a cooperative venture to assist in teaching these units in a general business or a consumer economics course.

Teacher aids. One approach to rising enrollments and shortage of educators is allowing teachers more time for their professional teaching work and less time on routine work better done by lower-paid workers. As evidenced by the following introductory sentences from a newspaper report, this is not just a practice in some schools, but also a growing trend in certain areas of the country:

> Nearly a third of Connecticut's school districts have teacher aids on their payrolls today. Seven years ago, only two towns in this state employed teacher aids. Today the figure is 58.[14]

This trend may sound like Utopia to the older B-A teacher who scored all tests, checked homework assignments, and performed routine work himself. It is now realistic to predict that the problem of increasing enrollments and teacher shortages may be met with the expanding trend to provide paraprofessional aids.

---

[14] *The Hartford Courant*, Hartford, Connecticut (March 4, 1968).

Television Teaching

Television is one of the newer tools of teaching. It offers help in facing problems caused by the increasing number of students, the smaller number of able teachers, and the overwhelming increases both in the amount and complexity of space-age knowledge. Through it, the best teachers can reach more people in places near and far. Through it, students can see and hear people at the work of the world, can see their own and other countries, and can whirl for a while in outer space—all without leaving the classroom.

The use of educational television is expanding rapidly. This is true for both closed-circuit and open-circuit television. Many new schools include provisions for a closed-circuit television system. While the extent to which high school bookkeeping-accounting will be taught through this medium is not clear, B-A teachers should be prepared for this developing trend.

Bookkeeping-accounting is a subject which lends itself to television teaching. The many visual aids which promote B-A understanding can perhaps be used more effectively over television than in the classroom. For example, a chalk-board or overhead-projector presentation of a work sheet is a large and complicated presentation. Thirty people sitting varying distances from the illustration may focus their eyes on thirty different places and see with different degrees of accuracy. Produced on a television screen, however, the parts of the work sheet being discussed may be brought into clear and isolated focus by the camera. All students' eyes are then looking directly at the illustration of the point being discussed.

Not all good classroom teachers are automatically good television teachers. Since television requires specialized knowledge and skills, future teachers of bookkeeping-accounting should include in their training program at least one course in audio-visual education. This course should provide practical experience in solving the problems of television teaching.

The planning required for television teaching. The amount of planning which must go into even one television performance is considerably more detailed and sophisticated than the lesson planning recommended for beginning teachers in Chapter 6. The preliminary planning requires:

1. Exercising good judgment in determining what is important enough to go on the air.
2. Timing and pacing each presentation for the time slot.
3. Planning and preparing precise visual support—charts, graphs, and other devices usually have to be approved by television technicians.
4. Anticipating questions that might be asked if the lesson was presented to a live audience.
5. Planning for students' off-television activity:

    a. Classroom setups
    b. Monitors
    c. Discussion topics and questions
    d. Evaluation procedures—tests, reports, etc.

6. Taping lectures and lessons so the teacher may make corrections and improvements.
7. Rehearsals before the camera using chalkboard, charts, demonstrations, overhead projector with transparencies, etc.
8. Lighting in the classroom for notetaking.
9. Arranging for quality of audio pickup.
10. Devising program to overcome a possible negative attitude caused by loss of personal contact.

One author states the benefit of television thus: "The major advantage accrues from the forced reorganization and reevaluation of the course content and teaching techniques. . . . The thorough preparation and the carefully planned presentation make better quality instruction a certainty." [15]

Just as accounting and other college courses are today being transmitted by closed-circuit television, so bookkeeping-accounting and business courses can be transmitted from a central location into different high school classrooms. Bookkeeping-accounting will be taught to interested people just as typewriting, shorthand, secretarial practice, and other high school subjects are transmitted by open-circuit educational television stations into American homes.

---

[15] Harold M. McGrath, "Teaching 'Introduction to Business' by Closed Circuit Television," *American Business Education*, Vol. XVIII (May, 1962), pp. 235-37.

Video Tape

The first commercially prepared set of video-taped lectures for use in teaching college accounting over closed-circuit television was announced in 1967. The description of their cost follows:

> The complete set of 60 video tapes sells at a net price of $10,200.00, f.o.b. Kent (Ohio). Each tape runs for approximately 45 minutes. The video tapes can also be purchased in a set of 30 tapes for the first half of the course and 30 tapes for the last half of the course. The two sets of 30 tapes sell for $5,100 per set. The two student lecture guides, one guide for each half of the course, sell at a net price of $3 each f.o.b. Kent.[16]

It is not known how many years it will be before similar tapes come within the range of high school budgets, but perhaps not as long as some may think. According to a recent report from San Jose State College in California, some television and video tapes are now being used in professional preparation of business teachers. A TV tape is used to record the student teacher's presentation and then played back for criticism by the practicing student and his colleagues. In this instance the tape is reported as costing, ". . . about $70 for a one-hour tape," and that such a ". . . single tape can be reused for about 100 passes before it begins to wear out." [17]

Programmed Instruction

Programmed instruction involves two elements—a program of teaching and a device which presents the program. The device may be a special textbook or a teaching machine. Like record players without records, and film projectors without films, the teaching machine is useless without a program. The value of a teaching machine is only as great as the value of the programs available for it. At this writing, there is only one programmed B-A textbook [18] published for the high school level. There is no programmed instruction in bookkeeping-accounting available for use with a teaching machine.

---

[16] Developed by Emmett W. Boyd and Rudolph Malandro, produced by Philip A. Maconber, Kent, Ohio.

[17] Richard S. Dale, "A New Use of Television in Business Teacher Education," *The Journal of Business Education*, Vol. XLIII (December, 1967), pp. 98-99.

[18] Frederick G. Comstuck (Subject Matter Consultant), *Beginning Bookkeeping*, Programmed by General Programmed Teaching Corporation, (Chicago: Encyclopaedia Brittanica Press, 1964), 1936 frames.

A program is a carefully arranged sequence of statements and questions, presented in a series of small units called frames, requiring specific responses from the student.

The essential elements of programmed instruction are as Schram states:

(a) an ordered sequence of stimulus items,
(b) to each of which a student responds in some specific way,
(c) his responses being reinforced by immediate knowledge of results,
(d) so that he moves by small steps,
(e) therefore making few errors and practicing mostly correct responses,
(f) from what he knows, toward what he is supposed to learn from the program.[19]

When programmed instruction made an appearance in the 1950's, quite a flurry was created among some educators and publishing companies. Many programmed materials were rushed onto the market so fast that they lacked adequate testing, and some proved to be weak or ineffectual for self-instruction. As a result a certain amount of skepticism developed about the value of this new form of learning. Now, however, because such materials are usually being adequately tried and tested before publication, a better quality of programmed instruction is coming off the press.

In addition to schools, business and industry is using programmed instruction. Self-study materials are commonly found in employee-induction programs and in-service training programs.

There is a place for programmed instruction in bookkeeping-accounting. Individual pamphlets would seem more appropriate than programmed textbooks. These individual pamphlets could cover one or more short units or topics: the fundamental bookkeeping equation; the meaning of debit and credit; how to post; how to adjust for depreciation expense, and so on. Materials in pamphlet form could be used:

(1) by the student who has been absent and needs help in catching up with the class

---

[19] Wilbur Schram, *Programmed Instruction Today and Tomorrow.* The Fund for the Advancement of Education. November, 1962, p. 2.

(2) by slow students or others who may have had difficulty learning from the teacher's presentation or the textbook's treatment of a particular topic

(3) by students with the ability to progress more rapidly than the average pace of the class

(4) as an aid in review.

Individual pamphlets are recommended because it does not seem realistic to ask or to expect high school B-A students to remain with this single method of learning throughout an entire B-A course. Programmed instruction, when used occasionally for a short period of time, offers a change in method which should prove helpful to both teacher and student.

The following is an example of a short unit of untested programmed instruction in bookkeeping.

EXAMPLE OF
PROGRAMMED INSTRUCTION
UNIT I
The Fundamental Bookkeeping Equation

– –

Instructions:

1. Cover the answers in the right-hand margin below with the edge of a textbook.
2. Study the introductory sentence.
3. Read the material in each frame and write your response.
4. Slide the textbook down the page just far enough so that you can check the correct answer with your written response.
5. If you made a mistake, pause long enough to analyze your error and to reflect upon the correct answer before proceeding to the next frame.

– –

ACCURATE AND UP-TO-DATE BOOKKEEPING RECORDS WILL SHOW WHAT A PERSON OR A BUSINESS IS *WORTH* FINANCIALLY—in $$$ and ¢¢¢.

1. The value of the things that a person owns helps to determine how much that person is _____.	*worth*
2. When a person does not *owe* anything to anybody, the total value of the things he owns is his financial _____.	*worth*

3. Mr. X does not *owe* anything to anybody. He *owns* $500 in cash plus things that could be sold for $200. Mr. X is worth a total of $_____.　　*$700*

---

4. Thus to find the financial worth of a person who does not *owe* anything to anybody, you add the total value of all of the things that he _____.　　*owns*

---

5. When a person does *owe* something to someone, then his *net* financial worth is found by subtracting what he *owes* from the total value of the things that he _____.　　*owns*

---

6. Mr. Y owns things worth $800. He also owes $50. Mr. Y has a *net* financial worth of $_____.　　*$750*

---

7. Thus to find the *net* financial worth of a person who both owns things and owes things, you subtract the total value of the things he owes from the value of what he _____.　　*owns*

---

8. When a person owes something to another, the value of what he owes is subtracted from the value of what he owns in order to find his _____ financial worth.　　*net*

IN BUSINESS—IN BOOKKEEPING AND AC-COUNTING—INSTEAD OF REFERRING TO *things owned, things owed,* and *net worth,* SPE-CIAL BUSINESS TERMS ARE USED.

---

9. Anything of value that belongs to or is _____ by a business is called an *asset.*　　*owned*

---

10. Anything of value owned is called an _____.　　*asset*

---

11. When a person or a business owes money to another, the one who _____ the debt is said to be *liable* for its payment.　　*owes*

---

12. Thus the debts for whose payment a person or a business is _____ are called *liabilities.*　　*liable*

---

13. Amounts owed are, therefore, called _____.　　*liabilities*

14. By subtracting the total value of what a *person* owes from the total value of what he owns, his _____ is found.

net worth

---

15. The net worth of a business is found the same way. The liabilities of the business are subtracted from its total _____ in order to find what in business is called *proprietorship* or *capital.*

assets

---

16. The assets of a business minus its _____ equals the *proprietorship* of the business.

liabilities

---

17. The assets of a business minus its liabilities equals the _____ of a business.

proprietorship

---

18. If a business owned assets worth $3,000 and owed liabilities amounting to $1,000, its proprietorship (net ownership or investment in the business) would amount to _____.

$2,000

---

19. Thus when a business has debts, the _____ is found by subtracting the liabilities of the business from its _____.

proprietorship

assets

---

20. In an earlier frame, the $50 that a PERSON *owed* was subtracted from the $800 that he *owned* in order to find his *net worth* of $750. In Frame No. 18 above, the _____ of a business were subtracted from its _____ in order to find its _____.

liabilities
assets
proprietorship

---

21. Since $3,000 (assets) minus $1,000 (liabilities) equals $2,000 (proprietorship), it is equally true that $3,000 (assets) equals $1,000 (liabilities) plus $2,000 (_____).

proprietorship

---

22. Using the number 3 to represent the value of assets, 1 for liabilities, and 2 for proprietorship, the following combinations of equations are shown.

$$A = L + P \quad P = A - L \quad L = A - P$$
$$3 = 1 + 2 \quad 2 = 3 - 1 \quad 1 = 3 - 2$$

In accordance with the above illustrations ......

assets = liabilities + _____.

proprietorship

23. In accordance with the equations illustrated in
    Frame No. 22, proprietorship = assets — _____.   *liabilities*

24. In accordance with the equations illustrated in
    Frame No. 22, liabilities = assets — _____.   *proprietorship*

25. Because the financial statement of a business called
    a *balance sheet* shows all assets listed on the left-
    hand side and all liabilities *and* proprietorship on
    the right-hand side, the fundamental bookkeeping   *assets*
    equation is written as follows: *liabilities*
    _____ = _____ + _____.   *proprietorship*

Modular Scheduling

There is a strong need today for ways of using valuable teaching time to better provide for the development of each individual
student's capabilities and to provide the necessary time for the
effective use of new educational media—television, programmed
instruction, audio tapes, and cooperative work experience.

One of the responses to these needs is the development of
modular scheduling—a method of class scheduling which makes
available both longer and shorter units of time, provides for both
large and small groups of students for various kinds of teaching,
and frees teachers from the inflexibility of a teaching day composed
only of forty- and fifty-minute periods. This type of scheduling
came into being as a result of experimentation in the efficient
utilization of school staff and instructional aids by a commission
appointed by the National Association of Secondary School Principals. The commission was appointed in 1956, named the Commission on the Experimental Study of the Utilization of Staff in the
Secondary School, and financed by the Ford Foundation.

The flexible schedules in participating high schools were based
on the use of a time module—an arbitrary period of time used
to build periods of varying lengths. Time modules usually vary
from ten to thirty minutes. A school using a thirty-minute module
may develop periods of any number of minutes divisible by thirty
—30, 60, 90, 120. School programs, scheduled in this manner,
might offer a schedule similar to the one in Figure 13–1.

Period	Monday	Tuesday	Wednesday	Thursday	Friday	Saturday
8:30	Large	Individual	Large	Large	Large	
9:00	Group	Study	Group	Group	Group	
9:30	Instruction				Small Group	
10:00						Individual
10:30	Small Group		Small			
11:00	Discussion		Group		Individual	
11:30	Large Group	Large Group	Large	Individual	Study	
	Instruction	Instruction	Group			
12:00	Lunch and Activities					
1:00		Small	Small	Small	Large	
1:30	Individual	Group	Group	Group	Group	
2:00	Study	Large				Individual
2:30		Group	Individual			
3:00		Individual	Study	Individual	Small	
3:30	Small Group	Study		Study	Group	

Figure 13—1. How a student might spend his time in the
secondary school of the future

Source: J. Lloyd Trump, *Images of the Future* (Urbana, Ill.: Commission
on the Experimental Study of the Utilization of the Staff in the
Secondary School, 1959), p. 12, as illustrated by Lester W. Anderson
and Lauren A. Van Dyke in *Secondary School Administration* (Boston:
Houghton Mifflin Company, 1963), p. 165.

The schedule of a first-year bookkeeping student at Simla
High School, Simla, Colorado, and reported by the bookkeeping
teacher, Curt L. Rickart, at a workshop conducted by the author
during the summer of 1968 at Western Colorado State College,
is shown on the following page.

Modular scheduling provides variations in the group size and
teaching time. The large groups listen and look; small groups discuss or practice; and individuals study or practice with or without
help. Basically, modular scheduling offers both teachers and students freedom to pursue many interests and achieve their highest
educational aspirations. But, with this freedom comes the responsibility to use time wisely and well. The student faced with a two-
hour or a twenty-minute block of "free" time must exercise mature
judgment in deciding what the best use of that time is. The teacher
given the time he desires, must now resist the urge to follow old
lesson plans. He must responsibly develop new techniques and set
his sights on higher achievement.

Student Schedule for Bookkeeping—20-Minute Modules

Module	Time	Monday	Tuesday	Wednesday	Thursday	Friday
1	8:40					
2	9:00	╲╳				
3	9:20					
4	9:40					
5	10:00	╲╳		╲╳		
6	10:20					
7	10:40					
8	11:00					
9	11:20					
10	11:40					
11	12:00	◄───	Lunch #I	───►		───►
12	12:20	◄───	Lunch #II	───►		───►
13	12:40	▓▓▓		▓▓▓		▓▓▓
14	1:00	▓▓▓		▓▓▓		▓▓▓
15	1:20			╲╳		
16	1:40				╲╳	
17	2:00					
18	2:20				╲╳	
19	2:40					
20	3:00			╲╳		╲╳

▓▓▓ Structured Modules—Bookkeeping Lecture		6 Mods.
╳ Unstructured Modules—Bookkeeping Laboratory		8 Mods.
	Total	14 Mods.

Figure 13—2.

Modular scheduling offers, timewise, a rare opportunity to provide for individual differences, but the individual differences themselves may well be the greatest difficulty in the administration of the program. Students of all ability levels who lack self-discipline and direction may waste the time completely. Teachers whose patterns are rigidly established in the old time slots may not change easily, if at all. As one author put it, "Flexible scheduling can be either a fad or a fundamental, depending primarily on whether or not such a schedule is an integral part of a faculty's planning for quality education." [20]

Modular scheduling is a complex process—so complex that a school of any size must turn to computers for scheduling to solve their particular problems. In addition, modular scheduling is a process that must be completely accepted by the whole school or not at all. Educational centers at places such as Stanford University [21] and the Massachusetts Institute of Technology [22] have been established to help schools develop modular schedules through the use of computers.

Automated Data Processing

The most outstanding business trend affecting B-A instruction and business education in general is automation of the office—the processing of data automatically. The effect this trend should have on the high school B-A course, as seen by this author at this time, is discussed in Chapter 24. Additional remarks follow.

Previous to 1956 the *Business Education Index* did not have a heading for automated data processing, and in 1956 this same index listed only eleven items under the heading *Automation*. Ten years later, in the 1966 issue of the *Business Education Index*, the subject heading was changed to Data Processing and the listing had increased more than ten times—to 121.

Some say automation is no longer a trend. They say that automated data processing is here to stay—that it is now a fait accompli. This is true. But, it is also true that (a) methods and equipment are changing; (b) equipment is being simplified, reducing cost; (c) and, because of lower cost it is coming within the financial range of more firms. (Smaller firms as well as public bookkeepers and accountants are recording data on cards or tape for processing at a local data center.) It is therefore obvious that

---

[20] Eugene R. Howard, "Modular Scheduling in the Senior High School—A means of Improving Instruction," *High School Journal*, January, 1965, pp. 282-88.

[21] R. N. Bush and Dwight W. Allen, *New Design for Secondary Education* (New York: McGraw-Hill Book Company, 1964).

[22] Complete report available from Educational Facilities Laboratories, 477 Madison Avenue, New York, New York   10022.

this trend has not fully run its course, and it is imperative that B-A teachers keep themselves up-to-date on new equipment, methods, and uses.

Continuing Use of Bookkeeping Machines

Some business educators watching this increasing use of automated equipment wonder if the result will be a decrease in bookkeeping and accounting machines usage. A recent comprehensive study of the present and possible future use of office machines in the State of Connecticut disclosed, among other things, that "The great majority of firms using bookkeeping and accounting machines indicated no discontinuance of their use at the present time."[23]

While this study was limited to one state (over 3,000 businesses of all types and sizes responded) it may well be indicative of practices in most other states.

STUDY QUESTIONS

1. What must a teacher do before he can become a formulator or conditioner of trends affecting the teaching of bookkeeping-accounting? Why is it important that he do these things?

2. What are some of the major provisions of the Vocational Education Act of 1963?

3. Why does the amount of federal funds spent for the training of office workers vary from state to state?

4. Why is it predicted that cooperative work-experience programs for bookkeeping students will increase?

5. What major advantage to high school business departments should result from the use of a lay advisory committee of local people?

6. Why should the requirement to identify the objective of students preparing for an office occupation improve both the educational and the vocational guidance in many high schools?

---

[23] Cletus Clow, *Business Education Curriculum Implications of Effects of Technology on the Types of Office Machines Used By Selected Connecticut Businesses,* Hartford: Connecticut State Department of Education, 1967, p. 7.

7. Why is it that more second-year courses in high school bookkeeping-accounting may be offered as a result of the Vocational Education Act of 1963?

8. Name three changing requirements for the preparation of business teachers which are the result of the Vocational Education Act of 1963.

9. What are the principal functions of the Educational Research Information Center (ERIC) located on the campus of Ohio State University?

10. Why do employers of bookkeepers usually prefer to hire junior college graduates instead of high school graduates?

11. Why, in general, should high school students who plan to attend a post-high school institution postpone their vocational training until after high school?

12. What are the reasons that caused the downgrading of the subject matter of bookkeeping and the establishment of low-level forms of bookkeeping courses?

13. What danger or harm is seen in the offering of low-level book-keeping or year-long record-keeping courses?

14. What reasons are given and what suggestions are offered for the teaching of record keeping to future office workers?

15. What is meant by *team teaching*?

16. What two factors could cause the medium of television to become more important in today's educational picture?

17. What is meant by *programmed instruction*?

18. How does modular scheduling lend flexibility to teaching?

19. What are some of the possible difficulties faced by teachers and pupils whose school shifts from a traditional school day of forty-or-fifty-minute class periods to a modular scheduling system?

20. What changes are continuing to take place in the field of automated data processing which indicate that as a trend it has not fully run its course?

DISCUSSION QUESTIONS

1. There is an old saying, "He who pays the fiddler calls the tune." Now that federal funds are being used for the vocational training of office workers, to what extent do you believe the federal government "calls the tune" on how those workers shall be trained? Do you see any need for concern about this?

2. What do you believe will be the greatest improvements to business education as a result of the Vocational Education Act of 1963?

3. Which of the following two requirements under the Vocational Education Act of 1963 do you believe would be most beneficial for vocational B-A students: (a) completing a suitable project, such as a practice set, or (b) participating in a cooperative-work-experience program?

4. What special problems do you see for the B-A teacher who establishes a cooperative-work-experience program for the first time?

5. It has been said, "There is something wrong with a high school business department that needs an advisory committee in order to do its job well." What is your reaction to this statement?

6. Some educators believe that business education will have greater stature if it is aligned with the academic rather than the vocational phase of secondary education. Which alignment do you favor? Why?

7. What are some of the advantages and disadvantages of not openly classifying high school students in such curriculums or "tracks" as *college preparatory, general, home economics, business, agriculture,* and so on?

8. A college insists on supervising and coordinating its student-teaching program which is a work experience plan. However, this same college offers no supervision or coordination to a required work-experience program in offices for business-teacher trainees. Is this a good policy? Explain.

9. Under what circumstances, if any, might a college-bound student be encouraged to enroll in a high school B-A course?

10. Explain why you believe it is best to teach record keeping: (a) as a unit in a clerical practice course, (b) as a half-year course, (c) as a full-year course, or (d) not at all.

11. Under what circumstances would you advocate the use of team teaching in a first-year B-A course?

12. Discuss the feasibility and the possibility of teacher aids being employed in a public high school familiar to you.

13. What duties could the B-A teacher be expected to assign to a full-time, adult teacher aid?

14. What do you see to be the advantages and the disadvantages of teaching high school B-A through the medium of closed-circuit television?

15. If good programmed instruction covering various first-year book-keeping topics were available in pamphlet form, would there be a demand for such materials?

16. What future do you predict for modular scheduling? Explain.

17. What length of module do you believe is best for high schools in general? for B-A classes in particular?

18. In what ways do you see modular scheduling having an effect on the day-to-day formal lesson plan method of teaching discussed in Chapter 6?

19. What future do you see for teaching automated data processing to high school students in: (a) a first-year B-A course, (b) a second-year B-A course, (c) a separate course devoted to ADP.

PROJECTS

1. Prepare a basic plan for the initial establishment of a cooperative-work-experience program for B-A students.

2. Prepare a paper comparing the similarities and the differences between a good student-teaching program and a good cooperative-work-experience program required of business teacher trainees.

3. Compare the contents of a modern record-keeping textbook with the contents of a modern bookkeeping-accounting textbook. Prepare a paper (a) indicating their similarities and differences, (b) justifying the teaching of such material, and (c) indicating the place for coverage of such subject matter in the curriculum of a specific high school.

4. Prepare a plan outlining the major team-teaching responsibilities for each of two teachers in a first-year B-A course.

5. Prepare a paper describing the duties that could be performed by an adult teacher aid assigned to assist a teacher who teaches both first and second-year B-A courses.

6. Prepare a detailed B-A lesson plan for recording on video tape. Indicate how this plan would differ from a similar lesson plan to be used in teaching a "live" class.

7. Choose a B-A topic which could be taught in a single 40-45 minute class period. Prepare a unit of self-teaching, programmed materials for this topic.

8. Prepare (a) a plan for establishing an "ideal" modular scheduling system for your school and (b) an outline in detail of the essential changes a B-A teacher should be ready to make under such a system.

9. Prepare a set of questions pertaining to current trends in automated data processing for use when interviewing a manager of a local data center. Write a report on the results of the interview.

10. After familiarizing yourself with programmed instruction, prepare a unit of self-teaching, programmed materials on a first-year B-A topic normally taught in a single class period or less. Experiment with the use and the testing of this material until you believe it is perfected.

SELECTED REFERENCES

Balter, Leslie. "The Multisensory Approach: Key to Programmed Instruction," *Business Education World.* XLVIII (December, 1967), 14.

Bangs, F. Kendrick, Principal Investigator. *Curricular Implications of Automated Data Processing for Educational Institutions.* Boulder, Colorado: University of Colorado, 1968. (Available from Executive Secretary, Delta Pi Epsilon, Gustavus Adolphus College, St. Peter, Minnesota 56082.)

Barton, Sister Ann Xavier. "Modular Scheduling in the Business Department," *The Journal of Business Education.* XLIII (April, 1968), 306.

Bennett, James C. "The Expanding Role of Television in Business Education," *The Journal of Business Education.* XLII (May, 1967), 335-336.

Buckley, John W. "Programmed Instruction: With Emphasis on Accounting," *The Accounting Review.* XLII (July, 1967), 572-582.

Bush, R. N., and Dwight W. Allen. *New Design for Secondary Education.* New York: McGraw-Hill Book Company, Inc., 1964.

Clow, Cletus A. *Business Education Curriculum Implications of the Effects of Technology on the Types of Office Machines Used by Selected Connecticut Businesses.* Hartford: Connecticut State Department of Education, 1967.

Cook, Fred S., and Daniel P. Brown. "Does Micro-Teaching Have a Place in Business Education?" *Business Education World.* XLVIII (May, 1968), 14-16.

Dale, Richard S. "A New Use of Television in Business Teacher Education," *Journal of Business Education*. XLIII (December, 1967), 98-99.

De Bellis, Charles A. "Team Teaching and Bookkeeping," *The Balance Sheet*. XLVI (April, 1965), 345-348.

Fairbank, R. E. *A Follow-up of New York State High School Bookkeeping Students*. Albany: The University of the State of New York, State Department of Education, 1967.

Georgiades, William. "Team Teaching: A New Star, Not a Meteor," *NEA Journal*. LVI (November, 1967), 14-15.

Gibbs, William E. "The Teacher and Programmed Learning," *The Balance Sheet*. XLVIII (May, 1967), 402-405, 420.

Halverson, Gaylon L. "Programmed Learning in High School Bookkeeping," *Business Education Forum*. XIX (October, 1964), 18, 23.

Howard, Eugene. "Modular Scheduling in the Senior High School— A Means of Improving Instruction," *High School Journal*. (January, 1965), 282-288.

Kane, Howard H., and Donald F. Ungurait. "The Accounting Telecourse: A Case History," *Collegiate News & Views*. XXI (March, 1968), 1-4.

Long, R. Charles. *A Study to Determine the Effect of the Vocational Act of 1963 Upon Business Teacher Education Programs in Selected Colleges and Universities*. Doctor of Education Study, University of North Dakota. As reported in *The Delta Pi Epsilon Journal*. X (February, 1968), 15-17.

McGrath, Harold M. "Teaching 'Introduction to Business' by Closed Circuit Television," *American Business Education*. XVIII (May, 1962), 235-237.

Schram, Wilbur. *Programmed Instruction Today and Tomorrow*. The Fund for the Advancement of Education, November, 1962, p. 2.

Schultheis, R. A. *The Potential Employability of Slow Learners in Recordkeeping Positions*. Unpublished doctor's thesis. Indiana University, Bloomington, 1966. As reported in *The Delta Pi Epsilon Journal*. X (August, 1968), 27-32.

Spanswick, Ralph Sterling. *An Investigation to Determine the Qualifications and Skills Desired, Accepted, and Actually Used in Manual Bookkeeping Jobs*. Doctor of Education Study, Northern Illinois University. As reported in *The Journal of Business Education*. XLIII (March, 1968), 252.

Tonne, Herbert A. "Trends in Business Occupations in the 1960's," *The Journal of Business Education*. XXXVIII (May, 1963), 314-316.

"Trends in Bookkeeping and Accounting Instruction in Junior and Senior High Schools," *Developing Vocational Competency in Bookkeeping and Accounting*, Eastern Business Teachers Association Yearbook, Vol. 40, Part II. New York: New York University Bookstore, 1967.

United States Department of Health, Education, and Welfare. *Administration of Vocational Education, Rules and Regulations*, Vocational Education Bulletin No. 1. Washington, D.C.: Superintendent of Documents, 1967.

Whitcraft, John E. "The Impact of the Vocational Education Act of 1963 on Business Education," *Administration and Supervision of Business Education*, Eastern Business Education Association Yearbook, Vol. 39, Chapter 6. New York: New York University Bookstore, 1966.

INTRODUCTION

Part I of this textbook is devoted to the broad and basic principles for teaching bookkeeping-accounting; to the importance of bookkeeping-accounting; its place in the curriculum; and B-A materials, resources, and teaching methods. It is hoped these first 13 chapters supply B-A teachers with the concepts, knowledges, and tools necessary to develop self-sufficiency and confidence in solving teaching problems.

Part II of this book gives specific suggestions for teaching selected B-A *subject matter*. This subject matter includes areas and topics most frequently questioned in the graduate and undergraduate B-A methods courses taught by the author over the past ten years.

It is not unusual to find beginning teachers and students in methods courses interested in and appreciative of ready-made plans for teaching specific B-A topics. This is understandable, and certainly the aspiring teacher is not only entitled to all the help he can borrow from the experience of others, but should be complimented for wanting to improve his competency. But, beginning teachers must understand that their own thinking and ingenuity are necessary for their fullest development as teachers.

In chemistry, formulas for mixing certain elements always produce the same results—mix two parts of hydrogen with one part of oxygen (H_2O) and the result is always water. In teaching there are no precise formulas that always produce the same results. This is because the elements that go into a lesson are never exactly the same. No two teachers act, think, or look alike—nor can they be made to act, think, and look the same. With varied experiences and therefore different values, no two teachers can ever teach exactly alike. Add to this the fact that no two students act or react exactly the same with identical interest, intensity, ability, etc.— and the point should be clear that what is best for one will not necessarily be best for another.

These are the reasons why all teachers must understand that their own thinking and their own planning is necessary for their best teaching and for their fullest development in their particular school. The lesson plans and suggestions given in Part II of this book are, therefore, primarily devices for the presentation of ideas that, if used, should be redesigned to fit the needs of the individual teachers.

GETTING STARTED—
THE FIRST WEEK'S WORK

Chapter 14

The importance of a good start by both pupils and teacher cannot be overestimated. During the opening day of the course and the first week, all-important impressions, student opinions, and student reactions are formed. Unfavorable reactions that take a few brief minutes or classroom periods to form may not be corrected or eradicated the rest of the year. With a good beginning, students inwardly say, "I like the teacher." "This course makes sense." "This is not going to be as tough as I thought." "I'm glad I signed up for bookkeeping-accounting." "I'm going to learn something in this course." Without forethought to develop a good beginning, such reactions as, "What's it all about?" "I don't like this teacher." "This is going to be too tough for me." can become the modus operandi for the student during his tenure in class.

What *is* a good beginning for a B-A class? It is the same as for any other course. The teacher introduces students to bookkeeping-accounting in a manner which

1. creates or reinforces interest in the subject;
2. builds rapport between himself and the students;
3. gets students participating, contributing, *doing;*
4. is businesslike and, at the same time, friendly and understanding;
5. builds confidence in the student and his ability to understand and to succeed;
6. builds respect for the teacher;
7. causes a student to feel that the teacher is personally interested and concerned about him and his success in the course.

Conversely, a bad start is an introduction to bookkeeping-accounting that results in the student becoming

1. timid, afraid, annoyed, or alarmed by the subject;
2. antagonistic to the teacher or the subject;
3. lazy or indifferent or disinterested;
4. sorry he enrolled in the course.

Good general teaching techniques for the first week are no different than for the second, the twentieth, or the fortieth week. However, during the first week the impressions formed and the learnings acquired can be more vital and more influential. For this reason both beginning and experienced B-A teachers are more concerned and detailed in their first week's teaching plans.

These generalities do not answer specifically the beginning teacher's questions, "But what do you *do* the first day, the second day, the first week?" Before the class time can be well planned for the first few days of the course, answers to the following questions should be secured.

1. What organizational procedures of the school are required the first day of the new year?
2. What textbooks and supplies (workbooks, paper, etc.) are available or can be made requirements in the class?
3. How long are class periods the first day?-the second?-the remaining days of the course?

These questions can be asked the day the teacher is employed and a department chairman or the principal will supply the answers. They must be answered before the teacher can begin planning for a good start. Procedures on the opening day vary from school to school. While one school has a teacher distributing books and supplies in each class, another school handles this in homerooms. In others, pupils secure books before or after school, or during free time at a central disbursing room. Some schools keep pupils in a homeroom from one to two hours in the morning filling out class cards and other forms, thus cutting down regular classroom periods for the rest of the day. Then there are a few schools that manage to start the first day of school on the same schedule as any other day in the year.

Even if the first day has abbreviated fifteen-minute periods, the teaching of bookkeeping-accounting can get off to a good start. Here are several suggestions to consider:

1. Familiarize students with the textbook. (See remarks and suggestions on pages 169 and 170.)

2. Lead a discussion on the topic "Who keeps records of business transactions?"

3. Condense your first day's lesson plan to fit the abbreviated time.

4. Ask class members to tell of any experiences they have had in keeping books.

5. Ask how many earned money during the summer—and whether or not they kept records of what they earned. Bring out how and why some bookkeeping was done as a result of their earning a dollar. Who keeps a record of their earnings or savings?

    —employer—payroll; bank—savings; government—income tax, social security; parent—budget.

6. Ask, "Even if you didn't earn any money this past summer, how did each of you cause bookkeepers some work?"

    —spending money at movies, pizza parlors, swimming pools, miniature golf courses, baseball games.

The decision as to what to do the first day and week is further qualified by (1) the needs of the students in your class; (2) the kind of textbook and materials available for use; (3) your basic beliefs about how people learn best.

The needs of students vary from school to school and what they should be taught will vary accordingly. The pupils in some schools enter a B-A course with only the vaguest conception of what a bookkeeper is or does, with the narrowest of understandings as to the advantages of learning bookkeeping or why people other than future bookkeepers study it. In other schools, students have learned before they enter the course the many advantages that can be derived from a knowledge of bookkeeping-accounting. They have a good general idea of bookkeeping-accounting and enter upon the study of bookkeeping-accounting with a high degree of intrinsic motivation.

Many schools prescribe specific textbooks and materials to be used. If the prescribed textbook does not seem to fit the needs of the students nor agree with the beliefs of the teacher, the teacher must adjust both available materials and beliefs held to best fit the situation. It is a rare occasion in any position in any field where all the factors are present to create the ideal situation. The best that can be done is to use to the fullest extent what is available and move in the direction of the ideal. In spite of difficulties, it is amazing how closely one can approach the ideal by having it as a goal.

The beliefs that a teacher has about the best methods of teaching will cause a difference in belief about what is best for students to learn. One teacher will believe that some of the things a B-A class needs to learn the first day are what he, the teacher, expects in the line of respect, attention, punctuality, and other behavior. Another teacher will prefer to let these learnings accrue for a future time when and if the situation for such teaching arises. One teacher will believe that what is in the first chapter of the students' textbook should be presented first for the students to learn. Another may feel that information in the preface or introduction of the text should be the first. Still another may first prefer to discuss the importance of bookkeeping-accounting to all people.

Thus can be seen some of the many variations for introducing students to bookkeeping-accounting and how difficult it is for one to prepare a master plan or to offer suggestions for teaching that all could use.

In spite of these foregoing qualifications for the plans that follow, the reader should be alerted to the following benefits which he can secure from a study of these plans:

First, and perhaps paramount, these plans give the inexperienced teacher a valuable opportunity to study the reasoning and thinking that an experienced teacher might put into his plans. The "Remarks" on the plans tell the reader *why* the teacher has planned to have students and himself do and say certain things. This column, in effect, reflects the teacher's ability to apply psychological principles of learning to his teaching plans. It gives the reader the opportunity to "hear" the planner "think out loud" as he proceeds with the formulation of his plan. *Beginning teachers rarely, if ever, are able to apply educational principles smoothly, correctly, and completely while thinking on their feet from extemporaneous, mental plans.*

Second, a study of these plans gives the reader the opportunity to examine his own philosophy regarding the need for and the degree of directness which he believes is best for introducing students to the technical terms and techniques of bookkeeping-accounting. For example, if he sees the need and subscribes to the belief of a motivational approach, he could start with and be benefited by ideas suggested in Lesson Plans #1 and #2. If he believes in a more direct approach, he might wish to borrow ideas from Lesson Plans #3 and #4, and introduce his students quickly and more directly to technical bookkeeping-accounting terms and practices.

A study of these four plans will readily disclose that they are prepared in a sequential order, starting with a motivational approach. Within four days, if all four plans or similar variations are used, the students will have been *introduced* to some initial technical terms and procedures of bookkeeping-accounting through what might be termed a composite "motivational-personal-equation-balance-sheet approach."

The sequential nature of these plans should not deter the teacher from deleting Lesson Plan I if a motivational approach is not desirable. A teacher could choose to start his class either along the lines of Lesson Plan #2, a personal approach; or Lesson Plan #3, the equation approach; or Lesson Plan #4, a balance sheet approach.

LESSON PLAN I

Introducing Students to Bookkeeping-Accounting

Title:	Motivating Students for B-A Study.
Aims:	To support and strengthen students' interests in the study of bookkeeping-accounting by broadening their understanding of why this subject is studied. To establish pupil-teacher rapport.
Supplies Needed:	Plain paper for students.

MOTIVATION

TEACHER	REMARKS:
"Each of you in this course may have different reasons for being here. It might be interesting for us to find out why you did enroll in this course. It might also be good for me to know so that I can better help you achieve your purposes."	Teacher shows interest in individual students, thus helping to build rapport.
"Will you, therefore, think for a minute and then write one or more of the reasons why you enrolled in this course."	This stimulates reflective thought; the first activity in bookkeeping-accounting is thus directly related to students' interests.
"You will not have to turn in your papers. All that is asked is that you write your real, your honest reasons, no matter what they are. Only you will see the paper."	The knowledge that the papers are not to be collected may encourage freer thought and expression and eliminate strain.
Teacher has *student* distribute paper. Gives students sufficient time to think and write down reasons.	Early and constant participation of students in classroom management builds a cooperative classroom spirit.
"Without looking at your reasons, I am going to try to list them on the chalkboard or overhead projector."	The presentation may be turned into a bit of a game creating the student attitude of "Can he list my reasons?"

PRESENTATION

Teacher writes heading on chalkboard, "Why High School Students Take a Bookkeeping Course."

Teacher lists and makes brief comments on the reasons similar to the following:

(Note: Rather than repeat constantly the phrase "chalkboard or overhead projector," it is understood that many teachers with access to an overhead projector will at times prefer to use it instead of the board.)

TEACHER

1. To be with a friend who is taking the course.
2. To prepare for a bookkeeping or office position.
3. To learn more about business practices in general.

"As we pause here for a moment, will all of you now place a check mark in front of each reason on your paper that I have written on the board?"

"How many of you now have check marks on your papers?"

REMARKS:

This reason presented first may inject a touch of humor and break the ice at the start of the presentation so that subsequent responses of students are more spontaneous and free.

"Suppose I put my list aside for awhile and let us see if you can complete the list."

A list of ten or twelve items is long and attention can be easily lost. Therefore, after presenting three, change the procedure and bring the students into action by asking for items from their lists.

STUDENT

Students state reasons they have on their papers, giving some explanation if they so desire.

REMARKS:

If students do not respond quickly to this suggestion, pass it by and continue making the list yourself.

Do not do anything in class to make anyone feel uncomfortable. Treat all answers with respect even though some may have small value.

More interest and status is given a student-compiled list.

Teacher expands list on board from students' responses or from his own list until all reasons such as the following items have been presented.

4. To help in the future study of accounting and business in college or elsewhere.
5. To help in a business I hope to own or manage: farm, beauty salon, store, garage or service station, etc.
6. Because my parents wanted me to take the course.

Teacher can give status or recognition to each response by a brief comment or question such as: "Why do you believe your parents

TEACHER

7. Because my secretarial course requires me to take a year of bookkeeping-accounting.
8. Because of guidance counselor's advice.
9. Because I need one more course for graduation and this fits in the free time I have.
10. Because I have heard it is an easy course.
11. To learn how to keep personal budgets, club records, etc.
12. Because I plan to teach business subjects.

"Do any of you have reasons still unchecked on your papers? Are you willing to have them listed here?"

List additional reasons if given.

REMARKS:

wanted you to study bookkeeping-accounting?" "Why do you think all secretarial students must take a year of bookkeeping-accounting?", etc.

APPLICATION AND SUMMARY

TEACHER

"On the board we have listed the reasons why people take bookkeeping-accounting. I wonder if this tells us anything about this subject?"

STUDENT

"1. Bookkeeping-accounting is an important subject to many people.
2. Since many people think it is important to study, it must be helpful.
3. It is a helpful subject to many people in many ways.
4. Many people have studied it successfully so it can't be too difficult to master."

REMARKS:

If students do not contribute all of these responses, the teacher could, himself, develop them and make these points clear.

HOMEWORK

TEACHER

REMARKS:

"Since our discussion here has indicated that bookkeeping-accounting is important to people, perhaps it might be well for us to discover further just how and why it is important."

"In preparation for tomorrow's work, will you talk to one or two adults and ask them 'In what way has bookkeeping been important to you?" (Teacher writes this question on board so that assignment will be clear to all.) *"You may ask the grocer, the newsstand man, the next door neighbor, the service station operator, your mother or father, or anyone that is convenient. After you have talked with them, write what they said and bring it to class tomorrow."*

Beginning teachers sometimes fail to be clear and "to the point" in making assignments. This homework assignment carries the discussion right out into the community, links school learning with the reality of everyday living, and has the student bring back into the classroom community reaction to the subject.

"After we have found what it is that makes bookkeeping-accounting important to people, then we will take the first steps necessary to learn how to keep books ourselves."

LESSON PLAN II

Introducing Students to Bookkeeping-Accounting

Title:

Motivating Students for Bookkeeping-Accounting Study—or—The Need for Records in Determining Financial Worth.

Aims:

To bring students to an understanding of
  (a) the meaning of financial worth,
  (b) how financial worth is determined,
  (c) the need for records (bookkeeping-accounting) in determining the financial worth of an individual or a business.

Supplies Needed: Plain paper and textbook, workbook, or mimeographed problems to be worked in class and for homework.

MOTIVATION

FIRST SUGGESTION FOR MO-
TIVATION—if homework assignment indicated in Lesson I was
given to students.

TEACHER

*"Yesterday we examined and dis-
cussed many reasons why people
study bookkeeping-accounting. Will
you give me a few of the reasons?"*

*"At the close of the period yester-
day, I asked you to try to find
out why people think that bookkeeping-accounting is so important.
Let us see what you found."*

Teacher calls upon individual
class members to tell whom they
interviewed and what replies were
received to the question, "In what
way has bookkeeping-accounting
been important to you?"

Teacher writes this question on
chalkboard and summarizes students' findings under it.

Teacher then refers to response
"So I know what I am worth,"
and proceeds to the *presentation*
section of the lesson:

STUDENT

"1. To help in a business I want to
run; to meet requirements of
secretarial course; because
guidance counselor recom-
mended it, etc."

REMARKS:

This will connect the start of today's lesson with what was done
yesterday and help reinforce learning.

STUDENT

(Common answers to be ex-
pected.)

"1. Helps me keep within my
budget.

2. So I know how much I can
spend.

3. So I know what income tax to
pay.

4. So I know where I stand.

5. So I know what I own.

6. So I know what I am worth."

REMARKS:

Students who do a homework assignment usually possess a psychological set or anticipation for reporting on this first. Teachers who
ignore or frequently postpone
these assignments are failing to
derive maximum motivational help
and learning from assignments.

SECOND SUGGESTION FOR MOTIVATION—Teachers who prefer this plan as their initial introduction could start their lesson and motivation with the following story:

TEACHER

"Recently, while I was riding on a bus, two men seated directly behind were discussing, in voices which I couldn't help overhearing, a third man."

"One asked the other, 'Do you know Johnny Bucker who lives over in Plainville?' His friend replied, 'Sure! Johnny is worth a barrel of money,' and for emphasis, added, 'A big barrel of money.' The other denied this loudly and exclaimed, 'Johnny isn't worth any barrel of money. Johnny isn't worth a cent.'"

REMARKS:

Story telling, if brief and to the point, can be an excellent device for getting attention and interest. If well done, it takes the students out of the class, out of themselves, and gets them thinking. It gives the teacher the opportunity to move easily and naturally to the presentation rather than introduce it with the deadening remark, "Today we are going to learn about—." Daily motivation or interest-getting need not, in fact should not, always be through the technique of connecting with the previous day's learning. Teachers should feel that they have "poetic license" to concoct a good story or illustration. This is an important phase in the creativeness of teaching—in lesson planning.

Teacher asks class, *"On the basis of these remarks, what do you think Johnny Bucker is worth?"*

"What is 'a barrel of money'?"

"Is it possible for a person to be worth 'not a cent'?"

STUDENT

"A great deal of money."

"Thousands of dollars, maybe."
"Hard to tell."

"No. You're always worth something."

REMARKS:

The questions here are suggestive for leading and controlling a discussion on a person's worth. The individual teacher, naturally, may choose to use different questions.

PRESENTATION

TEACHER	STUDENT
"How do we determine what a person is worth?"	"By what he does or what he has."
"How would you determine which people in our community are the most valuable, the most worthwhile to the community?"	"Find out the people who have done things that benefit other people in the community rather than just themselves."
"If we were to prepare a list of the ten people worth most to our community, would they also be the richest people in dollars and cents?"	"Not necessarily."

STUDENT: "By what he does or what he has."

STUDENT: "Find out the people who have done things that benefit other people in the community rather than just themselves."

STUDENT: "Not necessarily."

REMARKS:

The purpose of the discussion is to guide students to see for themselves that there is a difference between financial worth and social or moral worth. This extends their knowledge of the term *worth* and gives a sharper and more discriminatory meaning to the B-A term *financial worth*. Learning in this manner, through good questioning, is more effective than if the teacher simply tells students the difference. Telling does not always stimulate thought.

"Let us jot down on a sheet of paper three people who have contributed most to improving the community."

STUDENT

Students write names.

REMARKS:

This activity also gives some clue to the student's knowledge of the community in which he lives and indicates whether there is some need for a study of or reaching out into the community.

STUDENT

Student reads lists.

"Mary, would you like to read your list?"

Teacher writes names on board.

TEACHER

STUDENT

"John, yours?"

"Who else would like to read his list?"

Generally, the lists will be different and the teacher can then say, *"We each have different names on our list. Why do you suppose this is so?"*

"Yes, we may have different opinions about others."

"Because we know different people."

"Because we think differently."

REMARKS:

This point will be developed into the fact that because people's opinions vary concerning social and moral worth, there is no way to put a specific value on social and moral qualities.

"There is a term we apply to people whom we have listed as benefiting the community. We say they have 'social worth' or 'moral worth.'"

Teacher writes "social worth" and "moral worth" on the board.

"There is another term we use, too, to express a person's value in terms of what he owns. That is 'financial worth.'"

Teacher writes "financial worth" on the board.

"With which of these three 'worths' do you think bookkeeping-accounting is most concerned?"

STUDENT

"Financial worth."

"Yes, bookkeeping-accounting deals with records of a person's financial worth."

"Do you think a bookkeeper or an accounting clerk records social or moral worth?"

"No."

"Why not?"

"They are difficult to express in amounts. They are based upon opinion and cannot be exactly measured or recorded."

TEACHER

REMARKS:

"So let it be clear at the start of this course that bookkeeping-accounting is concerned with financial records only—not records of social or moral worth. These records are used to determine how much a person is worth financially."

"Let us see how a high school student, such as yourself, would determine his financial worth."

"Back there is a vacant seat. Let us say that Student John Doe sits there. What are the things we must consider in figuring out what he is worth?"

A fictitious student is suggested here since it eliminates the possibility of embarrassment or envy that might arise if a student from the class gives his personal financial state. Various students may suggest amounts, real or imagined, and thus John Doe becomes a composite of the student group. The closer you connect the topic to other students the better will be student interest and learning. You are also leading them *from* the familiar *to* the unfamiliar—a psychologically sound teaching procedure.

Teacher writes heading on board and guides student responses. FINANCIAL WORTH OF JOHN DOE—HIGH SCHOOL STUDENT. Teacher makes a list similar to the following:

Responses similar to the following could be expected.

STUDENT

Money in pocket	$ 1.00
Cash in bank	75.00
Clothes	190.00
Bicycle	35.00
Record player	30.00
Record collection	25.00
	$356.00

TEACHER

REMARKS:

If students raise questions of purchase price versus selling price for arriving at values, compliment them on their thinking and questions. Explain that part of the B-A course is concerned with learning how to record financial values. Without getting involved with depreciation say, "In this instance, we will list the price we think John Doe could receive if he sold his clothes, record player, or bike."

STUDENT

"How much is John Doe worth financially?" — "$356.00."

"How did you determine that?" — "By adding up the value of all things that he owns."

"Suppose John Doe owns all these things but also owes a friend $1.00. How much is he worth then?" — "$355.00."

"How did you arrive at that worth?" — "Subtracted what he owed from what he owned."

"That is a basic formula in bookkeeping. Let me write it on the board."

Teacher develops following formulas on board:

OWNS = FINANCIAL WORTH OF AN INDIVIDUAL

OWNS — OWES = NET FINANCIAL WORTH OF AN INDIVIDUAL

STUDENT

"When would the first statement (formula) be correct?" — "When the individual does not owe anyone anything."

"When would the second be correct?" — "When an individual owes something to someone."

TEACHER   STUDENT

Teacher writes the term *net* on
the board.

"What does the term 'net' mean?"   "The amount after the debts are
                                     subtracted."

                                     REMARKS:

                                     Teachers might prefer to delay
                                     introducing the term *net* until
                                     later in the course when gross
                                     and net profit are discussed. Be-
                                     ginning teachers must be cautious
                                     about the use of words, the mean-
                                     ing of which the students may not
                                     know. When such terms are used,
                                     meaning must be taught, too.

                                     STUDENT

"What are some of the advantages   "Ease of mind."
or reasons for one knowing exactly "Better management of income—
what he is worth financially or for might save more or try to spend
keeping accurate and up-to-date   more wisely."
financial records?"   "For reporting income tax to gov-
                                     ernment."
"EVERY person, EVERY business,   "Proof of bills paid."
can thus operate more efficiently "Reminder of what you owe."
if they are aware of how much   "To assist in borrowing."
they are worth."

APPLICATION

"Now suppose that we wanted to   STUDENT
find out how much John Doe's   List what he owns, find out what
father is worth. How would we   he owes, and the difference is what
go about it?"   he is worth financially.

                                     REMARKS:

                                     Here, the teacher is planting the
                                     seed of the concept that assets
                                     vary between individuals and dif-
                                     ferent businesses.

Teacher develops an OWNS and OWES column on the board.

TEACHER

"What are some items commonly owned by a parent, and approximately what are they worth?"

STUDENT

Car	$ 1,800
Tools	40
House	12,000
Furniture	1,500
Clothes	300
Money in bank	400
	$16,040

"What are some debts a parent might have?"

Bills	$
Electric	5
Gas	3
Store	20
Money borrowed	150
	$ 178

"Now figure the financial worth of John Doe's father."

"What is it?"

"Let us figure the worth of several other people."

Teacher assigns end-of-chapter, workbook problems, or mimeographed problems dealing with the financial worth of individuals.

"$15,862."

REMARKS:

Students figure financial worth of people in the problems, applying the new learnings.

Teacher walks around the room, inspects work, assisting where needed, and determines how well students have learned and how well they are able to apply the knowledge.

STUDENT

Students work at seats.

SUMMARY

"Let us now review what we have covered today."

"What do we mean by financial worth?"

STUDENT

"How much a person has in terms of money."

TEACHER

STUDENT

"How do we determine what a person is worth financially?"

"By subtracting what he owes from what he owns."

"State this in the form of an equation."

OWNS — OWES = FINANCIAL WORTH OF AN INDIVIDUAL

"If a person is said to be worth $500, does that mean he doesn't owe anyone anything?" Explain.

"No. True financial worth is what he is worth after subtracting his debts."

"What other kind of values do we have for measuring the worth of an individual to his family or his community? Illustrate."

"Social or moral values."
"When a person gives time and service to the community."

"What kind of values are shown in bookkeeping-accounting records?"

"Financial."

"State the reasons why an individual would keep personal financial records?"

"For help in computing income tax, better management of income, etc."

"State one reason why a business keeps financial records? Another? etc."

"To know what it owns."
"To know who owes it money."
"To know who owes how much money to it."
"To know whom it owes and how much, etc."

REMARKS:

Some teachers summarize a lesson by *telling* the students what they were to have learned that day. Requiring the students to answer summary questions assures the teacher of some degree of pupil activity and at the same time gives him a chance to test if what was taught is understood.

Occasionally it is well for the teacher to ask students to summarize the day's work without any suggestions or summary questions by the teacher.

TEACHER	REMARKS:
	Questions should be scattered throughout the class to bring all students into the activity, and to give the teacher a general feeling of the degree of his teaching success.
"Any questions? Any points not clear?"	Calling for questions *occasionally* can be a good technique. It invites participation and challenge and can assist in good rapport. BUT just because a class has no questions does not mean that all is clear and understood.

HOMEWORK

"So that you have additional experience and practice in figuring the financial worth of an individual, your homework assignment is to complete . . ." (This could be end-of-chapter problems, workbook problems, or mimeographed problems supplied by the teacher—just so they have further application of the day's learning.)

"Furthermore, you will please read and study pages . . . to . . . in your textbook. This will give you additional information on this topic."

"So I am sure that your assignment has been clear, I am going to ask Mary Jane Smith to repeat the two things assigned."

"Tomorrow we will first review your homework, and then we will look at some business terms book-keepers, accounting clerks, and secretaries use when referring to financial worth, things owned, and things owed."

Beginning teachers sometimes forget at the finish of the lesson to give the planned homework assignment. One way of eliminating this is to write the assignment for each class at a particular corner of the chalkboard. Students are told of this practice and held responsible for copying down the written assignment before leaving the class each day. While this eliminates overlooking the assignment, and is better than no assignment at all, it is certainly not as good as motivating or connecting the assignment *near the close of the period* with what has been done in class or what is to come the next day. A good close to a well-planned and well-taught lesson is a clearly understood assignment that keeps the new learnings in action.

TEACHER	REMARKS:
"If some of you are interested in reading ahead of the assignment, you will find some of the things we will discuss tomorrow on pages . . . and . . . ."	It is well to challenge and encourage students to study on their own. It gets some out of the habit of doing no more than the assignment.

LESSON PLAN III

Introducing Students to Bookkeeping-Accounting

Title: Assets, Liabilities, Proprietorship, and the Book-keeping Equation.

Aim: To help students reach an understanding of the above business terms.

Supplies Needed: Plain paper for students.

MOTIVATION

FIRST SUGGESTION FOR MO-TIVATION—if homework assignment indicated in Lesson II was given to students.

TEACHER	REMARKS:
"Yesterday we found out how to determine the financial worth of an individual. Let us review briefly how we determine what a person is worth."	This is a brief review for the purpose of recalling and establishing a connecting link between yesterday's and today's work.

"What is the formula we use in determining a person's financial worth? Robert Jones."

Teacher places formula on board.

STUDENT

"OWNS — OWES = NET WORTH."

REMARKS:

"You had some homework problems in which you figured the financial worth of a number of people. Let us turn to those now."

In the early part of the course it might be best to call largely upon students who raise their hands. Too much of this practice, however, can encourage lack of participation or laziness on the part

TEACHER

"What was your answer to problem #1? Mary Smith, do you have it? How did you get your answer?"

Teacher fills in totals of OWNS, OWES, and NET WORTH on board to test accuracy.

"How many of you had the same answer?" Compliment the class, if justified, by saying, *"Good work"* or some other such expression.

"If your answer was correct, place a check mark (∨) beside it. If it was incorrect, place an (x) beside it. That is how a bookkeeper indicates the accuracy of his work. We will follow this procedure whenever we check any of our work."

Check all or part of the remaining homework assignment by having answers reported by different students.

REMARKS:

of some students. A procedure that tends to keep everyone on his toes is stating a question, pausing for a moment until all the class has a chance to find the answer, then calling upon an individual. Homework is given value early in the course by immediate use in classwork. Homework ignored soon becomes homework not done.

STUDENT

(Since problems used will vary, student responses cannot be supplied here.)

Students look at papers.

REMARKS:

It is a well-accepted psychological principle that students work more satisfactorily as the result of a reward than as the result of punishment. When deserved, compliments are rewards.

Students check answers.

REMARKS:

This is a simple clerical skill that can be started early and developed into an automatic procedure. Students begin to feel important when they use vocational procedures.

It is not always necessary to check an entire homework assignment, especially if it is a lengthy one that would consume a large proportion of the class time. Checking a problem here and there will

TEACHER

REMARKS:

achieve the purposes desired. The teacher will have to use his judgment to determine when to check all the homework and when to spot-check it.

Proceed to the *presentation* section of the lesson.

SECOND SUGGESTION FOR MOTIVATION—Teachers who wish to start their course with an immediate introduction of assets, liabilities, proprietorship, and the bookkeeping equation may start here.

TEACHER

"In B-A work, we use special terms to describe what a person or a business OWNS, what is OWED, and what one is worth financially."

"Those of you who are planning to be secretaries will frequently hear these business terms or have them dictated to you. Some of you have already seen them in newspapers and books and are already familiar with them."

REMARKS:

This relates bookkeeping-accounting to the secretarial students in the class and to such everyday activities as reading the newspaper.

PRESENTATION

TEACHER

"Who can tell us the term used to define items of value that a person or business owns?"

STUDENT

"Assets."

REMARKS:

Even if no student knows the term, teachers should take every opportunity to give the students a chance to contribute, to participate, to *do*.

Teacher writes the term *assets* on the board.

STUDENT

"Name two assets that you own. Robert Brown? Mary Smith? James Harvey?"

"Books, bicycle, fountain pen, etc."

TEACHER	REMARKS:
"In bookkeeping-accounting we record only values that have financial or dollars-and cents values—things that can be sold or converted to money."	This is a review for those students who have been taken through the previous two lessons, and it is a quick presentation of the several concepts of the term *worth* for those students for whom it is the beginning lesson.
"People possess other things that are also called assets. For example, when Robert Brown named two assets which he owned, he spoke clearly and distinctly so that all of you could hear. Therefore, we can say that Robert possesses the asset of clear and distinct speech."	

	STUDENT
"If one of you had a weak voice and wanted to speak more strongly, could you buy Robert's?"	"No."
"Robert, therefore, possesses an important social asset that cannot be bought."	
"What are some other important social or moral assets that a person might possess?"	"Neatness, punctuality, cooperation with others, dependability."
"How much is each of these worth in dollars and cents?"	"Nothing" or "Immeasurable in dollars and cents. But they might help you get a job and make money."

	REMARKS:
"Yes, and therefore, these non-financial assets do have importance. Studies show that many times people in offices lose their jobs or do not receive promotions largely because they lack some of these social and moral assets."	Lack of desirable personal characteristics is in a large part responsible for loss of a job or lack of promotion. Business teachers must give emphasis to the teaching of personal characteristics in addition to skill building if they are to give realistic training for vocational and everyday living.

TEACHER

"Everyone has some social and moral assets. Can they be recorded as financial assets?"

"So in bookkeeping-accounting we deal only with what kind of assets?"

"So that we can be sure that all understand what financial assets are, will the girls in the class list five common types of financial assets owned by a wife or mother, and the boys list five common types of financial assets owned by a husband or father."

"Let us have one boy and one girl read their lists."

Teacher raises questions or asks class to comment on questionable items.

"We can see from the lists that different types of people own different kinds of assets. It is also true that different kinds of businesses own different types of assets. For example,

"Let us have the boys write down five common assets they think a garage, a farmer, or a doctor might own. And the girls prepare a similar list for a beauty shop or a public stenographer."

Have several lists read and discussed briefly.

STUDENT

"No, because the dollar-and-cents value cannot be measured."

"Financial."

Students write.

REMARKS:

Here the teacher is *testing* students to see if they understand and can *apply* what was taught. Thus the initial application in this lesson accompanies the presentation rather than follows it.

STUDENT

Items that might appear on the girl's list: jewelry, clothes, washing machine, stove. On the boy's list: tools, fishing tackle, car, golf clubs, bonds.

REMARKS:

The teacher here is also moving the students' experience one step out of direct personal contact but still within familiar territory.

Here the students' experience is moved out into the realm of business.

MEDIAL SUMMARY

TEACHER	REMARKS:
"Let us pause here a minute and review briefly what we have learned about things that people or businesses own."	It is desirable occasionally to pause during a presentation and conduct a medial summary rather than to let the entire summary accumulate until the close of the lesson. It checks the students' understanding of the presentation and helps him catch up with the knowledge offered before too much accumulates for him to grasp.

	STUDENT
"What are such things called?"	"Assets."
"Why do they differ from person to person? from business to business?"	"Because people and businesses differ."
"What is the difference between a financial or business asset and a moral or social asset? Illustrate."	"A financial asset can be expressed in terms of money. A moral or social asset can't be reduced to money terms but still has great importance to the possessor."
"Which type of assets does the bookkeeper record?"	"Financial."
"Why is this the only kind he records?"	"Because it is the only kind that can be reduced to money values."
"Does this mean that financial assets are more important than other kinds of assets?"	"No. Social assets are very important, too."
"What new business term can we now substitute for OWNS in this equation on the board?"	"Assets."

PRESENTATION (continued)

"Who knows the term used to define what a person OWES?"	"Debts?"

TEACHER

"Yes. There is, however, another term that covers all kinds of debts."

Whether supplied by a student or not, the teacher writes LIABILI-TIES on the board.

"The terms 'debts' and 'liabilities' mean essentially the same thing, but businessmen and bookkeepers more frequently use the term 'liabilities' because it is a more inclusive term."

"All of you have used the term 'liable' before. It is not new to you."

Teacher writes *liable* on the board.

TEACHER

"You may have forgotten to go to baseball practice or to a play practice, and so you say, "I forgot to go to practice and I'm liable to be put off the team or out of the play."

"The term 'liabilities' is built from the word 'liable' and has a somewhat broader meaning than the word 'debt.'"

"In your case you had an obligation to appear for practice and you are liable to be punished for not meeting your obligation."

"A debt is something you owe. Liabilities include not only debts you definitely owe, but also possible debts or losses you anticipate might reasonably occur."

STUDENT

"Liabilities."

REMARKS:

When students do not know the answer to a well-stated question, and it cannot be restated in a manner that will help students see the right answer more clearly, the teacher should tell the answer at once. This procedure avoids a tense, unpleasant situation created by a long silence or by belittling the students' knowledge.

Teachers who don't want chorus answers to general questions will find it easier to establish student response procedures early in the course.

REMARKS:

Here the unfamiliar term is being linked to a word that is familiar.

TEACHER

"We'll look more closely at this later in the course."

"Right now, who can give us some examples of common liabilities a high school student might owe?"

"That a parent might owe?"

"That a business might owe?"

"What word, a common business term, can we now substitute for OWES in this equation on the board?"

"That leaves us with one remaining word or phrase in our equation which we have not changed."

"What is another name for the owner of a business?"

Teacher writes *proprietor* on the board.

"If the proprietor of a business is the owner of the business, what do you think 'proprietorship' means?"

"Who knows another business term that means the same thing as ownership or proprietorship in a business?"

Teacher substitutes PROPRI-ETORSHIP for NET WORTH in the equation on the board.

It now should read: Assets — Liabilities = Proprietorship.

REMARKS:

Constant use of the chalkboard in writing new words and new terms is a necessary procedure in good teaching. The chalkboard is a most effective visual aid. If students not only hear, but also see, learning is more effective. The well-planned use of a chalkboard is an excellent review or summary device.

STUDENT

"Liabilities."

"Proprietor."

"Ownership."
"Capital."

"Net Worth."
"Capital."

REMARKS:

Depending upon teacher's preference or text being used, "Capital" or "Owner's Equity" could be used instead of "Proprietorship."

FURTHER APPLICATION

TEACHER	STUDENT
"This equation with the new terms is called 'The Bookkeeping Equation' and is basic to all B-A work."	
"Are there other ways that you can see of expressing the same idea?"	Assets = Liabilities + Proprietorship.

STUDENT

REMARKS:

If the students are not quick to answer this question, the simple arithmetic equation $5 - 1 = 4$ could be written on the board. Then through questioning and discussion develop the fact that this could also be written $5 = 1 + 4$ or $1 + 4 = 5$ relating the terms *assets, liabilities,* and *proprietorship*.

Write equations on the board as they are developed.

Liabilities + Proprietorship = Assets.

Assets — Proprietorship = Liabilities.

The teacher can save class time by having these equations placed on large cardboards. As they are developed, the proper cardboard can be produced and placed on the board rack. This saves writing time, and the cards can be used year after year.

"Let us practice computing the bookkeeping equation in the several ways we have on the board."

"Turn to the mimeographed sheets (or the textbook, or the workbook) and do the problems on page ..."

Students work out equations.

Teacher walks around the room, helping students where needed.

FINAL SUMMARY

TEACHER

"*Let us summarize our work to-day.*" Teacher asks question such as:

1. What is a common B-A term for the debts a business owes?
2. What common business term describes the net worth of a business?
3. What is another term that means the same as proprietor-ship?

STUDENT

Liabilities.

Proprietorship.

Capital or Ownership.

TEACHER

4. What is the bookkeeping equa-tion?
5. Teacher gives a few simple problems dealing with the equation that students are asked to solve mentally.
6. Teacher reviews questions listed previously in medial summary—particularly those which were not answered promptly or prop-erly before.

STUDENT

Assets = Liabilities + Proprietor-ship.

REMARKS:

Beginning teachers sometimes need to be cautioned to keep the ma-terial and questions covered in the summary within the realm of the new learnings.

HOMEWORK ASSIGNMENT

"*The bookkeeping equation is con-stantly involved in B-A work. If the bookkeeper's books are not in balance, they have mistakes in them. If the bookkeeping equation is not in balance, if the total amount of the assets does not equal the total amount of liabilities and proprietorship, something is wrong.*"

"*So that you learn to feel more 'at home' with the bookkeeping*

REMARKS:

Homework assignment continues the work of (the application of) the classroom.

TEACHER	REMARKS:
equation, you are asked to work the following problems in your workbook. These problems are similar to the work we have been doing today."	

"Is the assignment clear? Will you please repeat it, Robert Jones?"

LESSON PLAN IV

Introducing Students to Bookkeeping-Accounting

Title: Introducing the Balance Sheet

Aims: To bring students to an understanding of what a simple balance sheet is and how it is related to the bookkeeping equation.

Supplies Needed: Plain paper, textbook, workbook, balance sheet paper. A large poster of a balance sheet that could be placed before the group would be especially helpful also.

MOTIVATION

TEACHER	STUDENT
FIRST SUGGESTION FOR MO-TIVATION—if students were assigned homework indicated in Lesson III.	
"Yesterday we discussed what the basic bookkeeping equation was. Suppose you write it to see if you remember."	Students write bookkeeping equation on a piece of plain paper.
	REMARKS:
	This is a self-test. It gives the students a little time to think and recall the preceding day's work.
Walk around the room and discover who is writing the equation correctly, then ask several students who are writing it correctly to put it on the board. Try to secure different expressions of the equation.	Several students write equation on the board.

TEACHER

REMARKS:

Being sure the student is correct eliminates initial student embarrassment. This procedure also allows the slower student to correct himself without embarrassment.

"John and Mary have not written exactly the same thing on the board. Which one is right?"

"They both are. Both equations mean the same."

REMARKS:

"Yes, the meaning is the same. We have simply used different words or a different form of the equation. In one instance our own everyday words were used. In the other, business words were used. Here in another instance, the student has written $L = A - P$ instead of $A = L + P$."

This idea is preparatory to the concept that the equation and the balance sheet tell essentially the same thing in a different form.

"Let us turn to the homework to check the correctness of your equations and to see if you have any questions?"

"Jean, will you give us your answer to the first problem?"

Student gives answer.

"How many have that answer? Let's check it for correctness."

Students check work.

REMARKS:

Teacher does arithmetic on the board.

This helps review arithmetic procedure for those who may be weak in that phase.

"Check your work as we did yesterday—with a check ($\vee$) if it is correct; with an (x) if it is incorrect."

Students check work.

REMARKS:

This continues the application of a common office skill.

When finished checking homework, proceed to the presentation section of this lesson.

Students check answers, explain when called upon to do so, ask questions.

TEACHER   STUDENT

SECOND SUGGESTION FOR
MOTIVATION—if teachers wish to
start their course with this lesson
and an initial or direct balance
sheet approach.

*"A question that one hears many
times both in everyday life and
in business is, 'How much is he
worth?' "*

*"Suppose someone asked you,
'How much are you worth?' How
would you go about figuring it
out?"*

"List what I have, decide how
much each item is worth, and add
up the amounts."

*"Suppose you owe someone some-
thing? What do you do about
that?"*

"Subtract it from the value of what
I have."

*"So, in order to find out what you
are worth financially, you make
a list of what you own and subtract what you owe. This is a
basic bookkeeping equation."*

REMARKS:
Here the teacher summarizes for
the students.

Writes OWNS — OWES =
WORTH on the board.

*"Financial worth is only one mea-
sure of a person's worth. If a person
works hard for a club, a church,
or a community and helps people,
he is said to have social worth.
The bookkeeper, however, can't
put a money value on social worth,
so he is only concerned with financial worth."*

Although this is a brief explanation, it is designed to broaden
the students' concept of the word
"worth" and define the B-A meaning of the word.

*"Business uses special words to
express this basic equation we
have on the board. Does anyone
know what they might be?"*

Students may know one or two of
the words. If no one knows, give
the answer promptly. Avoid a long
silence that may be interpreted as
reproof for not knowing or cause
uneasiness.

TEACHER	REMARKS:
Teacher writes on the board AS-SETS — LIABILITIES = PRO-PRIETORSHIP.	
"Proprietorship is another word for ownership and net worth is another word for proprietorship."	This is another example of moving in teaching from the known to the unknown.
Write the three words on the board, bracket them, and write "same meaning."	This is another attempt to develop the basic idea that words or form may give the same facts in a different way.

PRESENTATION

REMARKS:

"When called upon to determine a man's financial worth, a bookkeeper prepares a statement called a balance sheet. Our task is to learn something about a balance sheet, which all bookkeepers at one time or another must prepare."	If a visual aid is used, the teacher can point to the form and be sure all students are looking at the same thing. When each student looks at his book, the teacher has little assurance that all students are actually looking at the correct item.
"Now let us see what a balance sheet looks like. This form (on the board, on a chart, or on a screen) is a balance sheet. Let us make a list on the board of what is contained in a balance sheet so that when we prepare one ourselves we can check and be sure we have all the parts."	This procedure exemplifies the psychological principle of teaching by presenting the whole and then moving to the parts.

	STUDENT
"What comes first?"	"The heading."
Write the word "Heading" on the board.	
"What is contained in the heading?"	"Name of the individual or the business."
	"Name of the form—balance sheet."
Write "Who" under the heading on the board.	"Date for which the statement is prepared."

TEACHER

Write "What" under the heading.

Write "When" under the heading.

"The heading of every financial statement should answer these three questions—who? what? when? If a statement is filed and then taken out later, it is worthless if it does not tell when it was done, or for whom it was done. Not having who, what, and when on the balance sheet would be like announcing an athletic game for the students to attend and not tell who was playing, or what kind of a game it was, or when it was to be."

"Now let us look at the body of the balance sheet. See if you can find the parts of the basic equation."

"What is the amount of the total assets here on the left side?" Point to visual aid.

"When you add the liabilities and the proprietorship, what is the amount here on the right side?"

"The amounts are the same, aren't they? The two sides of the balance sheet balance. That is why it is called the balance sheet. The two sides must always be in balance, always equal to each other, just as the equation is."

"The businessman wants to know not only what the total of his assets are, but what the specific items are, also. So here (pointing to visual aid) on the left side

REMARKS:

This procedure is also the beginning of analysis and interpretation in bookkeeping-accounting.

Again relating a basic bookkeeping procedure to something within the students' own experiences.

Students point out assets, liabilities, and proprietorship.

REMARKS:

Here the relationship between the equation and the balance sheet is specifically developed.

Students give amount.

Students give amount.

TEACHER

under the title 'Assets' they are listed. Steve, will you read the assets listed here?"

REMARKS:

The word "right" and "left" sides are used to emphasize the correct placement of the assets and liabilities.

Student reads.

TEACHER

"Suppose your balance sheet was for a garage. What other assets might appear on such a balance sheet?"

STUDENT

"Tools, equipment, etc."

REMARKS:

This question tests the students' understanding of the real meaning of the term "assets."

"On the right side, the liabilities are listed. Joan, will you read them?"

Student reads.

STUDENT

"You read several names. What does a name mean under liabilities?"

"That's a person we owe some money to."

"Suppose you were running a home and made out a balance sheet. What are some liabilities that might appear on it?"

"Mortgage, debt to a loan association, bill owed to grocer, etc."

"Now let's finish our list of items that appear on the balance sheet. We have the heading. What shall we call this big section?"

"The body."

"What is contained in the body?"

"Assets, liabilities, and proprietorship."

"Yes, just the same as in the equation, only in more detail. Look back at the balance sheet. How would the figures on it change if this business borrowed $500 cash from J. Smith?"

"The amount of cash would be increased by $500 and the liabilities by $500."

REMARKS:

There is enough new learning contained within the aim of this lesson without introducing new terms such as *debit* and *credit*.

TEACHER

STUDENT

"What changes would be needed to bring the balance sheet up to date if the business spent $100 for supplies?"

"Decrease the amount of cash by $100 and increase the value of supplies by $100."

"Would someone like to suggest a business transaction that would change the figures in the balance sheet?"

Students suggest several other changes, and teacher changes figures accordingly.

"Notice that although we change the figures within the balance sheet, the two sides always balance."

REMARKS:

Repetition to fix the idea.

APPLICATION

"Let us turn to page ... in the textbook. Here is another balance sheet. Let us do problem ... on page ... and see how well we can set up a balance sheet."

Students construct a balance sheet.

Teacher walks around room to see if students are performing assignment correctly—giving individual help as necessary, or stopping class to reteach any one understanding that appears weak.

SUMMARY

"Let us see what we have learned today."

Teacher asks questions similar to the following.

The replies of the students determine if further questions are necessary.

1. What is the form called that shows what a business is worth at a given time?

"Balance sheet."

2. What is contained on a balance sheet? — "The heading and the body."

3. Why is the heading important? — "It tells what the form is, for whom it was prepared, and when."

4. Why is the date in the heading important? — "It indicates on what day the different items listed were owned and owed."

5. What is it used for? — "To indicate what a person or business is worth at a given time."

6. Who prepares balance sheets? Why? — "Bookkeepers. To supply their employers with necessary information."

7. Why is the term "balance" used in the title of this financial statement? — "Total amount on left-hand side is equal to or balances with total amount on right-hand side."

8. How is the balance sheet related to the bookkeeping equation? — "Assets on left-hand side equal liabilities and proprietorship on right-hand side."

9. When is a balance sheet prepared? — "When a business (or individual) wants to know what it is worth—usually monthly or yearly."

10. Will the balance sheet change from one period to the next? — "Yes."

HOMEWORK

"Preparing a balance sheet is one of the most important B-A procedures. Therefore, so you have more practice in dealing with balance sheets, will you please work out problems . . . and . . . in your workbook, and come to class prepared to answer all of the questions on page . . . at the end of Chapter . . . ."

Students make note of homework to be done.

The words in a lesson plan do not begin to come to life until the teacher speaks them to the class. Just as an actor makes the lines of a play come to life, so the individual teacher makes a lesson plan come to life. A written lesson plan cannot fully express the personality of the teacher. He has to put his personality into the plan as he teaches. His own way of expressing himself, his own personal illustrations of points, his own humor, his own knowledge of what will appeal to his particular student group—all of these things make a lesson plan live. It is apropos, therefore, to say here again that these plans are suggestive outlines which must be modified to meet the needs and personality of the individual teacher.

STUDY QUESTIONS

1. Why is a good start at the beginning of a course so important?

2. What are five or six factors that one looks for in determining whether or not a good start has been made?

3. How, if at all, would general teaching techniques differ between the first and second week of a course? between the first and the twentieth week? between the first and last week?

4. Why is it that experienced as well as beginning teachers are probably more concerned with their first week's teaching plans?

5. What three things must beginning teachers know before they can plan most effectively for the first day of the school year?

6. In what ways do schools differ in the procedures followed in the classrooms on the opening day of school?

7. Suppose that during the opening day your teaching time is limited to 15 minutes for each class period. What could you and your B-A pupils do to make the most of this time?

8. What major benefit may the inexperienced teacher derive from the sample, introductory lesson plans shown in this chapter?

9. How can these four illustrative plans be of value to experienced teachers?

10. How can student participation in classroom management be secured the first day?

11. What motivational technique in Lesson I is used to show the value of the study of bookkeeping-accounting?

12. Give an example of a homework assignment that links school learning with the reality of everyday living.

13. Why should homework assignments be discussed or checked each day?

14. Why is story telling a good teaching device?

15. When should you avoid illustrations that concern members of the class?

16. Why is it important in lesson planning to consider the words you are going to use in your teaching?

17. Give several ways of summarizing a lesson.

18. If the class is silent when asked, "Are there any questions on the lesson?" what should the teacher not assume?

19. When is it best to give a homework assignment?

20. What are several ways in which students can be called upon to answer questions?

21. Why are compliments to students who have earned them desirable?

22. What is meant by "spot-checking" homework?

23. Why should business teachers give attention to the teaching of personal characteristics in addition to skill building?

24. Give an example of how a teacher can start the teaching of a B-A principle within the realm of student experience.

25. What is a medial summary?

26. When students do not answer a well-stated question readily, what should a teacher do?

27. How can a teacher avoid chorus answers to general questions directed to the class?

28. Give several uses of the chalkboard in teaching.

29. Give an example in teaching bookkeeping-accounting of moving from the known to the unknown.

30. Why is it more desirable to have all students look at a visual aid in the front of the room rather than an illustration in their textbooks?

31. Why is it said that a written lesson plan cannot fully reflect the personality of the teacher who prepared it?

DISCUSSION QUESTIONS

1. Why may it prove unsatisfactory or disappointing to try to use a lesson plan prepared by someone else?

2. Which of the four plans presented in this chapter comes closest to your preference for introducing students to bookkeeping-accounting? Why?

3. Would you prefer to use an approach other than those presented here? Describe it and tell why you prefer it.

4. How can a knowledge of psychology be helpful in teaching of bookkeeping-accounting? Give illustrations.

The PROJECTS found at the end of each chapter in Part I of this text are not continued in Part II. These end-of-chapter items were dropped from Part II because they would be the same or similar for most of the chapters in this latter part of the book. For example, the three most logical students' projects for each of these chapters would seem to be as follows:

1. Prepare your own set of lesson plans for the teaching of the subject discussed in this chapter.

2. Write a paper dealing with the special problems and possible solutions for the teaching of the subject matter discussed in this chapter.

3. After studying the available writings on the teaching of _____, prepare a paper summarizing your findings and stating your conclusions.

SELECTED REFERENCES

Lamb, Marion M. *Your First Year of Teaching,* Monograph 103. Cincinnati: South-Western Publishing Company, 1961.

Mickelson, Harold. "An Easy Introduction to Bookkeeping," *The Balance Sheet.* XL (January, 1959), 196-198.

Musselman, Vernon A., and J. Marshall Hanna. "Introducing the Course," *Teaching Bookkeeping and Accounting,* Chapter 7. New York: Gregg Publishing Division, McGraw-Hill Book Company, Inc., 1960.

Satlow, I. David. "Let Mental Hygiene Guide Your First Lesson of Any Bookkeeping Unit," *THE EBTA Journal.* III (Fall, 1964), 11-12, 22.

Wunsch, M. R. "The First Day in Bookkeeping and Accounting," *The Balance Sheet.* XLVIII (March, 1967), 304-306.

Chapter 15

Basic Importance of Debit and Credit

Since the principles of debit and credit are basic to all manual and machine bookkeeping-accounting, when to debit and when to credit is a basic unit in B-A instruction. Rules for debiting and crediting are based on logical reasons. Students can follow rules and turn in impressive papers, but learning *how* to follow rules without knowing *why* is ineffectual. The student must understand the underlying concepts before he can master bookkeeping-accounting.

Since individuality is a valued asset in a democracy, B-A teachers use a variety of procedures to develop the *whys* and *hows* of debit and credit. But, in spite of the individual methods used, the basic principles taught are the same.

What basic *whys* and *hows* of debit and credit should be presented and explored at this point? And, what are some suggestions for the successful teaching of these basics?

Procedural Outline

The following procedural outline is one path to a basic understanding of debiting and crediting of balance sheet accounts. The outline assumes that students have been introduced to the balance sheet and the bookkeeping equation previously. This material is suggested as a logical development of subject matter that can be incorporated in several lesson plans, and the words put into the mouth of the teacher are merely for variation of form. The lesson plans developed from this material should be a reflection of the individual teacher—his own words, his unique personality, with illustrations he feels are best for his students.

Learning Stages in the Outline

Incorporated in the procedural outline, starting below, are four learning stages. As the student progresses from one stage to the next, the full meaning of debit and credit is made clear. Debiting and crediting are reasoned actions for the students and not procedures based on a memorized set of "blind" rules.

1. To comprehend the need for accounts by
   a. Understanding what a business transaction is.
   b. Understanding how each transaction affects the value of two or more items (called accounts).
   c. Understanding the need for some systematic way of sorting and summarizing the changing values of things owned and owed.
2. To comprehend the meaning of account balances by
   a. Knowing why accounts have two sides.
   b. Knowing what the balance of an account is.
   c. Knowing the names given to each side of an account.
   d. Understanding the kinds of balances that assets, liabilities, and proprietorship always have.
   e. Understanding that the balance side of an account is always its increase side.
   f. Understanding that a decrease is always placed on the side of the account opposite the balance side.
3. To develop a formula for debiting and crediting different kinds of accounts.
4. To reinforce understanding of debit and credit through drill and application.

**A PROCEDURAL OUTLINE OF SUGGESTIONS
FOR TEACHING
WHEN TO *DEBIT* AND WHEN TO *CREDIT*
BALANCE SHEET ACCOUNTS**

	PROCEDURES—WHAT IS SAID AND DONE
Review the form and the content of a balance sheet presented in previous lessons	*"Let us see how well you remember what we learned the first week in bookkeeping-accounting."* *"Assume that Mr. James Howard decided to invest $4,000 of his savings and open a new self-service launderette."*

"On July 1, he deposits this $4,000 cash investment in the bank under the name of the new business, MODERN LAUNDERETTE. Write name on board. How would his balance sheet look at this time?"

Teacher constructs balance sheet on board according to the correct directions of the students. He points out (1) the need for a heading and the three items it contains, and (2) how the bookkeeping formula is included in the arrangement of the body.

Modern Launderette
Balance Sheet
July 1, 19—

Assets		Liabilities	
		& Proprietorship	
Cash	4,000		
		J. Howard, Cap.	4,000
Total Assets	4,000	Total Liab. & Prop.	4,000

"On July 2, the Modern Launderette spent $2,500 for 10 automatic, coin-operated washing machines."

"How can we change the July 1 balance sheet so it will reflect the business activity on July 2?"

LEARNING STAGES

Teacher records on the original balance sheet as the students indicate the necessary changes:

1. To comprehend the need of accounts by

Modern Launderette
Balance Sheet
July ~~1~~, 19--
     2

Assets		Liabilities	
		& Proprietorship	
Cash	1,500 ~~4,000~~		
Washing Equipment	2,500	J. Howard, Cap.	4,000
Total Assets	4,000	Total Liab. & Prop.	4,000

"Did this purchase of washing machines change the amount of the proprietorship?"

"What was changed?" (Bring out that there was an exchange of values—that as one asset was decreased by $2,500, another asset was acquired valued at $2,500.)

a. Understanding what a business transaction is

"What is the name or term applied to business activities such as investing in a business, and buying or selling something?"

Teacher writes term and definition on board. BUSINESS TRANSACTION—an exchange of one business value for another.

"Give some examples of business transactions you were involved in recently."

"Let us now see the Modern Launderette's business transactions for July 3 and determine how each of these transactions change the values of two items on the balance sheet."

b. Understanding how each transaction affects the value of two (or more) items.

As each of the next four transactions is considered by the class, the teacher calls for specific students to tell what values change on the balance sheet. As the student gives the right answer for a transaction, he is asked to come to the board and change the appropriate amounts on the balance sheet.

Trans. 3. Incurred a liability of $1,000 buying drying equipment from the Elmo Machine Company. Payment need not be made for 60 days.

Trans. 4. Paid rent for month of July, $200. Through questions and discussion lead the class to see this is an expense and that expenses reduce proprietorship.

Trans. 5. Bought furniture for use by customers. Paid cash, $100.

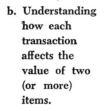

Trans. 6. Collected $55 from washing machines and $15 from drying machines—total income for the day, $70.

Through questions and discussion lead class to see that income increases proprietorship.

After all values and necessary amounts have been recorded, the balance sheet appears on the board as follows:

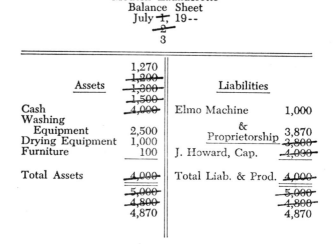

Modern Launderette
Balance Sheet
July ~~1,~~ 19--
~~2~~
3

Assets		Liabilities	
	1,270		
	~~1,200~~		
	~~1,900~~		
	~~1,500~~		
Cash	~~4,000~~	Elmo Machine	1,000
Washing		&	
Equipment	2,500	Proprietorship	3,870 ~~3,800~~
Drying Equipment	1,000		
Furniture	100	J. Howard, Cap.	~~4,000~~
Total Assets	~~4,000~~	Total Liab. & Prod.	~~4,000~~
	~~5,000~~		~~5,000~~
	~~4,800~~		~~4,800~~
	4,870		4,870

c. Understanding the need for some systematic way of sorting and summarizing the changing values of things owned and owed.

Teacher now pauses, refers to the rather messy balance sheet and asks students for their reaction to this unsystematic method of updating business records.

The *need* is established for some better method of maintaining current business records.

"Almost any suggestion that one might make would be an improvement. What ideas for improvement can any of you offer?"

(In some classes the students will have been introduced to accounts when they posted an opening entry earlier in the course. Nevertheless students do not acquire a complete comprehension of the use of accounts until the introduction of business transactions. The utilization of accounts to record the changing effects business transactions have on balance sheet items gives greater understanding for the existence of accounts.)

It is assumed that the students will suggest the need for a separate record of each item on the balance sheet.

2. To comprehend the meaning of account balance by

"Suppose we had a separate sheet of paper or an individual form for each item on the balance sheet. When we record on the form each value change affecting that item, the form would supply an up-to-date summary of how the item's value is changing through business transactions."

Teacher then uses the chalkboard to indicate (1) how the Modern Launderette cash changes might have been recorded, and (2) how the increases and the decreases to Cash might be totaled to find the value of cash on hand at any time. This second step is aimed at laying the groundwork for teaching what the account balance is.

Cash
+4,000
−2,500
− 200
− 100
+   70
1,270 on hand

"If, however, instead of mixing all of the increases and the decreases of cash together in one column, we placed the increases in one column and the decreases in another, we would have an even better system for finding the current value of this balance sheet item."

a. Knowing why accounts have two sides

Teacher demonstrates this by placing the title of the account over a large T on the board and writes the increases to cash on one side and the decreases on the other.

Cash	
4,000	2,500
70	200
	100

Teacher points out that an account is a B-A form used, not only for recording items in the opening entry, but also to sort and summarize changes caused by business transactions. For learning purposes, the changes in an account balance can best be shown by using this simple form called a T account.

b. Knowing what the balance of an account is

Teacher demonstrates the finding of an *account balance.*

c. Knowing the names given to each side of an account

"In business, instead of saying we 'increase' or 'decrease' an account, we say we 'debit' or 'credit' it."

"These terms are the names given to the two sides of every account."

The students, by correctly answering the following review questions, supply the teacher with the detail for completing the diagram on page 402.

"When opening an account, where is the account name placed?"

"Which side of an account is the debit side?"

"Which side of an account is the credit side?"

Name of Account	
Debit Side	Credit Side

For emphasis and reinforcement, teacher calls for chorus answers to the following questions:

"The debit side of any and all accounts is what side?"

"The credit side of any and all accounts is what side?"

"This is simple to remember—debits on the left, credits on the right. Never any exceptions. Debits —left, credits—right."

"If someone tells you to debit a certain account for $10, what is he asking you to do?"

"If someone credited an account for $5, what did he do?"

"Debit means one thing and one thing only—the left-hand side of an account."

"Credit means one thing and one thing only—the right-hand side of an account."

"We want to record increases and decreases in accounts. What relationship does this have to debiting and crediting?"

"*Let us look at the cash account on the board. Here we put cash increases on the debit side and decreases on the credit side.*"

"*I might just as well have reversed these entries and placed the increases on the credit side and the decreases on the left-hand or debit side.*"

"*The important question then is HOW DO WE KNOW WHEN TO DEBIT AN ACCOUNT AND WHEN TO CREDIT IT? The balance sheet can help us.*"

"*Let me show you a diagram which will help you remember the kind of balances that asset accounts always have, the kind of balances that liability accounts always have, and the kind of balance that the proprietorship account always has.*"

d. **Understanding the kinds of balances that assets, liabilities, and proprietorship always have**

"*Since accounts always increase on their balance side, this diagram will help you remember when to debit an account and when to credit an account.*"

While the teacher constructs the diagram shown on page 404, the students are instructed to complete a similar one on paper.

The teacher asks the following questions stressing certain points at appropriate stages in developing the diagram.

1. "*How many sides are there to a balance sheet?*"

   Draw a very large T on board and write "balance sheet" above it.

2. "*What kind of accounts are always shown on the left-hand side of the balance sheet?*"

   Write "assets" near the top of the left-hand side.

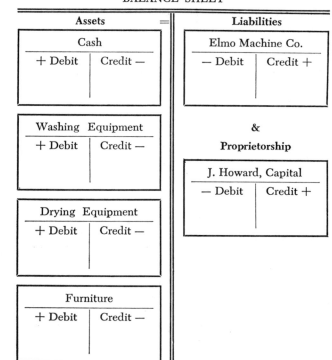

BALANCE SHEET

3. *"Name the Modern Launderette's asset accounts."*

On the left-hand side of the balance sheet draw and title a small T account for each asset named.

Explain that you are boxing in each of these T accounts with a margin to resemble separate accounts.

4. Asks questions similar to Nos. 2 and 3 regarding the liability and the proprietorship accounts.

5. *"Which side of all accounts is the debit side?"*

Write "debit" on left-hand side of all T accounts.

Emphasize that this is true for *all* accounts.

6. *"Which side of all accounts is the credit side?"*
Write "credit" on right-hand side of all T accounts.
Emphasize that this is true for *all* accounts.

e. Understanding that the balance side of an account is always its increase side

7. *"You remember that assets are listed on the left-hand side of the balance sheet. Now all you have to do is remember that all asset accounts have left-hand balances. Since they always have left-hand (debit) balances, they always increase on the left-hand (debit) side."*

"Therefore, when a business transaction causes the value of any asset to increase, the amount of the increase is always placed on which side of the T account?"
Insert a plus mark (+) on the left-hand side of each asset account in front of the word "debit."

f. Understanding that the decrease is always placed on the side of the account opposite the balance side

"When an asset decreases in value, should the amount of the decrease be placed on the right or left side?"
Insert a minus mark (—) on the right-hand side of each asset account following the word "credit."

8. *"You remember that liability accounts and the proprietor's capital account are listed on the right-hand side of the balance sheet. Since they also have right-hand balances, they always increase on the right-hand (credit) side."*

"Therefore, when a business transaction causes a liability account or the proprietor's capital account to increase, where will the amount of the increase always be placed?"
Insert a plus mark (+) on the right-hand side of the liability account and the capital account following the word "credit."

"When a liability or the capital account is decreased, where should the amount of the decrease be placed?"

Insert a minus mark (—) on the left-hand side of the liability and the proprietorship accounts in front of the word "debit."

3. To develop a formula for debiting and crediting different kinds of accounts

Repeated questions, discussion, and reference to the diagram emphasizes the following facts.

The *left-hand* side of *ALL* accounts is called the debit side.

The *right-hand* side of *ALL* accounts is called the credit side.

Accounts *increase* on their *balance side.*

Asset accounts *always* have debit balances

They increase on their debit side.
They decrease on their credit side.

Liabilities and proprietorship always have credit balances.

They increase on their credit side.
They decrease on their debit side.

(The depth of their understanding of accounting may cause some beginning teachers to be reluctant to teach that, "Asset accounts *always* have debit balances," or that liability accounts *always* have credit balances." It is true, on occasion, that these accounts may have contra balances. A customer may overpay his account. The bank account might become overdrawn. But these exceptions have no place in the introduction of debit and credit in this early stage in the course.)

4. To reinforce understanding of debit and credit through drill and application

"Earlier this week we recorded business transactions directly onto a balance sheet. The sloppy results emphasized the need for a more systematic means of sorting and summarizing business transactions. Therefore, we established individual accounts for each balance sheet item. Through debit and credit entries that record increases and decreases in these account balances, we are now maintaining a record of each item's current value."

"Using our diagram of T accounts superimposed on a large balance sheet, let us test our understanding of debits and credits. Let us see if we now know when to debit and when to credit each type of balance sheet account."

Ask students to imagine that each of the T accounts on the diagram is a separate page from a loose-leaf ledger and these pages are spread on top of a king-size balance sheet.

Teacher refers to earlier part of this plan and has class analyze one by one each of the five transactions of the Modern Launderette as follows:

Write Transaction No. 1 on board:

James Howard invests $4,000 in his new business, the Modern Launderette.

"What two accounts are affected by this transaction?"

"What kind of an account is Cash?"

"Asset account increases are recorded on which side of the T account—the debit side or the credit side?"

Teacher records the $4,000 debit to Cash in the T account on the chalkboard diagram. Pupils do the same on their diagrams.

"What kind of an account is James Howard, Capital?"

"How is its balance affected—increased or decreased?"

"Increases to the proprietorship account are recorded on which side of the T account—the debit side or the credit side?"

Teacher records the $4,000 credit to James Howard, Capital, T account on the chalkboard diagram. Pupils do the same with their diagram.

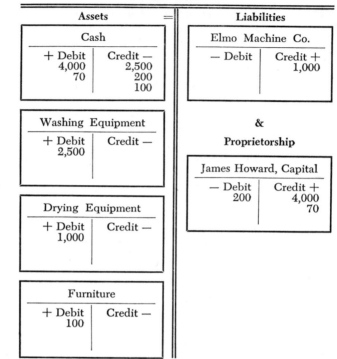

BALANCE SHEET

Teacher completes the next two transactions, repeating the same questions for each.

To vary procedures and test students, the teacher instructs the class to complete the remaining two transactions on their own.

After sufficient time, the teacher calls on a few students to explain how they recorded each transaction. The teacher constantly asks WHY after each student's response.

(Teachers in some classes who may wish to take this opportunity to plant the seed for understanding a trial balance should proceed as follows.

Ask the class, without reference to the term "trial balance," to prepare a balance sheet for July 3 from the account balances of the Modern Launderette and compare it with the messy results of the previous balance sheet. All teachers should realize that regardless of how many class periods are needed to bring their classes to an understanding of debiting and crediting accounts, appropriate drill and application work are also necessary.)

Absence of Expense and Income Accounts From Preceding Outline

Teaching students that expenses are debits to the proprietor's capital account and incomes are credits to this same account may seem questionable. Since this is not an on-the-job practice, how may we justify such teaching?

First, this is a learning situation, and the simpler the learning situation the better. Students know what a balance sheet is, and they are familiar with balance sheet items (accounts). Thus introducing debits and credits is limited to the three types of accounts on the balance sheet—accounts students recognize.

Second, this plan develops the basic B-A understanding that proprietorship is increased by income and decreased by expenses thus giving students a foundation to link to future learning— separate expense and income accounts.

Third, by limiting the debit and credit effect of transactions to balance sheet accounts only, special attention and greater emphasis can be devoted to expense and income accounts when introduced as a separate topic. Further support for this procedure is found on page 414.

Need for the Right Kind of Drills

Students need much practice in learning when to debit and credit an account—the analysis of transactions. Practice should not be just any drills. For example, "debit" means one thing and one thing only—the left-hand side of a standard account. "Credit" means one thing and one thing only—the right-hand side of a standard account. If drills on debit and credit are to be realistic and meaningful, they must relate to accounts, not journals. Students drilled at this introductory stage on placing debits in the left-hand column and credits in the right-hand column of a two-column general journal often are in a state of confusion when later introduced to combination or multi-column journals with debit and credit columns in no particular order.

The best drills for student understanding of debit and credit are those which strengthen ability to:

(a) classify accounts—identify asset, liability, and proprietorship accounts quickly.
(b) identify the kinds of balances that different kinds of accounts have.
(c) remember the increase-side and the decrease-side of accounts.

Finally to fix debit and credit principles, oral as well as written drills are essential. A good technique for oral drill is the use of flash cards with the entire class. Transactions are written on one side of the cards and the corresponding debit and credit T-account analyses are written on the opposite side of the cards. Various written drills are found in textbooks, but for the students introduced to debit and credit through the use of T accounts, drills using T accounts are best.

The Proper Order for Analyzing a Transaction

Students should be permitted to follow their own inclination when stating the credit and the debit of a transaction. Requiring a student to always state the account to be debited first is a carry-over from the days when all recordings were made in a two-column journal. Since the debit is always recorded first in the two column journal, this was, at one time, a reasonable teaching requirement. However, business transactions are rarely recorded in a two-column journal today, and there is no reason for continuing this debit-first mandate. Analyzing a transaction is just as meaningful without this ritualistic demand, and allowing a student to state the part of the entry he knows may enable him to determine the offsetting part more easily. Furthermore, if the student gives the credit part of a transaction first—so what? The credit of the transaction is half the answer—half the answer is better than total silence, and it shows what the student does know as well as indicate where he needs assistance.

Teachers and teachers-to-be schooled in the debit-first ritual might find it quite revealing to see how successfully the oral drills on debit and credit move along when this routine requirement is dropped. They will find that students at this stage of learning, where textbooks make frequent use of cash transactions, often use what happens to cash as their real "key" for recording a transaction. Thus if cash is paid out in a transaction, students will have the credit part solved first, whereas if cash is received, they will usually give the debit first.

STUDY QUESTIONS

1. Why is it important that beginning B-A students not only learn the mechanics of debit and credit, but the theory as well?

2. What four learning stages should the student go through when learning debit and credit?

3. Why have income and expense accounts been excluded in the procedural outline for introducing students to debit and credit in this chapter?

4. How can an instructor give his students sufficient practice in learning when to debit and credit an account?

5. Which drills are considered to be the best type to assign when introducing students to the meaning of debit and credit?

6. How can flash cards be used to help in the teaching of debit and credit?

7. When analyzing a transaction, should the student be required to always state the debit part of the transaction first? Why? Why not?

8. Why are cash transactions frequently used in the early stages of a student's introduction to bookkeeping-accounting?

DISCUSSION QUESTIONS

1. Do you believe that the chalkboard or overhead projector should be used when new B-A concepts are being introduced? Why?

2. What suggestions do you see in the outline on debit and credit in this chapter that might be of value to you as a teacher?

3. How important is it that the instructor constantly question the students, especially when presenting new material?

4. How many class periods should be devoted to teaching the theory of debit and credit?

5. If you were to convert the procedural outline in this chapter into daily lesson plans, how many days would you plan for teaching this material to an average-ability class?

6. Do you consider the use of the T account a helpful teaching aid? Compare it with the two-column general journal as an aid in teaching students the meaning of debit and credit.

7. If it were suggested that greater emphasis on and use of the bookkeeping equation could be included in the procedural outline illustrated in this chapter, how would you react?

SELECTED REFERENCES

Musselman, Vernon A. "Teaching Account Classification in Bookkeeping," *The Balance Sheet*. XLI (September, 1959), 14-15.

Weaver, David H. "Teaching the Analysis of Balance Sheet Transactions," *Business Teacher*. XLV (September-October, 1967), 4-5.

Chapter 16

Introducing Students to Expense and Income Accounts

Need for Special Attention to Expense and Income Accounts

Once a student has learned the need for accounts and has grasped the principles of debit and credit as they apply to *balance sheet accounts*, there is nothing difficult in teaching him the use of expense and income accounts. Most teachers agree with this statement. However, a "surface" understanding of expense and income accounts may lead to later trouble with closing entries. Therefore, the depth of understanding necessary for successful learning of closing entries should be provided in the teaching of expense and income accounts.

How to Introduce Expense and Income Accounts

The following outline offers some specific suggestions as to how students can be introduced to expense and income accounts after having first acquired a good understanding of the effect of business transactions on assets, liabilities, and proprietorship.

STEPS FOR INTRODUCING STUDENTS
TO
EXPENSE & INCOME ACCOUNTS

1. **Connect with previous learning**

   a. Review the procedure of the previous day or so—when expense items were being debited and income was being credited to the proprietor's capital account.

   b. Use the chalkboard to show in T account form the capital account of the Modern Launderette (used in illustrations of

Chapter 15). At the end of a month this account is "cluttered" with numerous debit (expense) and numerous credit (income) amounts.

2. **Show the need for separate expense accounts**

   a. Ask each class member to assume that he is the bookkeeper for the Modern Launderette, which has now been operating for several months. Mr. Howard, the owner, asks his bookkeeper, "How much was spent for machine repairs during the past month?"

   b. Bring out through questions and discussion the advantages of having separate accounts for the major or important expenses of a business. Indicate that the minor or infrequent expenditures are brought together under one account called Miscellaneous Expense.

   Students should be able to contribute some of the following advantages:

   —Helps the owner see more clearly how the money is being spent.

   —Supplies more details, thus a quick month to month comparison can be made of expenses.

   —Supplies detailed records for income tax purposes.

   —Helps in decision making.

3. **Show the need for separate income accounts**

   a. Mr. Howard, the owner, asks his bookkeeper (each student in the class), "How much of last month's income came from the washing machines and how much from the dryers?"

   b. Bring out through questions and discussion:

   —The disadvantages of recording income directly into the capital account.

   —Why it is helpful for the owner to know how much income the business is receiving from the washing machines and how much income the business is receiving from the drying machines.

   —That some businesses might need only one income account and that others, such as department stores, find it helpful to keep separate income accounts for each department.

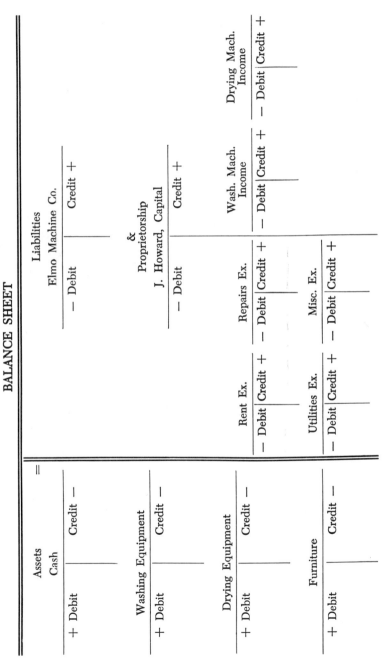

Figure 16—1.

4. STRESS the relationship of the expense and income accounts to the capital account. (A full understanding of this relationship is essential if the student, some weeks later, is to experience a ready introduction to closing entries.)

   a. Expand the diagram previously used to introduce debiting and the crediting of balance sheet accounts. Through illustrations on the chalkboard (See Figure 16–1):

      (1) Show expense accounts "nesting" below the debit side of the capital account.

      (2) Show income accounts "nesting" below the credit side of the capital account.

      (3) Stress the fact that these are *temporary proprietorship accounts.*

         (a) That their use keeps the capital account from becoming cluttered with numerous debit and credit entries.

         (b) That they supply the kind of information an owner or manager needs for the best management of a business.

         (c) That these accounts will never appear on the balance sheet.

         (d) That after these accounts supply the necessary detailed information, the difference between total expense and total income is found, and this single amount is placed in the balance sheet's capital account.

      (4) Supply students with adequate drill and application in recording expense and income transactions.

         (a) Point out that instead of *debiting* the capital account for expenses to decrease capital, a separate expense account is *debited.*

         (b) Similarly, point out that instead of *crediting* the capital account for individual income transactions to increase capital, a separate income account is *credited.*

Concluding Remarks

When students are *first taught* to analyze expense and income transactions, the teacher should insist on students answering WHY an expense account is debited and WHY an income account is credited; that expenses are recorded as decreases in proprietorship—debits; that incomes are recorded as increases in proprietorship—credits.

Good judgment indicates when such routine questioning has served its purpose—when to stop before boring the students. However, it is wise to occasionally repeat such questioning in the interval preceding the introduction of closing entries. Reinforcing the knowledge that these are temporary proprietorship accounts lays a foundation for closing entries.

STUDY QUESTIONS

1. How can the principles of debit and credit as applied to balance sheet accounts aid a student in understanding the use of income and expense accounts?

2. Why will only a "surface" understanding of income and expense accounts lead to trouble when closing entries are introduced?

3. List the four suggestions for introducing the income and expense accounts outlined in the chapter.

4. What are some of the advantages of separate expense accounts? Can you think of others not given in the text? Advantages of separate income accounts?

5. In introducing income and expense accounts, why is it important to stress the relationship of these accounts to the capital account?

6. On the diagram on page 415, why are the expense accounts shown "nesting" below the debit side of the proprietorship account and the income accounts "nesting" below on the credit side?

7. Why are income and expense accounts called temporary proprietorship accounts?

8. When asking students to analyze the debit and credit parts of transactions what "why" question should the instructor continually ask the students? What caution is offered regarding such questions?

DISCUSSION QUESTIONS

1. What teaching advantages, if any, do you see in asking class members to picture themselves as the bookkeeper in a business, even though the business might not actually exist?

2. What are the reasons for occasionally reminding students that income and expense accounts are temporary capital accounts?

3. While the bookkeeping equation is related in this chapter's presentation of expense and income accounts, what is your reaction to the suggestion that a more effective presentation would result if emphasis were given to relating income and expense accounts by expanding the initial bookkeeping equation as follows:

   Assets = Liabilities + (Proprietorship — Expenses + Income)?

4. If, in the above question, you favored more emphasis on the expanded equation, do you believe (a) that all high school B-A students could easily grasp this expanded equation, or (b) that those students who studied algebra would be more successful with this approach?

5. High school textbooks usually introduce students to income and expense accounts by illustrating businesses with several expense accounts but only one income account. Would the illustration of realistic businesses having several income accounts as well as several expense accounts aid teaching and understanding? Explain.

SELECTED REFERENCES

Weaver, David H. "Teaching the Analysis of Income and Expense Transactions," *Business Teacher.* XLV (November-December, 1967), 13, 27.

PROBLEMS OF TEACHING
THE WORK SHEET

Chapter 17

Reasons for Teaching the Work Sheet

The work sheet summarizes on one paper the results of most of the B-A work done during an entire fiscal period. This includes verifying the accuracy of the posting, figuring the necessary adjustments, finding the net income or loss, and summarizing information for presentation on the income statement and the balance sheet. It is obvious that teaching such an intricate procedure with all of its varied concepts needs a great deal of care and thoughtful planning. Therefore, it is not surprising that teachers find this procedure a difficult area to present.

An overall examination of teaching the work sheet will be presented first in this chapter. Then, in Chapters 18–23 a closer examination is made of teaching adjusting and closing entries.

The first essential for the successful teaching of any subject is a clear and full understanding *by the teacher* of what is to be taught. Otherwise student learning will be in spite of the teaching that is done rather than because of it. Therefore, in this instance, the teacher must have clearly in mind the purposes of a work sheet. Why do bookkeepers and accountants prepare work sheets? Why are students learning to prepare work sheets?

On the job the work sheet is the bookkeeper's "scratch pad." It can be a timesaver, a helpful short cut for summarizing and making available necessary information for completing the final steps or links in the bookkeeping cycle. The work sheet is a timesaver for supplying quickly important end-of-period information without first spending all the time necessary for recording adjusting and closing entries in the journal, for posting adjusting and closing entries to the ledger, and ruling and balancing accounts.

Visualize a bookkeeper at work the first day of the month. His employer enters the office and says, "Say, Joe, can you give me the net income for last month? I don't want the statements for a day or so, but I need the net income now."

Joe grabs an eight-or-ten column analysis pad and takes a trial balance. Then all necessary adjustments are made so he can arrive at the accurate net income for the period. Since all nominal accounts must be classified as income or expense before the net income can be determined, he next sets up a double Income Statement column and quickly extends the proper amounts to these columns. Joe knows that he would not have to classify the real accounts in a Balance Sheet column in order to get the net income for the period, but since this takes only a few extra minutes and gives him a further check of accuracy, he includes this major column on his work sheet also. Within a relatively short time he completes the necessary extensions and calculations. He then goes to his employer and says, "Mr. Howard, the net income for last month was $. . . . . . ." "Thanks a lot, Joe," says Mr. Howard, and Joe returns to his desk to continue his work.

If his employer changed his mind and wanted the financial statements at once, the information necessary to quickly prepare these reports is available on the work sheet. In the situation described, if the pressure of daily work prohibits closing the books and setting up the formal end-of-month statements right away, Joe can lay the work sheet aside. Within a day or so when pressure eases, he turns to it and prepares formal statements—balance sheet, income statement, etc.—makes the necessary adjusting and closing entries in the general journal, and updates the books. Without the use of the work sheet, Joe could not have quickly answered Mr. Howard, nor would he have easy access to all the information for completing the final B-A steps.

After this one example of the use of the work sheet in an office, let us turn to the classroom again. What are the objectives in teaching the work sheet? Even though most B-A teachers know them well, let us state them here for the purpose of clarity. They are:

1. To record a trial balance—proving that accounts in the ledger are in balance.
2. To adjust account balances not truly stated in the trial balance.

3. To classify accounts,
   (a) real amounts going to Balance Sheet columns, and
   (b) nominal amounts going to the Income Statement section.
4. To find quickly the net profit or loss for the accounting period.
5. To provide summarized information for quickly preparing
   (a) a balance sheet and
   (b) an income statement.
6. To provide a ready source for journalizing adjusting entries.
7. To provide a ready source for journalizing closing entries.
8. To use as a quick check against the post-closing trial balance
   (amounts and totals in Balance Sheet columns).
9. Finally, to give the student a bird's-eye view of the entire cycle
   being pulled together and culminated.

With the exceptions of Nos. 2 and 6, all these objectives are present when the student is first introduced to the six-column work sheet. Any teacher, experienced or otherwise, who studies this list of proposed new learnings knows that this is a big assignment. Probably the fact that it is a large learning unit is a major reason why the teaching of the work sheet is more difficult than many other B-A topics.

What elements cause the work sheet to be hard to teach? It is possible that when the difficulties are brought out into the open, they may not be so formidable after all.

Reasons Why Some Teachers Find the Work Sheet Difficult to Teach

1. First, the compiling of a work sheet involves new procedures and concepts. A full grasp of its purposes and advantages cannot be taught quickly—within a day or a week. One B-A methods teacher told his class that the work sheet was a single unit of learning and should be covered and taught within a single class period. In support of this, he referred to the Gestalt theory of learning that supports learning by wholes rather than atomistic, segmentary, or piece-meal learnings. The fallacy here is that the instructor also failed to quote a qualifying phase of the Gestalt theory which, in effect, says that the size of the "wholes," of the unit, must be within the grasp or comprehension of the learner. A house is a whole—a unit—but would one try to teach a carpenter how to build a house within one class period, one day, or one

week? Neither can we teach the work sheet in a class period or two. The above instructor might have been on more solid ground if he had proposed an introductory lesson set up on a "whole" approach to teach *about* the work sheet. But, his demands to teach the work sheet in one day were as fallacious as the teacher who writes an article claiming to teach the bookkeeping cycle the first day, or the typewriting teacher who claims to teach the highly organized skill of typewriting in one day.

2. A second reason for difficulty with the work sheet is that some teachers fail to knit all the steps into a unifying picture. That is, some teachers fail to convey to their students the purposes and advantages of a work sheet. It is necessary that the work sheet, like the B-A course itself, be taught in segments. It is equally necessary to present how each segment relates to other segments of the work sheet. And, it is also just as necessary to fit the learning of the work sheet into the over-all picture or cycle of bookkeeping. Students cannot be left to develop the relationships themselves, but must have specific help in establishing them.

3. Coupled with reason two is a third cause for student misunderstanding. Some students stumble and flounder over the learning of the work sheet because they have not been helped sufficiently to see the advantages and shortcutting that a work sheet offers. In such cases, students, after completing the work sheet, have been known to go back to the ledger for the information needed to compile the balance sheet and income statement. In another extreme case, the teacher had the students journalizing closing entries from an inspection of accounts in the ledger rather than from the ready information on the work sheet. If, in this latter instance, the teacher had done this with the aim of showing how this information was already centralized on the work sheet, the procedure could have been justified. This was not the case.

The work sheet is the accountant's "scratch pad." It is not a financial statement. Thus the work sheet may be prepared with a pencil. As indicated before, it is a timesaver, a helpful short cut for summarizing and making information readily available for completing the final links in the bookkeeping cycle. If students are not helped to see these advantages and to make use of them, the work sheet becomes a bookkeeping chore—merely something the teacher says they have to learn.

4. A fourth paramount reason for difficulty in teaching the work sheet is that some teachers fail to illustrate and demonstrate adequately and clearly.

When work sheets are taught, particularly the more difficult ones involving adjustments, most teachers who do not have an overhead projector and appropriate transparencies available will want to illustrate them on the chalkboard. This involves taking time to rule the board and write all the account names and amounts in the trial balance—consuming five to ten minutes of class time. Even if a student is assigned this task, many teachers probably feel frustrated at the loss of class time, or stretch their ingenuity to assign classroom work while this preliminary activity is being performed. On subsequent days, when the teacher wants to carry the chalkboard illustration beyond the adjustments, he must again write all the account titles and numerous amounts. This may take another five or ten minutes of a forty-minute period. As a result, some teachers, instead of "wasting" this class time, will teach the work sheet from an illustration already worked out in the textbook. When this is done, teaching becomes more abstract, and the student is cheated of seeing the work sheet come to life—developing account by account and from column to column.

5. Finally, inadequate testing can have a detrimental bearing upon the students' attitude and application for learning the work sheet. There is probably no single test in bookkeeping-accounting that more adequately and comprehensively tests a student's general knowledge and skill than a work sheet *problem test*.[1] Failure by the teacher to give problem tests periodically throughout the course as work sheets become more and more extensive lowers the value students give to the work sheet.

Methods of Teaching the Work Sheet

Teaching the Trial Balance Section of the Work Sheet

The work sheet is a form used to place in one complete overall unit the figures for the trial balance, the balance sheet, the income statement, the adjusting entries, and the closing entries. (See Figure 17–1 on page 425.)

---

[1] See pages 256-257 for additional remarks on problem-situation tests.

The trial balance is the first segment of the work sheet, and it is essential in the development of the work sheet. However, the trial balance has a purpose all its own—that of testing the accuracy of debit and credit account balances in the ledger. The importance of this test for accuracy is easily understood by students. As a result, the trial balance can be taught as an initial and separate segment before making reference to the work sheet. B-A teachers present the trial balance separately, since it is a learning unit small enough to be comprehended easily.

Immediately after the procedures for taking a trial balance have been presented and practiced, the relationship to the work sheet should be established. This is done by placing subsequent trial balances on the work sheet form and establishing this procedure as the initial step in developing a work sheet. The trial balance should be welded to the remainder of the work sheet and not maintained as a separate action. Students must learn quickly to take a trial balance *on* the work sheet, and not on separate two-column paper.

Until recently, it has been the general practice to teach students to list on the trial balance only ledger accounts containing a balance. Thus, the name of each account used for adjusting another account was written below the trial balance totals. However, in business, bookkeepers and accountants list the title of every general ledger account on the work sheet trial balance—whether the account has a balance or not. Because this latter method is used by modern accountants and because it is easier to teach students to make adjustments when all general ledger accounts are listed, it seems likely that listing all account titles will also become the popular procedure in the classroom.

Introducing Students to the Work Sheet

Work sheets vary in size and complexity. If we are to follow the psychological principles of learning, we should start teaching the simplest form and proceed gradually to the most complex.

Better B-A textbooks have improved the initial presentation of the work sheet by developing an abbreviated work sheet sometimes called a working trial balance. This initial presentation introduces only the trial balance, the classification of accounts, finding the net

C. K. Norris
Work Sheet
For Month Ended May 31, 19--

Account Titles	Acct. No.	Trial Balance		Adjustments		Income Statement		Balance Sheet	
		Dr.	Cr.	Dr.	Cr.	Dr.	Cr.	Dr.	Cr.
Cash	11	3,578.50						3,578.50	
Accounts Receivable	12	1,735.80						1,735.80	
Merchandise Inventory	13	14,828.00		(b) 13,888.50	(a) 14,828.00			13,888.50	
Supplies	14	166.40			(c) 30.40			136.00	
Prepaid Insurance	15	268.00			(d) 32.00			236.00	
Accounts Payable	21		2,968.70						2,968.70
C. K. Norris, Capital	31		16,172.00						16,172.00
C. K. Norris, Drawing	32	400.00						400.00	
Income & Expense Summary	33			(a) 14,828.00	(b) 13,888.50	14,828.00	13,888.50		
Sales	41		5,593.20				5,593.20		
Purchases	51	3,034.00				3,034.00			
Delivery Expense	61	86.00				86.00			
Insurance Expense	62			(d) 32.00		32.00			
Miscellaneous Expense	63	127.20				127.20			
Rent Expense	64	200.00				200.00			
Salary Expense	65	310.00				310.00			
Supplies Expense	66			(c) 30.40		30.40			
		24,733.90	24,733.90	28,778.90	28,778.90	18,647.60	19,481.70	19,974.80	19,140.70
Net Income						834.10			834.10
						19,481.70	19,481.70	19,974.80	19,974.80

Figure 17—1.

income or loss, preparing a simple balance sheet and income statement, journalizing closing entries, and the relationship of the work sheet to the bookkeeping cycle.

The Adjustments columns and the need for teaching adjusting entries are postponed until the second cycle. As a result, through the use of a service business with no merchandise inventory and no accrued accounts or deferred items to adjust, it is possible to cut down the number of new concepts introduced to the student in his initiation to the work sheet. An example of such a work sheet is Figure 17–2 on page 427. This abbreviated six-column work sheet can be taught in the following seven progressive steps.

1. The procedure and purpose of a trial balance.
2. What a work sheet is and how to classify income statement and balance sheet accounts.

When students are first introduced to a work sheet, some teachers find it helpful to label the debit and credit columns of the Income Statement columns "Expense" and "Income" respectively. Similarly, the Debit column of the Balance Sheet columns can be headed "Assets" and the Credit column "Liab. and Prop."

3. How to find the net income or loss on the work sheet.
4. How to prepare an income statement from the work sheet.
5. How to prepare a balance sheet from the work sheet.
6. How to journalize closing entries from the work sheet.
7. How a work sheet relates to and summarizes the culminating phases of the bookkeeping cycle.

The teacher decides according to the classroom situation how much teaching time each of these steps will consume.

There is little doubt that student introduction through this abbreviated form of work sheet is best, and the average class can be expected to learn this in about a week. Some weeks later, when a larger spiral of the cycle has been covered, the Adjustments columns can be introduced with a complete work sheet. New concepts and learnings can then be concentrated on work sheet adjustments. This has the advantage of teaching the work sheet in comprehensible stages rather than in one swoop.

In most high school textbooks the eight-column form is used to illustrate a work sheet with an adjustment section. (See Figure 17–1 on page 425.)

Hill-Top Motel
Work Sheet
For Month Ended August 31, 19--

	Account Titles	Acct. No.	Trial Balance Dr.	Trial Balance Cr.	Income Statement Dr.	Income Statement Cr.	Balance Sheet Dr.	Balance Sheet Cr.	
1	Cash	11	2,487.00				2,487.00		1
2	Housekeeping Supplies	12	564.00				564.00		2
3	Furniture and Fixtures	13	5,557.00				5,557.00		3
4	Office Equipment	14	465.00				465.00		4
5	Apex Plumbing Company	21		200.00				200.00	5
6	Motel Equipment Company	22		1,000.00				1,000.00	6
7	Charles Martin, Capital	31		6,700.00				6,700.00	7
8	Room Sales	41		1,621.00		1,621.00			8
9	Advertising Expense	51	35.00		35.00				13
10	Laundry Expense	52	85.95		85.95				14
11	Miscellaneous Expense	53	17.50		17.50				15
12	Rent Expense	54	200.00		200.00				16
13	Utilities Expense	55	109.55		109.55				9
14			9,521.00	9,521.00	448.00	1,621.00	9,073.00	7,900.00	10
15	Net Income				1,173.00			1,173.00	11
16					1,621.00	1,621.00	9,073.00	9,073.00	12

Figure 17—2.

Even though the simplified form of the work sheet is taught first, the teacher still needs to organize and present the material for the work sheet with adjustments clearly. He still needs to:

1. Present it in a unifying manner so that the segments are knit together, and the students not only grasp the importance of the segments but also their relationship to one another.

2. Make optimum use of a visual presentation so that the students see and feel the work sheet develop and "come to life."

3. Help the students to see the advantages, the shortcutting, and the uses made of the work sheet.

An Overall Presentation of the Work Sheet

In order that the teacher may have some specific assistance, a suggested outline for the teaching of a complete eight-column work sheet is presented below. Teachers who prefer to introduce a ten-column work sheet, including the Adjusted Trial Balance columns, should have no difficulty in placing this additional step in the following outline.

Unless the teacher has an overhead projector and specially prepared transparencies, teaching the work sheet usually requires a great deal of writing on the chalkboard. This takes time and slows down the presentation. In order to diminish this loss, the following outline is developed with the use of visual charts designed to save chalkboard-writing time and to present the subject more clearly. In the illustrations that follow, the permanent, visual material, which may be easily constructed by the teacher for repeated use, is indicated by the lettered sections. The material that would be written on the chalkboard during the presentations is shown in italics.

The visual material suggested is composed of five heavy posterboard sheets, approximately 44" x 18" in size. These five charts, in sections, contain a complete work sheet. They can be rested on the chalk tray of a chalkboard or can be hung from hooks. The new learnings in the presentation are then developed on the chalkboard (as shown in italics in the illustrations) at the right of the charts being used. These five separate charts contain:

I. A list of the account titles of the work sheet.

II. The Trial Balance columns of the work sheet.

III. The Adjustments columns.

IV. The Income Statement columns.

V. The Balance Sheet columns.

Such visual material gives flexibility to the use of work sheet columns and enables the teacher to have the student concentrate on the new essentials of a particular day's learning. This visual material also enables the teacher to devote his energies to the development and presentation of new procedures on the chalkboard.

Outline for Teaching the Work Sheet

Using the charts mentioned above (or an overhead projector with appropriate transparencies), the following procedures may be developed in classroom presentations.

Step 1. Teach the trial balance. On the last day devoted to teaching the trial balance, an applied homework assignment is given for completing a trial balance problem. The teacher uses this assignment the next day for introducing the work sheet. If the next day by oral check the teacher finds that a number of the students have errors in this assignment, he can reteach or review quickly on the chalkboard the compiling of a trial balance. (See Figure 17–3 on page 430.) If this is not necessary, the teacher could place the first two charts (a list of the account titles and the Trial Balance columns of the work sheet—Figure 17–4 on page 431) before the class. These show the finished homework assignment. Students inspect and compare with their completed assignment.

Step 2. Introduce the work sheet—its purpose and form. The class is motivated by connecting the trial balance homework problem, now before them, with the new learnings to be presented. If the visual aid is used, the teacher is ready to start the presentation more quickly. Through class discussion the students are led to see the following facts:

a. All the business transactions of C. K. Norris for the month of May have been recorded in the journal(s).

b. All of these entries have been posted to accounts in the ledger.

	Account Titles	Acct. No.	Trial Balance Dr.	Trial Balance Cr.
1	Cash	11	3,578.50	
2	Accounts Receivable	12	1,735.80	
3	Merchandise Inventory	13	14,828.00	
4	Supplies	14	166.40	
5	Prepaid Insurance	15	268.00	
6	Accounts Payable	21		2,968.70
7	C. K. Norris, Capital	31		16,172.00
8	C. K. Norris, Drawing	32	400.00	
9	Income & Expense Summary	33		
10	Sales	41		5,593.20
11	Purchases	51	3,034.00	
12	Delivery Expense	61	86.00	
13	Insurance Expense	62		
	Miscellaneous Expense	63	127.20	
14	Rent Expense	64	200.00	
15	Salary Expense	65	310.00	
16	Supplies Expense	66		
17			24,733.90	24,733.90

Figure 17—3.

    c. The trial balance proves that the accounts in the ledger are in balance—the debits equal the credits.

    d. An examination of the trial balance will not readily show Mr. Norris (1) what the business is worth at the end of May or (2) what net income or loss was incurred during May.

    e. The preparation of a balance sheet and an income statement are the next steps in B-A work.

    f. After bringing out the above points, explain briefly what a work sheet is and how it is used for summarizing the information required for these statements.

Insert on the chalkboard the heading for the work sheet and columnar headings for the balance sheet and the income statement—Figure 17—5 on page 432.

Step 3. Start to classify the amounts in the Trial Balance columns by extending them into the Balance Sheet columns. When a trial balance amount must be changed before it can be extended, through discussion show the class this amount must be adjusted. At

	Account Titles	Acct. No.	Trial Balance Dr.	Trial Balance Cr.

CHART I — CHART II

	Account Titles	Acct. No.	Dr.	Cr.
1	Cash	11	3,578.50	
2	Accounts Receivable	12	1,735.80	
3	Merchandise Inventory	13	14,828.00	
4	Supplies	14	166.40	
5	Prepaid Insurance	15	268.00	
6	Accounts Payable	21		2,968.70
7	C. K. Norris, Capital	31		16,172.00
8	C. K. Norris, Drawing	32	400.00	
9	Income & Expense Summary	33		
10	Sales	41		5,593.20
11	Purchases	51	3,034.00	
12	Delivery Expense	61	86.00	
13	Insurance Expense	62		
14	Miscellaneous Expense	63	127.20	
15	Rent Expense	64	200.00	
16	Salary Expense	65	310.00	
17	Supplies Expense	66		
18			24,733.90	24,733.90
19	°			
20				

° The term "net income" blocked out on visual aid.

Figure 17—4.

this point the need for the Adjustments columns on the work sheet becomes evident. Since the need is now felt and seen, now is the time to introduce and teach adjustments. (See Figures 17—6 and 17—7 on pages 433 and 434.)

Step 4. Teach adjustments. (The teaching of adjustments is detailed in Chapter 18.) Moving from the simple to the more complex, it seems best to introduce the adjustment of prepaid accounts before dealing with the merchandise inventory account.

The amount of time devoted to teaching adjustments at this time is dependent on the types of adjustments necessary to complete this introductory work sheet. However, regardless of whether the teacher finds it advantageous to spend one day or one week

C. K. Norris
Work Sheet
For Month Ended May 31, 19--

	CHART I		CHART II			Income Statement		Balance Sheet	
	Account Titles	Acct. No.	Trial Balance			Income Statement		Balance Sheet	
			Dr.	Cr.		Dr.	Cr.	Dr.	Cr.
1	Cash	11	3,578.50						
2	Accounts Receivable	12	1,735.80						
3	Merchandise Inventory	13	14,828.00						
4	Supplies	14	166.40						
5	Prepaid Insurance	15	268.00						
6	Accounts Payable	21		2,968.70					
7	C. K. Norris, Capital	31		16,172.00					
8	C. K. Norris, Drawing	32	400.00						
9	Income & Expense Summary	33							
10	Sales	41		5,593.20					
11	Purchases	51	3,034.00						
12	Delivery Expense	61	86.00						
13	Insurance Expense	62							
14	Miscellaneous Expense	63	127.20						
15	Rent Expense	64	200.00						
16	Salary Expense	65	310.00						
17	Supplies Expense	66							
18			24,733.90	24,733.90					
19	°								
20									

° The term "net income" blocked out on visual aid.

Figure 17—5.

C. K. Norris
Work Sheet
For Month Ended May 31, 19--

CHART I		CHART II							
		Trial Balance		Adjustments		Income Statement		Balance Sheet	
Account Titles	Acct. No.	Dr.	Cr.	Dr.	Cr.	Dr.	Cr.	Dr.	Cr.
Cash	11	3,578.50						3,478.50	
Accounts Receivable	12	1,735.80						1,835.80	
Merchandise Inventory	13	14,828.00		(b) 13,888.50	(a) 14,828.00				
Supplies	14	166.40							
Prepaid Insurance	15	268.00							
Accounts Payable	21		2,968.70						
C. K. Norris, Capital	31		16,172.00						
C. K. Norris, Drawing	32	400.00							
Income & Expense Summary	33			(a) 14,828.00	(b) 13,888.50				
Sales	41		5,593.20						
Purchases	51	3,034.00							
Delivery Expense	61	86.00							
Insurance Expense	62								
Miscellaneous Expense	63	127.20							
Rent Expense	64	200.00							
Salary Expense	65	310.00							
Supplies Expense	66								
		24,733.90	24,733.90						

Mdse. Inventory

Dr.	Cr.
14,828.00	(a) 14,828.00
(b) 13,888.50	

Income & Expense Summary

Dr.	Cr.
(a) 14,828.00	(b) 13,888.50

Supplies Expense

Dr.	Cr.
(c) 30.40	

Supplies

Dr.	Cr.
166.40	(c) 30.40
	30.40

Figure 17—6.

* The term "net income" blocked out on visual aid.

	Account Titles	Acct. No.	Trial Balance Dr.	Trial Balance Cr.	Adjustments Dr.	Adjustments Cr.
1	Cash	11	3,578.50			
2	Accounts Receivable	12	1,735.80			
3	Merchandise Inventory	13	14,828.00		(b) 13,888.50	(a) 14,828.00
4	Supplies	14	166.40			(c) 30.40
5	Prepaid Insurance	15	268.00			(d) 32.00
6	Accounts Payable	21		2,968.70		
7	C. K. Norris, Capital	31		16,172.00		
8	C. K. Norris, Drawing	32	400.00			
9	Income & Expense Summary	33			(a) 14,828.00	(b) 13,888.50
10	Sales	41		5,593.20		
11	Purchases	51	3,034.00			
12	Delivery Expense	61	86.00			
13	Insurance Expense	62			(d) 32.00	
14	Miscellaneous Expense	63	127.20			
15	Rent Expense	64	200.00			
16	Salary Expense	65	310.00			
17	Supplies Expense	66			(c) 30.40	
18			24,733.90	24,733.90	28,778.90	28,778.90
19	*					
20						

CHART I · CHART II

* The term "net income" blocked out on visual aid.

Figure 17—7.

on this objective, there is need for referring to the work of the previous day. Thus that part of the visual aid shown in Figure 17–7 can be brought into use on as many days as is needed in the teaching of adjustments—this at a saving of time for copying similar material on the chalkboard each day.

The trial balance in Figure 17–7 includes each account in Mr. Norris' general ledger regardless of whether it has a balance. As a result, the accounts needed for the adjustments are already available in the trial balance. Thus it is easier to teach the accounts needed for the adjustments and not necessary to teach students to write these accounts below the trial balance totals.

Step 5. Extend amounts that are now adjusted (the up-to-date amounts for each account) to the Balance Sheet and the Income

Statement columns. This can be done by using the sections of the visual aid shown in Figure 17–8 on page 436. (This step can be used in conjunction with step four.)

Step 6. Compute the net income or loss. At this point the work sheet is completed, but the teaching of the work sheet is not finished. The information now summarized on the work sheet, the all important application of the work, still remains to be taught. These applications may be presented in the following steps.

Step 7. Prepare the income statement from the work sheet. (See Figure 17–9 on page 437.) Note that by using the income and expense summary account for adjusting Merchandise Inventory, and by extending both the beginning and ending inventory amounts into the Income Statement columns, only the account names and the amounts in the Income Statement columns (CHARTS I & IV) are needed for preparing the income statement.

Step 8. Prepare the balance sheet from the work sheet. (See Figure 17–10 on page 438.)

In addition to showing how the balance sheet is prepared from the information on CHARTS I and V, the means of figuring the proprietor's capital can also be demonstrated.

Step 9. Record adjusting entries from the work sheet. (See Figure 17–11 on page 439.)

Step 10. Record closing entries from the work sheet. (See Figure 17–12 on page 440.)

Note that in preparing closing entries it is not necessary to refer to the Balance Sheet columns if there are no proprietor withdrawals.

It is not unusual for B-A personnel to face a deadline for submitting financial statements to their employers. Therefore, it is common practice to complete the balance sheet and the income statement before proceding with the final routine of adjusting and closing the accounts in the ledger. As a result, the recording of the adjusting and closing entries usually constitutes the last steps in the use of the work sheet—except of course as it is filed away for possible future reference.

C. K. Norris
Work Sheet
For Month Ended May 31, 19--

Account Titles	Acct. No.	Trial Balance Dr.	Trial Balance Cr.	Adjustments Dr.	Adjustments Cr.	Income Statement Dr.	Income Statement Cr.	Balance Sheet Dr.	Balance Sheet Cr.
Cash	11	3,578.50						3,578.50	
Accounts Receivable	12	1,735.80						1,735.80	
Merchandise Inventory	13	14,828.00		(b)13,888.50	(a)14,828.00			13,888.50	
Supplies	14	166.40			(c) 30.40			136.00	
Prepaid Insurance	15	268.00			(d) 32.00			236.00	
Accounts Payable	21		2,968.70						2,968.70
C. K. Norris, Capital	31		16,172.00						16,172.00
C. K. Norris, Drawing	32	400.00						400.00	
Income & Expense Summary	33			(a)14,828.00	(b)13,888.50	14,828.00	13,888.50		
Sales	41		5,593.20				5,593.20		
Purchases	51	3,034.00				3,034.00			
Delivery Expense	61	86.00				86.00			
Insurance Expense	62			(d) 32.00		32.00			
Miscellaneous Expense	63	127.20				127.20			
Rent Expense	64	200.00				200.00			
Salary Expense	65	310.00				310.00			
Supplies Expense	66			(c) 30.40		30.40			
		24,733.90	24,733.90	28,778.90	28,778.90	18,647.60	19,481.70	19,974.80	19,140.70
Net Income						834.10			834.10
						19,481.70	19,481.70	19,974.80	19,974.80

Figure 17—8.

C. K. Norris
Work Sheet
For Month Ended May 31, 19--

| CHART I | | CHART II | | CHART IV | |
| Account Titles | Acct. No. | Trial Balance | | Income Statement | |
		Dr.	Cr.	Dr.	Cr.
Cash	11	3,578.50			
Accounts Receivable	12	1,735.80			
Merchandise Inventory	13	14,828.00			
Supplies	14	166.40			
Prepaid Insurance	15	268.00			
Accounts Payable	21		2,968.70		
C. K. Norris, Capital	31		16,172.00		
C. K. Norris, Drawing	32	400.00			
Income & Expense Summary	33			14,828.00	13,888.50
Sales	41		5,593.20		5,593.20
Purchases	51	3,034.00		3,034.00	
Delivery Expense	61	86.00		86.00	
Insurance Expense	62			32.00	
Miscellaneous Expense	63	127.20		127.20	
Rent Expense	64	200.00		200.00	
Salary Expense	65	310.00		310.00	
Supplies Expense	66			30.40	
		24,733.90	24,733.90	18,647.60	19,481.70
Net Income				834.10	
				19,481.70	19,481.70

C. K. Norris
Income Statement
For Month Ended May 31, 19--

Income:		
Sales		5,593.20
Cost of Merchandise Sold:		
Merchandise Inv. May 1, 19—	14,828.00	
Purchases	3,034.00	
Total Cost of Mdse. Available for Sale	17,862.00	
Less Mdse. Inv. May 31, 19—	13,888.50	
Cost of Merchandise Sold		3,973.50
Gross Profit on Sales		1,619.70
Expenses:		
Delivery Expense	86.00	
Insurance Expense	32.00	
Miscellaneous Expense	127.20	
Rent Expense	200.00	
Salary Expense	310.00	
Supplies Expense	30.40	
Total Expenses		785.60
Net Income		834.10

Figure 17—9.

C. K. Norris
Work Sheet
For Month Ended May 31, 19--

CHART I		CHART V	
		Balance Sheet	
Account Titles	Acct. No.	Dr.	Cr.
Cash	11	3,578.50	
Accounts Receivable	12	1,735.80	
Merchandise Inventory	13	13,888.50	
Supplies	14	136.00	
Prepaid Insurance	15	236.00	
Accounts Payable	21		2,968.70
C. K. Norris, Capital	31		16,172.00
C. K. Norris, Drawing	32	400.00	
Income & Expense Summary	33		
Sales	41		
Purchases	51		
Delivery Expense	61		
Insurance Expense	62		
Miscellaneous Expense	63		
Rent Expense	64		
Salary Expense	65		
Supplies Expense	66		
		19,974.80	19,140.70
Net Income			834.10
		19,974.80	19,974.80

C. K. Norris
Balance Sheet
May 31, 19--

Assets		Liabilities	
Cash	3,578.50	Accounts Payable	2,968.70
Accounts Receivable	1,735.80	Proprietorship	
Merchandise Inv.	13,888.50	C. K. Norris, Capital	16,606.10
Supplies	136.00		
Prepaid Insurance	236.00		
Total Assets	19,574.80	Total Liab. & Prop.	19,574.80

Computation of Present Capital

Balance in proprietor's capital account, May 1,		16,172.00
Net income	834.10	
Less withdrawals	400.00	
Net increase in capital		434.10
Present capital, May 31,		16,606.10

Figure 17—10.

C. K. Norris
Work Sheet
For Month Ended May 31, 19--

CHART I / CHART III

Account Titles	Acct. No.	Adjustments Dr.	Adjustments Cr.
Cash	11		
Accounts Receivable	12		
Merchandise Inventory	13	(b)13,888.50	(a)14,828.00
Supplies	14		(c) 30.40
Prepaid Insurance	15		(d) 32.00
Accounts Payable	21		
C. K. Norris, Capital	31		
C. K. Norris, Drawing	32		
Income & Expense Summary	33	(a)14,828.00	(b)13,888.50
Sales	41		
Purchases	51		
Delivery Expense	61		
Insurance Expense	62	(d) 32.00	
Miscellaneous Expense	63		
Rent Expense	64		
Salary Expense	65		
Supplies Expense	66	(c) 30.40	
Net Income			
		28,778.90	28,778.90

General Journal

Date	Account Titles	Post. Ref.	Debit Amount	Credit Amount
19--				
May 31	Adjusting Entries			
	Income and Expense Summary		14,828.00	
	Mercandise Inventory			14,828.00
31	Merchandise Inventory		13,888.50	
	Income and Expense Summary			13,888.50
31	Supplies Expense		30.40	
	Supplies			30.40
31	Insurance Expense		32.00	
	Prepaid Insurance			32.00

Figure 17—11.

C. K. Norris
Work Sheet
For Month Ended May 31, 19--

		CHART IV Income Statement		CHART V Balance Sheet	
CHART I Account Titles	Acct. No.	Dr.	Cr.	Dr.	Cr.
Cash	11			3,578.50	
Accounts Receivable	12			1,735.80	
Merchandise Inventory	13			13,888.50	
Supplies	14			136.00	
Prepaid Insurance	15			236.00	
Accounts Payable	21				2,968.70
C. K. Norris, Capital	31				16,172.00
C. K. Norris, Drawing	32			400.00	
Income & Expense Summary	33	14,828.00	13,888.50		
Sales	41		5,593.20		
Purchases	51	3,034.00			
Delivery Expense	61	86.00			
Insurance Expense	62	32.00			
Miscellaneous Expense	63	127.20			
Rent Expense	64	200.00			
Salary Expense	65	310.00			
Supplies Expense	66	30.40			
		18,647.60	19,481.70	19,974.80	19,140.70
Net Income		834.10			834.10
		19,481.70	19,481.70	19,974.80	19,974.80

General Journal

Date	Account Titles	Post. Ref.	Debit Amount	Credit Amount
19--	*Closing Entries*			
May 31	Sales		5,593.20	
	Income and Expense Summary			5,593.20
31	Income and Expense Summary		3,819.60	
	Purchases			3,034.00
	Delivery Expense			86.00
	Insurance Expense			32.00
	Miscellaneous Expense			127.20
	Rent Expense			200.00
	Salary Expense			310.00
	Supplies Expense			30.40
31	Income and Expense Summary		834.10	
	C. K. Norris, Capital			834.10
31	C. K. Norris, Capital		400.00	
	C. K. Norris, Drawing			400.00

Figure 17—12.

The Advantages of Using Visual Aids

The steps outlined previously are essential for full understanding and application of an eight-column work sheet. Successful B-A teachers have in the past covered these steps without the use of the sectionally charted work sheet or appropriate transparencies and will continue to do so in the future. The individual teacher will have to analyze the use and value of such teaching aids in the light of his own techniques and preferences.

There are four main advantages in using visual aid material to teach the work sheet.

First, the sectionally charted work sheet or transparencies supply flexibility to the teaching. Only related sections of the work sheet that are applicable to the lesson need to be used.

Second, such visual material assists in knitting together all the segments of the work sheet. The student is helped to *see* and understand not only the segments but also the relationship of these segments to each other and the entire work sheet. The advantages of the work sheet are clearly presented.

Third, the visual aid charts (or transparencies) are based on the teaching principle "a picture can be worth a thousand words." There is nothing abstract about this type of teaching. The teacher shows and demonstrates. The pupil watches, questions, and *does.* The student *sees* the work sheet growing, developing into a useful tool and timesaver.

Fourth, the visual material saves time. The work sheet charts or transparencies eliminate the long period of board writing. Furthermore, they can be used repeatedly. Such timesaving and laborsaving devices lend themselves to a more complete job of teaching the work sheet.

Accordion Folding of the Work Sheet

Students taught to accordion fold the completed work sheet often find this an aid to understanding. This is done in a manner that permits the double columns of the completed work sheet to be folded against the *account titles* or the *trial balance* columns so that only the double columns needed are visible. For example, when the balance sheet is to be constructed, the double column showing the balance sheet figures is folded back beside the *account titles* column. The information necessary for preparing the balance sheet is made to stand alone, and the preparation of the statement is easily accomplished. A similar procedure can be used when the income statement, the adjusting journal entries, or the closing journal entries are made. Many students who apply this technique for a short time soon acquire a clear understanding of work sheet applications and short cuts.

Testing Student Achievement of the Work Sheet

A final reason why the work sheet is often poorly understood is inadequate testing. A good test can also be a good learning experience. Problem tests on the work sheet are essential to good testing and teaching. Teachers who fail to give good problem tests on the work sheet are cheating themselves of achievement information and are denying students valuable learning experiences. Furthermore, the absence of such tests in a B-A course could depreciate, in the eyes of the students, the importance of the work sheet.

If work sheet problem testing is so important, why do some teachers ignore or shy away from it? A common reason offered is that work sheet problem tests, if good, comprehensive ones, cannot be completed within a short class period of 40 to 45 minutes. This objection can be overcome by using the simple technique, or variations of it, described below and illustrated in Figure 17–13 on page 443.

A complete work sheet problem test as shown in Figure 17–13 is duplicated (or could be written on the chalkboard). Each of these problems, with simple directions, is attached to a sheet of eight-column analysis paper. On this paper are the account titles and balances. In less than a minute after the student receives this material he is at work on the problem. He does not have to spend five or ten minutes copying account names and amounts. All of the testing time is devoted to having the student complete the work sheet—from the major heading to columnar headings, the trial balance through adjustments, and so on until the final net income or loss is determined. If the teacher believes that his students know which accounts normally have debit or credit balances, he could duplicate the balances of the accounts directly into the Trial Balance columns on the analysis sheet and let the problem start with the Adjustments columns. Teachers soon find that within a 45-minute period some such problems could be expanded and constructed to include the journalizing of adjusting and/or closing

The Problem: On March 31 of the current year, the end of a monthly fiscal period, the accounts and their balances in the general ledger of Herman's Pharmacy were as shown in the first column of the attached eight-column analysis sheet. Inventories at the end of this monthly period showed that the pharmacy now owned merchandise worth $4,602, $243 worth of supplies, and $160 worth of insurance.

The Requirements: Complete an eight-column work sheet showing the net income or loss for the period.

Work Sheet Problem Test #3

1	Cash	$1,185							1
2	Accounts Receivable	743							2
3	Mdse. Inventory	4,537							3
4	Supplies	304							4
5	Prepaid Insurance	172							5
6	Accounts Payable	1,185							6
7	H. J. Herman, Capital	5,424							7
8	H. J. Herman, Drawing	400							8
9	Income & Expense Summary	—							9
10	Sales	3,080							10
11	Purchases	1,826							11
12	Delivery Expense	91							12
13	Insurance Expense	—							13
14	Miscellaneous Expense	56							14
15	Rent Expense	100							15
16	Salary Expense	275							16
17	Supplies Expense	—							17

Figure 17—13.

entries and the completion of a balance sheet or an income statement.

Work sheet problem tests involve to some extent all phases of the bookkeeping cycle. Teachers can make such tests very simple or quite comprehensive. These tests can be constructed with various requirements and can measure student understanding and ability to perform basic procedure, such as:

1. Journalizing—when the student does this mentally with adjustments or physically if the problem includes the requirement for recording adjusting and/or closing entries in general journal form.

2. Handling debit and credit balances of ledger accounts—as in a trial balance where the account balances are supplied, but it is not specified whether or not they are debit or credit balances.

3. Classifying accounts—as when the debit or credit balances of all accounts are extended to either the Income Statement or the Balance Sheet columns.

4. Preparing financial statements—as when the problem calls for the preparation of a balance sheet and/or an income statement to be completed from the work sheet information.

Some routine techniques, such as posting, ruling, and balancing accounts, would naturally be absent from work sheet problem tests, but there is plenty of other time for testing these skills.

When students experience work sheet problem tests the first and second time through the cycle, they will be more impressed with the status and importance of the work sheet and apply themselves more conscientiously than if they were tested only with "true" and "false" or other objective questions, such as placing check marks ($\sqrt{}$) in proper places on a facsimile work sheet.

Time Versus Emphasis in the Teaching of the Work Sheet

Educational psychologists tell us that subject matter presentation and practice should be balanced in time and emphasis. Like a clock or a watch, bookkeeping is made up of many wheels—topics —steps in the cycle. Some are large wheels, some small. A large wheel in a clock cannot be said to be more important than a small one, for, if you take one away, large or small, the clock stops—the cycle is broken.

It takes longer to teach certain topics than others. Teachers cannot take the above principle and say that it supports spending the same amount of time on each bookkeeping topic or step in the cycle. Then they would be achieving only a balance of time devoted to each step in the cycle but would be ignoring a balance in emphasis.

It takes more time to arrive at a balance of emphasis—of student achievement and understanding—in teaching the work sheet than the general journal. Teachers who are concerned with achieving both a balance of time *and* emphasis in their presentation of bookkeeping-accounting, might consider whether they are devoting the time and emphasis that it needs and deserves.

STUDY QUESTIONS

1. What causes the teaching of the work sheet to be more difficult than some other B-A areas?
2. Why do bookkeepers and accountants prepare work sheets?
3. Why is the work sheet referred to as the accountant's "scratch pad"?
4. What are the important objectives and understandings that teachers should strive to achieve in the teaching of the work sheet?
5. What are the five suggested reasons why some teachers find teaching the work sheet difficult?
6. What caution is mentioned regarding the introducing of students to the trial balance without mentioning its relationship to the work sheet?
7. What is the name given to an abbreviated six-column work sheet? Name the three double columns that comprise it.
8. Why has it become a common practice to introduce students to a six-column work sheet rather than to an eight- or ten-column work sheet?
9. What are the seven progressive teaching steps that the presentation of a six-column work sheet should include?
10. What is taught in each of the steps recommended for consideration in the teaching of an eight-column work sheet?
11. What are the teaching advantages of the visual aid illustrated in this chapter?
12. How could the B-A teacher present each of these steps without the use of the visual aid illustrated?
13. What special folding technique is suggested for helping students understand work sheet applications and short cuts?
14. Why is it claimed that work sheet problem tests are essential to good teaching and testing?
15. Why are work sheet problem tests ignored by some teachers?

16. What suggestions are given for overcoming teacher objections to work sheet problem tests?

17. What major phases of B-A work can be included in work sheet problem tests?

DISCUSSION QUESTIONS

1. What, in your opinion, makes the work sheet one of the more difficult B-A teaching areas?

2. Some teachers may have difficulty teaching the work sheet because its construction and applications are not crystal clear in their own minds. How do you react to this statement?

3. Contrast the educational arguments that would support a teacher's presenting an introductory day's lesson about the entire work sheet as compared with another teacher who would, in piecemeal fashion, teach the segments of a work sheet and proceed to relate each segment of the work sheet to every other segment.

4. After the trial balance has been learned, the teaching of the remainder of the work sheet can be done in either a horizontal or a vertical fashion. Students can be taught to extend the balance of each account line after line horizontally across the work sheet *or* they can be taught to proceed vertically completing each double column before proceeding to the next double column and so on across the work sheet. Which of these two methods do you believe is best? Why? Would your answer be the same for a six-column, abbreviated work sheet as for an eight- or ten-column work sheet? Explain.

5. When teaching the trial balance, which method is best from a teaching standpoint? (a) Teach students to list all accounts in the general ledger regardless of whether they have a balance. (b) Have students list only those accounts with balances and then when adjustments are made on the work sheet, write the names of accounts needed below the trial balance. Explain.

SELECTED REFERENCES

Freeman, M. Herbert. "Innovations in Teaching the Work Sheet," *Business Teacher.* XLV (March-April, 1968), 24-25.

Hazel, Dorothy. "Bookkeeping and Accounting: A Plan for Teaching the Work Sheet," *Business Education Forum.* XVI (December, 1961), 15.

Smith, Sue. "The Work Sheet Made Easy," *The Balance Sheet.* XLVI (May, 1965), 407.

TEACHING ADJUSTING ENTRIES— AN OVERALL VIEW

Chapter 18

Adjusting Entries as a Teaching Problem

In a survey [1] made to determine upon what topics B-A teachers in training should be given special help, experienced teachers ranked the teaching of adjusting entries third in a list of over 50 items. The two topics ranked above adjustments were "Getting Started—The First Week's Work" and "The Aims of Bookkeeping Instruction." Since the two higher-ranked topics center more on method, than subject matter, it can be said that in the subject matter areas of bookkeeping-accounting adjusting entries are most deserving of special attention.

Since adjustments are a major teaching problem and also affect the teaching of the work sheet, this chapter is devoted to adjusting entries in general. Each of the four chapters which follows is devoted to one of the four major types of adjustments.

General Learnings that Apply to All Adjustments

The three concepts or general understandings that apply to all adjustments should be made clear to the students.

First, certain accounts change in value each day—sometimes with each tick of the clock.

Example: If a business pays an *annual* premium of $365 for fire insurance, the prepaid insurance account (asset) would show a value of $365 on January 1. At the close of January 1, one day's worth of insurance ($365 ÷ 365 days) or $1 has been used or consumed. This $1 is now an expense of running the business, and

[1] Lewis D. Boynton, *A Methods Text in Bookkeeping for Secondary Teachers* (Doctoral dissertation, Columbia University, 1951).

447

the company now owns only $364 of insurance. Thus can be seen the change in value of an asset account, Prepaid Insurance, with the passage of a single day. It would be possible to mathematically determine insurance cost for each hour or each second. However, if bookkeepers or accounting clerks tried to keep such accounts in up-to-date, accurate balance each hour, each day, or even each week, they would have time for little else.

Second, it is not practical, sometimes not possible, to keep certain accounts up-to-date and in true balance at all times.

Third, it is sufficient to bring such accounts up to date—adjust them—only at the close of a fiscal period when a business determines where it stands, what it owns, and what profit was made.

When students acquire these general learnings about adjustments first, they then know WHY and WHEN accounts must be adjusted. There remains for them to learn WHAT accounts must be adjusted and HOW to adjust accounts.

Use of the Work Sheet to Introduce Students to the NEED for Adjustments

Students must see and feel the need for adjustments before they can apply themselves fully to learning adjusting entries. One of the best ways to bring this about is, after they have learned to prepare a six-column work sheet with no adjustments, to let them in collaboration with the teacher proceed to extend amounts on an eight- or ten-column worksheet. (See Figure 17–6, page 433.) When students understand that it is incorrect to extend certain amounts from the trial balance to the balance sheet and income statement columns, they are ready to learn adjustments. The teacher now puts the eight- or ten-column work sheet aside, and proceeds to teach one or more types of adjustments.

The Use of T Accounts and General Journal Entries to Teach Adjustments

By the full use of illustrative T accounts on the chalkboard or overhead projector the teaching of adjustments can be taken out of the realm of abstract teaching and made concrete. While all teachers know that the adjustments are first recorded on the work sheet before general journal entries and their postings are made, it is more abstract and difficult teaching to try to have students learn first to place the adjustments in the work sheet columns without first having them see and learn the adjustments in T accounts. After students see and understand the effect of adjustments on accounts, only then are they ready to make adjustments on the work sheet.

Kinds of Accounts Requiring Adjustment

Because the nature of the accounts that need adjusting are different, all adjustments cannot be made in exactly the same manner. In general, however, most adjustments may be grouped as involving:

1. Prepaid expenses and income received in advance
2. Merchandise inventory
3. Valuation accounts—allowance for depreciation and doubtful accounts
4. Accrued expenses and income

Each of these four groups has its teaching problems, and separate treatment is accorded each in the four chapters that follow. The outline on pages 450-451 is presented to refresh the reader's memory and to give a reference to some common accounts that are involved in adjustments.

The Order of Introducing Adjustments to Students

One of the most basic of all teaching principles is to move from the simple to the complex. In what order, therefore, should the four types of adjustments be introduced? Which is the simplest type of adjustment? Which is the most complex?

Perhaps some difference of opinion would result in the answers to these questions. But there seems little doubt that the majority of B-A teachers and students agree that adjusting the merchandise inventory account outranks the other adjustments in difficulty. Unlike other adjustments, this account requires two entries instead of one, and it requires a clear understanding of the inventory's relation to Purchases, Sales, and the income and expense summary

SUMMARY CLASSIFICATION AND EXPLA-

ACCOUNTS	DEFINITIONS
A. Prepaid Items 1. Prepaid Expense Accounts	Expenses paid before or during an accounting period, and not completely used up or consumed by the business during that period.
2. Prepaid Income Accounts	Income received before or during an accounting period, and not entirely earned by the business during that period.
B. Merchandise Inventory Account	An asset showing the value of merchandise on hand *at the beginning of a fiscal period.*
C. Valuation Accounts (Allowance Accounts)	Accounts used in calculating the estimated value of related assets. (Certain fixed asset accounts, such as Buildings and Equipment, decrease in value each fiscal period because of wear and tear—depreciation. This decrease in value is an expense to the business and must be recorded each period. Similarly, accounts owed to the business each fiscal period are frequently uncollectible and become an expense to the business.)
D. Accrued Items 1. Accrued Expense Accounts	Expenses incurred during an accounting period but not recorded before the close of the period.
2. Accrued Income Accounts	Income earned during an accounting period but not recorded before the close of the period.

NATION OF ACCOUNTS TO BE ADJUSTED

EXAMPLES	ADJUSTMENT NECESSARY
Supplies Prepaid Insurance Prepaid Interest Prepaid Rent	Set up related expense accounts to show the true expenses incurred for period under consideration.
Interest Received in Advance Rent Received in Advance	Set up related liability accounts to show income received but not fully earned as yet. (See Chapter 19.)
Merchandise Inventory	Adjust this account to show true value of merchandise on hand at the end of the accounting period —using the income and expense summary account for the adjustment. (See Chapter 20.)
Accumulated Depreciation Allowance for Bad Debts	Set up valuation accounts to adjust the value of the related assets to true current balance sheet value *and* set up related expense accounts to show the estimated expenses of these items for the period. (See Chapter 21.)
Salaries Payable Interest Payable Commissions Payable	Set up liability accounts to show expenses still to be paid *and* set up related expense accounts to show true expenses incurred for period.
Interest Receivable Rent Receivable	Set up asset accounts to show income still to be received *and* set up related income accounts to show true income earned for the period. (See Chapter 22.)

account. This multiple relationship creates the difficulties experienced in this adjustment. Yet in textbooks the adjustment of the Merchandise Inventory is presented first. Why is this so?

In the early chapters of B-A textbooks the simplest of bookkeeping systems are used for illustrations. Service-type businesses which can operate without inventories or other adjustment-type accounts are commonly used in textbooks to begin B-A study. The work sheet of these businesses, having no adjustments, can be limited to six columns.

When the merchandising-type businesses are presented, the first account on the trial balance in need of adjustment is Merchandise Inventory—the most difficult account to learn to adjust.

Textbook writers find it difficult to deviate from presenting the adjustment of Merchandise Inventory first. It is a normal, on the job practice to record the adjustments to accounts in the order given on the trial balance. The merchandise inventory account is the first calling for adjustment.

Also, when adjustments are made on the work sheet, the debits and credits are labeled in the adjustment columns with corresponding letters of the alphabet. This aids in locating all of the adjustment when the entry is journalized. The merchandise inventory account should be identified with the letter "a" since it usually precedes other adjustment accounts. This seemingly trivial clerical procedure is important in tracing and keeping order in the books. Authors feel that disturbing this order in the textbook presentation would only create confusion.

What can a teacher do to alleviate the difficulty in this area? Steps three and four on pages 430-431 offer a solution. The teacher is not bound by a textbook. Students may be introduced to adjustments through prepaid accounts instead of the Merchandise Inventory. Prepaid accounts are more common, and the concepts of their adjustment are easier to grasp. For example, the complementary accounts used in their adjustment—Supplies Expense, Insurance Expense, or Rent Received in Advance—are more discernible.

When the student has learned these simpler adjustments, the teacher can next teach the adjusting of Merchandise Inventory on the work sheet. If this procedure is followed, the alphabetic labeling of the adjusting debits and credits should be delayed until it can be taught in proper sequence.

In summary, when introducing students to the eight-column work sheet, prepaid items seem to be the simplest adjustment to comprehend, and it is recommended that these adjusting entries be taught first. Following the principle of going from the simple to the complex, the Merchandise Inventory adjustments could be presented immediately after the teaching of adjusting prepaid items. Some weeks or even months later, after the students have an opportunity to practice these two types of adjustments, they should have no difficulty with valuation accounts—depreciation and uncollectibles. Finally, because the additional concept and practice of reversing entries is taught at the time accruals are taught, it seems best to reserve the fourth type of adjustment for last.

STUDY QUESTIONS

1. Why has the author given special attention to adjusting entries?

2. When do B-A teachers first face the problem of teaching adjusting entries?

3. What three concepts that apply to all adjustments should be made clear to the student when introducing adjusting entries?

4. When is a good time to introduce the need for adjusting entries?

5. What place should the use of illustrative T accounts on the chalkboard or the overhead projector play in the teaching of adjustments?

6. Classify the four kinds of accounts that must be adjusted periodically. Are they all adjusted in the same manner?

7. In what order should the four types of adjustments be introduced to students? Why?

8. Which of the four types of adjustments do a majority of teachers find most difficult to teach?

9. Why is it that this more difficult adjustment is presented first in textbooks?

10. What kind of accounts does the author suggest as the easiest to adjust and, therefore, the first to be used for teaching adjustments to students?

DISCUSSION QUESTIONS

1. What is your reaction to the statement, "Because accountants are frequently called into small businesses to handle the end-of-period accounting work, it is not necessary to teach adjusting entries to high school B-A students?"

2. Do you believe that high school B-A students should be taught to record prepaid expenses as both an asset and as an expense, and to handle adjustments under both procedures?

3. Is it easier, quicker, and more effective to illustrate *the need* for adjustments on the overhead projector or on the chalkboard? Explain.

4. Is it easier, quicker, and more effective to teach (to demonstrate) the adjustment of an account on the chalkboard or on the overhead projector? Explain.

5. It has been said that we teach as we have been taught. How, if at all, will or should your teaching of adjustments to high school students differ from the way you were taught in your college accounting course?

6. When teaching adjustments, should the teacher first emphasize their relation to the work sheet or to the ledger, or should an attempt be made to jointly and equally emphasize their relation to both the ledger and the work sheet? Explain.

SELECTED REFERENCES

Garrison, Lloyd L. "Bookkeeping and Accounting: Adjusting Entries—Why?" *Business Education Forum.* XXIII (October, 1968), 16-17.

Musselman, Vernon A. "New Procedures for Teaching Adjustments," *Business Education Forum.* X (December, 1955), 12-13.

Weaver, David H. "Understanding—The Password to Learning Adjustments," *Business Teacher.* XLVI (September-October, 1968), 4-5, 20.

Chapter 19

The Simplest Kind of Adjustment—Prepaid Items

One of the simplest adjustments involves the advance payment of expenses such as rent, insurance, supplies, or interest.

An illustration of the learning involved in this type of adjustment is presented below. The detail in this example should provide teachers with ideas for use in planning their presentation of adjusting a prepaid expense account. (The example on page 447 shows another approach, using Prepaid Insurance.)

Example of Rent as an Expense and as a Prepaid Expense (Asset)

The proprietor of a proposed new shoe store wants to rent a certain vacant building on Main Street. The owner of the building agrees to rent the building and gives the following choice of rental terms:

1. $300 per month, payable in advance of each month, or
2. $3,000 per year, payable one year in advance.

Let us assume the proprietor of the shoe store does not wish to use $3,000 of his cash to pay a year's rent in advance. Therefore, he pays $300 in advance for the first month's rent. At this point the shoe store proprietor's bookkeeper has the choice of making either of the entries shown on the next page.

1. ⎰ Dr. Prepaid Rent   300
   ⎱   Cr. Cash   300
         Prepayment of rent for January

2. ⎰ Dr. Rent Expense   300
   ⎱   Cr. Cash   300
         Paid rent for January

Reason for debiting a prepaid item to an asset account.
In deciding which of the above entries to make, the bookkeeper
might reason as follows:

"This $300 is an expense of the business that has been paid for
in advance. It is an expense that has been incurred and prepaid
before the store is occupied, but will not be completely used until
the end of January. The shoe store now owns one month's worth
of rent valued at $300. Things owned are assets. As assets
are used, they become expenses of the business. In bookkeeping-
accounting we cannot call an item *both* an asset and an expense.
We cannot do this because an asset is something owned and an
expense is a cost of running the business—because assets appear on
the balance sheet, while expenses appear on the income statement.
I could, therefore, rightly call this an asset that will eventually be
used, and I could debit the $300 to an asset account and be
technically correct. Furthermore, if my boss asked me to prepare
an initial or opening balance sheet the day before the store opened
on January 1, I would have to list this $300 as an asset. I could do
this by showing $300 opposite an asset account called Prepaid Rent.
Yes, I could justify debiting this $300 to an asset account."

Reason for debiting a prepaid item to an expense account. The
bookkeeper continues his reasoning. "If I do debit this $300 to an
asset account now, what will be the situation at the end of January
when my employer definitely will ask me to prepare a balance sheet
and an income statement? Then my ledger and trial balance will
show $300 in the asset account Prepaid Rent. This will not be cor-
rect. What was 'Prepaid Rent,' an asset on January 1 worth $300, has
been used and is now an expense—a part of the cost of running
the business. Therefore, it is obvious that if I list this amount as an
asset at the beginning of January, at the end of January I will have
to remove the $300 from the asset account and place it in the
expense account. I could easily do this by placing the following
adjusting entry in the general journal:

Dr. Rent Expense 300
    Cr. Prepaid Rent 300
        To adjust the prepaid rent account.

Continuing to reason and think out loud, the bookkeeper arrives at the following conclusions:

1. "Yes, I could record this transaction to the asset, Prepaid Rent, adjust it at the end of January, and be technically correct."
2. "However, since this monthly prepaid rent is an expense that is consumed each month *before* I prepare the monthly financial statements, I could save time if I charged this as an expense at the beginning of the period."
3. "In general then, any expense—such as rent, insurance, supplies, or interest—incurred during a fiscal period and *completely used as a cost of running the business during that same fiscal period,* can and should be charged immediately to a proper expense account rather than to an asset account."

Up to this point in the illustration, a groundwork of understanding has been laid for what is to follow. *First,* the difference between an expense and a prepaid expense account should be clear. *Second,* there can be more than one way of recording a prepaid expense transaction—bookkeepers have decisions to make regarding such entries, and the proper choice can save time. *Third,* and perhaps most important of all, the student is being prepared to solve subsequent problems in a textbook which require him to alternate between adjusting the prepaid rent account and the rent expense account. It is worth mentioning here that some students who seem to easily learn a simple adjustment, encounter difficulty when a situation calls for a complete reversal of that adjustment. Many of these students may have *memorized* a few clerical steps and not really understood the adjustment.

Continuing example—adjustment of a prepaid item. This time we shall assume that the proprietor of the shoe store takes advantage of the yearly terms offered for rent and pays in advance the $3,000 *annual* rent. (Equivalent to $250 a month.) His bookkeeper is once again faced with the choice of one of the journal entries shown on page 458.

Dr. Prepaid Rent   3,000
   Cr. Cash   3,000
     Paid rent for year
         or
Dr. Rent Expense   3,000
   Cr. Cash   3,000
     Paid rent for year

The identical reasons given previously for charging the monthly $300 rent to the prepaid rent account can be used to justify the choice of the first of these two entries. After the bookkeeper gives full consideration to charging the $3,000 annual rent to the prepaid account, he says, "But previously, when paid monthly and charged to the rent expense account, I saved myself an adjusting entry. Can I do the same this time?" To clarify the situation, he sets up comparative situations with T accounts and studies the results. (See illustration of comparative methods on pages 460 and 461.) This time the bookkeeper reaches the following conclusions:

1. "An adjustment of accounts will be necessary whether I charge the original expense to Prepaid Rent or Rent Expense."
2. "Provided I make a proper adjustment, the end-of-the-month financial statements will be the same."
3. "It seems best to charge the original transaction to Prepaid Rent because

    (a) the remaining prepaid rent will then appear in this account from month to month, and
    (b) this will also result in all twelve of my end-of-the-month adjustments being identical.

However, I see why some bookkeepers might charge the original transaction to Rent Expense."

A Summary of the New Concepts Presented

This illustration shows WHAT two accounts are involved in adjusting prepaid rent and HOW the adjustment of this advance payment is made. It further shows WHY adjustments are necessary at the end of an accounting period. The following diagram details the WHY, WHEN, WHAT, and HOW of our example.

WHY
     1. Some accounts change in character with the passage of time. Prepaid expenses (assets) become true expenses as the asset is used up or consumed.

WHEN 2. These accounts are adjusted and brought up to date at the end of each accounting period.

3. Bookkeepers have choices to make. They can initially charge the prepaying of an expense to either a prepaid expense account, such as Prepaid Rent, or charge it directly to an expense account, such as Rent Expense.

WHAT 4. It is better to initially charge prepaid expenses that will be completely used during a fiscal period to the expense account rather than the asset account.

5. Prepaid expenses that are paid in one fiscal period but not completely used until a subsequent period must be adjusted.

HOW 6. This adjustment is made by debiting the complementary expense account of the prepaid asset and crediting (subtracting) the used up expense from the prepaid asset (or vice versa if the expense account was originally charged with the total payment). In this particular illustration the student learns that the complementary account for adjusting Prepaid Rent is Rent Expense. Subsequently, or later in the course, he would see similar relationships between such pairs of accounts as:

Asset — Expense
Prepaid Insurance — Insurance Expense
Supplies — Supplies Expense
Prepaid Interest — Interest Expense

The introduction to adjusting entries is all-important. It is obvious from the detail of the foregoing illustration that students are not going to master all the new learnings in a single introductory lesson. Skill as well as knowledge is involved in making adjustments. So, in addition to the need for a complete and clear presentation, the students need time to grasp and apply what they have seen and been told. And, students need drill and practice to reinforce the skills and knowledges related to adjustments.

Adjusting Prepaid Income (Income Received in Advance) Accounts

Adjusting a prepaid income account is introduced by first presenting a quick review, illustrated with T accounts on the chalkboard, of the adjustment of a prepaid expense account. A similar T-

METHOD I

When Charged to an Asset Account

Prepaid Rent		Cash	
Jan. 1　3,000			Jan. 1　3,000

If the bookkeeper uses the above method, Prepaid Rent does not reflect a true picture on January 30. One month of Prepaid Rent ($3,000 ÷ 12 months = $250) has been used as a cost of running the business and is now an expense. Thus the prepaid rent account should be valued at only $2,750 on January 30. This requires an adjusting journal entry that removes $250 from the prepaid rent account and places it in Rent Expense.

The bookkeeper makes the following entry:

　　　Dr. Rent Expense　　　　　　250
　　　　　Cr. Prepaid Rent　　　　　　　　250

Now both the asset account and the expense account dealing with rent reflect a true picture.

Prepaid Rent		Rent Expense	
Jan. 1　3,000	Jan. 30　250	Jan. 30　250	

The January 31 balance sheet will now list the current amount of Prepaid Rent, $2,750, and the income statement will show the correct rent expense for the period, $250.

One of the expenses of running the business for January was rent, and this item must be subtracted from gross profit. Therefore, had the bookkeeper failed to charge the January rent as an expense, net profit for the month would have been overstated by $250. In addition, the balance sheet for January would also be incorrect, since $250 of the $3,000 listed as Prepaid Rent would no longer exist.

METHOD II

When Charged to an Expense Account

Rent Expense		Cash	
Jan. 1 3,000			Jan. 1 3,000

If the bookkeeper uses the above method, his rent expense account does not reflect a true picture on January 30. Only $250 of this rent expense ($3,000 ÷ 12 months) has been used as a cost of running the business in January. The remaining 11 months' rent, $2,750, should be in an asset account called Prepaid Rent. This requires an adjusting entry that removes $2,750 from Rent Expense and places this amount in the asset account Prepaid Rent.

The bookkeeper makes the following entry:

        Dr. Prepaid Rent   2,750
            Cr. Rent Expense   2,750

Now both the asset account and the expense account dealing with rent reflect a true picture.

Prepaid Rent		Rent Expense	
Jan. 30 2,750		Jan. 1 3,000	Jan. 30 2,750

The January 31 balance sheet will now list the current amount of prepaid rent, $2,750, and the income statement will show the correct rent expense for the period.

Only $\frac{1}{12}$ of the yearly rent expense is applicable to the January accounting period. Therefore, had the bookkeeper neglected to transfer the remaining unused value of the annual rent payment to an asset account, net profit for January would have been understated by $2,750. Also, the January balance sheet would show assets at $2,750 less than their actual value.

account picture of the adjustment of a prepaid income account is then developed next to the prepaid expense illustration on the board. Thus the "connection with previous learning" is achieved by means of showing the relationship of prepaid income to prepaid expenses.

After the relationship of prepaid income and expenses has been established, the teacher proceeds to develop answers to the following questions:

(1) What is prepaid income?

(2) What accounts are involved in the adjustment of prepaid income accounts?

(3) What is the difference between prepaid income (liability accounts where income has been received but not yet earned) and earned income (income received that has been earned)?

STUDY QUESTIONS

1. Which is the simplest kind of adjustment?

2. What is the difference between an expense and a prepaid expense?

3. Explain the circumstances under which a bookkeeper may save himself an adjusting entry by recording a prepaid expense transaction as either an expense or as an asset.

4. What B-A concepts will a student have acquired when he can, with complete understanding, adjust an account in the ledger that contains elements of expense as well as elements of asset value?

5. What relationship exists between the teaching of how to adjust prepaid expense accounts and prepaid income accounts?

DISCUSSION QUESTIONS

1. Do you agree or disagree that adjusting the account Prepaid Insurance is one of the easiest adjustments to teach? Why?

2. Which of the two examples shown on pages 460 and 461 for recording the payment rent do you prefer? Why?

3. Should you teach high school students more than one way of recording and adjusting a prepaid expense? Why?

4. If you had no chalkboard and no overhead projector in your bookkeeping classroom, what ways can you suggest for teaching students to adjust Prepaid Insurance—their first lesson dealing with adjustments?

Search for Improved Ways of Adjusting Merchandise Inventory

Whenever a difficult phase or an extra-important topic in a subject is reached, educators make special efforts to find improved ways of teaching it. The importance of a good start in a B-A course, as stated previously, has resulted in the development of more than twenty approaches to the teaching of bookkeeping-accounting. Similarly, the difficulty of teaching how to adjust the merchandise inventory account has resulted over the years in the development of various ways for teaching this adjustment.

There is a difference of opinion as to which of the more common ways of adjusting the merchandise inventory account is easiest and best to teach. This difference will perhaps remain until either an outstandingly easier way is devised or until research discovers more effective ways of measuring comparative teaching methods. Since no agreement exists on which is the best or easiest way of adjusting the merchandise inventory account, what help can be given in teaching this adjustment?

Some Common Ways of Adjusting the Merchandise Inventory Account

The teacher's thorough understanding of the more common ways by which the merchandise inventory account is adjusted supplies him with a reserve of information and confidence that could be of immeasurable assistance in his chosen method of teaching this topic. Such knowledge gives him a reserve of understanding for answering students' problems and questions.

Four of the more common procedures for handling merchandise inventory at the close of a fiscal period are listed below.

1. Adjustment through use of cost of goods sold account.
   1.1 Using both the beginning and the ending inventory amounts
   1.2 Using the difference between the beginning and the ending inventory amounts

2. Adjustment through use of purchases account.
   2.1 Using both the beginning and the ending inventory amounts
   2.2 Using the difference between the beginning and the ending inventory amounts

3. Adjustment through use of income and expense summary account.
   3.1 Using both the beginning and the ending inventory amounts and placing both inventory amounts on the same line in the Income Statement columns of the work sheet
   3.2 Using the difference between the beginning and the ending inventory amounts

4. Adjustment through use of closing entries—the direct summary method.

How the data for adjustments given below would be shown on the work sheet and in T accounts under each of the foregoing procedures is illustrated on pages 466 and 467.

Data for Adjustments

Beginning inventory $5,000
Ending inventory 4,000
Purchases 2,000
Sales 3,500

Comments on Different Procedures of Adjusting Merchandise Inventory

Several observations and comments can be made about the various common procedures that are shown for adjusting the merchandise inventory account.

Procedure 1, using the cost of goods sold account. Early in this century the use of a suspense or clearing account called Cost of Goods Sold for adjusting Merchandise Inventory was a common practice. The fact that some recent editions of introductory college accounting textbooks are showing this method indicates that the popularity of this procedure may be returning.

The major teaching advantage that can be claimed for this procedure is that the steps used in this adjustment, when both the beginning and ending inventory amounts are used, are identical to the steps followed in preparing the cost-of-goods-sold section of the income statement. For example, the cost of goods sold is found by adding the beginning inventory to the purchases to find the goods available for sale, and then subtracting the ending inventory from this amount. The adjustment on the work sheet does exactly this. Furthermore, under this procedure the amount extended into the Debit column of the Income Statement columns of the work sheet ($3,000 in the illustration on the succeeding page) is exactly what the account title labels it—Cost of Goods Sold.

One objection to adjusting merchandise inventory through a separate suspense account called Cost of Goods Sold is that under this procedure all of the amounts needed for preparing the income statement will not be found in the Income Statement columns of the work sheet. Thus, the use of this method increases the difficulty of teaching the application of the work sheet in the preparation of the income statement. Another problem with this method occurs when more than the beginning and ending inventory amounts are needed for arriving at the cost of goods sold. For example, when a business has balances in such accounts as Purchases Discount, Purchases Returns and Allowances, and Transportation on Purchases, these amounts must be taken into account when computing the cost of goods sold. Therefore, the teacher using a cost of goods sold account for adjusting Merchandise Inventory is faced with the teaching of additional adjustments on the work sheet for such accounts as Purchases Discount, Purchases Returns and Allowances, and Transportation on Purchases.

Procedure 2, using the purchases account. Teaching high school students to adjust the merchandise inventory account through the purchases account was the most popular method during the 1930's and 1940's. Except for the fact that this method has the advantage of not requiring the use of a special suspense account for adjusting Merchandise Inventory, it has about the same advantages and disadvantages as making the adjustment through the cost of goods sold account—Procedure 1 above. While this adjustment through

COMMON PROCEDURES FOR ADJUSTING MERCHANDISE INVENTORY

Procedure 1

ADJUSTMENT THROUGH USE OF COST OF GOODS SOLD ACCOUNT

1.1 Using Both the Beginning and the Ending Inventory Amounts

ACCOUNTS	TRIAL BALANCE Dr.	TRIAL BALANCE Cr.	ADJUSTMENTS Dr.	ADJUSTMENTS Cr.	INCOME STATEMENT Dr.	INCOME STATEMENT Cr.	BALANCE SHEET Dr.	BALANCE SHEET Cr.
Merchandise Inventory	5,000		(b) 4,000	(a) 5,000			4,000	
Sales		3,500				3,500		
Purchases	2,000			(c) 2,000				
Cost of Goods Sold			(a) 5,000 (c) 2,000	(b) 4,000	3,000			

1.2 Using the Difference Between the Beginning and the Ending Inventory Amounts

ACCOUNTS	TRIAL BALANCE Dr.	TRIAL BALANCE Cr.	ADJUSTMENTS Dr.	ADJUSTMENTS Cr.	INCOME STATEMENT Dr.	INCOME STATEMENT Cr.	BALANCE SHEET Dr.	BALANCE SHEET Cr.
Merchandise Inventory	5,000			(a) 1,000			4,000	
Sales		3,500				3,500		
Purchases	2,000			(b) 2,000				
Cost of Goods Sold			(a) 1,000 (b) 2,000		3,000			

Procedure 2

ADJUSTMENT THROUGH USE OF PURCHASES ACCOUNT

2.1 Using Both the Beginning and the Ending Inventory Amounts

ACCOUNTS	TRIAL BALANCE Dr.	TRIAL BALANCE Cr.	ADJUSTMENTS Dr.	ADJUSTMENTS Cr.	INCOME STATEMENT Dr.	INCOME STATEMENT Cr.	BALANCE SHEET Dr.	BALANCE SHEET Cr.
Merchandise Inventory	5,000		(b) 4,000	(a) 5,000			4,000	
Sales		3,500				3,500		
Purchases	2,000		(a) 5,000	(b) 4,000	3,000			

2.2 Using the Difference Between the Beginning and the Ending Inventory Amounts

ACCOUNTS	TRIAL BALANCE Dr.	TRIAL BALANCE Cr.	ADJUSTMENTS Dr.	ADJUSTMENTS Cr.	INCOME STATEMENT Dr.	INCOME STATEMENT Cr.	BALANCE SHEET Dr.	BALANCE SHEET Cr.
Merchandise Inventory	5,000			(a) 1,000			4,000	
Sales		3,500				3,500		
Purchases	2,000		(a) 1,000		3,000			

Procedure 3

ADJUSTMENT THROUGH USE OF INCOME AND EXPENSE SUMMARY ACCOUNT

3.1 Using Both the Beginning and the Ending Inventory Amounts and Placing Both Inventory Amounts on the Same Line in the Income Statement Columns

ACCOUNTS	TRIAL BALANCE Dr.	TRIAL BALANCE Cr.	ADJUSTMENTS Dr.	ADJUSTMENTS Cr.	INCOME STATEMENT Dr.	INCOME STATEMENT Cr.	BALANCE SHEET Dr.	BALANCE SHEET Cr.
Merchandise Inventory	5,000		(b) 4,000	(a) 5,000			4,000*	
Income & Expense Summary			(a) 5,000	(b) 4,000	5,000	4,000		
Sales		3,500				3,500		
Purchases	2,000				2,000			

3.2 Using the Difference Between the Beginning and the Ending Inventory Amounts

ACCOUNTS	TRIAL BALANCE Dr.	TRIAL BALANCE Cr.	ADJUSTMENTS Dr.	ADJUSTMENTS Cr.	INCOME STATEMENT Dr.	INCOME STATEMENT Cr.	BALANCE SHEET Dr.	BALANCE SHEET Cr.
Merchandise Inventory	5,000			(a) 1,000			4,000	
Income & Expense Summary			(a) 1,000		1,000			
Sales		3,500				3,500		
Purchases	2,000				2,000			

Procedure 4

ADJUSTMENT THROUGH USE OF CLOSING ENTRIES—THE DIRECT SUMMARY METHOD

ACCOUNTS	TRIAL BALANCE Dr.	TRIAL BALANCE Cr.	ADJUSTMENTS Dr.	ADJUSTMENTS Cr.	INCOME STATEMENT Dr.	INCOME STATEMENT Cr.	BALANCE SHEET Dr.	BALANCE SHEET Cr.
Merchandise Inventory	5,000				5,000	4,000	4,000*	
Income & Expense Summary								
Sales		3,500				3,500		
Purchases	2,000				2,000			

* Instead of showing the amount of the ending merchandise inventory on the same line as the beginning merchandise inventory, a popular variation is to place the amount of the ending inventory on a line below the accounts in the trial balance and label this Merchandise Inventory (New).

Figure 20—1.

THE EFFECT ON ACCOUNTS OF COMMON
PROCEDURES FOR ADJUSTING MERCHANDISE INVENTORY

Merchandise Inventory		Purchases		Cost of Goods Sold	
Bal. 5,000 (b) 4,000	(a) 5,000	Bal. 2,000	(c) 2,000	(a) 5,000 (c) 2,000	(b) 4,000

Merchandise Inventory		Purchases		Cost of Goods Sold	
Bal. 5,000	(a) 1,000	Bal. 2,000	(b) 2,000	(a) 1,000 (b) 2,000	

Merchandise Inventory		Purchases	
Bal. 5,000 (b) 4,000	(a) 5,000	Bal. 2,000 (a) 5,000	(b) 4,000

Merchandise Inventory		Purchases	
Bal. 5,000	(a) 1,000	Bal. 2,000 (a) 1,000	

Merchandise Inventory		Purchases		Income & Expense Summary	
Bal. 5,000 (b) 4,000	(a) 5,000	Bal. 2,000		(a) 5,000	(b) 4,000

Merchandise Inventory		Purchases		Income & Expense Summary	
Bal. 5,000	(a) 1,000	Bal. 2,000		(a) 1,000	

After closing entries
have been posted

Merchandise Inventory		Purchases		Income & Expense Summary	
Bal. 5,000 4,000	5,000	Bal. 2,000	2,000	Mdse. 5,000 ⎫ Purch. 2,000 ⎬ 7,300 Sundry ⎭ Expenses 300 Net Income 200	Mdse. 4,000 ⎫ 7,500 Sales 3,500 ⎭

Figure 20—2.

Purchases has not completely disappeared from use, it is rarely found today in high school B-A textbooks or in introductory college accounting texts.

One reason that it is disappearing is because its procedures do not provide in the Income Statement columns of the work sheet all of the amounts needed for the preparation of the income statement, as do several of the more modern and popular methods described below.

Procedure 3, using the income and expense summary account. This adjustment through the income and expense summary account, *using both the beginning and ending inventory amounts and placing both inventory amounts on the same line in the Income Statement columns,* is perhaps the most common method of adjusting Merchandise Inventory today. Although some teachers question whether this method is as easy to teach to high school students as those procedures using the purchases account or the cost of goods sold account, its major advantage is that this method makes all of the amounts needed for the preparation of the income statement available in the two Income Statement columns of the work sheet.

The method of using the difference between the beginning and the ending inventory amounts to adjust Merchandise Inventory through Income and Expense Summary can claim the teaching advantage of completing this merchandise inventory adjustment more closely to the manner of other adjustments. However, any such advantage is offset by the disadvantage of not providing all amounts in the Income Statement columns that are needed for the preparation of the income statement.

Procedure 4, using closing entries—the direct summary method. When closing entries are used for adjusting the merchandise inventory account, they are planned on the work sheet as follows.

    (a) The transfer of the beginning merchandise inventory to the debit of Income and Expense Summary is indicated by writing the amount of the beginning inventory in the Income Statement Debit column.

    (b) The amount of the ending merchandise inventory is entered in the Balance Sheet Debit column to indicate the value of the asset at the end of the period. It is also entered in the Income Statement Credit column to indicate the credit to Income and Expense Summary.

Therefore, when the closing entries are made from the information on the work sheet, Income and Expense Summary is credited for the total of the Income Statement Credit column and the various accounts with amounts in that column are debited (closed) in a combined journal entry. Income and Expense Summary is debited with the total of the Income Statement Debit column and the various accounts with amounts in that column are credited (closed) in a combined journal entry.

An examination of current introductory college accounting textbooks indicates that this direct summary method of adjusting the merchandise inventory account may be increasing in popularity. If this is true, and if "we tend to teach as we have been taught," the future may see this becoming a popular method on the high school level.

Under each of the procedures of adjusting Merchandise Inventory illustrated on pages 466 and 467, the trading section of the income statement would appear the same:

Income:		
Sales		$3,500
Cost of Goods Sold:		
Merchandise Inventory, Beginning of Period ..	$5,000	
Purchases	2,000	
Total Cost of Merchandise Available for Sale	7,000	
Less Merchandise Inventory, End of Period ..	4,000	
Cost of Goods Sold		3,000
Gross Profit on Sales		500

Two cautions seem worthy of note at this stage. First, because of the time available for teaching high school bookkeeping-accounting and because of the psychological effect upon students, it would seem best for the average high school student to learn only one way of adjusting the merchandise inventory account.

Elementary B-A classes are no place to confuse students with alternate adjustments. Leave such teaching to the college accounting courses.

The exception to this caution would be where the class is comprised of some high-ability students who, in the judgment of the teacher, could profit from the challenge of learning more than one way of adjusting the merchandise inventory account.

The second caution is to teachers who might choose to teach a method of adjusting this account different than the method shown in the textbook their students use. These teachers are reminded that they must provide their students with ample supplementary reference and practice material dealing with the method taught. Otherwise, students could be frustrated by turning to their textbook, their major out-of-class source of help, and finding confusion rather than help.

Teaching Problems Related to the Teaching of Adjusting the Merchandise Inventory Account

Once again, as is true for teaching all adjusting entries, the student must first understand WHY the account must be adjusted. When this is learned, he has added one more account to his list of WHAT accounts must be adjusted. He already knows WHEN accounts are adjusted, so the teaching of the adjustment of the merchandise inventory account centers on but one problem— HOW? Because the adjustment of this account does not follow the pattern of previously learned adjustments, the one additional factor that causes this adjustment to be more of a teaching problem than that of other adjustments is WHY it is adjusted the way it is. In the first simple adjustments that students learned, they encountered little or no difficulty in understanding why one new account must be established for handling the adjustment of a prepaid asset account. However, there are more new learning factors and more old learning factors in adjusting the merchandise inventory than for any other adjustment. When teachers understand this and understand what the factors are, teaching difficulties become less formidable.

Learning Factors Involved in Adjusting Merchandise Inventory

The B-A teacher must emphasize both old and new learnings when teaching how to adjust the merchandise inventory account. Which are new, introductory learnings and which are old, acquired learnings will vary from classroom to classroom. The new will have to be taught, the old reviewed and reinforced as needed. The teaching procedures are listed in sequential order in the outline of factors presented below. The outline follows the most common procedure currently being followed—that is the adjusting of the merchandise inventory account through Income and Expense Summary, using both the beginning and the ending inventory amounts, and placing both amounts in the Income Statement columns. With minor variations this outline could be modified for explaining the method of adjusting the account through the purchases account or a cost of goods sold account.

The WHY and HOW of Adjusting Merchandise Inventory

I. WHY the merchandise inventory account needs adjustment.

A. Why the balance in the merchandise inventory account must show the new, the correct, the ending inventory figures and not the old, now incorrect, beginning inventory amount.

B. Why the purchases account was established and the kind of account that it is.

C. What the relationship is between the purchases account and the merchandise inventory account.

D. Why new merchandise was charged to Purchases rather than to Merchandise Inventory.

E. Why the sales account was established and the kind of account that it is.

F. What the relationship is between the sales account and the merchandise inventory and the purchases accounts.

G. Why, when a sale is made, Cash or Accounts Receivable is debited and Sales is credited for the total amount rather than crediting Merchandise Inventory or Purchases for the inventory (cost) value of the merchandise sold and crediting income or capital for the profit on the sale.

II. HOW the merchandise inventory account is adjusted.

    A. Remove the amount of the old, beginning inventory from the merchandise inventory account by transferring the beginning inventory amount to Income and Expense Summary.

        1. Debit Income and Expense Summary because the beginning inventory amount is a part of the cost of merchandise sold and all costs (and expenses) are summarized on the debit side of Income and Expense Summary.

        2. Credit Merchandise Inventory to complete the transferring (closing) of the beginning merchandise inventory to Income and Expense Summary.

    B. Record the new, ending inventory amount in the merchandise inventory account.

        1. Debit Merchandise Inventory for the amount of the new, ending inventory because this is the value of the asset which should be reported on the end-of-period balance sheet.

        2. Credit Income and Expense Summary for the amount of the new, ending inventory because this new, ending inventory amount is a deduction from the cost of merchandise available for sale.

This completes the adjusting of the merchandise inventory account. To some students it will be a mechanical procedure and without understanding unless the teacher helps them to see the relationship of these adjusting entries in the income and expense account to the other amounts that will subsequently appear in that account as well as on the income statement itself. This could be done by developing an illustration on the chalkboard or overhead projector showing an outline of the necessary amounts the income and expense summary account of a merchandising business must contain if its final balance is to result in a net income or loss for a fiscal period. (See outline on next page.)

If this seems difficult, it should be remembered that the first half of this outline, the WHY of adjusting the merchandise inventory account, is largely review of knowledge already acquired.

If we do not review and fix understandings and relationships, we force students to memorize the HOW of adjusting entries when they do not comprehend the WHY of the procedure.

INCOME & EXPENSE SUMMARY

Merchandise Available for Sale {	Beginning Inv.	5,000	New Inv.	4,000	} Cost of Mdse. Sold: 3,000
	Purchases	2,000			} Gross Profit: 500
			Sales	3,500	
Expenses {		200			} Net Income: 200
		75			
		25			

The fact that students need repetitive practice on this adjustment, as with all adjustments, should be obvious. Some students have to perform a half-dozen or more adjusting entries before they grasp the understanding and procedure. A few, when they are first learning to adjust the merchandise inventory account, probably memorize the steps in the adjusting method before they understand what they are doing. If this gives temporary comfort and satisfaction to some conscientious students, there seems little point in making a major issue of it at this time *provided* the teacher takes the responsibility of replacing memorization with comprehension. Rote memorization at any stage in bookkeeping-accounting should be discouraged. The only way the teacher can stop memorization by some students is to bring clarity of understanding to the problem.

Several mini-problems similar to the following one can help supply students with the repetition or drill which most need when learning to adjust Merchandise Inventory. If the teacher wishes students to concentrate on the adjustment of Merchandise Inventory, Instructions 3 and 5 of this problem could be omitted.

MINI-PROBLEM
(End of Fiscal Period)

The class of 1970 at Plainville High School by selling school pennants worked to raise money for a graduation trip to Washington, D. C. They started doing this in 1968 when they were sophomores. A trial balance taken by their class treasurer on June 30, 1969, at the close of their junior year was as follows:

CLASS OF 1970
WORK SHEET
For Year Ended June 30, 1969

Account Titles	TRIAL BALANCE DR.	TRIAL BALANCE CR.	ADJUSTMENTS DR.	ADJUSTMENTS CR.	INCOME STATEMENT DR.	INCOME STATEMENT CR.	BALANCE SHEET DR.	BALANCE SHEET CR.
Cash	445							
Mdse. Inventory	25							
Class 1970, Cap.		265						
I. & E. Summary								
Sales		410						
Purchases	200							
Expenses	5							
Total	675	675						
Net Income								

Instructions: 1. Complete the above work sheet. The ending inventory on June 30 consisted of 40 pennants @ 50¢ = $20.00.

2. Prepare an income statement.

3. Prepare a balance sheet.

4. Record the adjusting entries.

5. Record the closing entries.

STUDY QUESTIONS

1. When can we expect to see agreement on what is the easiest way to adjust the merchandise inventory account?

2. Why is it advisable for a B-A teacher to understand the various ways Merchandise Inventory is adjusted?

3. Describe four different major ways of adjusting the merchandise inventory account.

4. What is the advantage of adjusting Merchandise Inventory on the work sheet to show both the beginning and the ending inventory amounts in the Income Statement columns?

5. Why was it suggested that the direct summary method of adjusting Merchandise Inventory might become a popular method on the high school level in the future?

6. What two cautions are given the high school B-A teacher for teaching the merchandise inventory adjustment?

7. What are some basic B-A concepts that a student must know in order to understand fully why the merchandise inventory account needs adjusting?

8. How can the teacher present the adjustment of the merchandise inventory account so that it is not a mechanical procedure without understanding?

9. Why do students need repetitive practice with adjustments?

10. How can drills and mini-problems help students learn the adjustment of the merchandise inventory account?

DISCUSSION QUESTIONS

1. Which way of adjusting Merchandise Inventory do you believe is easiest to teach to high school students? Explain.

2. Which way of adjusting Merchandise Inventory do you believe is best for practicing accountants? Explain.

3. Under what circumstances would you favor teaching more than one way of adjusting Merchandise Inventory to high school students?

4. What is your reaction to the following statement, "Because we tend to teach as we have been taught, beginning high school B-A teachers tend to teach bookkeeping-accounting the way they were taught accounting in college."

5. Should memorization of a B-A procedure by a student ever be condoned by the teacher? Explain.

6. Describe ways of adjusting Merchandise Inventory other than those discussed in this chapter and evaluate each as a method for teaching to high school students.

7. What place, if any, do you see the use of mini-problems playing in your future teaching of adjusting the merchandise inventory account?

The Importance of Depreciation

Depreciation is the constant decrease in value of certain kinds of fixed assets because of the wear and tear on those items as a result of their use, the weather, and the passing of time. Depreciation is thus an operating cost, an expense of running the business. If it is not recorded:

1. The value of those assets that depreciate will be overstated on the balance sheet.
2. The capital of the business will be overstated on the balance sheet.
3. The total operating expenses of the business will be understated.
4. The net income on the income statement will be overstated.
5. As a result of such overstatement of income, additional expense will be created by overpayment of income taxes.
6. The cost of assets that depreciate will not be distributed evenly over the years of their expected life.

Therefore, the importance of recording this normal, constant, and common expense of most businesses must not be slighted in B-A courses.

Learning Problems Involved in the Teaching of Depreciation

When one breaks down the learnings that students must possess or acquire before they can be expected to handle the procedures for recording and reporting the results of depreciation, the problems which this topic presents to both teachers and students become clear and rather simple.

1. What is depreciation?
2. How is depreciation computed? Is this an exact or estimated measure of depreciation? of expense?
3. Which fixed assets depreciate and which do not?
4. How are accounts affected by depreciation?
5. How are financial statements affected by depreciation?
6. How can accounts that depreciate be adjusted without the use of a valuation account?
7. What is a valuation account? How and why is it used in adjusting accounts that depreciate?
8. How are these accounts that have been adjusted shown on financial statements?
9. How is the sale or other disposition of a fixed asset that has depreciated recorded?

These problems, listed in order of importance for learning, supply the teacher with objectives for teaching depreciation.

Steps in Teaching Depreciation

Teachers who have difficulty in the teaching of depreciation or who are trying to improve their teaching of this topic should examine their procedure in the order of the preceding outline and the following questions:

1. Do you first help your students achieve a competent understanding of the term and concept of depreciation?
2. Do you next help them acquire skill in computing depreciation— the arithmetical skills and concepts of the simple, straight-line method of figuring the amount of monthly, quarterly, semiannual, and annual depreciation? When this is done, students learn that someone must *estimate* the life of an asset; that someone must *estimate* its end-of-life or scrap value; that subtracting the scrap value from the total original cost of the asset will determine the total *estimated* lifetime expense of the asset to the business; that this total expense divided by the number of years the depreciation will be occurring will result in one common way of finding the estimated annual expense; and that this is readily converted into monthly, quarterly, or semiannual amounts to fit the bookkeeper's needs. Students cannot be expected to understand fully and apply the B-A procedures involved with the recording and reporting of depreciation until *after* they have a basic understanding of depreciation itself and of how it is computed.

3. Do you connect the adjusting entry for recording depreciation with previous learning? Previous adjustments? Do you help students see the relationship of adjusting a fixed asset account to a prepaid asset account, such as prepaid insurance, which also diminishes in value with the passing of time—and which students learned to adjust previously?

4. Do you teach the answers to the previous three questions before you introduce the major new B-A learnings that accompany the teaching of depreciation—

   a. the meaning, the reason, and the use of a valuation account?
   b. the method of reporting depreciation on the balance sheet?

As previously stated, the student cannot be expected to grasp and be able to apply the B-A concepts dealing with depreciation until after he has learned (1) the concept of depreciation itself, and (2) the arithmetical concepts for computing depreciation. Teachers who have trouble with this topic of depreciation should reexamine the approach they use in opening up this topic to students. Even though the term may be new to many students, they usually have a general knowledge of depreciation. They know that a bicycle, a pair of shoes, an automobile purchased last year is not worth as much this year. They know this from previous experience. The teacher could introduce (motivate) an initial lesson in this manner. Such an introductory lesson might well be devoted to the objective, "helping students to arrive at clear understandings of depreciation and how it can be computed"—making little or no direct connection with bookkeeping-accounting at all. Several days might profitably be spent on this objective.

The next comparison or connection with previous learning that the teacher could make is to compare the fixed asset which is depreciating in value with another type of asset which also diminishes (not depreciates) in value. A review of adjusting prepaid insurance or another prepaid expense account could be made. Some classroom discussion time could be spent developing answers to the following:

Why did we adjust the prepaid insurance account? How? What effect did this adjustment have on the account itself? on the balance sheet? on the income statement? How did we compute each month's, each quarter's, the semiannual, and the annual insurance expense? How do we figure depreciation? What is the difference

between Insurance Expense and Depreciation Expense? (Answer—
One is based upon true expense figures, the other based upon an
estimate of expense—of wearing away—wear and tear.)

Then the class could be asked to suggest an adjusting entry for
recording a prefigured amount of depreciation on a fixed asset
such as Buildings. Because of the above relationship made between
adjusting a prepaid expense account, which would be made by
debiting Insurance Expense and crediting Prepaid Insurance,
the class will almost invariably supply the following answer for
recording depreciation expense:

> Dr. Depreciation Expense
> Cr. Buildings

While this, of course, is not the final adjusting entry that the
student will learn for adjusting accounts that depreciate, it is a
helpful and sometimes necessary learning step leading to the
introduction of a valuation account.

This extra, related step in teaching the proper recording of
depreciation expenses might be challenged with "This is not in
accord with vocational bookkeeping practice, and you are teaching
something which has to be unlearned." Although this may seem a
valid objection, in this particular instance it is not. First, as far as
this step in the teaching of adjusting a fixed asset account takes
the student, it is not incorrect B-A procedure. The student himself
can see the two practices that are common in nearly all adjusting
entries dealing with asset accounts (except Merchandise Inventory);
namely, (1) an expense account must be established to record the
amount of the expense and (2) the asset account must be reduced
in an amount equal to that placed in the expense account. This
intermediary step can be of considerable help in leading to a subsequent understanding of why allowance or valuation accounts are
set up instead of a credit being recorded in the asset account that
is depreciating. Second, the teacher who might still, in spite of the
above facts, continue to say, "but this is not the way it is done
in business," is making the mistaken claim that teachers must never
use any learning device, technique, or practice that is not used
in business.

Up to this point, teaching students to adjust accounts that
depreciate is no more difficult than teaching them to adjust prepaid

items. Students have already acquired a background of understanding and practice as to why, when, and how some accounts are adjusted, and it is not difficult to relate this background to adjusting fixed asset accounts. However, when this stage is reached, when the valuation account itself is introduced, a real teaching challenge is frequently encountered. Teachers who understand the reason for this learning difficulty can clarify the procedure so the students can master it.

The Reasons for and the Use of Valuation Accounts

The balance of a fixed asset account should always show the original cost of the asset owed by the business. The amount of its periodic depreciation expense cannot be credited to the fixed asset account. Only when the assets are disposed of are the fixed asset accounts credited. Therefore, a separate valuation account is established for accumulating (crediting) the amount of the periodic depreciation. This account shows the amount by which the cost of the asset is distributed period by period. The balance in this valuation account is used to "value"—to show the current book value of the asset on the balance sheet.

Since the credit balance in this account is subtracted on the balance sheet from the original cost of the asset, it is used to arrive at the current book value of the asset. Because it is so used, it is called a valuation account. Therefore, the purpose of valuation accounts is for clarity and completeness of financial reporting.

Students have little difficulty in seeing the advantage of a balance sheet that reports clearly the original cost of a fixed asset less the total accumulated depreciation—as compared with a balance sheet showing only the current valuation of, let us say, a building. Show them such a comparison, and they will tell the teacher which balance sheet they would prefer to have presented to them if they were a proprietor, a partner, a stockholder, or a banker considering a loan to the business.

The teaching problem of recording the sale or other disposition of an asset that has depreciated. Here again the major problem is probably more of an arithmetic teaching than a B-A teaching problem. The wise teacher teaches the arithmetic involved before introducing the B-A procedure for recording the sale or other disposition of a fixed asset. Students introduced to depreciation with a clear understanding of the arithmetic involved should be expected to have less trouble in this area than other students. Furthermore, it is difficult to imagine teaching this problem well and quickly without frequent chalkboard illustrations showing the accounts affected and their changes resulting from the sale or other disposition of the asset.

A common student error in computing depreciation. A common error students make when taking an examination or preparing a work sheet is to compute and record depreciation expense in a greater amount, covering a longer period, than the problem requires. For example, the problem may give the annual rate of depreciation whereas the fiscal or accounting period is only a month or a quarter. Frequently students will compute accurately the annual depreciation expense, but fail to convert it to a correct amount for the shorter accounting period. The mistake is easily understandable and quite disappointing to both student and teacher. Perhaps such mistakes can never be completely eliminated, but teachers who merely shrug them off as "understandable" are not giving the problem the attention it deserves.

Teachers who encounter this problem should alert their students to its existence. One way this can be done is to relate the problem to that part of the work sheet heading which helps supply the answer to the problem—that section of the heading which tells the length of the accounting period and states, "For the month (or quarter, or year, etc.) ended June 30, 19—." In some classes where such mistakes as these frequently occur, the teacher is willing to accept work sheets containing headings with the statement "For the *period* ended June 30, 19—" instead of teaching that the length of the period should be stated. Then, when properly taught, cautioned, and conditioned, this phrase in the heading of a work sheet or in an examination problem becomes an important phrase or "danger signal" to alert and caution the student when computing depreciation expense.

Teaching allowance for bad debts. The handling of depreciation expense is usually taught before the expense of bad debts is presented to students. When this is so, the student who has a sound understanding of depreciation and its valuation account, Accumulated Depreciation, finds little difficulty in comprehending the manner of evaluating and recording the bad debts expense applicable to accounts receivable. There are really only two new understandings for students to acquire.

First, teachers should help students acquire a businessman's understanding of credit and WHY bad debts expense is a common problem for the businessman and the bookkeeper; that credit to customers, when judiciously handled by business, results in greater profit and service to customers and community; that credit to customers is essential in some businesses, helpful and profitable in others, and not always practical or necessary in still others.

The second problem is one of arithmetic. HOW the amount of bad debts expense is estimated, how it is computed, and why the rate or amount estimated may change occasionally or from period to period—as is not true in the straight-line method of computing depreciation. The estimate for bad debts is usually based on a percentage of charge sales or a percentage of the balance in the accounts receivable account at the end of a fiscal period. The amount of the percentage is usually based upon the amount of such sales that proved uncollectible during previous accounting periods of the business. As businesses change their policies of granting or collecting credit transactions and as periods of economic change affect businesses and their customers, it is sometimes necessary to raise or lower the rate or change the method for estimating bad debts expense. In most businesses, however, this change is told to the bookkeeper, and he only has to figure the estimate of loss on the basis of the rate or percentage figure supplied him.

STUDY QUESTIONS

1. Why must the depreciation of fixed assets be recorded?

2. What six effects would the failure to record depreciation have on the financial records of a business?

3. What nine simple learnings must a student acquire before he can be expected to handle the procedures for recording and reporting the results of depreciation?

4. The answers to what four leading questions are offered as helpful teaching suggestions for an orderly approach to the teaching of adjustments involving depreciation?

5. What suggestion is offered for teaching students the major reason why valuation accounts are used in B-A work?

6. What two suggestions are offered for teaching the recording of a sale or other disposition of an asset that has depreciated?

7. What is a common error that some students make when computing depreciation? How can they be helped to eliminate this error?

8. What two new understandings should students acquire when learning about the allowance for bad debts that they did not acquire when studying about accumulated depreciation?

DISCUSSION QUESTIONS

1. Some college accounting textbooks prefer the term *plant assets* to *fixed assets*. If *plant assets* is an emerging new term, to what extent should the high school B-A class use it?

2. How much time, if any, should the B-A teacher spend teaching or reviewing the arithmetic required for computing depreciation?

3. How many different methods of computing depreciation should be taught in the first-year B-A class? In the second-year class?

4. How much time, if any, should the teacher spend teaching about credit practices in business when introducing students to a chapter dealing with bad debts expense? Is this topic worthy of securing a credit manager from a local business as a guest speaker?

5. How many different ways should a student be taught for estimating the expense of possible bad debts?

6. How important is teaching about aging accounts, cycle billing, and the turnover of accounts receivable in first-year bookkeeping-accounting? second-year bookkeeping-accounting?

SELECTED REFERENCES

Hanna, J. Marshall. "How to Teach Depreciation," *Business Education World*. XLI (November, 1960), 28-29.

Strickler, Elbert C. "Bookkeeping and Accounting: A Plan for Teaching About Bad Debts," *Business Education Forum*. XVI (December, 1961), 12-13.

Watkins, Brenda. "Bookkeeping and Accounting: A Plan for Teaching Depreciation," *Business Education Forum*. XVI (December, 1961), 14-15.

The Teaching of Accrued Items

Teach the Adjusting of Accrued Items Last

Accrued items should be the last of the four kinds of adjustments presented to students. This is recommended because when accruals are taught the rather elusive concept of reversing entries is also usually taught. The dual teaching load of (a) adjusting entries for accruals along with (b) the reversing of such adjusting entries makes accrued items a more complex teaching assignment. If, however, reversing entries were ignored when accruals are first introduced, the adjusting of accrued items should not be found much more difficult to teach than their exact opposites—prepaid items, the easiest of all adjustments. When to ignore the teaching of reversing entries is discussed near the end of this chapter.

Teach the WHAT and the WHY of Accruals by Comparison

Teaching by comparison has long been recognized as a helpful way to speed learning. The student already knows about prepaid items and how they are recorded and adjusted. Accrued items are the opposite of prepaid items. For example, accrued expenses are paid *after*, not before, they have been consumed. Accrued income is received *after*, not before, it has been earned. Since students have already learned to adjust prepaid expense and prepaid income items, teaching should speed learning when done with such comparisons. WHY did we adjust the prepaid insurance account? HOW would the balance sheet and the income statement have been affected if we had not adjusted Prepaid Insurance? Similarly, what should we do about employees' salaries that have been earned in one fiscal period but will not be paid until the next period? How will the balance sheet and the income statement be affected if we do not record such facts?

Thus, teachers who have trouble teaching accruals or who are not satisfied with their students' progress might well reexamine the way they introduce students to accruals. Do they make good use of comparison—of connection with previous knowledge?

Teaching the HOW of Adjusting Accrued Items

One of the most common, simplest, and clearest situations that teachers can use to illustrate the need for and how to record (adjust) an accrued expense is the item of employees' wages or salaries. Nearly every year in nearly every business where employees are paid on a weekly or a biweekly basis, they will have earned salaries during the last few days of a fiscal period that will not be paid until sometime early in the next fiscal period. Stated another way, the business has incurred a salary expense in one fiscal period that will not be paid until the next fiscal period.

The following detailed formal lesson plan shows how a teacher, through the use of comparison and through the example of employees' salaries, could introduce students to an understanding of accruals and how an accrued expense is recorded.

LESSON PLAN

1. Title: Introducing students to accruals.

2. Aims: To (a) introduce students to accrued expenses,
              (b) show WHY and HOW accrued expenses are adjusted, and
              (c) teach the meaning of *accrual*.

3. Materials Needed: Workbook or other paper necessary for students to complete the application problem to be assigned.

4. Review: (Connection with previous learning)   Teacher writes the following transaction on the board or uses overhead projector to project it on a screen:

"January 1, 1969—Paid 3-year premium on fire insurance policy, $360."

"If the bookkeeper debited Prepaid Insurance for $360 when this transaction was recorded, what adjusting entry should be made at the end of the first annual fiscal period?"

Teacher records answer on board or overhead projector in T accounts as follows:

PREPAID INSURANCE		INSURANCE EXPENSE	
1/1/69 360	12/31/69 120	12/31/69 120	

"If this adjusting entry is not made, what will be wrong with the balance sheet of December 31, 1969?"

(Prepaid Insurance and Proprietorship, as a result of ignoring the expense, will be overstated by $120 each.)

Teacher compliments class (if deserving) on their remembering the HOW and the WHY of this adjustment of a prepaid asset.

Teacher emphasizes, *"This type of transaction illustrates that, regardless of the fiscal period in which an expense is paid, to secure accurate financial statements the expense must be charged to the fiscal period in which the prepaid expense is used or consumed."*

"Let us now consider a somewhat similar situation and see how you would handle it."

5. Presentation: Teacher outlines on the board or projects on a screen a calendar for the latter part of one year and the first few days of the next year as follows:

1969		DECEMBER			1969	
S	M	T	W	T	F	S
21	22	23	24	25	26	27
28	29	30	31 ◄	End of 1969 Fiscal Period		
1970		JANUARY			1970	
Start of 1970 Fiscal Period →			1	2	3	

"This business has a payroll expense of $100 PER DAY."

Teacher writes "$100 per day" on the board or projects it on a screen.

"Its employees work a five-day week and are paid every Friday."

"How much should be debited to the account Salary Expense on Friday, December 26—the last complete week in the year 1969?" ($500)

"What is the date when the employees will next be paid their weekly salary?" (January 2, 1970)

"How much will they be paid on January 2?" ($500)

"Is all of this $500 that will be paid in 1970 an expense of this new fiscal period?"

(No, some of it, $300, is an expense of the previous year.)

"If this entire $500 salary expense is charged to the 1970 fiscal period, what amounts on the December 31, 1969 balance sheet will be incorrect?"

(If this $300 expense in 1969 was not recorded before the closing of the books on December 31, 1969, proprietorship (net income) would be overstated by this amount—$300. Furthermore, since liabilities of $100 per day for these three days have been incurred, the liabilities would be understated by $300.)

"Here we face a problem similar to that of handling prepaid insurance—that of charging the correct amounts of an expense to the proper fiscal period."

"When a business pays for an expense such as prepaid insurance IN ADVANCE, what means are used to distribute this expense to the fiscal periods in which it is actually incurred?"

(By adjusting the prepaid asset at the close of the fiscal period so that the amount of the expense incurred during that fiscal period is charged to it.)

"We have, therefore, learned what to do when an expense, such as prepaid insurance, is paid BEFORE *its use. In this case, however, the expense incurred in one period is not paid until the next fiscal period—* AFTER *it has been used."*

"How many of you believe that you see what needs to be done to correct the situation?"

(Note: Up to this point in the plan, through connection with previous learning and through comparison with a prepaid expense, students have been led to see the problem and the need for (the WHY of) an adjustment. The next step in the plan is to try to get them to think through, to reason, and to tell HOW to make the adjustment. Therefore, conditioned by the answers to the above questions, the teacher might proceed as follows.)

"That is right—an adjustment must be made."

"What is the usual time for the bookkeeper to make adjustments?"

(At the close of the fiscal period.)

"What did the business incur in 1969 that was not recorded?"

(An expense. Also a liability.)

"Name the expense account needed for this adjustment." (Salary Expense.)

"Has this expense been paid?" (No)

"But the business is liable for the payment. Debts that a business owes are called what?" (Liabilities)

"Fine! Now name the other account needed for this adjustment." (Salaries Payable)

After first leading the students to a successful understanding of the adjustment, the teacher then demonstrates the adjustment with T accounts on the board or overhead projector as follows:

SALARY EXPENSE	SALARIES PAYABLE
12/31/69 300	12/31/69 300

Pointing to the Salary Expense account, teacher asks, *"What kind of an account is this?"* (Expense)

"What final changes will be made to this expense account before the start of the new fiscal period?"

(It will be closed and ruled.)

Teacher does this as follows:

SALARY EXPENSE		SALARIES PAYABLE
12/31/69 300	12/31/69 300	12/31/69 300

Pointing to the salaries payable account, teacher asks, *"What kind of an account is this?"* (Liability)

"How will this account appear in the ledger at the start of the new fiscal period?"

(It will remain the same—stay open.)

"On Friday, January 2, 1970, when the $500 payroll is paid, how much of this is a salary expense for the new fiscal period—1970?" ($200)

"How much of this $500 was an expense of the old, 1969 fiscal period?" ($300)

"How much of this $500, therefore, should be debited to the 'new' salary expense account for 1970?" ($200)

"Give me the complete entry."

(Debit Salary Expense, $200; debit Salaries Payable, $300; and credit Cash for $500.)

Teacher records entry in T accounts as follows:

SALARY EXPENSE		SALARIES PAYABLE	
12/31/69 300	12/31/69 300	1/2/70 300	12/31/69 300
1/2/70 200			

CASH
1/2/70   500

Through questioning, class is led to see that of the $500 weekly payroll (a) $300 salary expense incurred in 1969 was charged to 1969, and (b) $200 salary expense incurred in 1970 was charged to 1970.

Teacher prepares the class for a new learning (reversing entries) by pointing out, *"For the previous 52 weeks the bookkeeper ALWAYS debited Salary Expense for the full amount of the payroll. There is, therefore, a danger that with this type of adjustment he might forget to debit the liability account this week for part of the expense. But after we have a bit more practice with this type of adjustment, I will show you a trick that bookkeepers use that eliminates the possibility for such an error."*

(See pages 494-503 for remarks on teaching reversing entries.)

"When payment for an expense is made in one fiscal period that will not be completely used or consumed during that period, what do we call the expense?" (Prepaid Expense)

Teacher writes term on board or uses overhead projector to project on a screen.

"Here is a new term—a different kind of expense that we saw today."

Teacher writes term "Accrued expense" followed by the definition, "an expense that is incurred in one fiscal period but not paid during that period."

"Name some kinds of accrued expenses, other than salaries, that a business might have." (Interest, taxes)

"You should also know that some businesses have accrued income."

Writes term followed by definition, "Income that is earned in one period for which cash is not received until a later period."

"Examples include interest income, rent income, and subscriptions income that have been earned but for which no payment has as yet been received."

Write terms under definition of accrued income.

6. Application: Assign short problem, to be done in class, calling for a similar adjustment to that just demonstrated in class. If classroom has ample board space, assign students to do their work there. Thus, the teacher can see more readily if students can apply the period's teaching.

As further application, if time permits, cite the case of two businesses as follows:

"Business 'A' has a 1,000 gallon fuel oil tank which it pays to have filled at the start of the winter. Business 'B' heats its quarters with gas (or electricity) which it pays for at the end of the winter according to a meter reading."

"Which has a prepaid expense for its fuel? Explain."

"Which has an accrued expense for its fuel? Explain."

7. Summary: A further test of the students' grasp of the lesson is determined by their answers to such rapid-fire questions as the following:

"What is an accrued expense?

(An expense that is incurred in one fiscal period but not paid during that period.)

"How does it differ from a prepaid expense?" (It is paid AFTER, not before, it is used or consumed.)

"If no adjusting entry is made to record an accrued expense, how will the balance sheet be affected?"

(Liabilities for the period will be understated and proprietorship (net income) will be overstated.)

"How will the income statement be affected?"

(Expenses for the period will be understated and net income will be overstated.)

"When the adjusting entry for an accrued expense is recorded, what kind of an account is credited?" (Liability)

"When an accrued expense is recorded, what two kinds of accounts are involved?"

(An expense account and a liability account.)

"When an accrued expense is paid, what three kinds of accounts are involved?"

(An expense, a liability, and an asset.)

"What expenses other than salaries are common types of accrued expenses?" (Interest, taxes)

8. **Homework Assignment:**

1. To read and study pages ... to .... (Those pages in the chapter on accruals that would reinforce the day's teaching.)

2. To complete application problems ... and .... (Those problems that would be further application of the day's learning.)

9. **Teacher's Remarks:**

Other Teaching Suggestions for Introducing Accruals

The foregoing plan outlines a successful way for introducing students to accruals. As with most introductory lessons, however, it is not the only way. Nor is it necessarily the best for all teachers.

Another introduction could start with the teacher giving a brief description of the two most common methods of keeping accounting records—the cash basis and the accrual basis. Teachers find that this comparison can be a real interest-getter and the meaning of *accrual* is easier to teach when a comparison can be drawn with another procedure—the cash basis.

Still another type of introduction which also lends meaning, importance, and motivation to learning accruals is to first show the students how the accuracy of both financial statements is affected when accruals are not recorded. Furthermore, demonstrate that failure to record accrued expenses results in overstating the net income of the business and thus increases its taxes as a result of this overstated income.

Regardless of the choice of the first day's introductory coverage of accruals, the teacher who fails to make use of the following three comparison learnings in his complete coverage of accruals is cheating himself of some exciting and fruitful teaching as well as denying his students some interesting and speedier learning:

(a) compare accrued items with prepaid items
(b) compare the method of the cash basis with the accrual basis for keeping accounting records

(c) compare the results to financial statements when accruals are recorded with the results when they are not recorded.

Finally, just as the previous introductory lesson to accruals made good use of comparison by connecting accruals with previous learning, so subsequent lessons for introducing accrued income could be connected by comparison with this introduction to accrued expenses.

The Teaching of Reversing Entries

To Whom Should Reversing Entries Be Taught?

It can be a waste of time to teach reversing entries to all students enrolled in a first-year B-A course. Because this is a technical phase of bookkeeping-accounting, a so-called "trick of the trade," the learning of reversing entries might well be limited to those students whose major objective in the course is vocational.

As stated earlier in this text, the very large majority of students in most first-year courses are not planning to become vocational bookkeepers. They are there because they plan to work in business offices, and the first-year course should be aimed primarily at supplying them with an understanding of business and how it operates. Therefore, it seems doubtful if much is contributed to that objective by forcing nonvocational bookkeeping students to learn such a technical procedure as reversing entries.

Thus, it is suggested that the teaching of reversing entries might well be delayed for the predominately vocational second-year course in bookkeeping-accounting. Schools that offer only one year of bookkeeping-accounting should certainly not omit its coverage for all students, but could take the individual differences of students into account, their abilities as well as their reasons for being in the course, when teaching this topic.

When Should Reversing Entries Be Taught?

Those students who are to study reversing entries should be taught these entries *after* they have learned to adjust accruals and *after* they have learned to handle accruals without the use of reversing entries. Some teachers teach reversing entries at the same time they first teach students to adjust an accrued expense. In other words, they never teach or demonstrate how books can be and are at times kept by bookkeepers who adjust accruals without ever making a reversing entry.

For example, in the lesson plan illustrated earlier in this chapter, students were taught how to make an adjusting entry for an accrued expense and how to record the payment of that accrual in the next fiscal period without any reference to reversing entries. In this way, the learning of the adjusting entry for an accrued expense should be no more difficult to learn than the adjusting entry for a prepaid expense.

It is *after* the student has learned to handle accruals without reversing entries that he can best see the need for reversing entries—how reversing entries eliminate the need for remembering to debit a liability account when accrued expenses are paid—how reversing entries eliminate the need for remembering to credit an asset account when accrued income is received. It is, therefore, several days after the student is introduced to accrued expenses, or perhaps even after he is also taught the handling of adjustments for accrued income, that he might be introduced to reversing entries as shown in the outline of the following lesson plan.

LESSON PLAN

1. Title: Introducing students to reversing entries.

2. Aim: To show students WHY and HOW reversing entries are made.

3. Materials Needed: Two-column general journal paper.
Before start of class, place outline of the following end-of-year calendar on board or project it on a screen with an overhead projector.

1969		DECEMBER			1969	
S	M	T	W	T	F	S
21	22	23	24	25	26	27
28	29	30	31 ←		End of 1969 Fiscal Period	
1970		JANUARY			1970	
Start of 1970 Fiscal Period →				1	2	3

(Note: This calendar illustration is exactly the same as was used in the lesson plan "Introducing Students to Accruals" on page 487.)

4. Review: Teacher re-creates the same situation as that used at the start of the presentation in lesson "Introducing Students to Accruals." (See page 487.)

"You will recall that several days ago, when we first learned about an accrued expense, we used as an example a business that had a payroll expense that totaled $100 PER DAY."

Teacher writes "$100 per day" on board or projects it on a screen.

"You will also recall that its employees worked a five-day week and were paid each Friday."

"Remembering what you have learned about the importance of and the need for recording accruals, what is the adjusting entry that should be made on December 31?"

Teacher records the correct answer in T accounts as follows:

SALARY EXPENSE		SALARIES PAYABLE	
12/31/69 300			12/31/69 300

Pointing to the salary expense account, teacher asks, *"What kind of an account is this?"* (Expense)

"What final changes will be made to this expense account before the start of the new fiscal period?"

(It will be closed and ruled.)

Teacher does this on the board or projects it on a screen with the overhead projector.

Pointing to the salaries payable account, teacher asks, *"How will this account appear in the ledger at the start of the new fiscal period?"*

(It will remain the same—stay open.)

"Now, on January 2 the weekly payroll of $500 is paid. For the previous 51 weeks, when this same

transaction was recorded each Friday, what was the usual—the normal entry?"

(Salary Expense was debited and Cash was credited for $500.)

"How should this same $500 payroll transaction be recorded this time on January 2?"

(Debit Salary Expense for $200, debit Salaries Payable for $300, and credit Cash for $500.)

"Why is a different entry made this time?"

(Because $300 of this $500 expense had already been charged to Salary Expense for the previous fiscal period and only $200 of this expense is for the new fiscal period.)

Teacher points out that this is one correct way of handling the transaction and completes the illustration as follows:

SALARY EXPENSE		SALARIES PAYABLE	
12/31/69 300	12/31/69 300	1/2/70 300	12/31/69 300
1/2/70 200			

CASH
1/2/70 500

"A bookkeeper is as human as the next person. If for 51 consecutive weeks you had each time debited Salary Expense for the total of the payroll, how many of you think that there is a chance that you might do the same on the 52nd time?"

"How many would trust your memories to never forget this different entry?"

(Perhaps a few might indicate that they would never forget, but the students have been led to see that the chance of a mistake being made here could be quite likely. The need for reversing entries is now developed.)

5. Presentation: *"Today I am going to show you a technique that many bookkeepers use to help them eliminate such possible errors. This 'trick of the trade' enables the book-keeper to record the payment of the payroll on the first Friday of the new year* (teacher points to January 2 on calendar) *in exactly the same way he recorded all of the other payroll payments throughout the previous year."*

Teacher draws a double line beneath the three T accounts that were developed in the review and opens up three new T accounts as follows for illustrating and comparing this new procedure with the old.

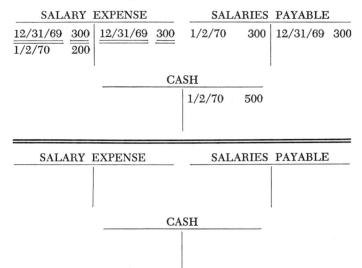

Through questioning and using two new accounts below the double line, the teacher again reviews and records

    (a) the December 31 adjusting entry for accrued salaries.

    (b) the December 31 entry closing Salary Expense.

The students are shown by comparison that there is no change, no new technique, in the handling of Salary Expense and Salaries Payable through the end of the fiscal period.

At this time—after the books have been closed for the 1969 fiscal period—the comparative accounts would be as follows:

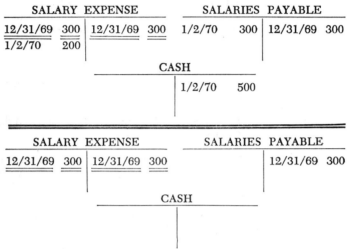

SALARY EXPENSE			SALARIES PAYABLE	
12/31/69 300	12/31/69 300	1/2/70 300	12/31/69 300

	CASH	
	1/2/70 500

SALARY EXPENSE		SALARIES PAYABLE
12/31/69 300	12/31/69 300	12/31/69 300

CASH

Teacher then explains and demonstrates a reversing entry—the entry made on the first day of the new fiscal period that reverses the December 31 adjusting entry that recorded the accrual.

The accounts would then appear as follows:

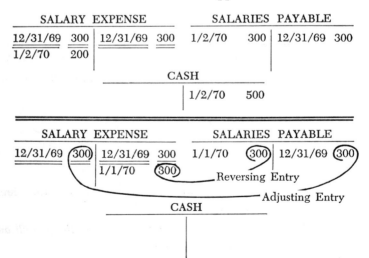

SALARY EXPENSE			SALARIES PAYABLE	
12/31/69 300	12/31/69 300	1/2/70 300	12/31/69 300
1/2/70 200			

CASH

1/2/70 500

SALARY EXPENSE			SALARIES PAYABLE	
12/31/69 (300)	12/31/69 300	1/1/70 (300)	12/31/69 (300)
	1/1/70 (300)		

Reversing Entry

Adjusting Entry

CASH

Teacher then reminds the class that the purpose of this new technique (reversing entry) is to eliminate the need for the bookkeeper remembering to charge only $200 of salary expense to the new fiscal period —that this "trick of the trade" enables the bookkeeper to make a normal entry on January 2—exactly the same kind of entry for paying the payroll on January 2 as for any other Friday in the year.

Teacher calls for a normal entry to record this $500 payment on January 2, 1970.

(Debit Salary Expense for $500 and credit Cash for $500.)

Teacher records the correct answer, thus completing the demonstration and the comparative illustration showing the two ways, as follow, for handling accruals:

(a) without using a reversing entry, and
(b) by using a reversing entry.

SALARY EXPENSE		SALARIES PAYABLE	
12/31/69 300	12/31/69 300	1/2/70 300	12/31/69 300
1/2/70 200			

CASH
1/2/70 500

SALARY EXPENSE		SALARIES PAYABLE	
12/31/69 300	12/31/69 300	1/1/70 300	12/31/69 300
1/2/70 500	1/1/70 300		

CASH
1/2/70 500

Pointing to the accounts above the double line, teacher asks,

"What was the total amount of the payroll on January 2, 1970?" ($500)

"How much of this $500 expense was charged to the year 1969?" ($300)

"How much of this $500 expense was charged to the year 1970?" ($200)

Teacher points out that by this method the bookkeeper had to remember to make somewhat of an "abnormal" entry on January 2—had to remember to debit Salaries Payable for $300 of this $500—had to remember NOT to debit Salary Expense for the entire $500.

Pointing to the accounts below the double line, teacher "forces" students to analyze and compare the two methods by asking the same questions as above.

"What was the total amount of the payroll on January 2, 1970?" ($500)

"How much of this $500 expense was charged to the year 1969?" ($300)

"How much of this $500 expense was charged to the year 1970?" ($200)

Teacher takes time here to again point out how the reversing entry on January 1 enabled the bookkeeper to make a normal entry on January 2, debiting Salary Expense and crediting Cash for $500—and how this resulted in only $200 being the net amount debited to Salary Expense for this first week in the new year.

Note: At the close of this simple introduction to reversing entries, the teacher might do well to indicate that if a business were limited in its accruals to a single item such as salaries payable, an alert bookkeeper might be able to remember to record the payment of a single accrual properly and thus not make use of a reversing entry. It would then also seem well to stress that it is common for businesses to have several accruals and that in such instances, as the students will see in subsequent assignments, the use of reversing entries is of real value to the bookkeeper.

6. Application: *"Now let us see if you are able to make proper use of a reversing entry."*

Teacher assigns for classroom work a similar problem to that illustrated in the above presentation calling for the recording of (1) accrued salary expense,

(2) closing entry, (3) reversing entry, and (4) payment of the payroll.

7. **Summary:**   Teacher has class turn to end-of-chapter material in their textbooks on page ... and calls on various students to answer appropriate questions and cases that relate to and help to reinforce the lesson just taught.

8. **Homework:**   Students to complete one or more end-of-chapter application problems in the textbook that will give them further application of the learnings taught in today's lesson.

9. **Teacher's Remarks:**

Students Must Understand Accruals to Understand Reversing Entries

Many students need more than a brief exposure to reversing entries in order to learn them. Just as there were students who needed repetitive practice with adjusting entries before they mastered them, so there are students who must be drilled on reversing entries before they acquire a clear understanding of them.

During the learning phase, some students are confused or are uncertain as to which of the adjusting entries should be reversed. When this is true, their basic trouble is their inability to identify the accruals—(1) the expenses that have been incurred during that fiscal period, but will not be paid that period, and (2) income that was earned in that period but will not be collected until the next. As a result, the teacher needs to center his teaching and help on assisting students to identify adjusting entries involving accruals.

One helpful way to assist students in identifying accruals is to have them participate in written and oral drills whereby they are asked to analyze the "data for adjustments" in numerous end-of-chapter problems. For example, work sheet problems involving adjustments of accruals are not only found at the end of the chapter on accruals, but also at the end of other subsequent chapters as well as in Supplementary Exercises at the end of the text. The teacher could direct the students to turn to certain such problems in their textbooks and require them to identify the data involving (1) accruals and (2) reversing entries.

Another help for students who have difficulty identifying the adjusting entries to be reversed is to point out that if the adjustments had not been made for the accrued expenses and accrued income, there would be *no accrued liabilities* and *no accrued assets on the balanced sheet.* Therefore, *the adjustments which opened up balance sheet accounts should all be reversed.*

STUDY QUESTIONS

1. Why should the teaching of accrued items be the last type of adjustments taught?

2. What previously learned knowledge can the teacher use when teaching the adjusting of accrued items?

3. What is one of the best examples to use when introducing a class to the need for adjusting accrued expenses?

4. Why should the students know both the WHY and the HOW of adjusting accrued income and expenses?

5. How does the lesson plan on adjusting entries make use of the comparison method of teaching?

6. Why is a summary recommended as the final step in a formal lesson plan?

7. What different ways are suggested for introducing students to the adjusting of accrued items?

8. What three comparison learnings should comprise a teacher's introductory lesson on the adjusting of accrued items?

9. Why is it suggested that the teaching of reversing entries might well be delayed until the student gets into a second-year course in bookkeeping-accounting?

10. How can the comparison technique be used when teaching reversing entries?

11. Can you find any evidence of this comparison method in the lesson plan presented on reversing entries?

12. What is the major problem students encounter when reversing entries are introduced?

13. What are some ways for overcoming the major problem students have when reversing entries are introduced?

DISCUSSION QUESTIONS

1. Which of the three ways suggested in this chapter for *introducing* students to accruals do you prefer? Why?

2. What do you like best about the lesson plan, "Introducing Students to Accruals," on pages 486-493? What do you like least about it?

3. Do you believe that all first-year B-A students should be taught how to adjust accrued items? Explain.

4. What changes would you make in the lesson plan, "Introducing Students to Reversing Entries," on pages 495-502, so that it would fit your own beliefs and techniques for teaching this topic?

5. Do you believe that all first-year students should be required to learn reversing entries? Explain.

SELECTED REFERENCES

Aichele, John M. "Do You Use the Calendar to Teach Accruals in Your Bookkeeping Class?" *UBEA Forum.* IX (December, 1954), 13-14.

Freeman, M. Herbert. "How to Teach Deferred and Accrued Items," *Business Education World.* XLI (December, 1961), 25-27.

Packenham, Edward S. "Toward the Elimination of Reversing Entries— A Teaching Note," *The Journal of Business Education.* XLIII (December, 1967), 118-119.

Rainey, Bill G. "Reversing Entries Made Easy," *American Business Education.* XV (October, 1958), 62-63.

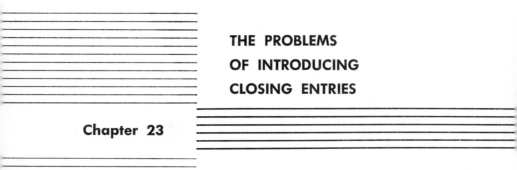

THE PROBLEMS
OF INTRODUCING
CLOSING ENTRIES

Chapter 23

The mechanics of closing entries are simple, but the understandings surrounding them are complex. It is the complexity of the understandings that make this a difficult teaching area.

Why Are Closing Entries Made?

The proprietorship account should show the *net* increase or decrease (net income or loss) that a business experiences during a fiscal period. So that the proprietorship account is not cluttered with the numerous fluctuations of the period, certain accounts are established to record transactions that decrease (expense accounts) and increase (income accounts) proprietorship. These income and expense accounts are called temporary proprietorship accounts because they temporarily hold information until it is summarized and transferred to the proprietorship account. Closing entries are the means of transferring the balances out of these temporary accounts and recording the *net* amount of profit or loss in the proprietorship account. Furthermore these income and expense accounts, or temporary accounts, are closed and ruled at the end of each fiscal period so that income or expense for one fiscal period is not included or confused with profit or loss of a previous or subsequent fiscal period. In this way a fresh start and a separate record of income and expense is kept for each subsequent period.

Businessmen want to know periodically how their businesses are prospering. The bookkeeper cannot supply such information readily and accurately *for each accounting period* unless he knows what the business started with at the beginning of the period and what the income and expenses were *for that period.* Thus the book-keeper must follow a technique at the end of each fiscal period that gives him an accurate count of present conditions and at the same time gets his records off to a clean, fresh start for the subsequent fiscal period.

It is the closing entries (after any necessary adjustments) and ruling and balancing, that enable the bookkeeper to bring his books into position for a fresh start for the next fiscal period.

In summary then, closing entries are needed

1. to transfer the net income or the loss for a period into the proprietorship account so that the proprietorship equity is accurately reported and shown each fiscal period.

2. to assist in the preparation of the income statement.

3. to close all open accounts containing elements of income and expense so that all such accounts are balanced, closed, and "emptied" for the period for a fresh start in the subsequent accounting period.

The Groundwork for Understanding Closing Entries Is Introduced Weeks Before Closing Entries Are Taught

The following is taken from the first paragraph of Chapter 16, "Introducing Students to Expense and Income Accounts," page 413.

". . . there is nothing difficult about teaching him (the student) the use of expense and income accounts. . . . However, a 'surface' understanding of the use of expense and income accounts may lead to later trouble with closing entries."

These introductory sentences to Chapter 16 give the major reason why that very brief chapter was included in this methods text-book—NOT because there is anything difficult about teaching the use of income and expense accounts, but because of the relationship of these accounts to the subsequent understanding of closing entries.

When students are first introduced to expense and to income transactions they are told that every time a business incurs an expense its proprietorship is decreased. Similarly, they are told that every time a business earns income its proprietorship is increased. Immediately thereafter, and for logical reasons, students are taught to debit expense accounts (instead of the proprietorship account) for transactions that decrease proprietorship and to credit income accounts (instead of the proprietorship account) for transactions that increase proprietorship. Then for the next month or so they concentrate on journalizing transactions, posting transactions, taking trial balances, and preparing work sheets.

The time between when students are first introduced to income and expense accounts and to closing entries is long. As a result, and unless the teaching during this time contains periodic reminders that expense and income accounts are temporary proprietorship accounts, this concept and relationship will have to be reviewed and strongly refreshed in the minds of the students before they can be expected to grasp the reason for closing entries.

The teaching of closing entries was also touched upon briefly in Chapter 17, Problems of Teaching the Work Sheet. The purpose of this chapter is to define closing entries, analyze in detail the reasons for and the techniques of closing entries and to offer other helpful suggestions for planning to teach this phase of bookkeeping that has proven a teaching block for some teachers.

What Are Closing Entries?

When an income or an expense or a mixed account contains postings of equal debit and credit amounts, it is in balance and said to be a *closed* account. One of the major and periodic steps in the bookkeeping cycle is, at the end of a fiscal period, to balance or close all accounts that contain elements of income or expense for that period. *Closing entries*, therefore, are periodic entries that have the effect of balancing all accounts containing elements of expense or income by transferring their open balances to a proprietorship account. These entries are made at the end of each fiscal period and are for the major purpose of bringing the ledger into agreement with the financial statements and to provide accounts that are suitable for the recording of transactions for the next fiscal period. This brief description or definition is the one most commonly associated with the term *closing entries*.

The term *closing entry,* however, is not entirely limited to the above description, but is also used in other situations by on-the-job bookkeepers and accountants. For example, a bookkeeper who receives payment in full of an account receivable can rightly refer to that entry, which has the effect of balancing this customer's account, as a closing entry—one which, at least temporarily, closes and balances this customer's account. Similarly, a depositor who withdraws all funds from his bank account has caused his account with the bank to be balanced and closed. Another type of closing entry that is not a periodic closing entry as described above, would be one in which a business disposes *completely* of a certain asset, such as all of its delivery equipment. The entry recording this complete disposal can rightly be termed a closing entry since the delivery equipment account has been balanced and closed as a result of the transaction.

One might attempt to infer from these illustrations that any entry which results in balancing an account can be called a closing one. Such a generalization could be supported with some degree of logic. It could, however, also lead to confusion in some instances. For example, each reversing entry causes a real account to be balanced. Therefore, if this broad concept were followed—that any entry which results in the balancing of an account is a closing entry—then a reversing entry would also be a closing entry. Any such attempt at a broad generalization to be all-inclusive of closing entries would seem to lead to confusion rather than simplification.

These other than end-of-period closing entries are mentioned here so as to give a complete answer to "What is a closing entry?" They are for the bookkeeping teacher's background and reference. The degree to which bookkeeping teachers wish to or are able to present clearly and without confusion this broader understanding, should be on the basis of individual teacher decision. It would seem wise for bookkeeping teachers to use the term *closing entries* with its limited meaning, and to alert only students with a vocational bookkeeping objective to the other on-the-job uses of the term.

All subsequent treatment of closing entries in this chapter will be devoted to and limited to those that are periodic, end-of-fiscal-period closing entries.

How Closing Entries Are Made—
Major Teaching Problems

The procedure for closing entries has changed since the turn of the century. The trend, both in business and in teaching, has been toward simplicity and away from the detailed, time-consuming entries of 25 and 50 years ago. For example, earlier in the century a *separate* general journal entry, with a written explanation for each entry, was required to close *each* income account, *each* cost account, and *each* expense account. Furthermore, it was the practice some decades ago to make separate entries closing Purchases Returns and Allowances and Transportation on Purchases into Purchases before making the subsequent separate entry closing the purchases account. Similarly, the account Sales Returns and Allowances was closed separately into Sales before the sales account was closed by another separate entry into the summary account.

The opposite extreme of this detailed method of closing each account by a separate entry is found in some college accounting textbooks today. This shows *all* income, cost, expense, and related accounts being closed into the summary account in a single compound closing entry.

While this latter practice may be fine for experienced bookkeepers and practicing accountants, it is certainly not a procedure that a teacher would want to use for introducing the average high school student to closing entries. Furthermore, it is believed that most teachers do not find the other extreme method of requiring a separate entry for *each* nominal account necessary. The most common practice, therefore, for introducing students to closing entries today lies between these two extremes. This is to teach them to make a separate closing entry for (1) all income accounts, and (2) for all expense accounts.

Later, when cost accounts such as Purchases, when minus-cost accounts such as Purchases Discount and Purchases Returns and Allowances, and when minus-income accounts such as Sales Returns and Allowances are introduced, it is a relative simple matter to continue to teach the closing of all such accounts with only two closing entries. These would be (1) a separate closing entry for all income accounts and other accounts with balances in the Income

Statement Credit column of the work sheet, and (2) a separate closing entry for all expenses, cost, and other accounts with balances in the Income Statement Debit column of the work sheet.

How Can Income and Expense Summary Be Introduced?

The next decision that a teacher faces is how to introduce the new income and expense summary account used for closing and for summarizing the balances in the nominal accounts into a single net income (or loss) amount. The problem here is to help the students see the need and the use of such a temporary "clearing" account.

Since students have been taught and reminded that income and expense accounts are temporary accounts that are subdivisions of the proprietorship, they may grasp more quickly the purpose and concept of closing entries if they are first shown the closing of the accounts directly into the proprietorship account. This enables them to see how the proprietorship account becomes cluttered with many postings and how such a procedure *does not summarize* in one amount the net income or the net loss for the period.

Textbooks would be criticized for illustrating this non-business practice of closing income and expense accounts directly into the proprietorship account. Teachers, however, as long as they do not waste time teaching things that must be unlearned, can defend this as merely an intermediary phase which omits temporarily a step in closing the books and leads to a demonstrated need for a summary account and thus a quicker learning of *all* of the steps.

What Place Does The Drawing Account Play When Introducing Students to Closing Entries?

The final decision that a teacher, as well as a bookkeeper, has to face about the *HOW* of closing entries is whether, after closing all income and expense accounts into Income and Expense Summary, (1) to close the net income or net loss now in Income and Expense Summary directly into the proprietor's capital account, or (2) to close the income and expense summary account into the drawing account and then close the resulting balance in the drawing account into the proprietor's capital account.

Both methods are correct. Both are currently popular. But the basic *teaching* problem here really centers more on when to introduce students to the drawing account than it does on whether to close Income and Expense Summary into Drawing or into Capital. By delaying the teaching of the drawing account until the second time through the cycle, the students have the decided advantage of having to learn only one new account instead of two when first being introduced to closing entries. Furthermore, when the drawing account is delayed for a later presentation in the course, students first learn a series of only three closing entries instead of four.

The trend at present seems to be to close Income and Expense Summary directly into the proprietor's capital account. If the business has a drawing account, it too is then closed directly into the capital account. Thus the capital account would show three important amounts: (1) the amount of the proprietorship at the beginning of the period, (2) the net income (or net loss) for the period, and (3) the total withdrawals by the proprietor. If, however, Income and Expense Summary is closed to Drawing and then the balance in the drawing account is closed to Capital, then the information in the proprietorship account would be limited to showing only two amounts: (1) the amount of proprietorship at the beginning of the period, and (2) the net increase or decrease to proprietorship during that period—this latter without knowledge of whether the change was the result of profit, of loss, or of the activity in the drawing account.

Visualizing the Teaching of Closing Entries

Teachers can speed progress and fix the learning of closing entries if they mark the pathway of understanding with symbols that point the way and with pictures that tell the story.

Essential to students' understanding of closing entries is the knowledge that income and expense accounts are *temporary proprietorship accounts*. Related to this is an understanding as to *why* income and expense transactions are itemized in these different accounts instead of in one proprietorship account,

Assume that the following diagram illustrating the relationship of income and expense accounts to the proprietorship account was first shown to students when income and expense accounts were introduced.

M. A. BURNET, CAPITAL

	19—	
	Oct. 1, Balance	2,751.50

AUTOMOBILE EXPENSE		FEES INCOME	
10/8	4.50	10/1	60.00
10/15	14.00	10/5	290.00
10/22	9.00	10/6	150.00
10/29	1ၑ.00	10/7	400.00
		10/9	320.00
MISCELLANEOUS EXPENSE		10/16	215.00
10/5	7.00	10/19	45.00
10/14	17.20	10/21	150.00
10/26	8.50	10/25	400.00
10/29	8.50	10/29	55.00
RENT EXPENSE			
10/1	120.00		

Figure 23—1.

A review, with this diagram on the board or overhead, is a most effective way (1) to remind students of the reasons for temporary accounts, and (2) to teach that the proprietorship account needs to be brought up to date at the end of each fiscal period. Having just previously used the amounts in the accounts for preparing an income statement, and with this picture before them, the students are helped to see that temporary accounts have served their purpose for one period and that the amounts recorded in them during the period should now be "emptied" into the one permanent proprietorship account.

After the students see the need for bringing the proprietorship account up to date, for "emptying" the balances in the income and expense accounts into the proprietorship account, and after they understand the advantage of showing the net income (or loss) in one amount in the proprietorship account, a picture that charts the overall process is helpful. A chart similar to the following is found in most high school textbooks.

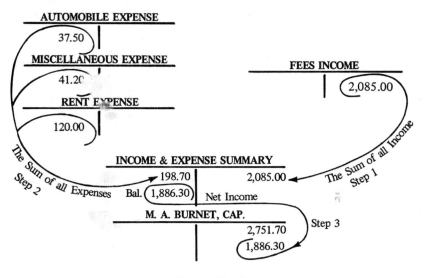

Figure 23—2.

The use of such a diagram at this early stage of learning closing entries is to provide a quick over-view of the process. It can give the brighter students a quick insight of the procedure. For others, perhaps its greatest value is to supply some initial feeling of the use of and the place of the new "clearing" account, Income and Expense Summary, in the process.

There are two reasons, however, why it would perhaps be best for the teacher not to dwell long on such a chart before the students have been led through at least one series of closing entries. First, while it has value for supplying a "feeling" of the process, as a *basic* teaching device it would perhaps be too abstract for some students. Second, it will have greater value for most students as a summary picture after they have performed closing entries under the guidance of the teacher.

The next important picture involved in the learning of closing entries shows the closing entries being made from the summary source for making such entries—the Income Statement columns of the work sheet. If charts or overlays similar to those described in Chapter 17, Problems of Teaching the Work Sheet, are used for introducing students to their first simple work sheet, the journalizing of the actual closing entries would be developed on the board or overhead projector as shown in Figure 23-3.

After the student *sees* the closing journal entries recorded from the information in the Income Statement columns of the work sheet, he next needs to *see* the effect of these entries on the accounts. It is, therefore, strongly recommended that the teacher continue to demonstrate on the board or overhead projector and let the students *see* the posting and *see* the few accounts involved being closed and *see* the "emptied" effect of each after being ruled.

The reader might point out that all textbooks show the above illustrations in some form or other and ask, "Why should the teacher perform this work which is already shown in the textbook?" One response could be, "Then why have a teacher?" But the important answer is that when this work is *developed* in front of the students, they see the whole process: (1) the need for closing, (2) the source of the entries, (3) the making of the entries, (4) the posting of the entries and thus (5) the closing of the accounts, and (6) the final ruling of the accounts to make them ready for use in the next period. Textbooks can tell what to do. Textbooks can show what should be done and what has been done. Teachers, however, can actually show the doing. Students are helped to learn by seeing the doing.

Summary of the Procedural Steps in the Overall Plan for Teaching Closing Entries

The major objectives in the plans for introducing students to closing entries are as follows:

(1) Review the reasons for the expense and income accounts—stressing they are temporary proprietorship accounts.

(2) Explain the need for bringing the proprietorship account up to date periodically.

(3) Teach the need for getting the ledger ready for the next fiscal period.

(4) Teach what is meant by a "closed" account by demonstrating when an account is closed and how it is closed by a journal entry.

CHART I

	Account Titles	Acct. No.	Income Statement Dr.	Cr.
1	Cash	11		
2	Automobile	12		
3	Office Furniture	13		
4	Professional Library	14		
5	Dennis Garage	21		
6	Meade-Lane	22		
7	M. A. Burnet, Capital	31		
8	Fees Income	41		2,085.00
9	Automobile Expense	51	37.50	
10	Miscellaneous Expense	52	41.20	
11	Rent Expense	53	120.00	
12			198.70	2,085.00
13	Net Income		1,886.30	
14			2,085.00	2,085.00

CHART III [1]

General Journal

Page - -

Date	Account Titles	Post. Ref.	Dr.	Cr.
	Closing Entries			
19—				
Oct. 31	Fee Income		2,085.00	
	Income and Expense Summary			2,085.00
31	Income and Expense Summary		198.70	
	Automobile Expense			37.50
	Miscellaneous Expense			41.20
	Rent Expense			120.00
31	Income and Expense Summary		1,886.30	
	M. A. Burnet, Capital			1,886.30

Figure 23—3.

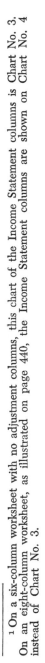

[1] On a six-column worksheet with no adjustment columns, this chart of the Income Statement columns is Chart No. 3. On an eight-column worksheet, as illustrated on page 440, the Income Statement columns are shown on Chart No. 4 instead of Chart No. 3.

(5) Lead students to see and suggest how income and expense accounts could be closed directly to the proprietorship account.

(6) Present the use of the new account, Income and Expense Summary. Show how this account is used as a "clearing account"—how it summarizes the net income or net loss and thus allows only one net amount to be transferred to capital rather than all of the individual balances in the income and expense accounts.

(7) Demonstrate the first step in the closing procedure—closing the income account into Income and Expense Summary.

(8) Illustrate the second step in the closing procedure—closing the expense accounts into Income and Expense Summary.

(9) Demonstrate the third step in the closing procedure—closing Income and Expense Summary into the proprietorship account.

In demonstrating each of these steps

(a) show that the information for the closing entry is taken from the work sheet, and

(b) show the closing entry being made in the general journal, and

(c) show the effect of posting the closing entries to accounts outlined on the board.

(10) Demonstrate how each and all of the accounts involved in the closing procedure will appear (a) after closing, and (b) after ruling.

STUDY QUESTIONS

1. Give three reasons why closing entries are needed at the end of each fiscal period?

2. Why is it necessary for a student to have a thorough understanding of income and expense accounts before introducing him to closing entries?

3. Why is there a need for giving students frequent reminders that income and expense accounts are only temporary proprietorship accounts?

4. What are closing entries?

5. Is the meaning of the term "closing entry" limited to those entries made at the end of the fiscal period balancing all income and expense accounts?

6. How has the teaching of closing entries changed in the past few decades?

7. What is presently the most common method used to introduce high school students to closing entries?

8. What two different methods are used for closing the Income and Expense accounts?

9. What kind of diagrams on the chalkboard or the overhead projector are suggested as helpful when introducing closing entries?

10. What caution is given about the overemphasis of diagrams and charts of closing entries before the student has practice recording closing entries?

11. Why is it important for the instructor, himself, to demonstrate the steps of closing entries even though these same steps are well illustrated in the textbook being used?

12. List briefly the steps in an overall plan for teaching closing entries.

DISCUSSION QUESTIONS

1. Is it easier to teach students *how* to close accounts or to teach them *why* accounts are closed? How should your answer to this question affect your planning for teaching closing entries?

2. What other ways than that suggested in this chapter can you think of for introducing the income and expense summary account to students?

3. Many, perhaps most, bookkeepers and accountants close all income and expense accounts with a single closing entry. What is your reaction about using this procedure when teaching high school students how to record closing entries?

4. Do you believe that high school students should be taught to close the income and expense summary account into the capital account or into the drawing account? Why?

5. After students learn to record and post closing entries, they are then taught how to rule and balance accounts. How do you respond to the claim that as a result of modern automatic data processing procedures, and as a result of the increasing popularity of ledger accounts with balance-column ruling, this outmoded ritual of ruling and balancing should no longer be taught?

SELECTED REFERENCES

Lager, Roger H. "How I Teach Closing Entries in Bookkeeping," *Business Education World*. XLVI (January, 1966), 200-203.

Schroeder, Lowell J. "The Teacher's Rule in Student Understanding of the Closing Entries," *Business Education Forum*. XII (April, 1958), 23-24.

Automated data processing is one of the latest in a series of developments that over the centuries have eased the task of handling information. Early man ticked off data on his fingers—the first digital computer. The ancient Greeks and Romans and the Chinese used the abacus to help them process data—another digital computer. Obviously, one's fingers are of little computational assistance in the information-demanding society of today; similarly, both the abacus and the electric adding machine are of limited use in handling the massive data processed by such agencies as the Social Security Administration and the Internal Revenue Service. Inasmuch as sophisticated, high-speed machines are required in order to handle sizeable tasks, automated data processing equipment has been developed.

The machines that have been developed, however, are not the last of the inventions that will ease the burden of laborious jobs. The amount of data in this world is so overwhelming that even newer, more sophisticated, and as yet unthought of data processing procedures must certainly come along and add to or displace today's computational machine wonders. One of the modern marvels being constructed has speeds of over one billion computations per second, but even it might be an outmoded machine shortly.[1]

Automated Data Processing in Everyday Life

Automated data processing has affected the life of everyone. The monthly punched-card bills from local utility companies, motor

---

[1] "Computers, Giant Brain," *The 1967 World Book Year Book* (Chicago: Field Enterprises Education Corporation, 1967) p. 279.

vehicle registrations, drivers' licenses, bank accounts, the MICR numbers on all checks, turnpike tollcards, credit cards, and the billing and mailing operations of record and book clubs are just some examples of how all individuals have come into contact in one way or another with automated data processing.

In a variety of ways, automation affects the jobs held by both common and professional workers. Factory procedures are automated as well as medical diagnoses. Automated data processing elements surround office workers and salespeople. Workers in small offices handle incoming purchase orders, checks, statements, credit memoranda, and bills, which are the output of automated data processing machines. Some workers in large offices may operate automated data processing equipment, others will prepare the data that is to be fed into such equipment, and still others handle the output.

In stores, salespeople use modern cash registers to record transactions on punched paper tape. This tape is then used in automated equipment for summarizing the day's operations. Sales tags are key punched. Handling customers' credit cards can be the first link in a subsequent chain of automated data processing procedures.

If a prospective office worker is to fit into today's business world, the obvious conclusion is that he must be adequately prepared to accept and to understand those automated data processing fundamentals that he will face both in the management of his personal business affairs and on his job.

Automated Data Processing in the High School Curriculum

Recognizing that automated data processing has become a part of everyday personal life and of vocational business life, one must conclude that formal instruction in this vital subject matter area must be a part of the high school curriculum. Since automated data processing enters into one's everyday life, every student, not just business students, should acquire a basic understanding and appreciation of the place and importance of it in today's society. The teaching of automated data processing on the appreciation level can be a part of the one or more required general education courses in the areas of social studies, general science, and general mathematics. As more and more teachers of general education subjects include appreciation-level understandings in their courses, business teachers will find it less and less necessary to start at this level when introducing their students to automated data processing.

Automated data processing will then appear in the *business curriculum* in two ways: (1) by relating it to the teaching of existing vocational subject matter; (2) by offering new job-training courses in automated data processing.

Developing Relationships in Existing Vocational Subject Matter

All potential office workers upon graduation from high school should have as a minimum accomplishment: (1) an appreciation of the automated processing of data and its relationship to their field of specialization; (2) a visual familiarity with the wide variety of automated data processing machines; and (3) a speaking acquaintance with the basic vocabulary of automated data processing.

Since bookkeeping and accounting courses are basically a study of the processing of data, the inclusion of automated data processing principles in such courses is a logical expectation. Another reasonable presumption is that B-A students, in contrast to other business students, would develop a higher degree of understanding and appreciation of the automated data processing field.

The relationship of automated data processing to other vocational business courses such as typewriting, general clerical, secretarial practice, office practice, and the distributive education field should be explored and included wherever possible in these courses.

Developing New Job-Training Courses in Automated Data Processing

There are many job opportunities in the data processing field. They range in difficulty from the routine, repetitive skill operations of the card-punch operator to the planning of a program for space flight. The former requires no more than a high school education with a relatively small amount of special training beyond that of learning to operate a typewriter and card-punch machine. However, the scientist or engineer programming a space flight may require several college degrees with highly sophisticated training in mathematics, and electronic computer programming.

Following is a list of job titles up to the rank of Junior Programmer for automated data processing positions taken from the *Dictionary of Occupational Titles* [2] along with abbreviated descriptions of their duties. This is a current list of beginning level jobs for which the high school may eventually provide specific training. However, this list also suggests that none of these jobs can justifiably be included as job-training objectives in a high school B-A course.

Title (Code Number)	Duties
Console Operator (213.382) (Digital-Computer Operator)	"Monitors and controls computer, loads programs, selects and aligns forms, loads tapes and/or disks, maintains control over daily operation of computer."
Card-Punch Operator (Key-Punch Operator) (213.582)	"Operates alphabetic and numeric key-punch machine, similar in operation to electric typewriter, to transcribe data from source material onto punch cards and prepunched data. . . ."
Data Typist (213.588)	"Converts alphabetic, numeric, and symbolic data into coded form on punch cards or tapes: Loads decks of punch cards or reels of magnetic or paper tape into machine. Moves switches to set up machine and auxiliary equipment to produce desired cards or tapes. . . ."
Tabulating-Machine Operator (213.782)	"Operates machine that processes data from tabulating cards into printed records: Wires and installs tabulating-machine plugboard (control panel), or inserts prewired control panel, using wrenches or screwdriver. . . . May tend machines that perform individual functions, such as sorting, interpreting, reproducing, and collating."

[2] U. S. Department of Labor, Bureau of Employment Security, *Dictionary of Occupational Titles,* Vol. I and II, 3d ed. (Washington, U. S. Government Printing Office, 1965).

Control Clerk (219.388)	"Keeps records for keypunch and tabulating department: Keeps records of all incoming and outgoing material processed in keypunch and tabulating departments. Assigns production codes and schedules due dates. . . ."
Junior Programmer (219.388) (Detail Programmer)	"Selects symbols from coding system peculiar to make or model of digital computer and applies them to successive steps of completed program for conversion to machine processable instructions. . . ." Documents less complex programs, writes instructions, tests programs, and debugs to a limited extent.
Coding Clerk (I, 219.388) (II, 219.688)	"Converts routine items of information obtained from records and reports into codes for processing by data typing or key punch units, using predetermined coding systems: Manually records alphabetic, alphanumeric, or numeric codes in prescribed sequence on work sheet or margin of source document for transfer to punch cards of machine input tape. . . ."
Tape Librarian (223.387)	"Classifies, catalogs, and maintains library of reels of magnetic or punched paper tape or decks of magnetic or punch cards used for electronic data-processing purposes. . . ."

The Time for Relating Automated Data Processing to Bookkeeping-Accounting Students

The best time for the teacher to relate automated data processing to bookkeeping-accounting is after the student has learned enough of the principles and procedures of manual bookkeeping to provide a background for seeing and appreciating the differences as well as the similarities. This could be anytime after the student has completed his first or second movement through the cycle—preferably after he has worked out a practice set satisfactorily. By that time, and any time thereafter, the student has had the experience of seeing all of the segments of the bookkeeping cycle being knit together; he has experienced the detail of journalizing, posting, preparing the work sheet and financial statements, closing the ledger, and preparing schedules of accounts receivable and accounts payable. With this background, it would seem that the student would have a basis for comparison of manual bookkeeping and automated data processing. He can better see and better understand differences in procedures for processing the same or similar data and see the similarities and sameness in results.

The foregoing is not to imply that teaching *about* automated data processing could not be integrated with the progressive presentation of the B-A course. When automated equipment, motion pictures, film strips, and other teaching materials that are tailored to this parallel approach become readily available, learnings about automated data processing might well be coordinated with the early teaching of manual bookkeeping principles and procedures. However, until such equipment is readily available to the teacher, and until some valid studies support the feasibility of such an approach, it seems logical to recommend a beginning background of manual bookkeeping and accounting before attempting to relate to other procedures. This recommendation is in accord with the common practice followed in most collegiate schools of business. Accounting and business administration majors generally complete one or more introductory accounting courses before being scheduled into an automated data processing course. When students understand that their introductory B-A course can be their entree to an automated data processing course, their attitude toward the importance of traditional bookkeeping and accounting may be improved.

An Approach for Relating Automated Data Processing to Manual Bookkeeping

Throughout the entire bookkeeping course the wise teacher presents the B-A principles and the procedural details along with an understanding that the details may vary from office to office and from year to year. However, the principles remain steady, and, once mastered, become the secure place from which all changes in detail may be viewed with equanimity.

The problem of teaching B-A students the relationship between automated data processing and manual bookkeeping is really only a segment of the larger problem of familiarizing the student with other common ways, the use of other tools than a pen, for processing business transactions—business data. The overall objective of a unit of instruction which includes teaching about automated data processing can be stated as follows: "To familiarize B-A students with faster ways of processing business data in volume."

The initial approach to this objective could be to remind students that business is always looking for ways to save money, to increase its income, to cut its expenses. Just as the use of a pen continues to be the best way for students in the classroom to learn to apply the principles of bookkeeping and accounting, so many small businesses find the use of the pen to be the most economical way for them to keep their records. Students need to understand why some businesses save money by using a computerized system for handling business data while other businesses do not have enough gross income to pay for the rent of such equipment. Students should also be helped to see that in between these two extremes are businesses which use other tools for processing data which for them are more economical than either the pen or the computer. Students should learn in the B-A class, not after they start working in offices, the kind of common tools other than a pen that are used for recording and processing business data.

Further Considerations for Teaching ABOUT Automated Data Processing

If the teacher agrees that (1) specific job training for automated data processing positions does not fall within the scope of his B-A course, but that (2) teaching the relationship of manual bookkeeping to automated data processing does fall within the scope of his B-A course, it would appear that the teacher has made his first big step toward the solution of this problem. But he then has other problems to solve—other decisions to make.

1. How deep shall he attempt to take his students in an understanding of this relationship?
2. How much time can and should he take from his first-year B-A course to teach this relationship?

Answers to the above questions will not and should not be the same for all B-A teachers.

Starting on page 526 is an outline of a ten-day teaching unit which has the objective of familiarizing B-A students with faster ways of processing business data. It is offered as a starting point for helping B-A teachers make their individual approaches and reach their individual solutions to this problem. New and beginning teachers are told that this outline is merely intended to be suggestive—experienced teachers will know this.

Following this outline are some suggestions for adapting it to various school situations. These suggested adaptations indicate to some extent why the author preferred to submit a ten-day teaching outline, which lends itself to more flexibility and easier adaptation, instead of a series of ten rigid, daily lesson plans.

Ten-Day Teaching Outline

Objective: To familiarize B-A students with faster ways of processing business data in volume.

First Day

SIMPLE SPEED-UP METHODS FOR PROCESSING BOOKKEEPING AND ACCOUNTING DATA

I. Objective

    A. To familiarize students with faster, non-machine ways of processing data

II. Introduction

    A. Methods of processing data constantly change and improve

    B. Examples of outmoded manual methods

        1. Recording individual closing entries with individual explanations when closing each income account and each expense account

        2. Recording in the Items column of an account the title of the other account involved in the transaction when posting

    C. Examples of speed-up B-A processes used in textbook

        1. Special journals

        2. Special ledgers

    D. Need for faster and improved ways of processing business data

        1. To keep management more completely and more currently informed

        2. To help a business keep up with or ahead of its competitors

        3. To handle large quantities of data more inexpensively and quickly as businesses increase in size

E. Estimates of differences in cost of processing business data
   1. Less expensive for most businesses to use some faster methods
   2. Certain equipment might prove too costly to use in smaller firms

III. Presentation—Speed-up methods in bookkeeping-accounting

A. "Write-it-once" principle
   1. Carbon paper
   2. NCR paper
   3. Carbonized sets
   4. Typewriter
   5. Autographic register
   6. Pegboard or writing board
      a. Application to payroll
      b. Application to inventory control
      c. Application to other records

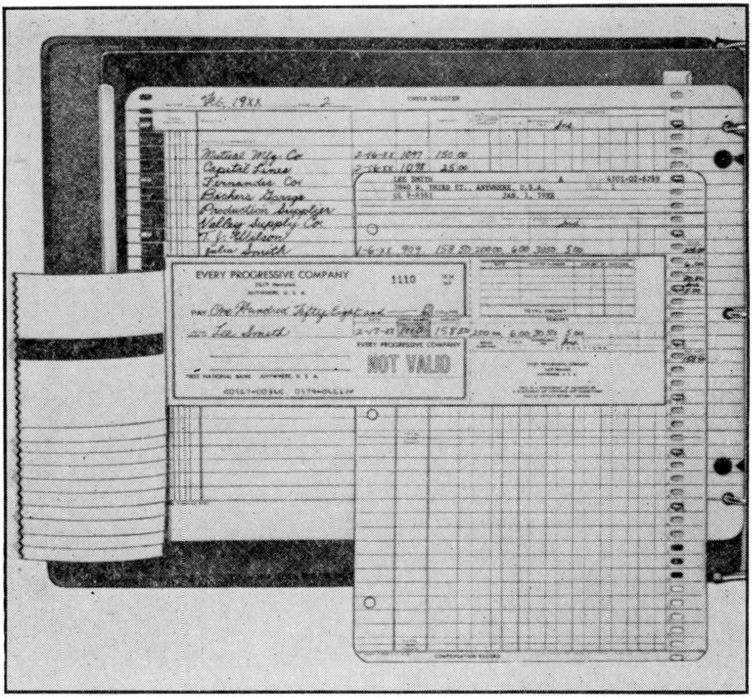

Post-Rite, a division of the Reynolds & Reynolds Company

Figure 24—1. A pegboard

B. Edge-notched cards
   1. Primary use as sorting device
   2. Use in schools
   3. Use in business
C. Estimate of training necessary for learning to use:
   1. Pegboard
   2. Edge-notched cards

Second Day

COMMON BUSINESS MACHINES USED FOR PROCESSING BOOKKEEPING AND ACCOUNTING DATA

I. **Objectives**

   A. To familiarize students with the more common machines used to speed the processing of bookkeeping and accounting data
   B. To introduce students to the processing of data automatically and to some related terms

II. **Introduction**

   A. Review speed-up methods for processing business data discussed yesterday

III. **Presentation**

   A. Common business machines in current use
      1. Adding-listing
         a. Ten-key
         b. Full bank
      2. Calculating
         a. Printing
         b. Non-listing
            (1) Key driven
            (2) Rotary
            (3) Electronic
      3. Bookkeeping and accounting
         a. General purpose
         b. Posting-billing
      4. Miscellaneous
         a. Cash register
         b. Time clock
         c. Teletype
         d. Automatic typewriter

Reprinted from Education Age with permission of
and copyrighted by Visual Products Division,
3M Company, St. Paul, Minnesota

Figure 24—2. A bank of teletypes at the Institute for Mathematical Studies
in the Social Sciences, Stanford University

B. Advantages of use of machines
    1. Speed in recording
    2. Speed in computation
    3. Accuracy
    4. Legibility

C. Disadvantages of using machines—reasons why some businesses
    limit their use of machines to adding and calculating machines
    1. Cost
    2. Special training needed for some machine operators
    3. Possible delays because of breakdowns

D. How some machines process data *automatically*
    1. Division on calculating machines
    2. Automatic typewriter such as a Flexowriter

E. Demonstration of *storage* of information in a machine
   1. Numbers to be added
   2. Subtotals on adding machines
F. Demonstration of *memory* of a machine
   1. Bookkeeping machine keeping track of cash balance
   2. Cash register keeping track of sales by department
G. Basic steps in all systems used for processing business data
   1. Input
   2. Processing
   3. Output
H. Training necessary to learn to operate the various machines presented
I. Cost factor when machines are used and not used for processing data

Third Day

DESIGN OF FORMS FOR AUTOMATED METHODS OF PROCESSING DATA

I. Objective

A. To demonstrate to students some of the planning necessary if machines are to prepare reports efficiently, correctly, and effectively

II. Introduction

A. Review some well-known forms and internal reports
   1. Checks and invoices, schedules of accounts receivable and payable, inventory sheets, sales analysis
   2. Reasons for size and format
      a. Ease of reading, filing, mailing, typing (printout)

III. Presentation

A. Who designs forms
   1. Individuals for personal use
      a. To keep account of cost and miles per gallon of gasoline for car, to record club dues, results of sport contests
   2. Individual office workers
      a. A typist when planning the centering and columnar arrangements for typing a balance sheet, a bookkeeper when analyzing sales data
   3. Systems planners when installing new office machines or new systems
      a. Forms prepared for specific machines in a specific business doing a specific job

B. The purpose of a form
   1. Arrangement of material in neat and logical sequence so user can comprehend and analyze data quickly
      a. Checks, invoices, payroll registers, bank statements, etc.
C. Considerations in form design
   1. Data needed
   2. Logical sequence of data
   3. Arrangement for easy reading and comprehension
   4. Size of paper or cards being used
   5. Machines and equipment being used—typewriters (6 lines per inch, 10-12 characters per inch), bookkeeping machines, ADP machines
D. Elements of form design for automated data processing
   1. Use of numbers
      a. Data usually organized according to numeric keys
      b. Machines, like people, can sort numbers more quickly than letters
      c. ADP systems usually use numbers rather than titles to identify accounts or other data being processed
      d. Numerical codes must be established for the data to be processed
   2. Each form design is basically controlled by machine on which it will be prepared
      a. Spacing chart needed for plotting form of final report
      b. Spacing chart predicts overall appearance of final report
E. System documentation
   1. Spacing charts and instruction sheets are a form of documentation
      a. Necessary for workers to understand and perform job
      b. Change as data to be processed changes
   2. Needed to train new employees and to remind them of all the routines they must perform

Fourth Day

INTRODUCTION TO PUNCHED CARD DATA PROCESSING

I. Objective

A. To introduce students to the punched card and to teach why and how business data are recorded on punched cards

II. Introduction

A. Everyday use of punched cards
   1. Utility company bills, record clubs, tests in schools, turnpike tickets

III. Presentation

    A. Why, in general, holes are punched into cards

        1. Converting information (data) to a language which a machine can "understand"

        2. Ability of machines to "read" holes

        3. Speed of processing information in punched cards

        4. Accuracy of machines in processing information

        5. Punched card can become a permanent record—can be used over and over again

        6. Enables machines, instead of people, to do routine, repetitive work

    B. How data are recorded in punched card form

        1. Card definition (areas or location)

            a. Face

            b. Edge (9 or 12)

            c. Corner (upper left, etc.)

        2. Punching locations

            a. Fields

            b. Columns

            c. Rows

            d. Digit positions

            e. Zones

        3. Recording data

            a. Hollerith Code

            b. Numeric characters (account numbers, amounts)

            c. Alpha characters (name, address)

            d. Special characters

    C. Meaning of *unit record*

        1. Unit—one, single

        2. Record—a collection of related items of data treated as a unit

            a. "Unit" indicates the related items are punched in a single card

            b. Machines which process a single transaction (one card) at a time are called unit record machines

Fifth Day

**PUNCHED CARD DATA PROCESSING—
UNIT RECORD MACHINES**

I. Objectives

    A. To introduce students to unit record machines that record, sort, and tabulate data, and print reports

B. To show some of the relationships of a manual bookkeeping system to a unit record system

II. **Introduction**

  A. Review

    1. Recording of data in punched cards

    2. Meaning of *unit record*

III. **Presentation**

  A. Meaning of *automated data processing*—ADP

  B. Relationship between some of the steps in processing information manually and processing it automatically—using unit record machines

Step No.	Manual Data Processing	Function	Automated Data Processing
1	Source Documents ↓	Initial Happening ↓	Source Documents ↓
2	Journal ↓	Recording ↓	Card Punch ↓
3	Ledger ↓	Sorting and Summarizing ↓	Sorter ↓
4	End-of-Period Schedules and Reports	Reporting	Accounting Machine

  C. Unit record machines and their function

    1. Indicated above

      a. Card punch (key punch)

      b. Sorter

      c. Accounting machine

    2. Other

      d. Verifier

      c. Interpreter

      d. Collator

      e. Reproducing punch

  D. Sorting unit records by different classifications

    1. Amount of sales for

      a. each item sold

      b. each salesman

      c. each sales territory

  E. Some machines controlled by wired panel

    1. Need for panel to be wired properly to derive an accurate printed report which is in accord with forms design

  F. Cost factor when processing data with unit record equipment

Sixth Day

FLOW CHARTING

I. Objective

A. To explain the importance of flow charts in an automated data processing system and introduce students to symbolic flow charts

II. Introduction

A. Review simple flow charts with which students are already familiar
   1. The bookkeeping cycle
   2. Posting
   3. Closing the ledger
B. Importance of these flow charts
   1. To visualize the total process
   2. To show steps necessary for completing a procedure or for solving a problem

III. Presentation

A. Methods of communication to tell someone else what machines are to be used and in what sequence they are to be used to process data and to prepare reports for business management
   1. Speaking
      a. Easy to do
      b. Difficult to remember
      c. Cannot be referred to at a later date
   2. Writing
      a. Can be referred to again and again
      b. Requires extensive effort and careful planning
      c. Requires careful and detailed reading to comprehend relationships of operations
   3. Flow charting
      a. Can be referred to easily
      b. Symbols used to visualize sequence and relationship of all operations
      c. Meaning of symbols used in flow charts must be learned by users
      d. Narrative
         (1) Symbol alone may not convey the entire procedure; therefore a brief description called the narrative is added and keyed to the particular symbol by number

B. Standard systems flow chart symbols for use with unit record installations

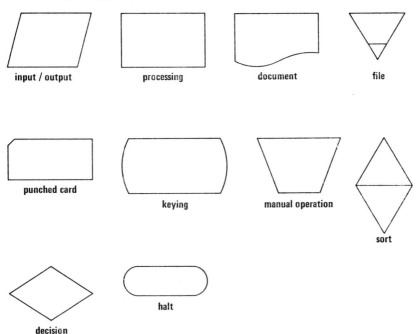

input / output	processing	document	file

punched card

keying

manual operation

sort

decision

halt

Seventh Day

COMPUTERS

I. Objective

A. To familiarize students with computers—the fastest large-volume data processing device yet developed

II. Introduction

A. Review purpose of flow charts
B. Flow charts in previous lessons were for unit record processing systems
C. Unit record systems require use of a different machine for each operation performed
D. The word *computer* implies several components connected together by electrical cables. Each component may perform a

separate function. One may "read" data into the memory of
the computer and another component may print the results of
calculations on to a report form

III. Presentation

    A. Types of computers
        1. Analog
            a. Used to control other machines and measure changes in
               degree rather than finite numbers
            b. Examples: thermometer, speedometer, oil dipstick, slide
               rule
        2. Digital
            a. Measure in exact amounts
            b. Examples: fingers, adding machines, cash registers, calcu-
               lators
            c. Most adaptable to business, therefore studied in detail
               here
    B. Characteristics of digital computers
        1. Electronic device—electrical circuitry does the arithmetic
            processing instead of wheels, counters or other mechanical
            apparatus
        2. Information can be stored or remembered by magnetizing
            tiny doughnut-like objects called cores. If the magnetic field
            in a clockwise direction were to represent the binary digit
            one, then the magnetic field in a counter-clockwise direction
            would represent the binary digit zero.
        3. Core storage in a computer as compared with storage in a
            unit record system
        4. Necessary computer components
            a. Device to read in data—card reader, disk drive, tape drive
            b. Device to read out data—printer, punch, disk drive, tape
               drive
               (1) Speeds of machines vary widely according to manu-
                   facturer and model
            c. Central processing unit—controls all computer functions
            d. Core storage—where data are retained in the computer
        5. Source of instructions for computers
            a. Computer program
               (1) Logic diagram (program flow chart)—guide for writ-
                   ing instructions for computer. All decisions to be
                   made by computer must be shown

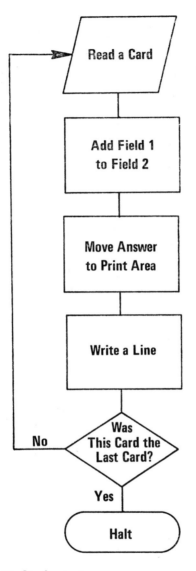

(2) Media for instruction
  (a) Punched cards
  (b) Paper tape
  (c) Magnetic tape
  (d) Magnetic disk

6. Storage of instructions
   a. Instructions are stored inside computer in the same manner as data are stored

(A study of programming will explain to a student how the computer knows the difference between data and instructions.)

Eighth Day

MEDIA USED FOR INSTRUCTING DATA PROCESSING MACHINES

I. **Objective**

   A. To make the students aware of some of the different media and devices which are used in automated data processing systems

II. **Introduction**

   A. Meaning of *media*
      1. The material on which data (and/or computer instructions) are recorded, e.g., paper tape, magnetic tape
   B. Media already familiar to students
      1. Source documents
      2. Punched cards
      3. Printed reports

III. **Presentation**

   A. Paper tape
      1. Will not store data as compactly nor be processed as quickly as magnetic tape
   B. MICR—Magnetic Ink Character Recognition
      1. Code on bottom of all checks
      2. Read by special machines—magnetic character readers
      3. Provides information on checks necessary for the automatic transfer to computers in order to debit and credit the proper bank accounts in the proper amounts
   C. Magnetic tape and disks
      1. Person writing instructions must know exactly how information is recorded and how to retreive it from tape or disk
   D. Mass memory
      1. Large scale computer storage
      2. Cannot be accessed as quickly as main computer storage
   E. Cathode Ray Tube—CRT
      1. Picture tube in home television set is a CRT
      2. Computers can be connected to a CRT and instead of printing output, display it on a picture tube

F. Light pen
   1. Used to draw on the CRT and send information back to the computer
G. Telephone
   1. Dial special number for computer giving stock information at the stock exchange. Also must dial the code number of the stock
   2. Dial other computers by means of a *data-phone*. This allows one computer to "talk" with another by means of electronic signals
H. Time-sharing
   1. Concept of several remote terminals such as teletypes connected by communication lines (probably telephone) to one computer. The computer is programmed to poll each terminal and act upon the request (special program) of that terminal. Allows one computer to serve several locations

Ninth Day

JOB OPPORTUNITIES IN AUTOMATED DATA PROCESSING

I. Objective

A. To acquaint the students with the various positions in the field of automated data processing and to explain the duties and educational requirements

II. Introduction

A. Help wanted section of large city newspaper
   1. Number and kind of positions available
   2. Salaries and working conditions mentioned

III. Presentation

A. Jobs, qualifications, and salaries listed
   1. Local newspaper or other local source
   2. U. S. Department of Labor publications
      a. *Occupational Outlook Handbook*
      b. *Dictionary of Occupational Titles* including
         (1) Data typist
         (2) Card-punch (key-punch) operator
         (3) Control clerk
         (4) Tape librarian
         (5) Tabulating-machine operator
         (6) Console operator

   (7) Coding clerk
   (8) Junior programmer
   (9) Business programmer
   (10) Chief business programmer
   (11) Systems analyst
B. Availability of training programs
C. Plan for tomorrow's field trip to a data center—the culminating experience to their study of faster ways to process data
   1. What to look for
   2. What questions to ask

Tenth Day

FIELD TRIP TO LOCAL DATA CENTER

(Note: Remarks on the taking of field trips by the B-A class are found on page 220 of Chapter 8, "School and Community Resources.")

Suggestions for Adapting the Ten-Day Outline

The preceding teaching unit is designed to familiarize students with faster ways of processing business data. It is suggested as a starting point for helping teachers make their individual approaches through which data processing can be integrated into the B-A course.

Curriculums from school to school provide varying amounts of training for B-A students on office machines including automated data processing machines. In some schools some of the material suggested in the foregoing outline will have been or will be covered outside the B-A class and need not be duplicated in the B-A course. Furthermore, a class of more able and selected students should quickly progress through an "average" B-A course and could well afford to spend more time and study this unit more thoroughly.

Many of the detailed day-to-day teaching procedures used when adapting this outline to the classroom will be the same or similar. It is particularly important that a wide variety of visual aids be utilized to bring this complex subject into the realm of personal experience. Just talking about automated data processing is not enough. When punched cards are discussed, examples should be available for students to see, touch, and use. Paper tapes, magnetic tapes, pegboards, calculating machines and so on should all be present in the classroom if at all possible, or at least visualized through the use of films, overhead projectors, and photographs.

A trip to a computer installation should be an integral part of such a unit of instruction. In fact, two field trips, one near the start of the unit and one at the end, is better than just one. When trips are made, careful plans are necessary for students to obtain the most useful information. All too frequently the tour guides at the data center, unless carefully briefed as to the specific intent of the trip, spend their time confusing and over-impressing students with the magical behavior of the machines rather than relating their function to what the student knows about bookkeeping-accounting.

When presenting the job opportunities in automated data processing, the teacher should not overlook the help available from a qualified guest speaker. The local chapter of the Data Processing Management Association (DPMA) could be an excellent source for securing such a person. The use of guest speakers is discussed on page 220 of Chapter 8, "School and Community Resources."

The foregoing outline should be modified and varied to suit the peculiarities of the individual situation. B-A students in some rural schools, for example, may not need as thorough an understanding of forms design, presented on third day of the outline, as B-A students in large urban areas with greater chances of working in large offices. Three or four days, instead of one, could be a better length of time devoted to punched card data processing if equipment and the situation justify the change. A similar remark could be made for each of the other topics in the outline.

In those schools or communities where a unit record system (including a 402 or 407 accounting machine) is available for visitation by a B-A class, there is potential for giving students a most effective experience in seeing the relationship between manual bookkeeping and automated data processing. In such an instance the teacher could:

1. Arrange to secure several decks of prepunched cards containing, for example, the same payroll data, the same accounts receivable data, and accounts payable data, the same inventory data, the same sales analysis data as will be processed by students manually when they complete an assigned practice set.

2. Arrange to secure a wiring diagram and wired panel for use with one or more such decks of cards.
3. Arrange to have the class see an accounting machine process *in minutes* the same data and produce *the same output* that they worked on manually.

As more schools obtain automated data processing equipment or have it made available to them, publishing companies will likely provide prepunched cards and wiring diagrams for such use with the practice sets that accompany their B-A textbooks. Furthermore, in schools which offer courses in automated data processing, appropriate projects in such courses could include the punching of certain decks of cards for the practice sets, working out the wiring diagrams, and wiring the necessary panels.

Summary

Business education is moving through a transition period in dealing with the coming of automated data processing to the high school curriculum. As late as 1960 a majority of educators were in agreement that the vocational training for most positions in data centers was for post-high school consideration. Viewpoints on this are being modified.

Today it is obvious that all future business workers need to be familiar with automated data processing. Different high schools will do this in different ways. The B-A course is one place where it could and should be done. The responsibility of the B-A course as it presently exists in the high school curriculum should be limited to teaching the *relationship* of automated data processing to B-A procedures. The understanding of basic B-A principles should not be sacrificed. Teachers should not be misled by their enthusiasm for automated data processing and starve their basic bookkeeping and accounting teaching by overindulging in unjustified automated data processing considerations.

The developments in the automated data processing field have created new jobs and therefore a new vocational training need which requires new courses as well as modification of existing courses. Specialized courses in automated data processing techniques should become a part of the vocational training program in high schools serving urban areas. The first-year B-A course could be a prerequisite for entrance to such courses.

Support for the belief that a first-year B-A course be a requirement for students enrolled in a high school data processing curriculum is found in the recommendations of the nation-wide study, "Curricular Implications of Automated Data Processing for Educational Institutions." [3] This extensive study recommends that a B-A course be included in the eleventh grade of a high school curriculum in data processing.[4] The following excerpts from Part I of the report supplement this recommendation.

Business and General Courses

Employment in business data processing departments requires more than technical know-how in machine operation. Background in how business is organized, how it operates, and how its records are kept is essential, together with good communications skills and knowledge of human relations. In order to provide these skills and knowledges, general background courses in business and the social sciences are an important part of a data processing curriculum.

The *Bookkeeping* course should be developed with an emphasis upon the use of electronic data processing equipment for compiling the records of a business. The emphasis in this course should be on a systems approach to accounting related to data processing accounting procedures.[5]

It is also desirable to point out in conclusion that one of the most certain things in life is change. The automated data processing field is an ever changing field, and the developments which are to come will inevitably be reflected in the high school curriculum. Bookkeeping-accounting and automated data processing teachers have a singular responsibility to their students to keep up to date from day to day in their subject matter field.

STUDY QUESTIONS

1. Give some examples of personal experience you have had with automated data processing.
2. What are some uses of automated data processing outside of business usage?

---

[3] Bangs, F. Kendrick, Principal Investigator. *Curricular Implications of Automated Data Processing for Educational Institutions.* (Boulder, Colorado: University of Colorado, September, 1968). (Available from Executive Secretary, Delta Pi Epsilon, Gustavus Adolphus College, St. Peter, Minnesota.)
[4] *Ibid.*, pp. 3 and 78.
[5] *Ibid.*, p. 80.

3. What students need to be provided with an appreciation level of understanding of automated data processing? Why?

4. What area of education should be responsible for teaching the appreciation level understanding of automated data processing? Justify this.

5. In what two ways will automated data processing appear in the business curriculum?

6. What should be the minimum accomplishment in automated data processing of potential office workers?

7. What is the present scope of job opportunities in automated data processing for high school graduates?

8. Name at least five titles of beginning jobs in automated data processing and tell what kind of work is done in each?

9. When should the relationship of automated data processing to bookkeeping be introduced in the B-A class? Justify your answer.

10. What overall objective can the B-A teacher set for a unit of instruction on automated data processing?

11. How might one introduce a unit of instruction on automated data processing?

12. What two difficult decisions must a teacher make after he has decided to teach his students something of the relationship of manual bookkeeping to automated data processing?

13. Name at least two factors which would require the suggested ten-day unit to be modified to meet the needs of the specific school situation.

14. How can some schools arrange to show quickly the relationship between the manual bookkeeping actually done in the classroom and automated data processing?

DISCUSSION QUESTIONS

1. Discuss the various ways in which automated data processing might appear in the high school curriculum.

2. Discuss automated data processing as a part of general education in the high school.

3. Discuss automated data processing as a part of vocational education in the high school business curriculum.

4. To what extent should automated data process training be deferred to post-high school institutions?

5. How extensively should a teacher attempt to lead his students to an understanding of the relationship of automated data processing to manual bookkeeping?

6. How much time in a first-year B-A course should students spend studying the relationship of automated data processing to manual bookkeeping?

7. What is the best course for teaching an *appreciation* of automated data processing to *ALL* high school students?

8. To what extent should B-A students be required to remember the standard symbols used in flow charting?

9. Are there any circumstances which might justify a teacher omitting any reference to automated data processing in his B-A course?

10. What topics would you add or delete from the suggested ten-day teaching outline presented in this chapter? Why?

SELECTED REFERENCES

Bangs, F. Kendrick, Principal Investigator. *Curricular Implications of Automated Data Processing for Educational Institutions.* Boulder, Colorado: University of Colorado, 1968. (Available from Executive Secretary, Delta Pi Epsilon, Gustavus Adolphus College, St. Peter, Minnesota 56082.)

Beckner, Caroline. "Who Should Study Data Processing," *Business Education World.* XLVIII (April, 1968), 10-11.

Boynton, Lewis D. "Manual Bookkeeping in an Era of Automation," *The Balance Sheet.* XLVI (September, 1964), 4-6, 44.

Brower, Edward. "Automation in Bookkeeping: A Problem of Timing," *Business Education Forum.* XXI (May, 1967), 24-25.

Caldwell, J. Edward. "Bookkeeping and Related Subjects," *Business Education for the Automated Office,* Eastern Business Teachers Association Yearbook, Vol. 37, Chapter 6. New York: New York University Bookstore, 1964.

Carpenter, W. G., and R. L. Nickels. "Setting up a Successful High School Data Processing Program," *Business Education World.* XLVIII (May, 1968), 9-11.

Gearhardt, George J. "Data Processing Instruction in Guilderland Central Senior High School," *The Journal of Business Education.* XLIV (October, 1968), 25-26.

Haga, Enoch. "Introductory Automation and Data Processing for All High Schools," *Business Education Forum.* XXII (May, 1968), 16-18.

——————. (ed.) *Automation Research*, Monograph 1. San Diego State College, San Diego, Calif.: Society for Automation in Business Education, 1965.

Hanna, J. Marshall. "Flow Charting in High School Accounting," *The Journal of Business Education*. XLIII (February, 1968), 198-201.

Johnson, Russell A., and Jackie G. Williams. "Data Processing in Beginning Bookkeeping," *Business Education Forum*. XXI (November, 1966), 18-19.

Kallaus, Norman F. "Integrating Data Processing Concepts in Business Classes," *Business Education Forum*. XXII (March, 1968), 22-23.

Kargilis, George. "Data Processing—A 'Must' for the High School," *Business Education Forum*. XXII (May, 1968), 14-16.

Lesak, Joseph A., and William G. Carpenter. "Accounting Students Learn Data Processing," *The Balance Sheet*. XLIX (February, 1968), 247-248.

McKenna, Margaret. "The Automated Office and Its Impact on Business Education," *Administration and Supervision of Business Education*, Eastern Business Teachers Association Yearbook, Vol. 39, Chapter 20. New York: New York University Bookstore, 1966.

McNutt, Sara Jean. "Teaching Data Processing," *Business Education Forum*. XXII (May, 1968), 21-23.

Parish, Clair R. "Data Processing Education," *The Journal of Business Education*. XLIII (December, 1967), 111-113.

Pearson, John E. "The Data Processing Jungle," *The Journal of Business Education*. XLII (April, 1967), 281-282.

Robertson, Leonard. "Symbolic Flow Charting as a Teaching Device," *The Business Teacher*. XLVI (September-October, 1968), 74-75.

Solomon, Martin B. Jr., and Nora G. Lovan. *Annotated Bibliography of Films in Automation, Data Processing, and Computer Science*. Lexington: University of Kentucky Press, 1967.

Witherow, Mary. "Communication Processing," *The Balance Sheet*. XLIX (April, 1968), 362.

Wood, Merle W. *The Teaching of Automated Data Processing in the High School*, Monograph 116. Cincinnati: South-Western Publishing Company, 1967.

Yourd, Bryce W. "Accounting, Data Processing, and the Psychology of Learning," *The Balance Sheet*. XLVII (May, 1966), 388-393.

A B-A methods text is devoted primarily to general bookkeeping-accounting teaching techniques and principles and to specific suggestions for teaching certain procedures. However, a teacher-education textbook should also give the teacher resources, guideposts, and evaluation material applicable to his field and the teaching profession in general. Therefore, the following general references, teaching guides, and appraisal form are presented in the appendixes.

Appendix I is a bibliography of publications pertaining to teaching which provides sources for enriching teacher knowledge and background. These are general references which provide more detailed discussion of many of the educational subjects covered in this text.

Appendix II is a list of good general teaching practices. The procedures in this list are common-sense rules that not only aid the beginner but serve as reminders to all teachers.

Appendix III includes a student-teacher evaluating form which indicates to the student teacher the qualities on which he will be judged. This appendix also gives pointers on self-evaluating as a person, a classroom teacher, and as a member of the teaching profession.

Appendix I

SELECTED REFERENCES
GENERAL

Alberty, Harold B., and Elsie J. Alberty. *Reorganizing the High School Curriculum*, 3d ed. New York: The Macmillan Company, 1962.

Andruss, Harvey A. *Ways to Teach Bookkeeping and Accounting*, 2d ed. Cincinnati: South-Western Publishing Co., 1943.

Business Education: An Evaluative Inventory, National Business Education Yearbook, No. 6, Chapters 5, 6, and 7. Washington, DC: National Business Education Association, 1968.

Dame, J. Frank, and Albert R. Brinkman. *Guidance in Business Education*, 3d ed. Cincinnati: South-Western Publishing Co., 1961.

Developing Vocational Competency in Bookkeeping and Accounting, Eastern Business Teachers Association Yearbook, Vol. 40. New York: New York University Bookstore, 1967.

Douglas, Lloyd V., James T. Blanford, and Ruth I. Anderson. "Teaching Bookkeeping," *Teaching Business Subjects*, 2d ed., Chapter 9. Englewood Cliffs, NJ: Prentice-Hall, Inc., 1965.

Good, Carter V. *Introduction to Educational Research*, 2d ed. New York: Appleton-Century-Crofts, Division of Meredith Publishing Company, 1963.

Hardaway, Mathilde. *Testing and Evaluation in Business Education*, 3d ed. Cincinnati: South-Western Publishing Co., 1966.

Harms, Harm, and B. W. Stehr. "Bookkeeping," *Methods in Vocational Business Education*, 2d ed., Chapter 7. Cincinnati: South-Western Publishing Co., 1963.

Johnson, H. Webster. *How to Use the Business Library*. 3d ed. Cincinnati: South-Western Publishing Co., 1964.

Lomax, Paul S., and Peter L. Agnew. *Problems of Teaching Bookkeeping*. New York: Prentice-Hall, Inc., 1938.

Lyon, Leverett S. *Education for Business*. Chicago: University of Chicago Press, 1931.

Musselman, Vernon A., and J. Marshall Hanna. *Teaching Bookkeeping and Accounting*. New York: Gregg Publishing Division, McGraw-Hill Book Company, Inc., 1960.

Nolan, C. A., Carlos K. Hayden, and Dean R. Malsbary. "The Bookkeeping Subjects," *Principles and Problems of Business Education*, 3d ed., Chapter 8. Cincinnati: South-Western Publishing Co., 1966.

Rahe, Harves. *Accounting—Bookkeeping—Recordkeeping Research Index*. New York: Gregg Publishing Division, McGraw-Hill Book Company, Inc., 1967.

Schorling, R., and Howard T. Batchelder. *Student Teaching in Secondary Schools*, 3d ed. New York: McGraw-Hill Book Company, Inc., 1956.

Selby, Paul O. *The Teaching of Bookkeeping*. New York: Gregg Publishing Division, McGraw-Hill Book Company, Inc., 1945.

Selected Readings in Business and Office Occupations—Designed Especially for the Classroom Teacher, National Business Education Yearbook, No. 5. Washington, DC: National Business Education Association, 1967.

Tonne, Herbert A. "Training for Bookkeeping Occupations," *Principles of Business Education*, 3d ed., Chapter 18. New York: Gregg Publishing Division, McGraw-Hill Book Company, Inc., 1961.

————, Estelle L. Popham, and M. Herbert Freeman. "Preparing to Teach Bookkeeping," and "Teaching Bookkeeping," *Methods of Teaching Business Subjects*, 3d ed., Chapters 17 and 18. New York: Gregg Publishing Division, McGraw-Hill Book Company, Inc., 1957.

Vocational Education, The Sixty-fourth Yearbook of the National Society for the Study of Education. Chicago: Distributed by the University of Chicago Press, 1965.

Appendix II

GENERAL METHODS OF TEACHING

Teachers differ in appearance, personality, and the effect they have upon students. There are, however, certain teaching practices, techniques, and characteristics which can be labeled as common to good teaching in any subject.

This appendix is devoted to these general teaching methods. While the topic cannot be completely covered in this outline, the listing of the following suggested procedures is a sincere attempt to assist in areas of trouble common to most beginning teachers. Ignoring one or two of these practices will not always make the difference between a good or bad teacher, but the more such techniques are followed, the closer one should come to his goal of good teaching.

Guideposts of Good Teaching

1. *Room conditions* and *arrangements* affect learning. Have the temperature of the room comfortable, the air fresh, the lighting adequate, the furniture conveniently arranged, and possible distractions at a minimum. Student lack of interest or lethargy can be the result of poor ventilation and lighting, or overheating.

Be sure everyone can see and hear all you do and say.

Make the classroom surroundings pleasing. Good teachers have eyes to see how a classroom may be made attractive and the initiative to improve those classrooms to which they are assigned.

The neatness with which a classroom is maintained is as much the teacher's responsibility as it is the janitor's.

2. *Student interest and attention* are essential to learning. Have everything ready before you start. Every hesitation, interruption, or delay is a distraction.

Secure the attention of every member of the group before you proceed. No attention, no results.

Be businesslike in starting on time. A strong example set the first week in September will frequently set the tone and behavior for the year. A teacher who delays getting his class started until five minutes after the bell each period is cheating his students of 15 hours of learning each year (180 days $\times$ 5 min. $\div$ 60 min. = 15 hrs.). This is the equivalent of over three weeks of class meetings during the year. Furthermore, constantly late starts require more and more prodding and appealing as the term progresses to get students under way. Tardiness, like punctuality, is a habit.

Do not proceed with a lesson until you have succeeded in arousing a feeling of need for the instruction. There is no use in giving a concert to an empty hall.

Make every pupil in the room feel that you are aware of his presence—slight no one. Look them "straight in the eye." Scatter your questions and bring all into the day's discussions and activities.

Permit no interruptions or distractions to interfere with your presentations. A one-minute interruption may require an additional ten minutes to get the class back to the same situation before the interruption.

Have something of importance taking place constantly. Pauses or "dead spots" allow attention to wander. No attention, no results.

Be alert to see that your class is following step by step. It is useless to proceed if some have been lost by the wayside.

3. *Personal mannerisms* **of the teacher can detract from student attention and learning.** Do not be a jitterbug. Avoid unnatural movements, gestures, and mannerisms that may prove distracting or even irritating to others. Anything that directs attention away from the presentation is detrimental to learning.

Common signs of nervousness in beginning teachers include: pacing the front of the room; juggling a piece of chalk or an eraser in one's hand; fingering a coat button, a piece of jewelry, or a pencil; jingling coins in a pants pocket while talking.

A recurring mannerism of speech that sets some students to counting the teacher's pet phrases instead of listening to what is being said include: punctuating *each* sentence with an "Ah," or an "Er-r-r"; accepting *all* students' answers and responses with one set remark such as "All right" or "O.K."; starting *each* sentence with "Now let us . . . ," or "All right, now let us . . ."; constantly saying "Any questions?"

4. *Good questioning* **provokes thought.** Good teachers are good questioners. Few beginning teachers can question well. The art of good questioning is acquired, not God-given.

Ask questions one at a time in a clear, concise manner. If you ask two or more questions at the same time, you lose or confuse students.

Address your questions to everyone in the group, pause for time for reflective thought, then call upon one student by name for the answer. If you call upon a student before you state the question, human nature will dictate to many in the class to do no thinking—"That's Johnny's question, I don't have to be concerned with an answer this time."

The results can be disquieting and weakening to the status of a beginning teacher who, after stating a question and saying, "Who will answer that?" gets dead silence as the response. To continue a general appeal for an answer, or to cajole the class with no favorable results can be embarrassing and detrimental to rapport. Then, to eventually signal out a student by name frequently causes that student to feel that he is being "picked on." After all, he indicated he did not know by keeping silent. What to do? First, until you get to know your class and its responsiveness, it would seem best not to use this technique of questioning. Second, if you use this approach and get no response, give the answer yourself rather than create tension by pressing for it.

Avoid group responses to questions. You are not training for chorus work.

Ask questions that require some thought before being answered. A student has a 50/50 chance of guessing the answer to a question calling for a "yes" or a "no" answer.

Use questions or challenging statements that arouse the curiosity of the students, that invite their participation, and that do not lend themselves readily to guessing an answer. The five W's of questioning aptly lend themselves to this principle. For example, "Why. . . ?", "Where . . . ?", "When . . . ?", "What . . . ?", "Which . . . ?." "How" at the start of a sentence, also helps to take the question out of the guessing category.

Insist upon complete statements in answer to your questions and, if necessary, follow through to be sure that you have understood the student correctly. This helps to make sure that the student really knows the answer and also helps the class to learn or know what the true, full answer is.

Ask only questions for which there is some likelihood of receiving a correct answer. There is no object in insisting on an answer when it becomes obvious that the class does not know. There is little educational value in a guessing contest.

Do not answer all the questions students ask of you. Refer some back to the class. To answer all questions personally is a common trait of beginning teachers. They probably feel that it gives them status, an opportunity to show how much they know, and proof of their ability to earn a teacher's salary. Actually, it is a poor teacher who, himself, attempts to answer *all* students' questions. Referring many students' questions back to the class helps keep the group alert to their classmates' contributions and questions. It gives students who know the answers a chance to "show their stuff." It can help bind the class into a cooperative, working team and away from the autocratic atmosphere set by a "know it all" teacher.

5. A teacher's *speech* is his stock in trade. Talk slowly. If you talk too fast, some pupils will miss part of what you say, and others will be lost by the wayside. Haste makes waste.

Enunciate clearly and distinctly. Remember that you are setting an example for others.

Slang, if used at all, should be used sparingly. Example is better than precept.

Never yell or speak unnecessarily loud. It only adds to the confusion and increases competition.

Speak directly to all members of the class—not to the floor, chalkboard, or ceiling. Look at the class—as you would like each student to address you when talking to you.

Sprinkle your speech with an abundance of examples, illustrations, and analogies and synonyms if you wish to put your ideas across. "For example," "for instance," "like this," "let me illustrate," and "in other words," are phrases that should occur in your speech.

6. *Visual materials* make learning and teaching easier. The *overhead projector* is becoming the most popular teaching tool in many bookkeeping classrooms. The current generation of bookkeeping teachers seem lost without it. In addition to providing most of the advantages of a chalkboard, commercially- and teacher-prepared transparencies for use on the overhead projector helps speed teaching and learning.

The *chalkboard* continues to be the most convenient teaching aid. It doesn't wear out nor cost you anything—use it freely. Write large, clearly, and legibly—so the last student in the last seat can see readily. On the overhead projector or the chalkboard:

Spell out new terms.
List and show the correct procedure for doing things.

List important rules, formulas, and statements.
Draw and show diagrams and flow charts.
Outline and show business and other forms.
Use colored chalk or ink.
Draw and show pictures and illustrations.
Give special class notices.
List assignments, tests, problems.

Use visual materials that are sufficiently large and clear for all to see without special effort or discomfort. A picture worth seeing should be seen by all.

Use pictures, charts, diagrams, models, and real objects themselves in explaining things. "One picture can be worth a thousand words."

Why go to all the trouble and take the time to give a wordy explanation of something that becomes obvious on sight?

It is frequently best to demonstrate first and then explain. This gives the student additional background with which to understand the explanation.

Keep the bulletin board attractive, neat, up-to-date, and inviting of attention. Do not let a bulletin board develop into a "catch-all" filing station. Do not thumbtack new notices or material on top of old.

7. *Vocabulary* should be adjusted to the student level. Good teaching starts on the student's level, not on the teacher's. It requires forethought, planning, and constant alertness for a bookkeeping teacher to gear his vocabulary to the level of the class. If he starts talking "debit" and "credit" before these terms have been taught, he will have discouraged and frustrated students.

Use a vocabulary within the comprehension of the class. Always explain new terms and strive to clarify those that confuse. Remember the new must always be in terms of the old. Students are not clairvoyants.

Tie in each new presentation or idea with experience or instruction that has gone before. This knowledge gives the new material background and setting.

8. The *speed of teaching* should be adjusted to the speed of learning. Beginning teachers frequently start their careers by covering too much ground at the expense of student understanding. It is usually more important to learn one topic well than be able to brag that, "We covered three chapters this week." A good test or two in September could help give the teacher an indication of his teaching effectiveness and of student progress. Make haste slowly.

Giving students an opportunity to talk, write, and otherwise be active in the classroom permits the teacher to observe whether or not his timing in teaching is accurate. If the students show by what they say and do that they comprehend what is being taught, then the teacher can assume that his speed of teaching is not too fast. If, however, the teacher spends all the classroom time talking, telling, and performing himself, he has no way of estimating the accuracy of his educational timing.

9. *The teacher's attitudes*—his friendliness or sternness, his smiles or frowns, his laughter or scorn—are as much a part of the curriculum as the courses he teaches.

An occasional smile and a touch of humor are good teaching techniques. If need be, work to develop a sense of humor. If the laugh is on you, grin and mean it. A smile does not detract from the efficiency nor the effectiveness of teaching. Neither a "killjoy" nor a comedian be.

Be friendly and apparently informal in your manner. Learn where the too friendly line is. Avoid a hard-boiled or "smart aleck" attitude.

Give your teaching an atmosphere of business, not one of amusement.

10. *Praise* is a far greater educational force than reproof. Encouragement is a teaching obligation owed to each student. All of us do better work when properly encouraged in our efforts.

Stressing a little thing that a student does well will bring greater educational results than harping on the many things he is doing wrong. False praise, though, is never practiced by the wise teacher.

Teachers, like students, are human. As such, they all vary. Kindness, however, is one quality that all good teachers have in common.

11. *Discipline* is an important phase of educational procedure. Discipline is a major concern and problem of beginning teachers. Too frequently the word is made synonymous with silence and

Hitlerian obedience. Educationally, probably the most desirable synonyms for discipline are self-control and orderly procedure. Two major factors in gaining and maintaining order in and out of the classroom are (1) the *personality* of the teacher and (2) the *philosophy* of the teacher, as expressed in his teaching methods, practices, and his classroom behavior. Factors of personality and philosophy are not, of course, separate and distinct. Much of one's personality is the outward expression of his philosophy. However, for purposes of discussion and dealing briefly with this problem of discipline, a dual classification is arbitrarily made. Some of those teacher traits that can have an important relationship to discipline are outlined as follows:

I. The Teacher's Personality
   1. physique
   2. appearance
   3. dress
   4. voice
   5. speech
   6. personal mannerisms

II. The Teacher's Philosophy
   1. the meaning of discipline
   2. sincerity of purpose
   3. industry
       —meticulousness in planning for instruction and arranging for pupil activity
   4. demands for a "quiet" or orderly room
   5. fairness
   6. fellowship
   7. striving for pupil self-discipline
   8. belief in the principle that a good teacher makes himself progressively unnecessary

The following remarks and specific suggestions are aimed at being helpful in considering this general, all-encompassing teaching problem as outlined above.

The type of order in a classroom should, of necessity, vary with the nature of the work being done. While one might expect to be able to "hear a pin drop" during a written examination, it would seem just as reasonable *not* to be able to "hear yourself think" in a woodworking class turning out projects with hammers, nails, power saws, and the like. A bookkeeping class would not, of course, be expected to match this latter extreme in decibels of sound, but would certainly seem in order if it equaled, and at times even surpassed, the undertone of noises commonly found in business offices.

There is no better guarantee against classroom disorder than able planning and good procedure.

Remain calm and composed. Keep a "cool head," at least outwardly, under all circumstances. "Flying off the handle" will only make matters worse.

Avoid getting into an argument. It will get you off the track and can get you into trouble.

Overlook minor faults or slips in behavior. You declare an open season on yourself when you show pupils that you are annoyed by trivial acts of theirs. Do not waste time playing the role of policeman.

Encourage honest effort and avoid unnecessary embarrassment and chiding, particularly in the presence of others. If it is necessary to talk severely to a student, it is usually best done in private. The memory is long and the end-results usually bad when a person is made a poor example before a group.

There is probably no better way for tackling a real or potential case of discipline than an after-school, friendly, man-to-man talk with the student. Such a procedure, after a study of the student's personal school records, gives the teacher an analytical rather than an emotional approach. Like a doctor, investigate and study the case before attempting to prescribe treatment for it.

Do not threaten or promise anything that you cannot or will not carry out. If you do, like the boy who cried "wolf," your threats will be ignored and your status and respect will be lowered.

It is unfair and unwise to punish an entire class or group for the infractions of one or two students.

Teaching is to arrange for and proceed with orderly learning. Only when classroom learning is being adversely affected and when the teacher feels that higher authority and help is essential, should students be sent to the principal's office. Good, cool judgment is necessary here. Teachers who permit serious infractions or incorrigible cases to continually infringe on class learnings are being unfair to the other students in the class. Teachers who constantly send students to the principal's office usually develop, in the eyes of the administration, reputations for being weak in handling discipline.

Poor physical condition of either the pupil or the teacher is frequently the cause of discipline problems. Many experienced teachers will agree that their worst days for discipline are when they themselves have lost sleep or are physically tired.

Teacher Growth Is a Continuing Process

Experienced teachers will recognize all, or most, of these foregoing summary ideas dealing with general methods of teaching. They know that these ideas are not the ideas or private property of any one author or person. Such ideas easily fall into the category of reasonable, common-sense teaching practices. They are read, in general, with understanding and agreement by both experienced and inexperienced teachers. They are not *learned*, however, by mere reading. They are learned only in practice—by doing. As they are learned in practice teaching assignments or on the job, teacher growth is taking place. Teacher growth is never complete, should never stop.

All growth is a continuing process, and all growth takes time. This is especially so in teaching. The good teacher is constantly evaluating, constantly improving even to the day of retirement. The good teacher recognizes that he cannot become *master* of successful teaching practices *except over a period of years*. He recognizes the need for establishing new values of time needed for his personal growth and professional improvement.

There is one unique distinction between a career in business and a career in business education. In business, a new employee's job is likely to be simple of operation and lacking in much responsibility. As he remains on the job and becomes familiar with it, his work gradually becomes more complex and his responsibilities are increased. A new teacher, on the other hand, begins his first year of teaching with a full schedule equal to and sometimes greater than that of teachers with twenty or more years of experience. They also frequently have a full quota of extracurricular responsibilities. There is no gradual growth in difficulty of assignment or responsibility. As a result, the most difficult time for a teacher is his first year. After the first year, a program of improvement can be planned; and, if there is constant evaluation and action to improve, then the longer he teaches, the better he becomes and the easier he is able to make his work. A knowledge of this fact should (1) cushion reasonable discouragement resulting from difficulties, mistakes, and teacher learning of the first year, and (2) encourage subsequent teacher growth.

Teacher growth involves among many elements these four basic essentials:

1. The teacher must have an interest and desire and inner self-discipline to move toward improvement. It is easy to get into a rut in teaching and do the same thing in the same way for years on end without being conscious of having gone to sleep professionally.

2. The teacher must be able to recognize areas in which he needs to improve. He must be willing and able to be objective about analyzing himself.

3. The teacher must be willing to accept objective help and suggestions. We are all too frequently blind to our own weaknesses and shortcomings. Helpful observation and supervision should, therefore, be welcomed. It is essential to maximum growth.

4. The teacher must recognize that teacher growth goes beyond classroom techniques and methods and reaches into every experience which contributes to making an interesting, vital person.

Appendix III

EVALUATION OF STUDENT TEACHERS

A methods textbook, like most methods courses, concentrates on specific activities most easily learned: daily preparation, materials of instruction, the use of teaching plans, utilization of available resources, motivation of learning, keeping updated, and providing for individual pupil differences. Other qualities of a successful teacher are not easily taught and learned. These qualities include personality traits an individual has been acquiring and reinforcing over the years. For example, one's voice, tact, initiative, self-confidence, sense of humor, sincerity of interest in others are traits that require more than a methods textbook or course to change. But personality traits can be changed and improved providing, of course, that (1) the individual is aware of his shortcomings, and that (2) he has a strong desire to improve.

Most people are too close to their own shortcomings—personality traits as well as other weaknesses—to be aware of them or to be able to evaluate them objectively. This is why observation of student teachers by experienced, capable, and understanding classroom teachers is so helpful. This is why some school systems require experienced teachers to be observed and evaluated periodically by their supervisors.

When a person's work is to be evaluated, it is basic that he know what is to be appraised. This is as true for the evaluation of student teachers and experienced teachers as it is for the evaluation of pupils in a B-A class. Although the evaluation form which follows was designed for rating student teachers, it contains items usually considered when evaluating teachers in general.

FORM FOR EVALUATING
STUDENT TEACHERS

Student Teacher's Name _____

Student Teacher's Major _____ Minor _____

Subject(s) student teacher taught under your direction _____

School and Town _____

Student teaching from _____ 197__, to _____ 197__

Check the criteria listed below with an "X" in the appropriate column. The words outstanding, above average, etc. indicate that the student teacher being evaluated has that degree of competence on that item as a *beginning teacher*. Explanation of the grading system will be found on the next page where the composite grade is recorded. You are not required to rate all factors if you believe you are not in a position to do so.

	A Out-standing	B Above Average	C Average	D Below Average	F Unsatis-factory
Student Teacher as a Person					
Appearance, (dress, cleanliness, posture)					
Voice (pleasant pitch, clearness)					
Health (adequate energy and vitality)					
Initiative and self reliance					
Tact, courtesy, poise					
Kindness, sincerity and sense of justice					
Sense of humor					
Receptiveness to criticism					
Student Teacher as a Classroom Teacher					
Knowledge of subject matter					
Familiarity with materials of instruction					
Utilization of library and other resources					
Sensitivity to needs and interests of students					
Discipline or class control					
Administration of classroom routines					
Daily preparation					
Formulation and use of teaching plans					
Skill in carrying on a discussion					
Ability to make learning meaningful and concrete					
Rapport with adolescents					
Ability to motivate learning					
Use of English language—Oral, written					
Student Teacher as a Member of Profession					
Acceptance by faculty members					
View of responsibility as extending beyond classroom					
Has a developing professional attitude					
Consistency of practices with verbalized beliefs					
Potential for future growth					
Sense of responsibility to students, cooperating teachers, college supervisor					

Please give your frank opinion of the ability, potential, and limitations of this student teacher in terms of teaching. This statement is most helpful to superintendents and principals considering the person for employment.

_____

_____

_____

_____

_____

_____

_____

_____

Please continue on other side if additional space is needed.

Arrive at a recommended grade for student teaching after considering the sum of the qualities, the comments, and judgments made above:

> **A** (superior or outstanding)
>
> **B** (above average)
>
> **C** (average)
>
> **D** (below average, required to repeat student teaching)
>
> **F** (failure)
>
> **Inc.** (given only when student is forced to withdaw from student teaching through circumstances not connected with teaching.)

RECOMMENDED GRADE IN STUDENT TEACHING _____

If you were in a position to employ this student as a full-time regular teacher, would you: (Check one.)

Employ him eagerly? ☐ With satisfaction? ☐ With some misgiving and reluctance? ☐ Only if no one else were available? ☐ Not even consider him? ☐

Indicate your opinion as to the best placement for this person as a beginning teacher:

Large City School ☐   Large Regional School ☐

Medium Size School ☐   Small Rural School ☐

Signature(s) of Cooperating Teacher(s) completing this report:

_____   _____

If this report is made by a College Department Supervisor, he or she please complete this item:

Your Name _____ Department _____